VILLAGE
ATHEISTS

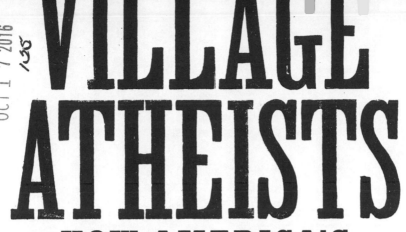

VILLAGE ATHEISTS

HOW AMERICA'S UNBELIEVERS MADE THEIR WAY IN A GODLY NATION

LEIGH ERIC SCHMIDT

PRINCETON
UNIVERSITY
PRESS

PRINCETON
& OXFORD

Published by Princeton University Press
41 William Street, Princeton, New Jersey 08540

In the United Kingdom: Princeton University Press
6 Oxford Street, Woodstock, Oxfordshire OX20 1TW

press.princeton.edu

Jacket design by Chris Ferrante.
Jacket illustration courtesy of Dover Books, ed. Carol Belanger Grafton.

Library of Congress Cataloging-in-Publication Data

Names: Schmidt, Leigh Eric, author.
Title: Village atheists : how America's unbelievers made their way in a Godly
nation / Leigh Eric Schmidt.
Description: Princeton : Princeton University Press, 2016. | Includes
bibliographical references and index.
Identifiers: LCCN 2016011082 | ISBN 9780691168647 (hardcover : alk. paper)
Subjects: LCSH: Atheism—United States—History—19th century.
Classification: LCC BL2747.3 .S37155 2016 | DDC 211/.80973—dc23
LC record available at https://lccn.loc.gov/2016011082

British Library Cataloging-in-Publication Data is available

This book has been composed in Scotch Modern

Printed on acid-free paper. ∞

Printed in the United States of America

1 3 5 7 9 10 8 6 4 2

For Jasper

CONTENTS

ILLUSTRATIONS

PREFACE

WHEN THE BOY SCOUTS OF AMERICA LIFTED ITS BAN ON gay scout leaders in July 2015, after years of contention, the move was widely seen among progressives as one more step forward in the struggle against discrimination. Secular activists, however, were quick to note that another vigorously contested ban—against the membership, employment, and leadership of atheists and agnostics—remained very much in place. In the very DNA of the organization is the assumption that every Boy Scout needs to have a religious faith in order to belong to the group and be a model citizen. As the association's guidelines declare, "No member can grow into the best kind of citizen without recognizing an obligation to God." While that founding principle is now applied expansively—seemingly any theistic affirmation will suffice—the line that still cannot be crossed is the one that separates religion from irreligion, faithful citizenship from public unbelief. The express elevation of the godly over the ungodly within the Boy Scouts of America is, of course, hardly a peculiarity of that organization. From presidential candidates paying their obeisance to Jesus and the Bible to ministers offering prayers to open Congress or bless town board meetings, the upper hand very much belongs to the God-affirming, not the God-denying, in American civic life. This strong partiality for religious profession runs deeps in the nation's history, but so do secularist challenges to these preferential conventions.[1]

In the late nineteenth century the figure most associated with disputing the country's obligatory godliness was the village atheist, a freethinking contrarian whose angular nonconformity had taken on almost mythic qualities in American culture by the 1920s and 1930s. As the personification of an unbelieving minority, the village infidel defied the widespread presumption that civic responsibility and social trust depended on religious association. The rights, liberties, and protections of citizenship extended equally to the irreverent and atheistic, so the secularist dissenter

proclaimed; public morality and sound government did not hinge
on sworn allegiance to God. That argument proved a hard sell
time and again. The prosecution of blasphemy and obscenity revealed the legal quandaries of overt unbelievers with particular
force, but other impediments, including bans on atheists holding public office or testifying in court, recurrently cropped up.
Such hindrances underlined the routinely marginalized status of
freethinkers and unbelievers in American culture. In the United
States avowed secularists were a minority, and secularism as an
express ideology, though built on fantasies of triumph over religion, lacked anything like imperial sweep or hegemonic force. Imagining themselves as the vanguard of enlightened rationality in
a nation saturated with Christian piety, village atheists found the
secularist future ever receding, even chimerical. The age did not
belong to them. Instead, what these willful infidels all too often
discovered was their own vulnerability to majoritarian demands
for religious deference—that they could get hauled off to jail for
peddling the wrong book, giving the wrong speech, circulating
the wrong cartoon, or even sending the wrong postcard. Capillar-
ies of unbelief in a body politic long inhospitable to them, village
atheists sustained a vision of secular enlightenment in the face of
much discouraging evidence.

The susceptibility of unbelievers to public rebuke and ostracizing disfavor is an important part of the story in the pages that
follow, but it is far from the full story. The nineteenth-century
Protestant moral order, while powerful, was fissured with division. For every evangelical watchman who thought that crushing
infidelity was an imperative, there was a more irenic churchgoer
who considered tolerance the principled (or, at least, more prudent) approach to forthright secularists. Much cultural work went
into drawing a bold line between religion and irreligion—and
then policing it accordingly—but, in the everyday world of village
atheists and their more devout neighbors, the room for blurring
was considerable. Infidel orators were usually tolerated, and even
sometimes applauded; a local freethinker could win the respect of
the Baptist minister (and vice versa); a secularist could weary of
irreligion and turn back to the church or to spiritualism; a cradle

Congregationalist could migrate into Unitarianism, then outright unbelief, and yet end up an initiate in the Theosophical Society. The sharp rhetoric with which infidels and Christians confronted one another often crowded out those subtleties and instabilities. Certainly many freethinkers and evangelicals saw this as a war without a middle ground, but forbearance and mutual recognition nonetheless frequently emerged amid the Manichean oppositions. What follows, then, is not a story of inevitable secular advance or unchecked Protestant dominance, but one of recurring friction and negotiation—the charged terrain that atheists and unbelievers have long occupied between tolerance and intolerance, civility and incivility, equal and unequal citizenship in American culture. While it often proved difficult for outspoken freethinkers to make their way in a God-loving nation, they nonetheless resolutely laid claim to equal standing in the American polity—frequently enough with the support of liberal-minded compatriots among the faithful.

Though framed in a broad chronological perspective that ranges from the seventeenth through the early twenty-first centuries, *Village Atheists* by no means attempts to recount the whole history of American unbelief. Instead, the book for the most part settles into the late nineteenth century, the epoch in which the village atheist as a recognizable American personage took definitive shape. It offers a pointillist group portrait, looking closely at a small handful of figures, all of whom exemplify critical aspects of American secularist experience: Samuel Porter Putnam, an ex-minister who, in dubbing himself the "Secular Pilgrim," became a Puritan antitype in his journey from evangelical Calvinism to this-worldly atheism; Watson Heston, a hardscrabble cartoonist who created the iconography of freethinking secularism and whose derisive images forced liberals to ruminate on their own incivility; Charles B. Reynolds, a Seventh-day Adventist evangelist turned crusading infidel whose trial for blasphemy made vivid the ongoing clash over irreligious freedom and the equal citizenship of unbelievers; and Elmina Drake Slenker, an atheist with Quaker roots, whose arrest for obscenity highlighted the legal jeopardy freethinkers frequently faced when they extended their emancipatory ambitions to marriage, gender, and sexuality.

Taken together, these sketches capture the dilemmas of a quotidian secularism—the tensions between combat and courtesy, candor and dissembling, irreverence and respectability that marked the everyday lives of America's unbelievers. By way of conclusion, the book turns to the strict church-state separationists of the early-to-mid-twentieth century—from Charles Lee Smith to Vashti McCollum, from Joseph Lewis to Roy Torcaso—who paved the way as plaintiffs and activists for the Supreme Court's axial reconsideration of the liberties and protections accorded nonbelievers in American culture. In a string of cases stretching from 1948 to 1965, freethinking secularists finally gained a measure of legal vindication. Those victories notwithstanding, atheists and agnostics still frequently felt themselves culturally isolated and mistrusted, even abhorred, politically quarantined within a God-trusting, Bible-believing nation.

As the case of the Boy Scouts of America suggests, the civic status of nonbelievers very much remains an unresolved question in the nation's public life. Even if atheists, humanists, and free-thinkers are now "coming out" in growing numbers—in an explicit borrowing from the vernacular of the gay rights movement—this "openly secular" campaign has hardly lessened certain stigmas. A 2014 Pew survey, for example, still found atheism to be the "top negative" among voters when considering potential presidential candidates, easily outstripping marijuana use or an extramarital affair. Yet, all the news of tenacious prejudice and distrust is ineluctably mixed—as it was in the past—with signs of tolerance, fair-mindedness, or even shrugging indifference. When, for instance, the Pro-Bowl NFL player Arian Foster candidly admitted his solidarity with the New Atheists (Bill Maher, Richard Dawkins, and company) in an ESPN "confession" in the summer of 2015, there was no appreciable backlash. Foster's hometown *Houston Chronicle* responded to the news with the headline "Arian Foster Is an Atheist. So What." Tokens of outright admiration—the American romance with go-it-alone individuality—were also detectable in the journalistic scripting of Foster's irreligious narrative. With shades of the village infidel in the background, the ESPN writer Tim Keown cast Foster as a brave (and very isolated) freethinker in the midst of a Bible Belt culture that still routinely fuses evangelical Protestantism to football as part of the very mechanics of team-building. Keown could not help but root for the one athlete self-reliant enough to have questioned his college coach's requirement at the University of Tennessee that players all attend church together. This book tramps into the thick of such cultural ambivalences—the persistent apprehensions and occasional allures of atheism; in doing so, it teases out a history tugged between religious coercion and irreligious freedom, between the incomplete sway of a Christian majority and the imperfect liberties of a secularist minority.[2]

◆

This project has been long in the making, and my debts are necessarily many. At Harvard I had the exceptional research assistance of Eva Payne and Kip Richardson as the project first began to take shape from 2009 to 2011. I also had the good fortune in 2011 to be invited to contribute to a Festschrift in honor of Edwin Scott Gaustad that Bill Leonard was orchestrating for *Perspectives in Religious Studies*. Ed was a Baptist who shared the church-state views of Jefferson and Madison; he was also an esteemed colleague and cherished mentor. The piece I wrote for that collection, "A Society of Damned Souls: Atheism and Irreligion in the 1920s," was my first stab at writing up some of this research. Part of that contribution has been reworked in the epilogue to this book. More recently, the Mormon History Association offered me the chance to give the 2013 Tanner Lecture, which, in turn, appeared in print under the title, "Freethinkers, Mormons, and the Limits of Toleration," in the *Journal of Mormon History* in 2014. A small portion of that essay appears here in revised form as a tiny piece of chapter 2.

In the fall of 2011, I moved from Harvard to Washington University in St. Louis to help launch a major new initiative, the John C. Danforth Center on Religion and Politics, which has generously supported my research for the last several years. The Danforth Center has provided an extremely rich collegial environment in which to work: Cassie Adcock, Darren Dochuk, Sarah Barringer

Gordon, R. Marie Griffith, John Inazu, Mark Jordan, Rachel Lindsey, Elizabeth McCloskey, Laurie Maffly-Kipp, Lerone Martin, Andrew Rehfeld, Mark Valeri, and Abram Van Engen have helped make it quite an intellectual collective, however nascent and fluid. The Center hosts a biweekly colloquium in which we share our work-in-progress, and I have gained much from those discussions and the wider company of scholars the colloquium engages, including our graduate and postdoctoral fellows. Suzanna Krivulskaya, a History PhD student, and Hannah Wakefield, an English PhD student, have contributed their considerable research skills to this project for which I am grateful. Debra Kennard and Sheri Peña, with their warmth and professionalism, have made the Center an exceptionally congenial place to work. It is a great pleasure being in the same suite of offices with them.

I received critical fellowship support for this project from the American Council of Learned Societies and the John Simon Guggenheim Memorial Foundation, which allowed me to focus in a sustained way on the research and writing of this book. It is an immense gift to be afforded the time for scholarly work, and it is with profound gratitude that I acknowledge both of these grants. I have also much appreciated the feedback I have received at various lectures and conferences, including events at Emory University, Florida State University, the Smithsonian Institution, the University of Toronto, Northwestern University, Carleton University, and the University of Missouri. In each of these places I have met with a bounty of intellectual engagement and searching inquiry. Many colleagues at these and other institutions have been especially supportive in sharing their own work or offering critical commentary, including Penny Edgell, Christopher Grasso, E. Brooks Holifield, Pamela Klassen, and Kathryn Lofton. Likewise, I have benefited from the wisdom and patience of Fred Appel at Princeton University Press. He has been waiting for me to deliver another manuscript for quite a while now and ended up with this one instead. He has only been generous and supportive about the switch.

Certain archives and repositories have proven indispensable for finding my way into this history: the Library of Congress, the

Huntington Library, the New York Public Library, the University of Illinois Library, the Special Collections Research Center at Syracuse University, the Rush Rhees Library at the University of Rochester, the Widener Library at Harvard University, the Harold B. Lee Library of Brigham Young University, the Seeley G. Mudd Manuscript Library at Princeton University, the Wisconsin Historical Society, and the Center for Research Libraries. I have profited as well from a network of historians who have been critical interpreters and collectors of freethought material, notably Timothy Binga, Roderick Bradford, Fred Edwords, Tom Flynn, Fred Whitehead, and Bill Young. Through correspondence with them I became keenly aware of the considerable resources still to be plumbed for understanding the multilayered history of agnostics, humanists, and atheists in the United States. Those with especially keen knowledge of particular denominational collections have also assisted me at various junctures, including Stanley Hickerson of the Adventist Research Center at Andrews University, Chris Anderson of the United Methodist Archives at Drew University, and James Hazard of the Friends Historical Society at Swarthmore College. Dannel McCollum graciously invited me into his home and shared with me the papers of his grandfather Arthur Cromwell, as well as his thoughts on the legacy of his mother, Vashti McCollum. Freethinkers, I learned along the way, never much liked Thanksgiving, but writing this history of American atheists and unbelievers has nonetheless left me deeply grateful to all those who have helped sustain my scholarly life over the last seven years.

My sixteen-year-old daughter, Ella, recently reviewed my literary output over the last quarter century and noted that her younger brother, Jasper, was the only member of the family left unmentioned in a book dedication. She found this an unfortunate slight in need of correction. At age eight, Jasper hardly seems the village atheist type. Still, as I also learned along the way, secularists had very high hopes for the *Little Freethinker* (to borrow the title of a journal aimed at forming their own progeny). I have similarly high hopes for Jasper, whose keen curiosity matches that of his older siblings, Zachary and Ella. Count this very tiny part of the family ledger balanced.

VILLAGE
ATHEISTS

THE MAKING OF THE VILLAGE ATHEIST

"OURS IS A LAND WHERE PEOPLE OUGHT TO BE RELIGIOUS," a Minneapolis newspaper opined with prescriptive assurance as Easter Sunday neared in 1904. Faith and reverence were American bedrock, the paper avowed; from the White House down to the humblest home, religious allegiance was the norm. As the solemn observances of Holy Week unfolded across the city, the paper found it hard to imagine atheists and unbelievers ever being incorporated into American civic life on equal terms: "We claim religious freedom for our strongest plank in [our] national foundations, but irreligious freedom is another matter entirely. Let a man believe what he likes. Let him believe, however." That citizenship and civil liberties were somehow contingent on religious belief, that religion was to be expressly privileged over irreligion—the Minnesota paper presented these as perdurable propositions governing American public life.[1]

A decade and a half later the persistence of this perception—that being irreligious was essentially un-American—sent the budding literary critic Van Wyck Brooks looking for inklings of deviance, if not deliverance. Brooks turned to Mark Twain to provide the needed relief, but found him instead complicit in the national fondness for religious faith—a dissembler all too fearful of public disapproval to give his unbelief full and frank expression. Emphasizing Twain's self-censoring evasions and posthumous deferrals, Brooks looked beyond him to an abstracted paragon, the village atheist, as the bearer of a "vital, restless, critical, disruptive spirit" in American cultural life. A forthright nonconformist, the village atheist offered a glimmer of intellectual independence and plainspoken dissent amid the chilling sanctimony and complacency that Brooks saw dominating the culture of his youth. "There is no type in our social history," Brooks solemnly concluded in 1920, "more significant than that ubiquitous figure, the 'village atheist.'" [2]

Brooks did not dwell on the particulars of this type. Notwithstanding his gesture toward "our social history," his readers could easily have come away thinking that the village atheist was anything but "ubiquitous"—that, indeed, the figure consisted in little more than an isolated character or two in Twain's *Pudd'nhead Wilson* (1894). In that novel Judge York Driscoll presides over a local Society of Freethinkers, a group that after four years in operation has exactly two members. Driscoll's small-town Missouri household is comprised of his wife and his widowed sister, both good Presbyterians, who have the community's approbation entirely on their side but whose piety has left the judge undeterred: he still ventures "to go his own way and follow out his own notions."[3] Behind an imagined character like Driscoll, behind the romanticized type that Brooks held up, was a culture of unbelief full of flesh-and-blood freethinkers and ungodly lecturers, all of whom confronted—with incredulity and spleen—religious claims that they were dangerously unfit for equal citizenship in an avowedly Christian nation. Theirs proved a long, contentious struggle in a country where the majority of their compatriots claimed to place much trust in God and very little in them.

The prejudice against atheists and unbelievers went deep. Even as prominent an architect of religious liberty as John Locke had been unable to imagine widening the circle of toleration enough to include the godless: "Those are not at all to be tolerated who *deny the Being of God*," Locke declared in his touchstone *Letter Concerning Toleration* (1689). "Promises, Covenants, and Oaths, which are the Bonds of Humane Society, can have no hold upon an Atheist. The taking away of God, though but even in thought, dissolves all." Public order, in Locke's view, was compatible with religious diversity—with a polity that included various kinds of

Christians, as well as Jews and Muslims—but not with overt irreligion. "Those that by their Atheism undermine and destroy all Religion," Locke concluded, "can have no pretence of Religion," and thus they could have no basis for claiming the "Privilege" of religious toleration. Those who rejected God were in Locke's estimate "the most dangerous sorts of wild beasts"; they were "incapable of all society." Such theological and political propositions carried life-and-death implications. In 1697, eight years after Locke's *Letter Concerning Toleration*, Thomas Aikenhead, a twenty-year-old student at the University of Edinburgh, was hanged for giving vent—in the company of fellow students—to a series of profane and atheistic rants against the scriptures, Jesus, Hell, and the Trinity. Aikenhead's execution made this much plain: even as the principle of religious toleration gained traction in late seventeenth- and early eighteenth-century Britain, irreligious freedom lagged far behind.[4]

The mother country very much provided the legal template for its North American colonies: sacrilege remained criminal, and atheism anathema. Offenders who cursed in God's name, scoffed at the scriptures, or otherwise mocked sacred things often landed in court, and the punishments meted out for such blasphemies could be severe, including public whipping, tongue-boring, and imprisonment. Though no one in the colonies was put to death for denying Christ's divinity or rejecting God, the law nonetheless looked upon such disavowals as potentially capital offenses. In one case in Massachusetts in 1654, a soldier, Benjamin Sawser, had drunkenly pronounced that "Jehova is the Devel" and that he "knew noe god but his sworde." As the court deliberated whether Sawser's egregious outburst constituted a capital crime, he made a jailbreak before a final punishment could be meted out.[5] Even when fines rather than prison sentences were at stake, religious contempt was taken quite seriously. The disorderly Elijah Leach found that out in Plymouth in 1765, when he indecently exposed himself to "divers of his majesties good subjects" and also loudly declared that he "did not care a turd for God in Heaven." For showing off his "private members" he was fined ten shillings, but for his "irreverent speeches" he was fined forty shillings.[6] The prevailing legal strictures in the British colonies criminalized ungodliness in a host of ways, and such regulations—aimed at blasphemy, profane swearing, and Sabbath-breaking, among other things—kept barefaced scoffers ever susceptible to prosecution as threats to public morality. Under these constraints blatant infidels remained few and far between in British North America.

Added to the legal proscriptions on irreverence was the social impropriety of overt unbelief. A classic mid-eighteenth-century guidebook to gentlemanly manners, the Earl of Chesterfield's *Letters*, made plain the reputational norms favoring religious profession: "Depend upon this truth, That every man is the worse looked upon, and the less trusted, for being thought to have no religion; . . . a wise Atheist (if such a thing there is) would, for his own interest, and character in this world, pretend to some religion." Irreligion was not good form; it was disrespectable and indecorous; the polite gentleman knew that "the Appearances of religion" mattered acutely as a marker of public credibility; it was useful, in other words, to be seen in a prominent church pew on a Sunday.[7] This was not a social calculus designed to make an evangelical's heart soar, but it was perhaps enough to secure the churches' hold on well-heeled parishioners and keep the infidels at bay. At the end of the century, in 1794, the revolutionary pamphleteer Thomas Paine fumed in the *Age of Reason* over the "mental lying" involved in keeping up this facade. "Infidelity does not consist in believing, or in disbelieving," he argued. Rather, it consists "in professing to believe what [one] does not believe." It was time, he insisted, to stop all the posturing deference to Christianity, its scriptures, clergy, and steeple-houses, and instead to avow openly a deistic natural philosophy untethered from biblical revelation. Paine's anticlerical candor cost his American reputation dearly, so much in fact that upon his return to the United States in 1802 he looked more the social pariah than the hero patriot. The full-throated defamation of Paine's character—a vile, beastly, drunken, loathsome, atheistic rogue—only served to confirm the practical wisdom of Chesterfield's advice.[8]

Another generation later, in the 1830s, Alexis de Tocqueville saw the same sort of social qualms reinforcing the preferment that religious association enjoyed in the new republic. In most instances, Tocqueville thought, Americans professed "the doctrines of Christianity from a sincere belief in them," but "a certain number," he surmised, did so because they feared being "suspected of unbelief." The point to Tocqueville was not how sizeable this clandestine bunch of nonbelievers was, but instead that the new nation's social, religious, and political mores kept incredulity furtive; only an infidel few risked public rancor. Tocqueville had a tale from early in his visit in 1831 to illustrate why most skeptics found it best to keep their cards close to their chest: a witness in a New York courtroom, when called to the stand, had daringly declared that he "did not believe in the existence of God or the immortality of the soul." The judge was dumbfounded to have discovered a living, breathing atheist anywhere, let alone in his own courtroom, and moved quickly to reestablish order. Pronouncing the United States to be "a Christian country," the judge maintained that he had no choice but to disqualify the witness whose testimony, in light of his irreligion, would lack all credibility. That was far from an isolated case. The question of whether witness competency depended on a belief in God (as well as on a belief in eternal rewards and punishments) haunted American courtrooms into the twentieth century. With the weight of public opinion—and, often enough, judicial opinion as well—on the side of religious profession, Tocqueville found the conclusion unavoidable: American Christianity, having turned disestablishment to its advantage, held significant sway over the nation's social and political institutions, so much so that unbelievers found it routinely advisable to keep quiet about their irreligion. As one newspaper moralized in 1834 about "a professed atheist" who had died in a laboratory explosion, supposedly the very day he had publicly disavowed God, "If men cannot believe, will not believe, let them be silent."[9]

Tocqueville was right about the fusion of Protestantism and republicanism in a new order based on voluntary associations, but all along it was equally evident how much the churches continued to depend on prior forms of establishment to maintain religion's elevation over irreligion. Several state constitutions, during

the nation's founding epoch, had kept explicit religious tests on
the books. Pennsylvania (1790), Tennessee (1796), and Mississippi
(1817), for example, each made belief in God as well as a future
state of rewards and punishments a condition of holding public
office. Massachusetts (1780) and New Hampshire (1784) had gone
further, enshrining specific Christian tests for elected representatives. Devisers of Connecticut's constitution had belatedly come
around to the notion of disestablishing the state's Congregational
order in 1818, but that broadened endorsement of religious freedom
did not extend to the expression of libelous views against Christianity. Blasphemies against God, the Bible, or the Holy Trinity
remained punishable with fines up to $100 and imprisonment up
to one year. A judge in New Haven handed out a six-month sentence in the county jail to one William Cannon for blasphemy
in 1826; James Granger got a full year from a Litchfield judge
in 1829. The state legislature dismissed a bill in 1836 that would
have allowed atheists to testify in courts of law. Right through the
Civil War, the aftermath of which forced another round of constitutional revisions, the civic standing of unbelievers looked shaky,
if not perilous. The new state constitutions of Maryland (1867),
North Carolina (1868), Arkansas (1874), and Texas (1876) loftily
proclaimed the rights of religious conscience, even as they specifically barred those who denied the being of God from holding
positions of public trust. Only in 1961 in *Torcaso v. Watkins* did
the Supreme Court dispatch as unconstitutional the proposition
that atheism could be used as a civic disqualification.[10]

The effectiveness of Christian uses of legal, political, and social
coercions to quiet infidels and atheists only went so far, however.
Building a confessedly Christian nation atop the epochal articu-
lations of religious liberty produced during the revolutionary era
proved an inherently unstable enterprise. The Virginia Act for
Establishing Religious Freedom (1786), the brainchild of Thomas
Jefferson, had enjoined that religious opinions and beliefs should
in no way diminish, enlarge, or affect a citizen's civil capacities.
Jefferson later specified in his *Autobiography* that the bill was expressly intended to reach beyond the religious to the irreligious,
that it comprehended within its mantle of protection "the Jew

and the Gentile, the Christian and Mahometan, the Hindoo and infidel." This Jeffersonian principle reverberated widely. In 1788, two years after the passage of the Virginia bill and three years before the ratification of the First Amendment, the Vermont editor of the first post-Revolution imprint of Locke's *Letter Concerning Toleration* found it necessary to offer some improvements on the original—prominent among them was the deletion of the entire paragraph denying toleration to atheists and unbelievers; prior colonial editions through 1764 had simply left the recommended ban intact. In the legal and intellectual ferment that followed in the Revolution's wake, proponents of the civil equality and religious liberty of freethinkers and infidels established a political beachhead that endured for their secularist heirs in the nineteenth century.[11]

The proposition that religious freedom extended to the openly irreligious had a strong appeal among Jeffersonians, even as it struck fear into the hearts of Federalists. Sharp divergence on this point came into full display in the conflict over one of Jefferson's bolder pronouncements in his *Notes on the State of Virginia* (1785). "It does me no injury for my neighbor to say there are twenty gods, or no god," Jefferson brashly remarked. "It neither picks my pocket nor breaks my leg."[12] Jefferson's Federalist opponents were eager to conflate his deism with atheism, and that infamous passage long fed the attack machine. "Polytheism or atheism, 'twenty gods or no god,' is perfectly indifferent in Mr. Jefferson's good citizen," a Presbyterian minister fumed in reply. "A wretch may trumpet atheism from New-Hampshire to Georgia; may laugh at all the realities of futurity; may scoff and teach others to scoff at their accountability; it is no matter, says Mr. Jefferson, 'it neither picks my pocket, nor breaks my leg.' This is nothing less than representing civil society as founded in atheism."[13] Jefferson was not—in his theology or his politics—an atheist, but he was clear on this point: that religious liberty, free expression, and equal citizenship should be unencumbered by particular theistic limits, Christian or otherwise. Such sweeping rights of conscience in matters of religious opinion collided head on with long-standing warnings that deism, atheism, and infidelity constituted intolerable public dangers. That Americans were free to worship any number of gods or to refuse to worship any god at all was a crucial Jeffersonian counterthrust—a fissure that freethinkers and unbelievers were repeatedly able to exploit against establishment-minded Protestants. As one infidel editor asked in 1857, "Suppose a man to hold publicly that there was *no* God; that the world as we see it, is the result of a fortuitous concourse of atoms; what then?" With Jefferson's vaunted rhetorical dig in mind, he answered with a brusque follow-up question: "Does it break my leg or fracture my skull?"[14]

The irreligious continued to face legal, social, and political disadvantages throughout the nineteenth century, but those burdens were not necessarily insurmountable. The playing field upon which believers and unbelievers skirmished was often more level than it initially appeared—a Jeffersonian terrain as much as an indelibly Protestant one. Take the example of the Jewish infidel Ernestine Rose. When a Congregational minister in Bangor, Maine, named G. B. Little tried to keep her from speaking there in 1855, he thought he had an easy target. Over the last decade Rose had become infamous for speeches celebrating Tom Paine and heralding women's rights; horrifying reports of her "ribaldries" aimed at Christianity preceded her; if she were allowed to lecture in Bangor, Little imagined it would simply be another occasion for her to air her "choicest blasphemies." So, the minister and his allies pulled out all the stops: "We know of no object more deserving of contempt, loathing, and abhorrence than a *female Atheist*. We hold the vilest strumpet from the stews to be by comparison respectable." It was ugly, and it backfired. Bangor had a lecture hall that could seat two thousand; it had never been filled to capacity—until Rose arrived. "They have never had such a large audience here before," one reporter noted, "and I doubt whether they will soon again, as the curiosity and desire to see her, 'a *female atheist*,' was most intense." An accomplished polemicist, Rose was in her element. Denouncing the "bigotry and intolerance" of her opponents, Rose admitted that she stood before the world "unprotected" by "a *profession* of religion," but insisted the lack of that "cloak" in no way diminished her right to the public expression of her opinions. The crowd was "uncommonly attentive, and remarkably enthusiastic"; Rose was warmly welcomed back for a second night. "Poor parson Little," one of her sympathizers remarked, "was made littler than ever!" Ever unapologetic in her unbelief, Rose would grandly deliver on the *"female Atheist"* taunt six years later in 1861 when she gave a rousing address in Boston entitled "A Defence of Atheism."[15]

In winning the round in Bangor, Rose illustrated an important point apt to get lost amid all the invidious rhetoric elevating the godly above the godless: namely, that liberality and forbearance frequently prevailed even for overt atheists and infidels. The *Boston Investigator*, a freethinking weekly that offered Rose unflagging support, reprinted a piece it found especially encouraging from "a religious newspaper" in 1860: "An Atheist is not to be tabooed" or "thrust out of the pale of humanity," the writer argued, no matter how aggrieved "our Puritan forefathers" might be at the thought of tolerating the irreligious. "By all means let the Atheist have free speech; let him address the public ear by the press and by the platform." More often than not, though, such acceptance of the public infidel remained grudging and calculated: not an endorsement of the equal rights of atheists, but a realization that clamping down on the ungodly only culled more attention to their blasphemies—just as it had for Rose in Bangor. The Protestant historian Robert Baird exemplified that reluctant acquiescence to tolerating the irreligious in his formative *Religion in America* in 1844: "It is sometimes the best way to silence a noisy, brainless lecturer on atheism, to let him alone." Baird was quite sure that nothing about the Constitution had been intended to grant the "rights of conscience" to "atheism, irreligion, or licentiousness," but nonetheless conceded that the "universal enjoyment" of religious freedom meant that "even the Atheist may have his meetings in which to preach his doctrines." Baird very much wanted to quell infidels, deists, and atheists—or, at least, to keep them hidden away in "private haunts" and "secret retirements"—but he wound up, almost in spite of himself, acknowledging their civil liberties as American citizens. Pragmatic calculation combined with a Jeffersonian logic on the principle of religious freedom to temper Baird's unmistakable longing for coercion.[16]

As Baird's ambivalence suggested and as Rose's career demonstrated, liberality and forbearance were only part of the story. In 1853 in Hartford, Connecticut, one of Rose's lectures on the Bible degenerated into a mob scene as hissing students from nearby Trinity College repeatedly disrupted the proceedings. The sheriff had to be called in to restore order. With good reason, Rose remained seriously doubtful that unbelievers operated on an equal political and social footing with their religious neighbors. She took particular aim at the Massachusetts courts where—"within the shadow of Bunker Hill"—a witness of unblemished character could be disqualified for being an atheist, while the testimony of any "believing scoundrel" was counted trustworthy. Even in her own activist circles, it was far from certain that her infidelity would not prove a disqualifying blot. At the National Woman's Rights Convention in Philadelphia in 1854, Rose's bid for the presidency was almost derailed by "the objection that she was an atheist." Some suggested she not be allowed a place on the dais at all. Only Susan B. Anthony's strong rejoinder turned the tide: "Every religion or none should have an equal right" to the convention's platform. (A thorough Jeffersonian on this point, Anthony took the view that the women's rights movement was open to "representatives of all creeds and no creed—Jew or Christian, Protestant or Catholic, Gentile or Mormon, pagan or atheist," but that was far from the consensus among fellow suffragists who frequently scorned leaders like Rose and Elizabeth Cady Stanton for their infidelity.) Such debates about the public status and civic trustworthiness of unbelievers recurred throughout the century in a wide range of settings—from legislatures to schoolhouses to courtrooms to women's rights organizations and far beyond. The density of engagement between the religious and the irreligious was as palpable as it was perpetual—a trysting of fear and animosity with fair-mindedness and tolerance.[17]

Rose, who had immigrated to New York in 1836, returned to London in 1869 after more than three decades of reform activism in her adopted country. Had she stayed, she would have seen her irreligious critique of reigning orthodoxies come into much fuller expression in the century's final quarter. A solid contingent of freethinkers—among them Abner Kneeland, Frances Wright, Gilbert Vale, Thomas Herttell, Horace Seaver, and Rose herself— had kept Tom Paine's torch burning in the decades before the Civil War. Establishing a small handful of infidel journals and associations, they had consistently managed to raise the hackles of evangelical moral reformers quite out of proportion to their numbers. Their antebellum labors—in Boston, New York, and Philadelphia, among other locales—laid the foundation for the luxuriant proliferation of freethinking lecturers and outright atheists in the 1870s and 1880s. At an Infidel Convention in New York City in 1860, the assembled company (Rose included) had dreamed of creating "a staff of Infidel lecturers" to counteract the effects of Christian evangelization. At the time, these gathered unbelievers could find only a couple of lecturers to commission, but twenty-five years later American freethinkers had a bounty of them—several dozen orators ready to grab the headlines away from famed evangelists and Christian-nation campaigners.[18] Secularist publishing ventures expanded congruently, and the organizational structures of the cause—at national and local levels—were significantly elaborated. As freethinkers surged in cultural visibility in the late nineteenth century, so did their liberal secular claims on American public life: that free speech should supplant blasphemy as a legal principle, that religious tests in courts and statehouses should end, that the public schools should be free of religious instruction, that the absence of religious belief should have no effect on the rights and protections of citizenship—all these secularist demands, and more, gained renewed and vigorous articulation.

No one better exemplified the broader fascination that open unbelief had come to possess by the late nineteenth century than the infidel orator Robert Ingersoll. The disillusioned son of a Presbyterian minister, Ingersoll had immense gifts on the platform and routinely sold out his coast-to-coast lecture tours from the late 1870s through the 1890s. "It was impossible to look round upon the crowded audience that assembled to hear Colonel Robert Ingersoll's lecture last night," a stunned reporter for the *Sacramento Daily Union* wrote in 1877, "without feeling that such a gathering, for such a purpose, denoted a change in popular beliefs far greater and more radical than is generally supposed to have taken place. Less than a generation ago it would have been impossible for any man to have delivered that lecture without sacrificing his reputation and social standing. He would have been denounced on all sides as an unprincipled infidel, an 'atheist,' and a wicked, Godless creature." While the world had not changed as much as this gaping reporter suggested—Ingersoll was still habitually condemned for his unbelief—his extraordinary career nonetheless suggested that infidel lecturers had gained people's ears to a degree that often confounded their critics. Even many Christians, the Sacramento reporter marveled, listened appreciatively as Ingersoll's arguments struck "at the root of their old beliefs"; they seemed somehow satisfied with his assault on orthodoxy and the Bible—as if he were making manifest their own "drifting doubts." Ingersoll hardly made atheism popular or mainstream, but his high profile was a clear indication of the new cultural prominence that unbelief had achieved by the last quarter of the nineteenth century. Out of the shadows of Ingersoll's celebrity, the village atheist would emerge as a recognizable American character, a self-assured dissenter openly at odds with the nation's evangelical verities.[19]

A word about naming. Nineteenth-century unbelievers tried out various designations for themselves—with inherited terms like "freethinker" and "atheist" finding company with newer labels like "liberal" and "agnostic." At an Infidel Convention in Philadelphia in 1857, those in attendance stumbled over the growing confusion in nomenclature. "The time is now come for the Unbelievers, Infidels, or Liberals (or what name soever we may call ourselves by) to stand forth"; so began one resolution that came to the floor. This uncertainty over naming created a long discussion. "Infidel" was a slur (akin to "atheist") that some thought should be resisted with more positive constructions of free inquiry, though most wanted to wear the badge proudly. "Liberal" was seen as the more irenic and encompassing term, but some thought it made resolute unbelievers look too amenable to religious associations and alliances (with, say, spiritualists or Unitarians). Two years later in 1859, when that small infidel association met again in Philadelphia, a resolution was floated suggesting that a new term of British coinage, "secularist," be adopted as a more inclusive label than "atheist" or "infidel." The assembled roundly dismissed that idea as "rank cowardice," a lexicographer's softening concession to Christianity, but their opposition did not prevent some infidels from trying out the new designation. The naming problem remained endlessly cloudy. One freethinker, puzzling in 1884 over the most appropriate label, wanted to "add a name of my own" to the mix of options; he recommended "true Americans" (it did not catch on). A journalist, looking back in 1933 on the irreligious agitators of the previous century, made light of all this slipperiness: "They could never even agree on what to call themselves. Freethinker, Rationalist, Agnostic, Atheist, Liberal, Secularist, Monist, Materialist—take your choice!"[20] And that was to say nothing of Philanthropist, Positivist, Humanist, or Humanitarian.

However baffling in their profusion, the various tags were recognizably bound together through a set of shared attributes. Those commonalities included: (1) a rejection of Christian orthodoxy and biblical authority that passed from deism into atheism; (2) a very strict construction of church-state separation; (3) a commitment to advancing scientific inquiry as the pathway to verifiable knowledge and technological prowess; (4) an anticlerical scorn for both Catholic and Protestant power; (5) a universalistic imagining of equal rights, civil liberties, and humanitarian goodwill; and (6) a focus on this world alone as the domain of human happiness and fulfillment. Most freethinkers saw the sundry labels at their disposal as mutually reinforcing, as shorthand condensations of these overlapping aims, principles, and objections. A correspondent to the *Boston Investigator* in 1882, for example, wrote to ask the editor: "I would like to know if Secularism and Atheism mean the same thing?" To which the editor replied: "They mean the same so far as concerns any useful and practical purpose."[21] The various appellations were, in short, interdependent and routinely transposable. Everyday interchangeability trumped fine distinctions, no matter how often one contributor or another tried to sharpen the political or metaphysical significance of a given marker.

The use of the label "village atheist" in the pages and title of this book warrants particular comment and contextualization. The earliest reference to "the village atheist" occurred in an 1808 review of the work of the British clergyman and poet George Crabbe. His collection of *Poems* (1807) included "The Parish Register," a richly descriptive account of the local characters surrounding an Anglican vicar in rural England. The *Monthly Review* called particular attention to Crabbe's "masterful delineation of the village atheist," though the poet had actually used the phrase "rustic Infidel" to depict this neighborhood lout:

Each Village Inn has heard the Ruffian boast,
That he believ'd 'in neither God nor Ghost;
'That when the Sod upon the Sinner press'd,
'He, like the Saint, had everlasting Rest.

The picture Crabbe painted of the "rustic Infidel"—a hearty companion of roadhouse quaffers, a libertine who considers "the Marriage-Bond the Bane of Love," a supremely "Bad Man" who conflates "the Wants of Rogues" with "the Rights of Man"—possessed, to say the least, none of the nonconformist romance that Van Wyck Brooks's depiction projected a century or so later. What "The Parish Register," first published in the United States in 1808, did suggest was that the village atheist's ancestry wound its way back into long-standing forms of impiety and profane living. Crabbe combined the scoffing irreverence of the tavern—the vulgarities of a Benjamin Sawser or an Elijah Leach—with the pigeonholes made for the deistic infidelity of Tom Paine and his acolytes. That combined image of sloshed blasphemer and Bible-ridiculing deist followed freethinkers out of the late Enlightenment deep into the nineteenth century. When Yale professor Henry A. Beers published his *Outline Sketch of American Literature* in 1887, he depicted "the village atheist" as a figure much like the one in Crabbe's register—irreverent, half-educated, and pugnacious, with a well-thumbed copy of Paine's *Age of Reason* in hand to inspire his harangues of the faithful.[22]

Depicting the "rustic Infidel" from a churchly vantage point, as Crabbe did, cast the character in an entirely unflattering light. Soon, though, the village atheist began to look almost appealing in the hands of more heterodox observers. In his "Divinity School Address" in 1838, Ralph Waldo Emerson suggested an emerging variation when he presented "the bold village blasphemer" as a figure before whom the creaking orthodox minister can only quake when they meet in the street: "The village blasphemer sees fear in the face, form, and gait of the minister." The radical Unitarian urge to applaud the "village infidel" as a daring heretic only grew more robust after the Civil War; both William Channing Gannett and Minot J. Savage sang the personage's praises as an emblem of earnest doubt, humanistic striving, and intellectual integrity. By the 1880s and 1890s, these paired locutions—"the village atheist" and "the village infidel"—had become recognizable labels in the copious vocabulary employed to describe America's resident freethinkers and secularist dissenters. Both coinages retained a distinctly literary feel that carried particular appeal for poets, novelists, and critics. For example, Harry Leon Wilson's turn-of-the-century novel *The Seeker* featured a character named Milo Barrus, whom Wilson identified upfront in his list of characters as "the village atheist." The head of a band of "care-free Sabbath loafers," Barrus was "so bad a man that he loved to spell God with a little g."[23]

By the 1910s and 1920s, the notion of the village infidel or atheist came to possess a noticeably nostalgic aura. When Edgar Lee Masters included a poem entitled "The Village Atheist" in his *Spoon River Anthology* in 1916, he offered only a graveyard epitaph for the talkative, contentious freethinker. Likewise, when the liberal Protestant minister Herbert S. Bigelow published *The Religion of Revolution* the same year, he presented a chapter in tribute to "a village infidel" whom he had dreadfully feared in his rural Ohio boyhood. Revisiting the town, the minister looks for the old freethinker—an apostate who had seen the Christianity of Bigelow's youth for the "contracted" and "shrunken" faith that it was—but mournfully finds that the man has been dead "these many years." As with Masters and Bigelow, Van Wyck Brooks was also looking backwards in 1920 to the heterodox provocations of the previous generation. Twain's hero, the silver-tongued Robert Ingersoll, was for Brooks a leading measure of plainspoken irreligious dissent, the great exemplar of the "crude atheism" that Twain had hungered to express. Ingersoll's death in 1899 had portended to many of his admirers the end of an era, and Twain himself had felt the loss keenly. "Except for my daughter's, I have not grieved for any death as I have grieved for his," the novelist wrote in a letter of condolence to Ingersoll's niece. Village atheists had lost their colonel in 1899, and that made their decline in the next century seem all the more inevitable.[24]

Soon, the elegiac note became even more pronounced. "The village atheist who used to corner the parson by asking where Cain got his wife is becoming extinct," journalist George Seibel wrote in the *American Mercury* in 1933. Seibel had grown up listening to infidel orators like James L. York and W. S. Bell, and he fondly recalled those "enemies of Yahweh" of a half century ago—among them, the nurseryman-turned-publisher D. M. Bennett, the "learned blacksmith" John Peck, the "atheist watchmaker" Otto Wettstein, and the erudite naturalist Felix Oswald with his traveling menagerie of pet monkeys. Seibel very much missed these "odd characters" with all their quirky methods of staging God's funeral.[25] Of course, village infidels were not quite the bygone relics Seibel made them out to be. Publisher Emanuel Haldeman-Julius, for example, was still cranking out heaps of freethought pamphlets in the 1930s from his perch in Girard, Kansas, and playing the part of the village atheist with visible delight. But, Seibel's nostalgia, not his historical exactitude, was what mattered—the felt loss of the village infidel's maverick individuality to churchgoing convention and Fundamentalist reaction. For literary sophisticates and sage pundits, the waning of the village atheist became one more sign of the continuing sway of the country's George Babbitts and Elmer Gantrys.[26]

Village Atheists grounds itself between the rustic infidels of the late Enlightenment and the romanticized nonconformists of the 1920s and 1930s. It trades not in literary representations or typecast characters, but in the flesh-and-blood freethinkers who made the village atheist such a culturally resonant figure in the first place. Like the rest of the options that had emerged by the end of the nineteenth century to describe the nation's secularist dissenters, the appellation "village atheist" was pliable. This extends as well to how the expression is employed in this book: it refers not only to overt atheists well-rooted in small towns, but also to a wider run of agnostics, infidels, and freethinkers, many of whom proved quite peripatetic and even cosmopolitan. That *Time* magazine in 1943 could proclaim the Baltimore-based journalist and satirist H. L. Mencken the nation's "outstanding village atheist" suggests the phrase's untethered, figurative qualities. Like Mencken or Ingersoll, the freethinkers given focal attention in these pages—the itinerant secularist Samuel Putnam, the combative cartoonist Watson Heston, the tent-preaching blasphemer Charles B. Reynolds, and the obscene atheist Elmina Drake Slenker—were far more than small-town cranks. They all began their careers with local performances of their unbelief and then built infidel personas of far-flung notoriety upon those religious ruptures. They became public atheists, in other words, but ones whose ministries always remained deeply entwined with their village kin. Indeed, their reputations depended on the strength of that kinship—on how their own expressions of infidelity resonated with their dispersed and often isolated comrades from Maine to Oregon.[27]

Above all, the notion of the village atheist is used to call attention to the quotidian qualities of American unbelief: that is, to how the struggle over God, revelation, and religious affiliation unfolded at the grassroots rather than in universities or literary bohemias—in Boonton, New Jersey, or Snowville, Virginia, or Carthage, Missouri, rather than at Columbia University or in Greenwich Village. Much of the story about the origins of modern atheism has been told, understandably, as a history of ideas, particularly of the ways in which Christian theologians effectively abetted unbelief through a series of compromises—with natural philosophers, deistic rationalists, and humanistic moralists—that gradually depleted the faith of its intellectual particularity and potency. Needless to say, telling the history of unbelief from the perspective of Christianity's self-inflicted wounds reveals little about the stakes involved for freethinkers and secularists themselves. It leaves the plebeian world of the village atheist almost entirely untouched.[28] American freethinkers emerged from an intricate web of everyday encounters—with itinerant evangelists, neighborhood converts, fiery populists, crusading reformers, spiritualist mediums, and hard-bitten sinners. The religious estrangements that vexed them were not philosophically abstracted; they were visceral, relational, and densely particular. They were rarely sophisticated metaphysicians worrying over the niceties of epistemology, but instead aggrieved contrarians stunned at the moral shabbiness of scriptural stories or the manipulative theatrics of popular revivalists. Their myriad alienations—from the God of the Bible, from the religious regulation of marriage and sexuality, from pious restraints on Sunday recreations, from equations of social respectability and moral trustworthiness with church membership—were hardly ethereal, but rather earthy in their lived concreteness. Village atheists, by self-profession, minded this world, not things spiritual, and their stories are told here with that mundane materiality very much in view.

A word as well about the larger storyline. A secularist narrative retains its temptations—slowly, but surely, over two-plus centuries, religious freedom has widened to include the irreligious, and, consequently, unbelievers have come to enjoy the rights and liberties of American citizenship equally with their believing counterparts. From this perspective, the liberal secularist principles that nineteenth-century freethinkers forwarded eventually carried the day; the outworking of a wall-of-separation logic in the courts has effectively materialized a secular polity neutral to the claims of believers and nonbelievers. The secularist plotline has gained additional traction in recent years from accruing sociological data that indicates a boom in the number of Americans who count themselves as having no religion at all. That demographic cohort had swollen by 2014 to about 23 percent of the U.S. population, and, while an internally diverse lot, these religious "Nones" suggest that the strong partiality once accorded religious identification has lost significant ground; it is socially acceptable now to sidestep religious adherence entirely—that is, to be "nothing in particular."[29] Nonbelievers, it would seem then, are not only constitutionally protected, but also culturally normalized. "We are a nation of Christians and Muslims, Jews and Hindus, and nonbelievers," President Barack Obama proclaimed in his first inaugural address in 2009.[30] His words had a fine Jeffersonian ring—with one notable exception. Obama exchanged "nonbeliever" for "infidel," a signal in itself perhaps of neutrality's triumph. That presidential acknowledgment, made during one of the nation's most hallowed ceremonies, could be taken as a teleological marker. The nonreligious have finally ascended to equal civic standing with their faith-espousing compatriots.

The secularist storyline has its merits and attractions as well as its clear limitations and gaping holes. Church-state jurisprudence is ever-evolving and necessarily unsettled, always awaiting the next spate of litigation over state-funded chaplaincies, faith-based initiatives, or reproductive rights to sort through the nation's religious-political entanglements. Groups such as the Freedom from Religion Foundation and the American Humanist Association, even with precedents like *Torcaso* in hand, remain quite accustomed to setbacks in the cases they fight on behalf of atheists and agnostics. Indeed, the very supposition of neutrality—that the government cannot be in the business of overtly favoring believers over nonbelievers—has been roundly disputed at the Supreme Court level in recent decades; Justices William Rehnquist and Antonin Scalia often took particular umbrage at the legal challenges posed by "devout atheists" and were expressly hostile to the notion that the state could not accord preference to civic religious observance over irreligious objections. "We are a religious people whose institutions presuppose a Supreme Being," the Supreme Court had announced in *Zorach v. Clauson* in 1952, and, frequently enough, judicial decisions are still handed down—on everything from the "under God" phrase in the Pledge of Allegiance to prayers before municipal meetings—that make this theological-political congruence sound like the nation's accepted orthodoxy.[31]

The convolutions in the legal landscape are matched by the thorniness of survey data. To be sure, the religious "Nones" are growing rapidly in number, but outright atheists remain a highly suspect minority when it comes to everything from gaining the trust of voters to winning over prospective in-laws. A 2006 study, for example, tested two propositions with its interviewees: "This Group Does Not At All Agree with My Vision of American Society" and "I Would Disapprove if My Child Wanted to Marry a Member of this Group." Atheists won on both scores—39.6 percent and 47.6 percent, respectively; they readily outdistanced other minorities, including Muslims, gays, recent immigrants, Jews, and African Americans. Those prejudicial judgments routinely make themselves felt in the lives of nonbelievers. A follow-up study in 2012 found that 42.9 percent of self-identified atheists and agnostics reported experiencing discrimination on account of their irreligion over the previous five years—whether in familial and social relationships, at school, or in the workplace. Even with the end of the Cold War and the diminished specter of "godless communism," atheists and freethinkers still inspire plenty of fear and loathing. They are often still relegated to a place beyond the pale of equal citizenship and social trust.[32]

Safe to say, any neat linear narrative about the public fate of American nonbelievers quickly breaks down—not only because of the ongoing conflicts and ambivalences that characterize the contemporary scene, but also because of the religious-secular contortions that have been evident throughout the nation's history. Has an entrepreneurial religious marketplace, for example, driven the country to remarkable heights of religiosity, making it appear eccentrically God-fearing compared to most European nations? Or, have secularizing forces—in higher education, in entertainment and the arts, in science and medicine—brought about a gradual de-Christianization of American public life? Good historians are able to make compelling cases for both sides of this argument because these contradictory trends have long coexisted.[33] The question then is not whether secularism has been advancing, while religion has been retreating (or vice versa), but rather how the two have interacted, overlapped, coincided, and clashed. The religious and the secular, belief and unbelief—these are not zero-sum games, but relationships of tangled complexity, fluctuating rivalry, and constitutive mutuality. The underlying presumption that the nation's history must be headed one way or another—through an unfolding process of secularization or Christianization—remains hard to relinquish, but the history told here purposefully occupies the uneasy space between those persistent narrative devices. Only a tensile plot, shorn of both Protestant hegemony and secular inevitability, can make sense of the relational interdependence and volatility that has long subsisted between believers and nonbelievers in American culture.

A word finally about numbers. Notwithstanding the recent upward trend for the religious "Nones," including the 7–8 percent of Americans who identify openly as atheist or agnostic, the unshakeable impression is that unbelievers remain—as they have always been—a negligible presence in a deeply religious nation. (Mark Twain's joke about Judge Driscoll's Society of Freethinkers mustering only two members in four years typifies that perspective.) Certainly infidels and freethinkers constituted a distinct minority in nineteenth-century America, as do avowed atheists and agnostics in the early twenty-first century, but the number of unbelievers was not inconsequential then—just as it is not inconsequential now. In the census of 1890, the first to collect extensive data on religious identification, formal church membership stood at about 35 percent of the population. The Methodist layman H. K. Carroll, the statistician overseeing the religious returns for the census, was confident adherence rates were actually much higher than that once attendees who were not full-fledged communicants, including young children, were added to the picture. Those adjustments more than doubled the aggregate number of Protestant adherents and made the country appear overwhelmingly Christian—indeed, about 80 percent Protestant (when Catholics were grudgingly added, the number rose to about 90 percent). Even with Carroll's optimistic Protestant reading of the census data, however, five million people were still left "belonging to the non-religious and anti-religious classes, including freethinkers, secularists, and infidels." Though Carroll continued to insist that there were "but few real atheists" in the United States, he had to admit that 8 percent of the population appeared to be "an active or passive opponent of religion." That in itself was a hefty number. If the irreligious had somehow constituted their own denomination, they would have had as many communicants as the Methodists did in 1890, and far more than the Presbyterians.[34]

Carroll was right that, by all kinds of measures, American Protestantism was growing and flourishing at the end of the nine-teenth century—in the value of property holdings, in the seating capacity of churches, in the number of ministerial recruits and for-mal members. Yet, even as his statistical compilations reassured him of the continuing ascendancy of evangelical Christianity, he had to admit that his confident projections masked another prob-lem: namely, many who counted themselves Christians "seldom or never [went] into a house of worship" and were essentially "indif-ferent to the claims of religion." This gap between profession and practice had caused the Unitarian pastor Octavius Frothingham to remark in 1878 that there were "no statistics to describe the numerical or geographical extent" of unbelief. "It is larger than can be expressed in figures," he argued, because "a great many who are present in the churches" were actually secret unbelievers, thus making "ecclesiastical connections" an unreliable measure of Christianity's hold on the culture. "Unbelief is more widely spread now than it ever was;" Frothingham declared, "it is more general; it comprehends more classes of people; it embraces more orders and varieties of mind." The minister was not offering this estimate as a jeremiad, a call for revival, but instead as some-one who, as an outré Unitarian, knew intimately the "beliefs of the unbelievers." Ballyhooed adherence rates inflated Protestant dominance, Frothingham maintained, while disguising the extent of religious disaffection, indifference, and doubt.[35]

Likely Frothingham, as a post-Christian liberal, overestimated in his turn the extent of clandestine unbelief and the fragility of American faith, but he was certainly right about this much: plenty of his fellow citizens still found it prudent to hide their skeptical misgivings behind at least nominal church affiliation. Re-ligious membership retained the benefits of public respectability, while open expressions of infidelity carried corresponding social risks. As a routinely excoriated minority, freethinkers and atheists knew that it behooved them to tread warily, even as they bemoaned that imposed caution. The testimony of a lonely infidel in Zanesville, Ohio, was suggestive of the minority status and social marginality that so often accompanied professed unbelief. Writing in 1854 to the *Boston Investigator*, he noted how pleased he was to learn about the cadre of British liberals, led by free-thinker George Jacob Holyoake, who had recently come up with a new name for their unbelief, "secularism." "For many years I have been one of that much-abused class called Atheists," he confessed, "but I never liked the name. In youth I was taught it was some hideous monster, and I cannot yet get rid of the idea that there is something derogatory in it when applied to me among my Christian family." As a small-town infidel, he felt all "alone" in Zanesville, while everyone else around him seemed to have one religious society or another with which to identify. "With a new name and some good design to work by," he hazarded, "I believe I could organize a small community here that are now wandering in the mazes of doubt." Though some of his fellow infidels were quick to cast the proposed name change as a sign of weakness, the secularist badge provided this Zanesville atheist with a little dash of hope that he might yet overcome the civic isolation that was part of his everyday experience. Protestant dominance may have been less secure than the high rates of church adherence suggested, but that proved small consolation for avowed atheists who continued to feel keenly their peculiarity. Open unbelievers, like the Zanesville secularist, remained accustomed to being outliers.[36]

However often atheists and freethinkers pronounced that history was on their side—that the triumph of scientific rationality and secular statecraft was assured—there was finally no getting around their minority status. The social costs associated with unbelief—and the pressures to keep quiet about it or to blunt it with one humanistic gloss or another—remained high throughout the nineteenth century, and well beyond. In one of Emanuel Haldeman-Julius's "Little Blue Books" from about 1930, freethinking lawyer Frank Swancara pointedly asked, "Have We Religious

Freedom?" Studying at length the debilities America's unbelievers faced, Swancara very much doubted that they enjoyed liberty
of conscience, certainly not in the same way that mainstream
Protestants did. "The atheist or agnostic must keep still, and
allow the religious public to regard him as a silent believer," Swancara yet claimed of his own era. To the "orthodox majority," the
unbeliever who openly disclaimed God or disparaged the Bible
remained "but a monster, in human form," odious to his or her
Christian neighbors. For America's village atheists, secularism
did not define their communities, let alone their age. Harboring
dreams of metaphysical conquest and political mastery, they settled instead for filing a series of minority reports. Often their
secularism proved but a petition for the toleration of their monstrosity, an appeal against the boycotting of their aberrant godlessness, a nonconformist case for irreligious liberty in a country
long wary of the free exercise of unbelief. Rough-edged figures
who worked against the grain of a godly nation, village atheists
negotiated their way into American public life through decades of
engagement and conflict. It is time now to give their secularist
stories a fuller hearing.[37]

CHAPTER 1

THE SECULAR PILGRIM

---◆---

OR, THE HERE WITHOUT THE HEREAFTER

SAMUEL PORTER PUTNAM WAS "BRED IN BLOOD AND BONE" in the orthodoxy of New England's old Congregational order. His father, Rufus Austin Putnam, was a Harvard graduate, class of 1822, who spent his entire career in the parish ministry. The wandering son recollected his steady father—he "never yielded one iota of his orthodox convictions"—with almost formulaic images of severity. Rufus had been as austere and unloving as the Father God he extolled: "He seemed a kind of grand shadow in my childhood. I do not remember that there was ever a flash of real sympathy between us." The scattered farmers of Chichester, New Hampshire, would gather each Sabbath to hear the patriarch preach his undiluted Calvinism: "All were fellow-travelers to eternity, and heaven was the goal," Samuel recalled. "Only a few, however, expected to get there, and the terrors of hell-fire were expatiated upon with fear and trembling." Decades afterward, Putnam expressed only bitterness toward the long Sabbath services of his childhood and the haunting fright of his father's sermons: "Many a night I awoke crying with terror," scared that his prayers for a "new heart" would come to naught and that he was among the damned. To a small boy, in that tiny church under his father's care, Protestant orthodoxy had felt inescapable and overpowering. If there were any village atheists in this New Hampshire crossroads, the pastor's son never met them: "To be an Infidel at that time, in that place, was an almost unheard-of monstrosity."[1]

FigURE 1. Samuel Porter Putnam, from Samuel P. Putnam, *400 Years of Freethought*
(New York: Truth Seeker Co., 1894), plate at p. 518. Author's Collection

In penning *My Religious Experience* (1891), Putnam imagined his life story as a Puritan counternarrative, a testimonial anti-type. To be able to give a credible account of regeneration was at the heart of his evangelical Calvinist upbringing; he had heard about the marks of genuine conversion "all the years of my child-hood." But, when it came time to relate his own experience, he self-consciously plotted a reverse pilgrimage from the one his father had projected for him. Among the few books besides the Bible that the young Putnam remembered being explicitly encouraged to read was John Bunyan's classic allegory, *The Pilgrim's Progress* (1678). Bunyan's Christian—a model Puritan saint—anxiously traverses a treacherous, narrow, temptation-laden path to get to the Celes-tial City. Among the distractions Christian encounters is Atheist who, scoffing at the dreary journey the pilgrim has undertaken, has stopped looking for Mount Zion and is heading back to the City of Destruction. Bunyan's saint, of course, remains true to his faith and quickly moves past Atheist, whose only remaining god is this world. In narrating his religious experience, Putnam effec-tively rewrote that archetypal Protestant narrative from Atheist's viewpoint. No longer a sojourner making his way in the light of eternity, Putnam became an itinerant freethinker, "a confirmed Materialist and Atheist," and a paradigmatic American secular-ist. His was an earthbound pilgrimage, not a celestial one. Put-nam's self-chosen sobriquet—"the Secular Pilgrim"—made that Puritan antithesis unmistakable.[2]

Putnam saw his "passing from the heart of orthodoxy to Free-thought" as a liberating progression, but that hardly made it a straightforward process. It was, as Putnam acknowledged, "a varied journey," not a linear march from religious authority to secular enlightenment, but an unsteady dance with his Protestant inheritance. In hindsight, the end point of his countervailing pil-grimage into atheism may have looked foregone, but it unfolded in multiple stages—with at least two switchbacks into the faith and three separate stints in Congregational and Unitarian ministries. For a long time, Putnam was not sure whether he wanted to ex-tricate himself from Christianity entirely or instead to reimagine

it on liberal Protestant terms; even his split from evangelical Calvinism never looked so much like a neat divorce as a family psy-
chodrama. Having haltingly removed himself from the pulpit's
long shadow, he would try out a series of public reinventions: as
a customs official, a novelist, a traveling lecturer, an editor, and
a historian. Around one self-transformation, however, he built an
elaborate secret—his momentary boldness as a free lover. All narratives are unfaithful, but Putnam's relation of his religious experience proved doubly so. He studiously hid the sexual implications
of his infidelity as well as the vulnerabilities of his secular identity behind a facade of atheistic assurance and finality.[3]

To say that Putnam's secular pilgrimage was paradigmatic
warrants some specification. The snaking route by which he re-
linquished his evangelical Calvinism for atheistic materialism involved all the major conduits of secularism's formal articulation:
(1) liberalizing religious movements that pushed within and then
beyond Protestantism—Unitarianism and the Free Religious Association were key institutionalized expressions; (2) organized
forms of freethinking activism—the National Liberal League and
American Secular Union stood out; and (3) expanding media platforms to spread the secularist message—coast-to-coast lecture
circuits and successful weekly journals, including the *Index* and
the *Truth Seeker*, were critical. Putnam was a wayfarer through
all of these religious fluctuations and irreligious developments.
"When . . . I think of the seminary, and orthodox pulpit, and
Liberal ministry, and the Secular pilgrimages, and the immense
theological and metaphysical spaces I have traversed," Putnam
remarked on a roving lecture tour in 1886, "I feel about a million
years of age. It has been a round-about journey, during which
God, heaven, and hell have disappeared like so many sparks, and
only the earth remains." That could have been the epitaph for the
secular pilgrimage Putnam embodied and exemplified: only the
earth remained. The empyrean horizon of the hereafter dimmed
to vanishing in the fleshy immediacy of the here-and-now. And
yet Putnam's journey also disclosed the very fragility of that
disappearance—how much work was required to keep the celes-

tial from reinserting itself into his own allegory of secularism's triumph.[4]

———————◆———————

Putnam recalled his mother, Frances, more fondly than he did his father. She was "more companionable," more "open to the sunlight and beauty of this world." The big meals Frances prepared for Sunday evenings marked the reentry of some bodily delight after a full day at the meetinghouse; apart from a little whittling on the sly between the morning and afternoon sermons, Putnam considered his mother's Sabbath fare the day's only consolation. Not that she was anything less than a faithful churchgoer, the proper helpmeet for her husband's ministry, but Samuel saw in her a greater ease with earthly enjoyments, tender emotions, and mundane responsibilities. The son recalled Monday washdays, for example, as glittering and happy by comparison to Sabbath observances; his mother presided over the duties in which "things seemed real" and his father over the errands that seemed impalpable. Putnam here traded on a series of familiar gender oppositions in which his father was cerebral and remote and his mother corporeal and sociable, but his observations were nonetheless suggestive. His mother was "a good cook," and, late in life, Putnam was ready to set down those Sunday meals as his first taste of a secular pilgrimage—a gustatory indication, within his strict Sabbatarian upbringing, of how freeing it would be to have religious obligations give way to fleshly appetites.[5]

Putnam's debt to his father also remained substantial, far more so than the son cared to admit. All the jeremiads about diminished clerical authority notwithstanding, the Congregational ministry remained an esteemed learned profession in antebellum New England. Rufus Putnam's vocation depended on serious study and substantial intellectual training, and he had a library fit to undergird his calling's scholarly, literary, and apologetic demands. As a youth, Samuel delved into his father's books for hours on end. A miscellany of theology, literature, and history, the collection belied Putnam's flat depiction of his father's blinkered dogmatism.

Among the books the son found, for example, were histories of ancient Greece that left him agape at the glories of Athens (as opposed to Jerusalem). He discovered as well the works of William Ellery Channing, the champion of New England's liberal Christian vanguard, the herald of both Unitarianism and the wider Transcendentalist ferment of Ralph Waldo Emerson and company. The father was by no means one of Channing's acolytes, but, as a learned minister, he had to be well versed in the theological debates that were then agitating the Congregational churches in order to shore up his own evangelical Calvinism. The son, by contrast, took Channing's sermons as a breath of fresh air; they filled him "with a strange feeling of relief." In the "top loft of the big old parsonage," the son read against the grain of his father's orthodoxy and bubbled with a youthful enthusiasm for more. Once he had his hands on Shakespeare, for example, the Bible seemed so "vastly inferior . . . in wealth of thought and life." His father's library, Putnam reminisced decades later, "was the nearest to heaven I ever got in my childhood."[6]

By his mid-to-late teens, when Putnam was at Pembroke Academy prepping for his 1858 matriculation at Dartmouth College, his reading had turned decisively to Romantic poetry. He became fixated, above all, on Percy Bysshe Shelley, a poet notorious for his heterodoxy (Shelley had been expelled from Oxford for authoring a pamphlet entitled *The Necessity of Atheism*): "I was saturated with his genius," Putnam effused. He described Shelley as "my Bible and my religion"; he claimed to have experienced a "new birth" through Shelley's "brilliant revival of the Pagan and Greek spirit." It was, of course, the opposite of the conversion for which his parents had long been praying—anti-Christian, pantheistic, if not atheistic, in its vivid rebellion. Once at Dartmouth, Putnam relished his Promethean revolt all the more and saw his irreligion as part of a heady adventure. The lingering "orthodox influences" at the college—chapel prayers and professorial admonitions—left him entirely untouched; he was blithe about the Bible's irrelevance to his new life. Dreamy and impulsive, with Shelley as his guiding spirit, Putnam was sure that "the bands of the Puritan faith were broken" and that he would "never be anything else but an Atheist."[7]

Thirty-some years later Putnam would look back with embarrassment on his "unreal and fantastic college life" and the "sentimental Infidelity" that had seized him: "My unbelief was the romance of sentiment." He felt, in hindsight, as if he had been a Transcendentalist caricature, gasping at sunsets and starry nights and listening to the melodies of forests and fields. "They who are Infidels as I was at college, merely through the emotions, are not always able to stand the onslaught of the churches," he admitted, "for anything built upon emotion is apt to be swept away by emotion." He had not been schooled in Enlightenment infidelity—in Hume, Voltaire, or Paine—but instead had "come out of Christianity" much as Ralph Waldo Emerson had, on a counter-Enlightenment "wave of feeling." The problem, as Putnam ultimately came to see it, was that his romantic pantheism still valued religious feeling and soulful epiphany, and, in that, it was "too much like sentimental Christianity." It had taken the fifty-something infidel a very long time to see his collegiate mistake for what it was—that "religious feeling, as feeling, is wrong"—but the seriousness of that intervening intellectual struggle made him no less forgiving of his youthful naïveté. "The last superstition of the human mind," the mature Putnam somberly averred, "is the superstition that religion in itself is a good thing." The retention of transcendental aspiration, in whatever guise, was what ultimately needed to be dissolved.[8]

The grizzled atheist of 1890 had it in for the callow infidel of 1860 because of what happened next. The Civil War broke out in 1861, and the idyll Putnam had been living was swiftly blown apart. Leaving Dartmouth his junior year without graduating, he enlisted as a private in the Union Army. His father had been a staunch reformer—active in temperance, missionary, and anti-slavery societies—and the son, even in his religious estrangement, knew intimately the strenuous demands of the New England conscience. Samuel went off to war with exalted purpose and high enthusiasm—to fight for "absolute principle," to put an end to slavery, to save the nation. He served first in the Fourth New York Heavy Artillery before being promoted in early 1864 to captain in the Twentieth U.S. Colored Infantry, a post he held until the end of the war. Camp life and the battlefield, especially "marching and counter-marching for days and weeks" in the Shenandoah Valley, came close to destroying him. "It is well enough to talk about inward strength and self-reliance," he observed, but those shibboleths made no sense of the absolute dependency upon the circumstances of army life that he now felt. The war's "prison-house" of dull routine and horrific violence left Putnam with one strangely Christian verity intact: "We cannot live upon what we are in ourselves."[9]

On one forced march toward Washington, Putnam was over-taken by fever, hunger, thirst, and blinding pain. Suddenly, he found his "whole life's history" flashing through his mind "with astonishing distinctness," as if in that moment he were drowning. And that is when it happened—when the "sentimental Infidelity" of his college days proved no bar against the vast onrushing of devout emotion:

> Home came before me with its sweet scenes, and mingled with the pictures the teachings I had received from father and mother; the milder aspect of religion, not the wrath of God or the fires of hell, but the love of Jesus. . . . With overwhelming power sounded the appeal I had so often heard: "Surrender to Jesus." I was looking at the cross shining against an ineffable halo. There was no fear in my emotions. It was simply attraction. . . . Suddenly out of my weakness, my suffering, the pain, the weariness, and the despair, my heart cried out, "I surrender!" There was no reserve.

Even thirty years later, when he was once again an atheist, Putnam remained in awe of this visionary episode, his battlefield surrender to Jesus. In a twinkling he had been saved; he had been transformed: "That one can pass in a moment from darkness to light, from the deepest misery to the brightest joy, by a belief in Jesus, has been a fact in my own life." What to make of that fact—what interpretation to give this experience—absorbed him for the remainder of his days. That he ultimately settled on "nat-ural causes" to explain this epiphany did not make the transformation any "less real." The fruits of the experience were, in this case, as tangible as a Monday washday.[10]

———————◆———————

Putnam's surrender to Jesus reconciled him to his childhood faith and dramatically reoriented his life aspirations. After he left the Union Army in June 1865, he decided to follow in the vocational footsteps of his father, and he headed off to Chicago Theological Seminary to train for the Congregational ministry. He went as an evangelical Calvinist much in the mold, he said, of "the theology of my parents." While his new birth had given his faith an emotional imperative, those warmhearted feelings were necessarily filtered through all the catechesis of his upbringing. Doctrine very much shaped experience—as was evident when Putnam reflected on the theological underpinnings of his own conversion: "So far as the phenomenon of the 'new birth' was concerned," he concluded, "the theologians were right. It came about just as they said it would." Putnam went to seminary having made the standards of evangelical Calvinist piety and learning very much his own. He led with the heart perhaps, but he talked up as well the intellectual delights of the profession—the "leisure and position" it would afford him to "learn all there is to learn." The other professions, he insisted, required too much specialized knowledge; the minister's calling was a summons instead to "universal inquiry" into "all philosophy, all poetry, all art, all history." His freethinking companions of the 1880s and 1890s might wonder why "any man of intelligence" would choose to enter the Christian ministry, but Putnam would never issue an apology for "the ideal ministry" he had imagined for himself in the wake of his wartime experience.[11]

That the reality would fall well short of the ideal was surely a given. Putnam found theological study corrosive to his religious affections; the seminary's "intellectual gymnastics" seemed to him anything but universal. They were, rather, trivial, the equivalent of counting angels on pinheads or distinguishing "betwixt tweedle-dee and tweedle-dum." Putnam's romantic and evangelical sensibilities combined to make formal theological training appear inherently artificial and businesslike. Prayer meetings felt like rehearsals—as if Putnam and his fellow students were practicing their ministerial roles rather than pouring out their souls. Similarly, the seminary's professor of homiletics, Putnam lamented, "had no spontaneity. . . . He made me a mechanic, but not an artist. He could not convey to me one wave of impulse." Professor of Hebrew Samuel Colcord Bartlett was no better: "Under his instructions I could be nothing but a theological martinet. Any real feeling was impossible." Indeed, it was Bartlett especially who seems to have reawakened Putnam's animus against orthodoxy; he reserved for Bartlett images of coldness and gloom—"a frowning precipice," "a strong-willed Puritan"—reminiscent of those he employed to describe his father. He felt from Bartlett only "the terror of the Almighty" and "nothing of the loveliness and sweetness of Jesus" that had been at the heart of his conversion. If this were all the seminary had to offer, Putnam concluded, he might well "have sloughed off orthodoxy before I graduated" and abandoned his vocational plans.[12]

Putnam was kept on track for the Congregational ministry by his growing awareness of liberalizing forces within Protestantism itself. The seminary's third and final professor, Joseph Haven, was the initial broker for Putnam of those wider intellectual developments. A well-respected moral philosopher, with a distinguished career at Amherst College already behind him, Haven modeled for Putnam a theological adroitness by which the "old doctrines" were made "mellow and humane." It was almost certainly through Haven that Putnam was introduced, as part of his theological studies, to the work of Horace Bushnell, a fount of liberal Protestant theology. By the mid-to-late 1860s, Bushnell was firmly established as an intellectual luminary among those American expositors directly engaging the work of Samuel Taylor Coleridge and Friedrich Schleiermacher, particularly their theological turn to experience and feeling as the ultimate ground of the Christian faith. In redirecting attention from the logic of theological systems to the spiritual immediacy of Christian consciousness, Bushnell also reimagined the inspiration of the scriptures— the Bible, he claimed, was to be engaged as a poem of the spiritual

life, not as a storehouse of Baconian facts. In the view of his orthodox critics, Bushnell played fast and loose with theological language; he showed a stunning disregard for doctrinal exactitude
on issues as fundamentally important as the Trinity and human
depravity; he took a perverse delight in the polysemy of Christian symbols and texts. The very things that troubled Bushnell's
detractors—lions of Calvinist orthodoxy like Charles Hodge and
Bennet Tyler—only made the Hartford pastor more appealing to
Putnam. A salve for Putnam's own frustrations with theological
rationalism, Bushnell provided the exasperated seminary student
with a more capacious and fluid orthodoxy.[13]

The one book of Bushnell's that Putnam especially saw as a
liberal Protestant lifeline was *The Vicarious Sacrifice, Grounded
in Principles of Universal Obligation*, which appeared in 1866
while he was in the midst of his studies at Chicago Theological Seminary. Putnam had been struggling with the doctrine of
the atonement, particularly the notion that God had wrathfully
demanded his Son's death on the cross as a substitutionary penalty for the sins of humanity. Putnam was far from alone in finding that "old doctrine" to be "cruel" and "barbaric"; it seemed
to turn God into "an iron despot" whose sense of justice was
wildly distorted by anger and malice. Bushnell had struggled for
more than two decades to reinterpret the doctrine in moral terms
he himself could accept; *Vicarious Sacrifice* was the culmination
of those efforts. Putnam read and reread the book, finding comfort in how effectively Bushnell reimagined the import of Christ's
sufferings and the qualities of God's character. In Bushnell's
hands, the atonement signified not the satisfaction of God's ven-
geance, but was instead an exemplification of divine love and
compassion. In Putnam's recapitulation of Bushnell, this was "a
love so infinite, so tender, so sympathetic, that God himself . . .
suffered as the mother suffers in the wrong-doing of her child. She
suffers not any penalty, not any consequence of sin, but suffers as
love must suffer when it sees a loved one perishing." The gender
switch—God himself becomes a mother herself—was telling not
only in relation to Putnam's familial and religious formation, but
also as an indication of the larger liberal Protestant reimagining

of the faith in more nurturing, maternal, and altruistic terms. Putnam saw now through Bushnell's exegesis that the cross was a "revelation of love, gentleness, grief, and undying sympathy." This view of the atonement, Putnam felt, had "a wonderfully softening effect" on the doctrines of evangelical Calvinism tout court—from original sin to eschatology. As Putnam saw it, Bushnell's theology allowed him "to preserve my humanity," while staying within orthodox denominational bounds.[14]

Graduating from seminary in 1868, Putnam was ordained to the Congregational ministry and went out to preach the gospel very much on the pattern of a liberalizing orthodoxy. Happy to be putting dry theological speculations behind him, he entered upon his new vocation with enthusiasm: "I really thought that I had found my life work." He quickly accepted a call to be the pastor of two small churches in the neighboring communities of De Kalb and Malta, Illinois, seventy miles west of Chicago, and spent the next three years happily working back and forth between the two villages. The salary was small, but the labor felt important. "As the result of my efforts," Putnam fondly recalled, "a new church building was erected on the prairies of Illinois. I looked upon this with glowing hope." The Jesus who had appeared to him on the forced march to Washington, the loving Savior who exemplified the "ideal perfection" of tenderness and sympathy, remained his guide. The point of his ministry was to bring his congregants to model their own Christian character on the nurturing kindness and compassion of Jesus, to feel the moral influence of the Lord's "soft and feminine" nature in their own lives. Putnam hoped, at least for now, to be the Horace Bushnell or Henry Ward Beecher of the rural hinterlands, the bearer of a delicately modified orthodoxy that kept pilgrims within the familiar denominational bodies rather than pushing them beyond the Protestant fold.[15]

The shine of Putnam's ministerial aspirations soon began to dim. However much he might have wanted to put old theological conundrums out of his mind, they continued to plague him: Could he really wrap his mind around the doctrine of total depravity? And, if not, what became of the necessity of regeneration and the new birth? And what about such infamous doctrinal horrors as the damnation of infants—who could have ever believed that the baby "on the mother's breast" was "fuel for hell"? As Putnam despaired, "There seemed to be no end to the struggle" of adjusting and then readjusting "my theology." But those doctrinal quagmires were only half the problem. In the humdrum of his pastoral labors, he came to the realization that church members were pretty much on a level with nonmembers: "Were the saints any better than the sinners?" he wondered doubtfully. His most faithful congregants started to seem lackluster and uninteresting; talking with them about the crops, the weather, and the good of their souls made for "fearfully dull companionship." Their descriptions of their heavenward pilgrimages seemed both sepulchral and clichéd: "A little travel the other way might have improved the cheerfulness of the procession," Putnam dryly remarked. Amid his grave pastoral visits he began to yearn for the livelier company of sinners, for the social enjoyments of "real human beings" who did not worry overmuch about the state of their souls. Not only was his orthodox theology continuing to disintegrate, but also his sense of calling to the Congregational ministry was rapidly evaporating.[16]

Putnam's next move into the Unitarian ministry was logical enough. When he made the switch in 1871, Unitarianism had been the standard path out of New England's Congregational orthodoxy for a half century. It allowed him to hold onto his broadest religious principles about God, Jesus, immortality, and human possibility without binding him to a creed. "I need not be afraid to express in its pulpit any intellectual conclusion to which I might arrive," Putnam rejoiced of his newfound liberty. Unitarian latitude did not free the church of controversy, of course; it just pushed the lines of dissent and division farther out on the liberal spectrum. Putnam quickly found himself in the thick of a debate about whether being Unitarian required the retention of the Christian name. He sided, at least initially, with those who viewed Unitarianism as the height of a liberalized Christianity— elastic, progressive, and cosmopolitan, but still at heart Christian in name and spirit. That preponderant view was espoused by the

foremost Unitarian churchman of the period, Henry Whitney Bellows, and Putnam respected his leadership immensely. Putnam
also felt, though, the pull of a smaller bunch of radicals who, in
1867, had formed their own dissenting band known as the Free Religious Association. Taking up the torch of the Transcendentalist
nonconformists of the previous generation, this group moved in
expressly post-Christian directions. They proffered a universalistic theism ostensibly freed from any Christian identification; they
mixed pluralistic religious inquiry with a supreme confidence in
scientific advancement. From 1871 to 1875 the Unitarian ministry
was Putnam's home, with pastorates in Ohio and Nebraska, but
the whole time he felt suspended more than settled, poised in
the tense space between a very liberal Protestantism and an expressly post-Christian identity.[17]

In these years Putnam gradually moved into closer fellowship
with the post-Christian radicals and the Free Religious Association. Among the leading spokesmen for this wing of Unitarian
come-outers was Francis Ellingwood Abbot who had started up
a journal called the *Index* in 1870—a weekly that would become
one of the primary platforms for defining liberal secularism as
a movement. Putnam credited Abbot with a "vast influence" on
him in these transitional years and began to write regularly for
the *Index*. To preserve his Unitarian credentials Putnam also remained a frequent contributor to Bellows's *Liberal Christian*, but
such fence-sitting did not mesh well with Abbot's approach to
ecclesial politics. Having failed to get the National Conference of
Unitarian Churches to renounce their Christian allegiance, Abbot
turned around and refused the name *Unitarian* for the last two
churches he pastored—they became Independent Societies with a
stated commitment to free inquiry. Those congregational exper-
iments fared poorly, and Abbot left the ministry for good in 1873
and turned to philosophical and political pursuits. An early proponent of Darwin's evolutionary theory, Abbot wanted all theological speculation subsumed into the methodological rigor of the
sciences. That God-of-Science side of Abbot's work, though, held
little attraction for Putnam, at least at this point. He actually
went on record in the pages of the *Index* against Abbot's wholly

scientific theism, wanting still to preserve room for the feelings of faith, for "the sweet, strange mystery" of things spiritual and infinite. Abbot welcomed the debate but was never going to yield on the point that God's fate was now in science's hands.[18]

Putnam was instead drawn to Abbot's political preoccupation with strict church-state separation. Abbot had first promulgated "The Demands of Liberalism" in the *Index* in April 1872; it was a nine-part petition calling for "our entire political system" to be "administered on a purely secular basis." Bible reading in the public schools, religious oaths in courtrooms, tax exemptions for church property, government-funded chaplaincies, state proclamations of religious festivals, and laws enforcing Sabbath observance—all these things needed to go. This secular program became Abbot's rallying cry: "ORGANIZE! LIBERALS OF AMERICA! The hour for action has arrived." He saw American liberty as especially imperiled by the political ambitions of certain evangelical Protestant groups that had begun lobbying in the wake of the Civil War for constitutional recognition of the United States as an expressly Christian nation. These efforts included a proposed revision of the Preamble to include acknowledgment of not only God, but also the Lord Jesus Christ and the Holy Scriptures as the basis of the country's civil government. Working to mobilize liberals of all stripes as a political counterweight to such ecclesial ambitions, Abbot led a massive petition drive against the proposed constitutional changes—a secularist campaign that helped keep this particular Protestant cause from gaining traction in Congress. He also began promoting the organization of local Liberal Leagues around the country to make known secularism's "Nine Demands" at municipal and state levels. These groups, in turn, became the basis for the formation of the National Liberal League at the nation's centennial celebration in Philadelphia in 1876. Abbot was elected the association's first president, with an illustrious lineup of religious liberals and freethinking secularists onboard—from Robert Ingersoll to Elizabeth Cady Stanton to Isaac Mayer Wise. By 1880, the league had over two hundred local auxiliaries dotting the country; by 1885, it claimed a membership of thirty thousand.[19]

Putnam was no more than a minor foot soldier in the initial rise of the Liberal League movement, but he had gotten cozy enough with Abbot's post-Christian band of secularist agitators to cause him trouble with his Omaha congregation. One of Abbot's colleagues, a freethinker named B. F. Underwood, had determined to promote the formation of local Liberal Leagues by turning secularism's claims into a traveling exhibition. On tour in 1875, Underwood had a list of twenty-one "RADICAL LECTURES" that were his stock-in-trade, including "What Liberalism offers as a *Substitute* for Christianity," "Evolution *versus* Christianity," and "Fancies and Fallacies about God." Underwood arrived in Omaha that spring, and Putnam invited him to speak from his Unitarian pulpit. Not known for his soft touch, Underwood delivered "an out-and-out Materialistic and scientific lecture," rife with atheistic provocations that turned Putnam's congregation against him. Putnam now faced a dilemma. In full sympathy with the liberal secular politics of Underwood and Abbot, he had also inched his way toward seeing the wisdom of renouncing the Christian name and taking a public stand as "anti-Christian" or "at least non-Christian." If being in the pulpit meant that he had to dissociate himself from the *Index* circle and profess beliefs he no longer accepted, then could he really stay in the Unitarian ministry? Deciding to take his stand with the radicals, Putnam resigned from his Omaha charge effective June 1, 1875. By then, he had already skipped town for Boston, "the Mecca of all Liberal pilgrims," to be a featured speaker at the annual meeting of the Free Religious Association at the end of May. There he rubbed elbows with the leading radicals—Abbot, of course, but also such New England literati as Octavius Frothingham and Thomas Wentworth Higginson. About a week later, still in Boston, Putnam tendered a letter of withdrawal from the whole of the Unitarian Association, wishing "to be no longer called a Unitarian or Christian minister."[20]

In announcing that decision Putnam set his sights on becoming a player, like Underwood, in "the Liberal lecture field." Having cast off (for the moment) "the empty and objectionable prefix of Reverend," Putnam seemed more than ready in mid-1875 for a trial run at an explicitly secular identity. He began to cultivate ties with D. M. Bennett, founding editor in 1873 of the *Truth Seeker*—a banner freethought paper with a more uncensored edge than Abbot's higher-born *Index*. Of the many free-thinking journals created in the decades following the Civil War, the *Truth Seeker* would be the most enduring and influential, with a national network of agents, subscribers, and aficionados. In one of Putnam's earliest pieces for Bennett's paper, which appeared just a few months after his resignation from the ministry, he extolled manliness over godliness, trying to establish a masculine pose against the gentler, more nurturing qualities that he had long prized in Jesus: "A manly man we know, but a 'godly' man, what is he?" Putnam asked. He also pointed to the real-world focus of his emergent secularism—earthly attainments were all that mattered, not airy pursuits of eternity: "Do not follow after a huge fantasy in the heavens," he advised. For his part, Bennett did what he could to support Putnam in his new venture, urging like-minded liberals to come out to hear him wherever he visited and reminding subscribers that the task Putnam was undertaking would not be easy. "The Liberal element is still unpopular; we are yet comparatively few in numbers," Bennett acknowledged. "The churches are populous, rich, and powerful, and their members still affect to turn up their noses and contemptuously scorn those who dare to think for themselves. It costs something yet to be an Infidel." Putnam, relying on his ties in the West, looked toward Nebraska especially and the work of Liberal Leaguers in Lincoln, Omaha, and Fremont. His lectures, he hoped, would help bring "the latent Liberalism" of that state into predominance.[21]

It did not take long for Putnam to regret deeply the course he had taken. Bennett was no doubt right that it remained a difficult road to abandon the church for the freethought lecture field—indeed, significantly harder in 1875 than it would be just a few years later after Robert Ingersoll had taken the country by storm. (The number of freethought lecturers touring the country went from a small handful to close to sixty between 1875 and 1885.) Perhaps, as one of his naysayers remarked at the time, Putnam had not found "Infidelity as profitable as expected" and was simply getting queasy about his prospects for solvency. Certainly, the

thought of taking up a routine job filled him with the dread of an
unrepentant romantic: "Go into business and forget all my aspirations, all the delights of study, leave the ideal world entirely?"
he asked in despair. The would-be Secular Pilgrim had obviously
thought that he was ready to make his way apart from any religious community and to propound hither and thither the liberal
secularism of Abbot and Underwood. Instead, for all the hopeful
glosses he wanted to put on the "strange changes" of his life, he
felt increasingly lost and disoriented, "tossed upon a sea of uncertainty," no longer "anywhere at home." Less than a year into
his renunciation of the Unitarian ministry, he began looking for a
way to return to that profession with its high spiritual and intellectual ideals, even if it meant reidentifying himself as a Christian. Years later, in another bout of hindsight, Putnam would see
this "little loosening of the bonds of integrity" as "a mistake," an
unwarranted compromise, but in the perplexities of the moment
he happily reaccepted Christianity in the poetic, idealistic, and
affective terms that had long been alluring to him. Taking "the
verity-giving power of human emotion" as his guide, Putnam re-
verted to the Unitarian pulpit after a short but anguishing time
without the anchor of a vocational identity.[22]

Called to a church in Northfield, Massachusetts, in early 1876,
Putnam returned to a Transcendentalist register of a "rapt spirit"
in the face of nature's mystical resplendence. He drank in the lu-
minous landscape of the Connecticut River Valley with a soul released from the "shadows of the night" into communion with "the
Everlasting Yea." He now wore the Christian badge without fret-
ting, even as he gushed, as other religious seekers of the era were
wont to do, about being much else besides—"a kind of Buddhist,"
"somewhat of a theosophist, a pantheist, 'god-intoxicated,' like
Spinoza." Putnam had resigned from the Unitarian church under
the impetus of Underwood's scientific materialism, only to repent
of his decision in deference to a romantic theism of noble feelings
and individual epiphanies. "God his sweetness gives, we know
not how," he wrote in one poem at the time. "It comes ineffably
from our own heart." Or, in another: "We shall know that beauty
still is strong— / That there is heart and life, the good, the fair; /

That God is smiling in the sunny air." None of this squared with the freethinking radicals for whom Putnam had been willing to go to the mat in mid-to-late 1875. Constancy was not the mark of his secular pilgrimage—or of most secular pilgrimages of the era. Putnam zigzagged his way out of and into and out of and into any number of things—atheism included.[23]

In *My Religious Experience* Putnam spoke only glowingly of his ministry in Northfield, which lasted into early 1879. "If I could have had my choice," he wrote, "I would have cherished this beautiful faith. I would not have let it go." Two things happened, however, that forced him to relinquish the agreeable appointment in Northfield, only one of which he chose to discuss in narrating his convoluted journey into infidelity. The expressed reason was that once again an atheistic materialism had overtaken his theological dream-world, this time chilling for good the spiritual feelings and sympathies of his Transcendentalist faith. He presented this renewed loss of faith as another moment of stormy spiritual crisis and intellectual reorientation: "The utter falseness of my philosophy of feeling was burned in upon my soul with agonies unutterable." Human emotion no longer seemed at all reliable as "a truth-discoverer"; the heart's affections now seemed partial and tyrannical—blind guides compared to science and reason. In abandoning feeling and emotion, Putnam no longer had the requisite props for his theism or his morality. He had long relied on the sentiments as the inspiration for ethical action, recurring especially to the example of how important sympathy and fellow-feeling were in galvanizing the abolitionist fight to end slavery. Likewise, he had relied on ineffable experiences of awe, beauty, and love to intuit divine reality and presence. A sentimental God and a sentimental ethics had gone hand in hand, and now Putnam found both of those moorings slipping away. These losses, he admitted, were painful and disorienting, but ultimately necessary and liberating. Dethroning both God and the affections would allow him to dispose of two despots, twinned enemies of freedom and rationality. In elevating science as the "one method of knowledge" and sweeping away the transcendent, Putnam saw himself as having finally arrived at the summit of "modern scientific

Atheism," "the profoundest result of the human mind." Romantic disillusionment, as much as enlightened rationality, pushed him back into unbelief.[24]

The intellect's triumph over God and the affections—that is how Putnam presented the denouement of his Northfield ministry twelve years after the fact in *My Religious Experience*. But, he left an important piece out of this part of his narrative, an indication of the studied avoidance and secrecy that had become second nature to him over the intervening years. Putnam featured his parents in at least modest detail in his spiritual memoir, but he never once mentioned that he had gotten married in 1868 and had fathered two children. Indeed, by 1891, he had rendered his wife, Louise; his son, Harry; and his daughter, Gracie, entirely invisible in his public presentations of himself and acted as if he had been a single man all along. The roots of that familial desertion dated to early 1879, when his infatuation with one young woman in his congregation became a matter of public notice and scandal. Rumors of his lechery flew; his wife left with the children to live with relatives; and the parish wanted him out, which Putnam obliged by resigning that winter. Having fallen in love with another woman and having felt the sting of gossip and public disgrace, he had ample reason to conclude that the sentiments were harsh masters—"blind and terrible, unreasoning and irresponsible." A little cold rationality was perhaps just the antidote Putnam needed for having acted, as one newspaper account put it, "the part of a big fool" in pursuing so ardently the affections of a young member of his flock.[25]

The chastening of the sentiments was, however, not Putnam's first response to the crisis. Instead, he tried to play the scandal out as a referendum on conventional morality and the divine dictates that Christians used to demand obedience to stifling customs and traditions. For that line of argument, he turned to free-love ideals as the necessary corrections of the "present marriage institution." Though he would also erase this radical gesture from *My Religious Experience*, he nonetheless launched his bark, in the immediate moment, toward the sexual radicalism of Victoria Woodhull and Ezra Heywood. "I fling my fortunes with the advanced radical reformers," Putnam wrote by way of explanation in April 1879, two months after his forced resignation at Northfield. "Even as religion must be free, even so must marriage be free," he claimed in typical free-love parlance. Marriage, as currently constituted, was "a relic of barbarism, the child of Orthodoxy"; it was a form of bondage, ownership, and subjection. The "finest affections" of the human soul were degraded through the legal, social, and religious coercions that enforced the maintenance of loveless and even brutish marriages. The point was not to destroy the institution, but to transform it—to open and elevate matrimony through "nobler ideals" of perfect love, true happiness, and full equality. "I admit that I have gone against the average moral standard of the community," Putnam confessed, "but in doing so I have appealed to a higher standard, to a more delicate perception of what constitutes a pure and noble life. . . . I appeal from the average moral sentiment of today to the enlightened judgment of the future." The "new morality"—free of coercive authorities, divine and human—would enfold marriage and sexuality into the rights of private judgment and individual conscience.[26]

For all intents and purposes, the Northfield episode and Putnam's response to it placed him beyond the pale of the church. Even radical post-Unitarians like Francis Abbot wanted nothing to do with liberals who unfurled the free-love banner and appeared to authorize libertinism. Abbot himself excoriated Putnam and his "rotten ethics" at some length in the pages of the *Index* that March. "If his experience had only taught him the folly, misery, and wrong of the 'free-love' which thus broke up his family and drove his poor wife in sorrow from her home,—if he had only set himself in earnest to retrieve his tarnished character and make what reparation he could for the evil he had wrought,—we should never have referred to the matter here, but should have drawn over it . . . the veil of pitying charity and silence," Abbot wrote indignantly. Putnam had instead decided to celebrate the course he had taken—his leaping off "the treadmill of conformity." He even had the gall to chide Abbot for a failure of nerve in being unwilling to apply the principles of free inquiry and private conscience to marriage and sexuality just as much as to the Bible and theology.

In short, Putnam had mutated into precisely the kind of liberal whom Abbot wanted to keep from tainting the National Liberal League and the Free Religious Association.[27]

While free-love radicalism certainly had resonance among some secular liberals in the late 1870s, it was intensely divisive. The more upstanding freethinkers, including Abbot and Robert Ingersoll, were insistent on drawing the line on any connection to the marriage reformers in order to keep them from sullying the freedom-from-religion cause. Realizing that the reputational costs of free-love candor were even higher than those for plain-old irreligion, Putnam soon removed his avowal of marriage reform and sexual freedom from public view. Thereafter, he kept his free-love beliefs clandestine, so secret indeed that when they were thrust back into the public spotlight upon his death in 1896, they became a much bigger bombshell than the local scandal in Northfield had been. Putnam's retreat into circumspection somehow gained him one last short stint in the Unitarian ministry in Vincennes, Indiana, at the end of 1879, but there was really no going back at this point. How convincing could he possibly be in the pulpit? A budding atheist and a disillusioned sentimentalist, with a free-love skeleton in his closet, Putnam was a man very much in need of a new vocation.[28]

Putnam was more of a lost soul than anything else when he "drifted" to New York City in early 1880. He came with few prospects, without his estranged wife or his two children, and without his Northfield soulmate. Indeed, he had only a hazy sense of wanting "to devote himself entirely to Liberalism outside of all churches and creeds"—an ambition without a corresponding occupation. He inevitably struggled to make ends meet. Living alone in an attic room, he tried out bookkeeping and other odd jobs, earning just enough for very meager fare. Before too long, though, he found steady employment at the Custom House as a civil servant. It was exactly the kind of bureaucratic labor that he had despaired of falling into just a few years earlier, but it paid well and afforded him some security amid the sea changes, professional and familial, he had experienced in the last year. A regular paycheck also allowed him to embrace the city with new hope and energy. Marveling at the teeming metropolis, Putnam gushed over its cosmopolitan worldliness: its museums, libraries, parks, and theaters; its thronged wharfs, department stores, slums, and street processions; its "infinite variety of faces, of gestures, of talk, of costume." Apart from his civil-service job, he started working on a new repertoire of freethought lectures and began making appearances on various secularist platforms. A commentator at the time noticed Putnam's gradual adjustment of his speaking style as he made the transition from minister to orator: he had arrived in New York "poor as the church mouse," with "the flowery declamation of a sermonizer," but was now rapidly "getting down to scientific hard pan." Even as Putnam tried to retool himself, the role of freethinking lecturer appeared little more than a side avocation. The Custom House was his bread and butter.[29]

New York offered Putnam a whole new circle of intellectual and religious renegades with whom to associate, and he made the most of those possibilities. Building on his prior ties to *Truth Seeker* editor D. M. Bennett, he moved quickly into the middle of Manhattan's secularist ranks. He connected directly, for example, with physician Edward Bliss Foote, one of the period's most important activists for free speech, as well as positivist T. B. Wakeman, a leading proponent of Auguste Comte's humanistic philosophy and a lawyer zealous to prosecute the case for secularism. Putnam gained first-hand knowledge as well of Felix Adler's Ethical Culture Society movement, even eyeing it as a possible outlet for his talents—a fledgling enterprise in which liberal-minded "teachers of humanity" were (as Putnam saw it) superseding the clerical profession. Most of all, though, he delighted in the fellowship of the Manhattan Liberal Club, a haven for the city's social, political, and religious iconoclasts, including the utopian individualist Stephen Pearl Andrews and the visiting British secularist Charles Watts. Putnam called the club a "throng of intellectual athletes," "a congregation of 'cranks' of the first order"; its spirit of free inquiry and vigorous debate on every conceivable topic captivated him. Shorn of religious community, he found in the club an alternative camaraderie, a place to mingle with the city's "choice revolutionary spirits," a balm for the loneliness he had initially experienced upon arriving in Manhattan. Buoyed by these new connections, Putnam soon felt enthused by the possibilities that New York City presented for constructing a humanitarian fellowship atop the ruins of Christian revelation.[30]

During these in-between years, as Putnam was attempting to fashion a distinctly secularist identity for himself in New York, he found inspiration in one figure above all: the infidel orator Robert Ingersoll. A top draw on the lecture circuit, Ingersoll had soared into national prominence after crisscrossing the country with his freethinking critiques of Christianity and the Bible in the late 1870s. New York City was, of course, a featured stop for him from one year to the next, and in 1885 the Peoria lawyer would make a mansion in Manhattan his home base of operation. Putnam did not give a precise date or place when he first heard and met Ingersoll—the "master influence in my life, more potent than all others"—but it was not long after his move to New York. The great infidel had given an especially rousing pair of lectures in the city in April 1882, in which he jousted with the Presbyterian T. De Witt Talmage, pulpit prince of Brooklyn. Talmage had been launching furious attacks on Ingersoll, "the champion blasphemer of America," and Ingersoll now returned the favor with withering blasts at "Talmagian Theology." Thousands turned out to hear Ingersoll, and the city's freethinkers delighted in his boldfaced challenge of one of American Christianity's most celebrated expositors. Whether Putnam met Ingersoll in the course of these lectures or on another occasion—Ingersoll had also lectured in New York the previous year on "The Great Infidels"—the two would become well acquainted by the middle of the decade through their shared work on behalf of the National Liberal League. Putnam found in Ingersoll a new professional paragon, the personification of "the worldly man" the ex-minister wanted to become.[31]

In *My Religious Experience* Putnam narrated his encounter with Ingersoll with epiphanous effect. As a moment of darkness-clearing transformation, Putnam's account of hearing Ingersoll mirrored his war-time experience of seeing the haloed cross of Jesus:

> I cannot describe the sensations of wonder and delight with which I listened to him for the first time. It was my own thought given to me in floods of living light. Here was the interpretation of myself, like the glory of a summer day. The discord was over; the confusion of thought and feeling at an end. The shadow of religion disappeared forever. Life I accepted simply as it was; the life of this world; the life of man.

Ingersoll had replaced Jesus as a way to interpret, measure, and imagine himself, so Putnam confidently avowed at a decade's remove in 1891: "Thus ends my religious experience under the sway of this generous heart, this brilliant mind." Suddenly, completely, Ingersoll had liberated Putnam from religious preoccupations and desires. He saw clearly now that all his searching after God had been a waste, a fool's quest: "It is not a good thing to strive after God, for there is none. It is not a good thing to labor for heaven, for there is none." Like Atheist in *Pilgrim's Progress*, Putnam was now able to reverse course and settle upon earthly realities as the sum total of existence. Ingersoll was the final hinge in the Secular Pilgrim's journey. As one door slammed on religious aspirations and illusions, another swung open for an unblinking atheism and materialism.[32]

Putnam got ahead of himself in the closing pages of *My Religious Experience*. Ingersoll had great oratorical gifts but not the magical powers to vanquish in a twinkling all of Putnam's struggles with religion. However much Ingersoll changed Putnam's life, the ex-minister still had to fashion his secular pilgrimage in increments and by degrees. This was quite evident in one of his first literary efforts after coming to New York, a poem entitled "Ingersoll and Jesus," which the Truth Seeker Company published in pamphlet form in 1882. Couched as a dream, the piece imagines "the natural Jesus" who, walking the earth again, is predictably miscomprehended by every latter-day Christian he chances to meet, including "a cold blue Presbyterian" and a "cultured Unitarian." Only upon meeting Ingersoll does Jesus recognize "a

brother" who shares his love of humanity and his disgust at outward pomp. From there the poem unfolds as a dialogue in which
Jesus and Ingersoll agree on one point after another:

> Said Robert, "I for man would work,
>   His earthly needs to-day;
> What makes him better here and now—
>   'Tis for this world I pray,
> Not for another in the sky,
>   Of which we cannot know;
> The living present is our goal."
>   Said Jesus, "That is so."

Ingersoll and Jesus share, from one stanza to the next, an "electric
sympathy"—an intense mutuality by which they recognize one
another as prophetic complements seeking "the same light." As
Ingersoll tells Jesus, "Here's my hand and heart. / The truths you
speak I feel." Putnam may have harmonized Jesus and Ingersoll
largely on the infidel's terms, but the poem nonetheless suggests
an author still thoroughly steeped in religious sentiments and ideals. Putnam's realignment with Ingersoll did not keep Jesus from
frequenting his poetic dreams or from being an ethical inspiration
of his secularism.[33]

Ingersoll's oratory may have cut through Putnam's post-North-
field confusion, but it hardly provided him with a blueprint for
a new career as a freethinker. Putnam still thrashed about for
direction. This was evident in his experiment at becoming a novelist for the cause. Inklings of his literary ambitions had surfaced
during the latter part of his Unitarian ministry, when he tried
his hand at poetry in the pages of the *Index* and the *Liberal
Christian*, as well as in a stand-alone volume entitled *Prometheus*.
While Putnam continued to keep up his occasional versifying, he
now put more effort into creating "the romance literature of Freethought," as one reviewer in 1883 labeled his new dalliance with
fiction. To be sure, writing romances was an inauspicious choice
of genres for someone ostensibly bent on desentimentalizing the
world, but that did not stop Putnam from plunging forward.[34]

All told, Putnam produced three novels, each of which wrapped freethinking characters into a larger romance: *Gottlieb, His Life* (1879); *Golden Throne* (1883); and *Waifs and Wanderings* (1884). Gottlieb, a good but religiously indifferent man, turns heaven and hell on end through his humble example of love and service; the Celestial City vanishes as Jesus brings God the Father around to Gottlieb's ethical humanism. Golden Throne, a California mining town, serves as the backdrop for ill-fated love, last-minute rescue, and rough justice (meted out by the town brawler known as Big Dick); all the while Ingersoll stands forth as a shining example for the local freethinkers and indifferent Christians: "I want to hear that man," says one. "I want to see him face to face. He has done more good than any living human being." Another quickly chimes in: "Ingersoll is our man. He knows the spirit of the age." For its part, *Waifs and Wanderings* turns to slavery, the Civil War, and Emancipation for its suspense. It foregrounds a slave named Columbus, who heroically saves the Union cause on the battlefield, and an emancipated slave named Amy, whose noble womanhood is matched by her unswerving atheism. "I have prayed, and no answer has ever come to my prayer," Amy remarks in refusing to affirm God's existence in order to testify in a court of law. "I have had to rely on myself, otherwise I would have been crushed." Putnam's novels garnered him some praise in freethought journals, but they showed few signs of popular success. Providing American nonbelievers with their own romance literature was hardly an occupation unto itself, but his efforts nonetheless inched him down the path toward a new calling as a full-time promoter of liberal secularism.[35]

Putnam's burgeoning involvement with freethought as a lecturer and writer paid off in late 1884, when he was elected Secretary of the National Liberal League (shortly to be renamed the American Secular Union). This role, which Putnam held for the next three years, made him the league's chief organizer and put him side by side with Ingersoll, who became the group's president the same year. Serving as the league's secretary allowed Putnam to resign from his appointment at the Custom House and hit the national lecture circuit in imitation of Ingersoll's far-ranging itineraries: "Sure I am that I never could have met with so cordial a reception and generous appreciation," Putnam would remark of one of his early tours across Montana, "if Ingersoll had not already aroused the sympathies and thoughts of these people with his earnest speech." Besides following in Ingersoll's footsteps, Putnam would join forces with the roving London freethinker Charles Watts, a founding organizer alongside Charles Bradlaugh and George Holyoake of British secularism. Touring together for a time, Putnam and Watts made North America their combined mission field—from Altoona to Toronto, from Montreal to Kansas City. Mostly, though, Putnam set out on his own cross-continent tours, establishing himself as an indefatigable traveler on behalf of the cause; by the early 1890s, he claimed to have logged over a hundred thousand miles as a lecturer and to have taken his secular gospel to all but four states and territories, as well as to a large swath of Canada. It was out of the relentlessness of these travels especially that Putnam came to see himself as the Secular Pilgrim par excellence.[36]

Ingersoll's eminence as a freethought lecturer remained unsurpassed, but Putnam's stature in the movement came to possess its own distinct luster. In 1887, Putnam ascended to the presidency of the American Secular Union, a validation of his labors as secretary of the organization and an honor that put him in the same rank with mentors like Abbot and Ingersoll who had inspired his turn to liberal secularism in the first place. Even as he maintained his unremitting schedule as a lecturer, Putnam kept expanding his portfolio. He next tried his hand at editing. Relocating from New York to San Francisco, Putnam collaborated with journalist George E. Macdonald in 1888 to start a weekly entitled *Freethought* on the model of D. M. Bennett's *Truth Seeker*. This venture failed after three-plus years of publishing, and Putnam returned eastward to further the cause in Chicago and Washington, DC. In late 1892 he took up the reins of another secularist organization, the Freethought Federation of America (headquartered in Chicago), which focused its energies on the politics of church-state separation. Putnam also lobbied for secular causes in the nation's capital, testifying before a House committee in 1893 in favor of the Sunday opening of the World's Fair, and before another in 1896 against the latest evangelical effort to amend the Constitution to acknowledge God's supreme authority over the nation's political affairs. Both of his congressional committee appearances showed his abiding commitment to Abbot's original Nine Demands of Liberalism. From New York to California, Putnam established himself as a secularist watchdog, especially on blue laws and the Sabbath question. His convoluted journey out of the ministry had led him to a busy career of freethinking activism; moving beyond his village rebellions in Chichester, New Hampshire, and Northfield, Massachusetts, Putnam had become a well-established public atheist and secularist.[37]

In the last years of his life Putnam's godless rhetoric grew more hard-bitten and vitriolic as his frustrations with Christian moral legislation deepened. One of his last battle cries for the Truth Seeker Company was a less-than-subtle pamphlet entitled *Religion a Curse, Religion a Disease, Religion a Lie* (1893). It contained such pungent lines as "Religion is a fungus growth upon humanity"; "Religion has been simply and solely evil"; and "Religion is a big burning boil, preachers are pimples, churches are cancers, and piety is pus." It had taken him decades to wring the religious feeling out of his own life, and Putnam now exhorted fellow secularists to face the barren indifference of the universe with an atheist's stoical courage. He no longer searched for consolation or transcendence, content now to confront the hard facts and ugly realities of the world. "God is born of agony, of suffering, and of pain—the fiction of the imagination to console the bitterness of man's estate," he proclaimed with a strong dose of nihilistic pessimism. "Millions are constantly wrecked, and torture of the mind and body, more or less, is the fortune of every human being. In a blind and miserable way people try to escape reality—shut their eyes and dream of heaven. It is like taking an opiate. It weakens, while it cures not the ills of life." Putnam saw clearly that God was "a lie, a cruel lie, a damned lie"; that there is no "infinite justice" or "infinite love" in the order of things; that the divine had been annihilated. Science, to be sure, stepped up to provide enlightenment and explanation, but it offered him objective truth without subjective comfort. Embracing its guidance might well make it possible to win a little more health and welfare in this world, but, in the larger scheme of things, science was not so much ameliorative as sobering. It allowed rationalists to face their doom free of religious sentimentality. *My Religious Experience* culminated in this bleak atheistic posture, the Celestial City having dimmed into an "infinite abyss" without "a gleam of hope."[38]

———————◆———————

Having already staged an atheist finale in his spiritual autobiography, Putnam still had one last act to perform as the historian of the secularist movement. *400 Years of Freethought* (1894) was, in many ways, his grandest gesture; it was an 874-page testament to the cause in the heyday of liberal secularism's formation. When donning the historian's hat, Putnam proved far more optimistic and forward-looking than he had been in the closing pages of *My Religious Experience*. Existential pessimism about the cosmos was one thing, but, in the far narrower circumstances of human history, there was still reason to be hopeful about advances in scientific knowledge, applied technology, and secular education. The gradual demystification of the world—the steady advancement of rationality that could be traced from the martyrdom of Giordano Bruno to the celebrity of Robert Ingersoll—was, as Putnam pictured it, a lesson in progress and enlightenment. Having promised his subscribers a book monumental in size and scope, Putnam had even taken a year-long break from his lecture tours in order to synthesize all the materials he had gathered into a full-scale history. Unlike so much of what he had tossed off for the cause over the years—his week-to-week "News and Notes" for the *Truth Seeker, Boston Investigator*, and *Freethought*, for example— this history was written with the long view in mind: "I have satisfied my intellectual conscience in this book," Putnam averred on the eve of its publication. Here was "a vast and inspiring picture" that captured the brilliance of freethinking philosophers, poets, political revolutionaries, and scientists from Spinoza to Hume, from

Gibbon to Shelley, from Paine to Garibaldi, from Galileo to Darwin. Here was a full-scale secularist history to replace the sacred history—the biblical chronicle of the Creation, the Fall, the Cross, and the Last Judgment—that had dominated his evangelical Calvinist upbringing.[39]

Putnam's twin emphases on "representative geniuses" and on the deep-rooted clash between science and religion hardly set his history apart. The framework was familiar from such entrants as John William Draper's *History of the Conflict between Religion and Science* (1874) and Andrew Dickson White's *The Warfare of Science* (1876), as well as from biographical works like James Parton's *Life of Voltaire* (1881). What made Putnam's history original was his depth of knowledge of the American scene, which allowed him to dislodge the intellectual history of European rationalism and replace it with a democratic history of American secularism. A little more than halfway into his big history, Putnam shifted his focus to the United States and, in making that move, he also altered his justification for writing the book. The history of freethought consisted not only in "the biographies of celebrated persons," but also in deep acquaintance "with the rank and file." He wanted to write a history of secularism as "a mighty life among the people," as an account of men and women "whose lives will never be known unless they are known in the pages of this book." He wanted to take his history out of the realm of "glittering abstraction" and ground it in the "every-day living" of all those liberal-minded folks he had gotten to know through lecturing in villages, towns, and cities across the country. "History to-day," he remarked, "has ceased to be a history of kings and princes and so-called great men, and has become a history of the people, and the history of Freethought should also be a history of Freethought people." The 140-plus portraits that Putnam included as an addition to his 874 pages of text captured this abrupt change of direction with splendid visual effect. Here was a picture gallery in which celebrated freethinkers (Spinoza, Hume, and Voltaire) were completely crowded out by local activists (Katie Kehm Smith of Portland, Oregon; Otto Wettstein of Rochelle, Illinois; and R. L. Baker of Fort Fairfield, Maine). In this democratic tableau,

Mattie Krekel of Missouri and J. D. Shaw of Texas very much held their own against the titans.[40]

Putnam's rank-and-file impulse did not eliminate the problem of selectivity. If anything, his profession of democratic inclusion only served to heighten the expectations of his readers and make them second-guess his choices: "Who to name and who not to name among the great number, past and present, of progressive workers and thinkers was a very delicate question to decide," one reviewer observed before specifying three missing figures whose absence could not have been mere oversight. Among the slighted was James L. York, "the Ingersoll of the Pacific coast," an ex-Methodist preacher whom Putnam viewed as a buffoonish speaker, long on comic effects and short on civility. The reviewer thought that Putnam's bias had gotten in the way of impartial judgment in the case of York—a lecturer who had, after all, pursued the liberal mission field as far away as Australia and New Zealand and who had led the charge in California long before Putnam had arrived there. The absence the reviewer had noted of two other figures—B. F. Underwood and Albert Leighton Rawson—signaled a more substantive line of demarcation. Underwood's credentials as a pioneer for the cause were impeccable, and his influence on Putnam stretched back two decades. But, Underwood and his wife Sara (also quite active in the movement, including as author of *Heroines of Freethought* in 1876) had become more and more invested in spiritualism, including the psychical practice of automatic writing. That betrayal of materialism was enough to get both of the Underwoods excluded from Putnam's history. For his part, Rawson had an even more glaring problem with consistency. A free-speech notable as the head of the National Defense Association, a close comrade of D. M. Bennett's, and a regular at the Manhattan Liberal Club, Rawson was also an artist, biblical scholar, occultist, Masonic ritualist, Muslim adept, and convicted thief. No matter how much time Rawson had spent among New York's freethinkers, Putnam was not going to profile someone whose identity—religious and otherwise—looked as slippery as Rawson's did.[41]

Putnam's own journey into unbelief was hardly a tale of fixity, but he wanted to steer his pilgrimage and those of his fellow travelers to an irreversible end point—one in which a secular politics and an atheistic philosophy were permanently joined together. Perhaps no one disturbed Putnam's designs more than his good friend George Chainey, a Methodist preacher turned Unitarian minister turned infidel lecturer (all before he reached age thirty). Chainey was making his break with Unitarianism at the same time Putnam was in 1879 and 1880: "We were on the same road, and saw things in the same light, and reached the same conclusions," Putnam warmly recalled of their earlier friendship. Seeing himself as having overleapt all ecclesiastical fences, Chainey headed from Indiana to Boston to take charge of an emerging congregation of freethinkers, agnostics, and lapsed Unitarians. In 1881 he started a journal called the *Infidel Pulpit* as a forum for his post-Christian reflections on the times and soon launched another one called, simply enough, *This World*. Known for his dramatic flair (he had contemplated a life on the stage), Chainey looked every bit the golden boy ready to play a leading role in the construction of a humanistic, post-Christian religion. When a couple of years later the British secularist Charles Watts chose four American freethinkers to profile for his London audience as representative leaders of the cause across the pond, Chainey was among them (Underwood, Ingersoll, and T. B. Wakeman were the other three). If Putnam had written *400 Years of Freethought* a decade earlier, Chainey without doubt would have figured prominently in it.[42]

But secularist hopes for Chainey came crashing down at a New York convention of freethinkers in September 1884. Ascending the rostrum ostensibly to speak once again in favor of "Ingersollism," Chainey instead proclaimed his wholesale conversion to spiritualism. Renouncing the "hell-broth" of agnosticism, atheism, and materialism, Chainey testified movingly about his ecstatic encounters with spirits, including a newfound guardian angel named Lily Dove. The speech sent his assembled colleagues into paroxysms of outrage and derision: "St. Paul's flop-over was apparently a well-considered act" compared with Chainey's "headlong jump" into spiritualism, so the *Truth Seeker* reported bitterly. Within the year Chainey had left Boston for Oakland, California, where he and medium Anna Kimball started a theosophical journal called the *Gnostic*. Years later the *Truth Seeker* was still ridiculing Chainey's journey from freethinking infidelity into "Spiritualism, Theosophy, Rosicrucianism, hermetic philosophy, and esoteric culture." By one account, he had finally slid all the way back to Methodism; by another, he had gone on to become the channel for a revelatory text called *Shusan*. One thing was certain—the canon of American secularism could not accommodate him. Chainey's secular pilgrimage had matched Putnam's story as closely as any-one's had, but the awakening to freethinking infidelity was sup-posed to have been the end of the story. Having overturned the teleology of Putnam's trek into atheism, Chainey needed to be written out of the history of American freethought: Putnam's no-tice of him was reduced to one line—a man who had glittered with promise but who had "lost his grip on the material world." As an embodiment of the serpentine pathways between secular and religious liberalism, Chainey was a standing reminder of un-belief's makeshift qualities. For Putnam to banish Chainey was to conceal the transience and instability of newly minted atheist and infidel identities, including his own.[43]

In creating his democratized portrait of the nation's "Free-thought people," Putnam certainly found plenty of wayfarers who fit the evolutionary progression he wanted to make the standard. At the alphabetical head of his biographical sketches was Captain Robert C. Adams, another New England son of a devoutly ortho-dox Congregational minister. Like Putnam, Adams had penned an account of his reverse pilgrimage. His *Travels in Faith from Tradition to Reason* (1884) was a testament to the slow process by which he had lost hold of Protestant Christianity and turned to in-fidelity. Put to sea at a young age, Adams became intensely aware of religious variety and deeply suspicious of Christian missions. During his years as a sailor he remained very serious about the devotional study of the scriptures, but he gradually lost confidence in the Bible on account of the wild disagreement of its Protestant interpreters. Following the path of radical Unitarians like The-odore Parker and deistic critics like Tom Paine, Adams finally renounced the Christian church and took his stand with scientific naturalism and worldly cosmopolitanism. The solidarity Putnam felt with Adams—from his rupture with evangelical Calvinism to his radical avowal of freethought—was obvious. Putnam saw himself in Adams, another Puritan antitype, a model for the pilgrimage into secularism. His was "a progress," Putnam concluded, "which every honest mind must make if born into the old faith and born also to think."[44]

Any number of other liberal-minded wayfarers fit the bill as well for Putnam: W. S. Bell, a Methodist preacher who passed through Harvard Divinity School and the Universalist ministry on his way to the Ingersollian lecture circuit; Henry Bird, a natal Episcopalian who left the church and found refuge as an open atheist leading the Newark Liberal League; Susan H. Wixon, a youthful rebel from orthodoxy who took it upon herself to develop a freethought literature for children; and Elizur Wright, an evangelical abolitionist who through his disillusionment with proslavery Christianity ended up an atheistic actuary tirelessly promoting the Nine Demands of Liberalism. Putnam's history recounted dozens of life stories like these in order to typify the secular pilgrimage. They allowed him to put a period after atheism and infidelity rather than an ellipsis. Mirroring the narrative resolution he had brought to his own religious experience, such exemplars tidied up the messy contingencies of unbelief, the spiritual clefts in the pristine secular landscape. George Chainey was gone, so were the Underwoods and Albert Rawson. Even for those freethinkers who remained, Putnam included, the religious intricacies and shadings of their own secularism had been largely cleaned up. Captain Adams, after all, had along the pilgrim's way been involved in the evangelical mission of the American Seaman's Friend Society and had undergone believer's baptism in a New Jersey lake with the Plymouth Brethren. Putnam took the zigzagging perplexity out of liberal secularism and mapped it as a triumphal march forward.

Two years after the publication of his carefully filtered history, Putnam's own life would end in a jumble of intrigue and scandal.

Having returned to the lecture circuit with restless vigor after the book's appearance, Putnam had just finished up a gig in Chicago when he headed to Boston in early December 1896 to speak (yet again) at Paine Hall and other liberal haunts. He traveled with a twenty-year-old woman named May L. Collins, an aspiring freethought lecturer from Lexington, Kentucky, who was seen as an up-and-comer in secularist ranks. She had recently published *A Plea for the New Woman* with the Truth Seeker Company, regaled audiences with a poem she had penned entitled "The Battle Hymn of Freethought," and already had lectures slated at such esteemed venues as the Manhattan Liberal Club and the Brooklyn Philosophical Association. Putnam was by now at age fifty-eight an elder statesman in the movement, an inspiration to such youthful protégés as Franklin Steiner and Katie Kehm Smith; he was clearly favorably impressed with Collins, a forceful speaker who was unabashed in expressing her radical religious and social views. Whether his relationship with Collins was anything more than professional is impossible to know, but that it might have been became a matter of intense public speculation.[45]

On Friday evening December 11, the two of them had been out socializing with other avant-garde Bostonians. Putnam had escorted Collins back to her apartment house on St. Botolph Street and lingered in her room; the janitor found both of them dead the next morning, the victims of an undetected gas leak. Tragic and unseemly at the same time, such circumstances surrounding the demise of a notorious infidel and his young acolyte were tailor-made for scandalmongering. Libertinism is exactly what the godly expected of freethinkers, and it took little time for "the ghouls of press and pulpit" (as the *Truth Seeker* depicted the mudslingers) to feed people's imaginations with all kinds of sensational stories about the degraded morality of Putnam and Collins. Lasciviousness was only part of the thrill: Was Putnam a murderer who had drugged his paramour? Or, was he a thief after a supposed stash of diamonds? Or, was this a misbegotten love affair that had ended in a double suicide? As a Minneapolis headline asked, "Collins-Putnam: Was It a Case of Double Suicide or Murder and Suicide?" Incriminating details emerged out of thin air: one teetotaling minister, in a screed entitled "Atheism and Its Awful Results," ventured that the two were overly fond of claret and had been out drinking all afternoon. So it went from one moralizing tidbit to the next. Defenders of the duo scrambled to get the "facts" out—that their bodies had been discovered "fully clothed," that the bedding was undisturbed, that Putnam had not even removed his overcoat, that their deaths were entirely accidental, and that there was simply no indication of foul play or illicit relations. An official report from the Suffolk County medical examiner corroborated these points, but that hardly settled the character question in the minds of the pair's detractors. Was this friendship as "honorable" as the comrades of Putnam and Collins insisted? It proved a question impossible to put to rest.[46]

Vindicating Putnam and Collins became a lot harder for friends and colleagues when H. L. Green, the Chicago-based editor of *Free Thought Magazine*, broke ranks within a month of their deaths. Though he had collaborated with Putnam on various projects over the previous fifteen years, Green had also long harbored doubts about his colleague's moral worthiness as a spokesman for freethinking secularism. This scandal confirmed for Green crucial flaws in Putnam's character—"fatal mistakes" that all decent, respectable, upstanding freethinkers should acknowledge and disclaim. In Green's view, the gas leak was beside the point; "free love and whisky" were the real killers of Putnam and Collins, and the tandem's complicity in those two great evils required exposure. As part of substantiating his charges, Green turned his obituary notices about the pair into a lengthy editorial indictment of Putnam especially—an epitaphic "warning to Liberals of this country to never again jeopardize their worthy cause by putting it in charge of a man or woman . . . whose life has the defects pointed out here."[47]

For the drinking charge, Green relied on a *Boston Globe* report that two bottles of whisky were found in Collins's room— one drained and the other nearly so—along with a quarter-empty bottle of French Benedictine. The question of whether any of that liquor had been consumed on the ill-fated evening mattered little; the putative presence of those three bottles was evidence enough of deplorable drinking habits. Green had, moreover, collected reports from several "reliable persons" (unnamed) that they had seen Putnam on a number of occasions "more or less under the influence of intoxicating liquor." Putnam's closest associates admitted that he was no teetotaler (one friend suggested that the time spent in California had accustomed Putnam to enjoying wine with dinner but wondered what crime there was in that). That Putnam fell short of strict temperance standards was clear enough, but whether that made him the drunk that Green pictured him to be was anything but obvious. "I feel sure that no one ever saw S. P. Putnam," free-speech champion Edward Bliss Foote wrote, "so affected by liquor of any description as to render him stupid, silly, or unsteady in his gait." Infidels, Tom Paine most famously, had long been lampooned as drunkards; one typical temperance tract took its title from the deathbed realization of a habitually besotted atheist: *I Am Afraid There Is a God!* Ironically, in Putnam's case, it was a fellow freethinker who most effectively reinforced the caricature of entwined intemperance and infidelity. To spare virtuous secularists guilt by association, Green pushed hard for a posthumous repudiation of the Secular Pilgrim and his young whisky-drinking companion.[48]

The free-love accusation was the more damning charge of the two—a jolting retrieval of Putnam's old domestic woes as well as his disreputable views on the marriage system, both of which he had kept well hidden from public view since the scandal in Northfield in 1879. Green first met Putnam about the time his marriage was falling apart, but Putnam was already passing as "a single man" with no acknowledgment of "his wife or children or home affairs." It was four years later, at a freethought convention in Rochester in 1883, that Green first became convinced that Putnam was leading a secret life as "an honest convert to the doctrines of free love." Having seen Putnam leaving a hotel with an unknown woman, Green did some snooping and discovered that the two had checked in as husband and wife under assumed names. When Green told Putnam's friend George Chainey about his discovery, Chainey reportedly dismissed the information as old news: Putnam's free-love partnership with the woman had been going on for quite some time. Not only that, but Green also heard from another source that Putnam had made the calculation to keep his radical views on marriage and "social liberty" a secret to avoid compromising his secularist labors on behalf of freethought. Green took that as studied hypocrisy—that Putnam lacked the transparency and courage of an Ezra Heywood or a Moses Harman, radicals who were forthright about their espousal of free-love principles and who were willing to go to prison for their convictions. To cap it all off, Green even dug up the court records from Putnam's divorce which showed that when his wife, Louise, had finally filed to have the marriage dissolved in 1885, it was on the grounds of adultery. With that *coup de grace*, Green raised his hands in triumph: "We hardly think it necessary for us to present more evidence to show that Mr. Putnam was a firm believer in the free-love theory of marriage."[49]

And yet Green could not stop himself from presenting even more evidence. From the hotel episode in 1883 and the divorce certificate of 1885, he leaped forward to the associates surrounding Putnam and Collins at the time of their deaths. Among those with whom they had been out that tragic evening was Moses Hull, the notorious author of *That Terrible Question; or, A Few Thoughts on Love and Marriage* in which he had endorsed spiritualized sexual partnerships apart from conventional wedlock. Also, the room in which Putnam and Collins had died turned out to be part of a flat occupied by Josephine and Flora Tilton; along with their sister Angela Tilton Heywood, they were social radicals of the first order, leading activists for women's rights and marriage reform. Their abode, Green insisted, was "known far and wide as the headquarters of the free lovers in Boston." At this point Collins, too, came in for her own share of suspicion as a reputed intimate of Lillian Harman. The daughter of Moses Harman, Lillian was part of the circle responsible for *Lucifer the Light Bearer*, the most notorious marriage-reform journal of the day; she was also infamous for defying the marriage laws of Kansas and cohabiting in an equal and loving partnership with Edwin C. Walker (the couple served jail time for that relational experiment). Collins had been seen, Green reported, palling around with Harman in Chicago before traveling to Boston with Putnam; an alarmed acquaintance claimed to have argued with Collins about her budding avowal of Harman's principles but to no avail. The pieces all fit together in Green's view: Collins had joined the ranks of the sex radicals in seeing marriage, under its reigning social and legal formulations, as an oppressive institution, especially for women; Putnam, a closet free lover, was utterly at home in these circles and had been for years; together Collins and Putnam had fallen into a free-love union and then perished in the midst of it.[50]

While Green had hardly proven that Putnam and Collins were themselves lovers, he had disclosed all too many of Putnam's guarded secrets: his broken marriage, his neglect of his two children, his early advocacy of free-love principles, his evident penchant for extramarital relationships, and his ongoing affinities with marriage reformers and sex radicals. Green concluded that Putnam's "damnable doctrine of free love" had led to a life of appalling irresponsibility and "libertinism"—a charge his admirers considered "the grossest calumny," even as they were forced to acknowledge that Putnam had indeed held "advanced views on marriage, divorce and the sexual relation." In attempting to rid "respectable Liberalism" of the millstone of the Putnam-Collins scandal, Green's discordant obituary notice aimed to sweep freethinking secularism clean of any association with free-love advocates. On questions of marriage and sexuality, Green agreed with Ingersoll and Abbot: liberals and secularists needed to remain safely domestic. (As Ingersoll remarked to Walt Whitman on his last visit to the poet's home, "Walt, the mistake of your life was that you did not marry. There ought to be a woman here.") Freedom from religion and full secularization of the state—those were the emancipations that mattered; liberating marriage and sexuality from religious strictures and legal inequalities—those were the schemes of dangerous social incendiaries. The specter that Green raised—that the Secular Pilgrim in his journey out of orthodoxy had ended up a dissolute apostle of "Sex Freedom"—agitated freethinkers for the better part of a year. The simmering scandal was certainly a posthumous adjudication of Putnam's character and leadership, but it was also a referendum on the reach of secular liberal politics: was the "entangling alliance between Free Thought and Free Love" to be abominated or embraced? Green and company desperately wanted that alliance broken, but they could never purify their cause of questions about sexual freedom and marital equality.[51]

In *My Religious Experience* Putnam had been careful to conceal the fact that his secular pilgrimage also entailed sustained questioning of the marital and sexual standards with which he had grown up. He ended that narrative in a settled atheistic posture—as if he had managed to arrive, through a long and arduous process of awakening, at a stable rational identity. Perhaps he had, but much suggested that in his "perpetual protest against puritanism" the Secular Pilgrim had struggled to find solid footing beyond religious affiliation and affirmation. Almost always on the road, he had little sense of home after the mid-1880s; his self-chosen moniker was a token of his rootless itinerancy, a man of many roles and way stations. Cut off by his renunciation of Christianity from all but one family member—a sister who kept up ties with him despite his infidelity—Putnam had few close relations. Neither of his grown children attended his funeral. One of his old friends and most esteemed colleagues, Charles Watts, made a point of staying away from Putnam's memorial service so as to avoid the free-love taint and its rudderless associations. To be sure, many freethinkers stuck by Putnam in memoriam and dismissed the scandalmongers: Green's withering indictment, after all, was filled with hearsay and rumor, and his obsession with exposing Putnam's private life had more than a whiff of Anthony Comstock's prying moral vigilance. The contumely heaped upon Putnam as "an adulterer, a drunkard and a hypocrite" rang with panicked hyperbole, and yet it was also evident that his secular pilgrimage had produced as much social, religious, and sexual confusion as it had clearheaded enlightenment and consistency. For much of his life, Putnam had been awash in "a sea of uncertainty," necessarily more adrift than anchored.[52]

Having reversed the direction of Bunyan's allegory, the Secular Pilgrim traveled on without a heavenly beacon, without the urgent question—"What shall I do to be saved?"—importuning him.

That Putnam cut himself loose from the Christian narrative of
redemption did not mean, however, that he was somehow doomed
to aimless wandering; his secular pilgrimage, after all, was born of
intense striving, not shiftlessness. The Atheist in Bunyan's story
laughs at Christian and his companion Hope, but his laughter
stems from a dark familiarity with the pilgrim's journey. Atheist
has been out looking for the Celestial City for twenty years, facing
the perils of the salvific trek far longer than Bunyan's resolute pilgrim, and has found nothing. Putnam's worldliness was a result
of like dedication and disillusionment; his ultimate determination
to find sustenance only in the material, the secular, and the bodily
was anything but capricious. Whatever his failings and however
meandering his travels, Putnam finally decided to fix his gaze on
this world alone—in all its delight and horror. Having refocused
his vision, he imagined a liberal secularist future free of the theological concerns that had kept him for so long headed in the
wrong direction. It was a future, in other words, in which pilgrims
would no longer have to be pilgrims at all; they would simply be
denizens of the here-and-now, uncompelled by the hereafter. "We
must be Infidel to Another World, to Future Existence, to what is
not of the Here and Now," one of Putnam's atheist comrades had
insisted. Thus divested of eternal concerns, Putnam imagined a
secular existence without religious remainder.[53]

To abandon Bunyan's allegory—the pattern by which the
saints proceeded through this world as strangers and pilgrims in
search of otherworldly redemption—was to jettison a fundamental structuring device of the Christian life. Few (if any) texts besides the Bible had exercised a more enduring influence on American Protestant culture than *Pilgrim's Progress*. Throughout the
nineteenth century it retained immense currency as devotional
template, literary commonplace, and also visual treasure-trove.
Just as the Bible itself was published in ever more sumptuously
illustrated editions as the century wore on, so too was Bunyan's
allegory. Pictorial embellishments of the fable made the disparity
between Christian and Atheist all the more vivid and portentous.
One engraving, for example, pictured Bunyan's pilgrim plainly
clothed, carrying a Bible, and tilting his eyes heavenward, the very

embodiment of Christian perseverance and self-denial; by contrast, Atheist was depicted as a fop, dressed in superfluities,
blindly beckoning Christian and Hope into an abyss (Figures 2,
3). With the beacon of the Celestial City pulling them onward, the
pilgrims were quickly able to turn their back on Atheist's hell-
ish chasm. The pit of unbelief, the engravings accentuated with
graphic force, was no match for the glory of the hereafter. Who
in their right mind would join Atheist on his reverse pilgrimage
away from Mount Zion back to the City of Destruction?

All along secularists countered Bunyan's deeply etched pattern of the sanctified life with any number of ripostes. Inverted
narratives of irreligious progress, like those of Putnam or Robert
Adams, were certainly prominent among them. The rejoinders,
though, took other forms as well, such as the allegorical antitype
D. M. Bennett published in 1878, *Chronicles of Simon Christianus
and His Manifold and Wondrous Adventures in the Land of Cosmos.* In this tale all of Bunyan's pious Christian characters are
turned into religious babblers, satirized with appellations such as
PraisetheLord, Godlyguts, and Fearohell. A freethinker named
Truthseeker offers the Christian pilgrim a "strong rope" of "Rational Conversation" to pull him out of the theological mists and
quagmires; a scoffer named Blunt makes short work of preachers
and scriptures alike. A beast called Priestcraft uses a wind machine to obscure "the Plains of Science" in a cloud of dust, but the
allegory's moral remains undimmed: people are being cheated by
deceptive promises of a paradise to come; they need to "cultivate
the country that they had." Once removed from the religious fog,
the wanderer would then be able to settle into this world and
pursue knowledge, prosperity, happiness, and benevolence with
unblinking focus. Always dragged back by one pious guide or
another, Simon Christianus could never quite free himself from
celestial fantasies, but that failure only made the fable more
pointed. The return of religion always threatens to derail the Car
of Freethought and pull the wayfarer back into the Vale of Superstition. Successful navigation of the atheistic route is far from
assured. It requires a perseverance surpassing that of Bunyan's
pilgrim.[54]

FIGURE 2. "I saw a man clothed with rags." John Bunyan, *The Pilgrim's Progress* (Philadelphia: Henry Altemus, 1890), 24. Author's Collection

FIGURE 3. "Then Atheist fell into a very great laughter." John Bunyan, *The Pilgrim's Progress* (Philadelphia: Henry Altemus, 1890), 127. Author's Collection

FIGURE 4. Watson Heston, "A Religious Phantasm—Using a Fact to Illustrate a Fiction," *Truth Seeker*, 25 Jan. 1896, 49. Center for Research Libraries

FIGURE 5. Watson Heston, "Traveling by Faith,"
Truth Seeker, 14 March 1896, 161. Center for Research Libraries

Just as secularists refashioned Bunyan's "Old Allegory" on their own terms with counterpoised characters like Godlyguts and Truthseeker, they also created visual representations to contradict pious imaginings of what the elemental encounter between Christian and Atheist looked like. This was especially evident in the cartoons of Watson Heston, whose work provided the quintessential pictorial expression of American secularism. In one of Heston's illustrations, entitled "A Religious Phantasm—Using a Fact to Illustrate a Fiction," the pilgrim points toward the Celestial City, while the freethinker's handy field-glass confirms it to be a mirage, a scientific tool thus proving "the falsity of the Christian heaven" (Figure 4). Materialist knowledge, if properly applied, would spare the believer from even embarking on a trek through the desert of orthodoxy. In another example, the Christian pilgrim is pictured "Traveling by Faith" on a treadmill, this time tricked by his own eyepiece of faith into seeing the New Jerusalem in the clouds. The secularist, firmly planted to the side, looks on knowingly at the pointlessness of the wayfarer's chimerical efforts (Figure 5). Heston liked to picture the choice between the "The Orthodox Route" and "The Freethought Road" as patently obvious, the former leading into the darkness of superstition and the latter into the light of reason.[55] Putnam had often displayed equal confidence about the ultimate outcome of his own religious journey, but the forsaking of orthodoxy had also occasioned in the Secular Pilgrim much anguish, vacillation, and uncertainty. Heston, the rib-tickling cartoonist, would show none of that equivocation as he traveled the infidel path with a bellicose swagger. And, yet, that very assurance—the manly bravado of secularism's inevitability and superiority—often proved little more than a mask used to disguise the social vulnerabilities and futurist illusions of Heston's own village atheism.

CHAPTER 2

THE CARTOONIST

OR, THE VISIBLE INCIVILITY
OF SECULARISM

WATSON HESTON, SELF-TAUGHT ARTIST AND ROUGH-EDGED freethinker, had a lot of hard luck. Born into an Ohio farm family in 1846, the youngest of nine children, he lost two of his brothers in the Civil War. Not long thereafter he left home, trying to make a go of it as a book peddler before retooling himself as a roving painter and photographer. After several years on the road he got married and settled in Carthage, Missouri, but he never prospered. He had his wife, Lottie, to bolster him but no children; sometime after his father's death in 1873, his mother migrated to southwestern Missouri to join his financially pinched household. While many townspeople looked to the numerous Protestant churches of Carthage—Baptist, Methodist, Presbyterian, Christian, Episcopal, and Congregational—to provide a sense of belonging, moral direction, and otherworldly solace, Heston refused to darken the door of any of them. For a time he found some fellowship in a local auxiliary of the National Liberal League, one of only seven in the state of Missouri in 1880. An infidel lecturer, W. F. Jamieson, had swung through town in 1878 to debate a Disciples of Christ minister, and his visit had helped inspire the formation of this small outpost of Liberal Leaguers. The club lasted only a few years, though, and Heston was soon left again to his own devices—a village atheist with a marginal occupation to support his household.[1]

"I am poor physically and financially, but rich in mental freedom from gods and devils, the creeds and isms of superstition,"

FIGURE 6. Watson Heston, from Samuel P. Putnam, *400 Years of Freethought* (New York: Truth Seeker Co., 1894), plate at p. 852. Author's Collection

Heston wrote in July 1884. That self-appraisal was included in a letter to the editor of the *Truth Seeker*, E. M. Macdonald, who had taken charge of the journal after D. M. Bennett's death in 1882. Having signed up for a trial subscription to the paper three months earlier, Heston was delighted with the irreligious communion he discovered therein: "I feel that it is as indispensable to me as the blood of Christ is to the Christian." Admitting that he had almost no money in hand, he hoped that what he could scrape together would keep the paper coming: "One dollar is my pile now, so date my subscription as far ahead as it will pay for, and by that time I may earn a few more cart-wheel 'In-God-we-trust's,' and thus swap my trust in God for a better trust in THE TRUTH SEEKER." That was a bit of an inside joke. Secular liberals objected to the motto "In God We Trust" being placed on American coinage, an inscription that Congress had first blessed during the Civil War as a rallying cry for the Union cause. Downtrodden, from the hinterlands, Heston showed the Manhattan-based editor that he knew the currency of freethinking activism. The very way he had dated the letter—July 3, 284—had also established him as an initiate. He was using a secular calendar, enunciated two years earlier by a congress of freethinkers meeting in St. Louis, set not by the birth of Christ but by the death of Giordano Bruno at the hands of the Inquisition in 1600. Reinventing Bruno as "the great Liberal of his age," freethinkers were in the midst of monumentalizing the Italian heretic. American secularists enthusiastically joined in fundraising for the erection of a memorial statue in Rome at the spot of his execution—an ambition realized in 1889. Year one of the modern era, Heston already knew from his perch in southwestern Missouri, was dated to Bruno's *auto-da-fé*.[2]

Heston may have been dispirited about his finances, but that hardly diminished his pluck. He was sure the reason that Carthage's Liberal League had died aborning was because of diffidence and dissembling. Several of those involved, he explained to Macdonald, had been "moral cowards" who stood "in awe of that miserable ogre, *popularity*." They were simply "too timid about hurting the feelings of their Christian friends to take an aggressive course," and that equivocation had alienated the most ardent free-

thinkers (like himself) and led to the group's collapse. Such faint-
heartedness, Heston wanted to make plain, was not an attribute
he shared, and he had a tale to prove it—a showdown that had
occurred during a recent stay of his in "the little, rusty, moth-
eaten village" of St. Johns, Ohio. A Christian acquaintance had
singled him out for his irreligion before a gaping crowd in front
of the post office: "I was the first real live Infidel they had ever
seen." Describing himself as always "outspoken and in earnest on
politics and religion," Heston claimed to have turned the scene
into an impromptu public debate and to have scared off his orthodox challengers: "No one felt like taking up the cross to fight for
Jesus." A lot of this was bluster and posturing, of course. Heston
was offering a testimonial to his own contrarian courage as a sin-
gularly defiant unbeliever, brave enough to face down soul-saving
preachers and godly townspeople even when fellow liberals shied
away from the fight. He wanted the take-away to be his wholesale disregard for pious convention, his indifference to the costs
of being known publicly as an infidel, but the letter revealed as
much about the isolation unbelievers felt and the social risks their
impious attitudes entailed. His boat-rocking views certainly were
not winning him many friends—or much business—in Carthage,
Missouri, or St. Johns, Ohio.[3]

Four months later, in November 1884 (or 284 by his calendar),
Heston wrote the editor of the *Truth Seeker* again, and now his
circumstances were even worse. He had been deathly ill in the
interim and was flat broke. Though he very much wanted to extend his subscription to the paper—"my chief mental food and
consolation"—the only way he could do so was on trust: "Fifteen
cents in cash would be a bonanza to me just now." He still struck a
pugnacious pose, announcing he would rather "die in the gutter"
than pander to Christians and thereby receive their favor. The
next day was Thanksgiving, and he derided the holiday's aura
of divine beneficence and pious gratitude: "I have no turkey—no,
not even so much as a poor old frozen-toed rooster—to offer up
as a burnt offering! ... Really I am sorely puzzled what to return
thanks for, and shall postpone it until God shows me more favors

than he has of late. Oh, for a cyclone of manna! Or, if it is all the same to him, I'll take mine in 'flapjacks,' with butter on." Heston's sarcasm about the arbitrariness of God's bounty was trenchant, but it hardly cut through the gloom that he felt hanging over his prospects as an artist and photographer in Carthage: "I stand a poor chance to get a situation here." Even other liberals in the community had written him off as "too radical."[4]

When Heston penned these letters to Macdonald in 1884, he was little more than a struggling, small-town crank. He had no national standing at all among freethinkers and secular liberals. His venting seemed designed primarily as an appeal to keep his subscription going on a shoestring, but it proved much more productive than that. Seeing Heston's second letter about his dire circumstances, an old friend, L. C. Tidball, now in Sheridan, Wyoming, tried to intercede on his behalf. Tidball wrote Macdonald a letter puffing Heston's artistic talent as an untapped resource for the secular cause: "In portrait and landscape painting he has no superior," Tidball claimed, "and as a cartoonist he is equal to *Puck*," an allusion to a pioneering American weekly devoted to satire and caricature. The friend urged some "rich Liberals" to commission Heston to paint upon canvas "the growth, the present attitude, and the future of Freethought," an epic of reason and liberty triumphant. "Leave the designs to him;" Tidball assured, "he has the ability to originate." The testimonial came from a comrade—and a satisfied customer: a portrait Heston had done of the Russian anarchist and atheist Mikhail Bakunin was on proud display in Tidball's home. Bakunin's reputation was at that moment on the rise with American freethinkers; a translation of his *God and the State* had recently appeared through the handiwork of the radical individualist Benjamin Tucker, whose journal *Liberty* had provided the woodcut upon which Heston based his portrait. Bakunin's depiction of atheism as essential to both human freedom and social revolution had generated excited discussion in liberal ranks, and his work took on an almost aphoristic quality for hardboiled secularists of the era. Among Bakunin's favored expressions: "If God existed, it would be necessary to abolish him."

For a friend in Wyoming to invoke "a fine picture" of a Russian nihilist was, it turned out, the perfect way to vouch for the artistic gifts of a village atheist in southwestern Missouri.[5]

Tidball's hyperbolic endorsement of Heston's abilities may well have been what helped the cartoonist turn the corner. A couple of months later, in March 1885, Heston wrote Macdonald again, now in much better spirits. He reported cheerfully on his reverse "missionary work among the pious heathen" of Carthage—labors that consisted primarily in circulating freethought literature (from Paine's *Age of Reason* to the latest issue of the *Truth Seeker*). Heston expressed particular approbation for the writings of John R. Kelso, a Methodist minister turned freethinker, whose way of "dissecting the moldy carcass of Christianity" filled the artist with glee. Kelso's *Bible Analyzed* had appeared the previous year, and Heston found its "straight from the shoulder" attack on orthodoxy exactly the right approach for "all true Liberals" to pursue. Heston also passed along to Macdonald a newspaper clipping that raised suspicions about an infidel-baiting preacher named Clark Braden. A wayfaring evangelist, Braden built his career around badgering freethought lecturers, including Ingersoll, Putnam, and B. F. Underwood, often through face-to-face confrontation. Among the infidel initiatives Braden was bent on destroying was the town of Liberal, Missouri, a secularist experiment in community-building about forty miles from Carthage that boasted a well-appointed library and lecture hall but lacked the encumbrance of any churches, preachers, or saloons. Having dirt on evangelists like Braden was certainly useful for the *Truth Seeker*'s larger enterprise, but that was not the crucial part of this budding exchange. Instead, it was the artwork that Heston now started sharing with Macdonald.[6]

Though Heston clearly needed steady work of some kind, the *Truth Seeker* seemed an unlikely vehicle of employment. Except for the occasional pictorial advertisement or decorative masthead, the paper had since its founding in 1873 carried no visual embellishments. The weekly's editorial cadre had done nothing to compete with other richly illustrated periodicals of the day, or even to keep pace with its chief British rival, George W. Foote's

Freethinker, which had included comic Bible sketches almost from its inception in 1881. The paper's unadorned appearance changed with the issue for May 2, 1885, less than a year after Heston first wrote Macdonald: half of the cover page was given over to Heston's art, a caricature entitled "The Modern Balaam," based on a story told in the Book of Numbers (Figure 7). That biblical chronicle presented the cartoonist with some low-hanging fruit: Balaam, a spiteful prophet, fails to recognize a sword-wielding angel of the Lord in the roadway, even though the donkey upon which he is riding does. When the ass intentionally falters to try to get Balaam to notice the angel, Balaam remains unseeing and instead thrashes the long-suffering animal with a stick. The donkey, now miraculously enabled by the Lord to speak, asks Balaam: "What have I done unto thee, that thou hast smitten me?" Finally cognizant of the angel, Balaam falls abjectly to the ground, and the ass is vindicated. Heston, capturing the story midway through, turns it into an anticlerical parable: Balaam, symbolizing latter-day ministers and priests, is beating his donkey, an emblem of the oppressed laity, with a switch marked "HELL." The bedraggled beast looks plaintively at the viewer—how could the clergyman, the modern Balaam, fail to see the liberating angel so near in the path? There she was, plain as day, brandishing reason's sword. Her feathered wings announced a full roster of freethinking journals to overmatch the cleric's sermon-stuffed pockets, with the *Truth Seeker* taking pride of place on the topmost quill. Surely, Heston suggested, the modern Balaam was about to get his own comeuppance.

The sensation was immediate. Demand for the issue shot up, and excited letters poured into Macdonald's office. "The picture representing priestcraft seated on the people is the truest likeness that has ever been got up," effused a reader from Centralia, Illinois. "It is simply immense." Another subscriber, certain that images were a more forceful medium than words, declared Heston's Balaam "the best hit in the way of a cartoon I ever saw." A Jewish barber in Detroit requested one for display in his shop, and a reader in Oneida, New York, had already commissioned an artist to recreate the image on canvas for his parlor. A man in New

FIGURE 7. Watson Heston, "The Modern Balaam,"
Truth Seeker, 2 May 1885, 273. Center for Research Libraries

Jersey reported that the cartoon crystallized his own prior experience as a Christian in a way that words never had: "I was like a donkey-man, with a Presbyterian priest on my back, directing all my ways and actions." For more than forty years he had been a "submissive donkey," badgered by his wife into making financial sacrifices for the sake of the church and its minister, until finally "I began to kick." Readers wanted the cartoon enlarged for framing; they wanted it turned into a chromolithograph; they wanted to use it to confront Christian friends and family members; they wanted it made into a broadside for conspicuous display in public places; they wanted it multiplied as a leaflet in order "to scatter thousands of them around the country." Macdonald, surprised by the strong response, met the requests he could, making the cartoon available as a stand alone print for ten cents and also offering it for sale in lots of one dozen, one hundred, and one thousand. He also assured his subscribers not to worry—more of Heston's illustrations were, indeed, in the pipeline.[7]

The next offering, entitled "A Short Lesson in History for Christians," appeared two months later in July, and this time Macdonald, anticipating high demand, was ready with bulk copies of Heston's latest contribution. The drawing possessed the panoramic sweep that Tidball had vouched was part of the artist's repertoire—a grand juxtaposition of the teachers of science and the tyrants of superstition (Figure 8). One side emphasized Catholic oppressiveness (Galileo being forced to recant; Bruno being burned at the stake; Luther being excommunicated); the other showcased Protestant benightedness (Presbyterian Thomas De Witt Talmage charging Ingersoll with blasphemy; the Salvation Army parading through the streets in an evangelistic clamor). The men of science and invention all looked serious, imperturbable, and self-possessed in the face of the haranguing men of the cloth. Freethinking secularists imagined a long, bitter, and ongoing war between science and religion; they wrote volume upon volume about such inveterate hostilities; Heston condensed that protracted prose into the terse immediacy of a single image. "As a short and easy lesson in history for Christians," Macdonald crowed upon its publication, "the picture is worth a whole library."[8]

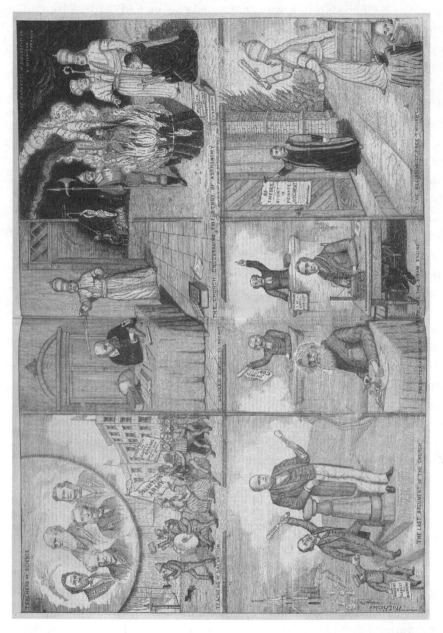

FIGURE 8. Watson Heston, "A Short Lesson in History for Christians," *Truth Seeker*, 11 July 1885, 440–41. Center for Research Libraries

Suddenly Heston's fortunes were looking up. By the summer of 1885, Macdonald was referring to him possessively as "our artist," advertising "The Modern Balaam" and "A Short Lesson" as indispensable emblems for the cause, and reprinting favorable press notices of the caricaturist's work from across the country, as well as from Toronto and London.[9] More importantly, Macdonald was now laying the groundwork—financial and otherwise—to relaunch the *Truth Seeker* as an illustrated weekly. Within a half year, Macdonald was ready to plunge ahead, and, with the first issue of 1886, the new pictorial venture began. Hedging his bets at the start, Macdonald had drawings from a handful of artists ready to utilize, but Heston's work quickly crowded out the others. That first year Macdonald devoted forty-five covers to Heston's caricatures; the following year all fifty-two. Jubilant subscribers pronounced Heston a prodigy, a brick, a Gatling gun, a jewel, a grand artist, a Hogarth, an equal of the celebrated cartoonist Thomas Nast, a second Voltaire. "I am just 'proper proud' of Watson Heston," a subscriber from Irwin, Iowa, gushed in June 1886, "that great genius, painter, poet, preacher, politician, and philosopher, all combined." Heston was fast becoming, as the *Boston Investigator* would characterize his repute just a few years later, "the artist-hero of Liberalism."[10]

Over the next decade and a half, through April 1900, Heston was a prolific cartoonist for the *Truth Seeker*. He provided the cover art for over six hundred issues of the journal and created a similar number of comic Bible sketches, which usually appeared on the paper's back page. Like "The Modern Balaam" and "A Short Lesson," the later cartoons often took on a life of their own apart from the journal—in scrapbooks; at newsstands, bookstores, and barber shops; on the walls of taverns, doctors' offices, and lecture-halls; and in freethinking pamphlets and tracts. The Truth Seeker Company published four different, stand-alone collections of them between 1890 and 1903; they were the company's signature productions, the picture books of American unbelief. Even after Heston's tenure at the *Truth Seeker* ended, his cartoons continued to circulate widely among secularists: Etta Semple's *Freethought Ideal* took them up in Kansas, as did Charles

Chilton Moore's *Blue Grass Blade* in Kentucky; they also became the stock-in-trade of the British freethinker J. W. Gott's controversial publishing ventures. Distinguished for being the last person imprisoned for blasphemy in England, Gott used Heston's cartoons as his own journal's trademark, devoting whole issues to them and even marketing some as pictorial postcards.[11]

By the time of his death in 1905, at age fifty-nine, Heston had produced an incomparable iconography of American secularism. His lifework had been the visualization of a secular republic, the bountiful provision of emblems—of enlightened rationality, anti-Catholicism, women's emancipation, anti-evangelicalism, scientific progress, intellectual freedom, and strict church-state separation—designed to render freethinking liberalism tangible. While very much a minority report—a village atheist's view of Christian America—his pictures made manifest far more than his own angular vision of dissent. Barbed, uncivil, filled with animosity and spleen, glinting with hope and indignation, they made secularism visible. In a movement that relied heavily on texts and oratory for spreading the word, Heston's cartoons massively enlarged visual satire as a medium and a mnemonic of American freethought. At the same time they compelled secular liberals to reflect upon the proper limits of ridicule and caricature as tools of disenchantment and to ponder the public implications of deliberately offending their religious neighbors. The cartoonist's art was a sword, and Heston's success forced secularists to gauge the wisdom of wielding or sheathing it.

◆

Modernity may have begun for American freethinkers with Bruno's execution in 1600, but the new era, it is safe to say, had gotten off to a slow start. To get from Bruno's martyrdom to his monument had, after all, taken nearly three centuries—a tortuous and protracted process of enlightenment. Nineteenth-century secularists associated the seventeenth and even much of the eighteenth century with the continuing reign of ecclesial tyranny and superstition—with the persecution of dissenters and the suppression of blasphemers, with despotic state churches and unremitting

religious conflict, with fiendish delight in the sufferings of the un-
redeemed. That the old epoch of sanctified violence still haunted
the new freethought era was apparent in the cartoon Heston drew
at the end of December 1892 to bring in the New Year. A character
representing Christianity grasps hold of Father Time with one
hand, while still carrying the sword of persecution in the other
(Figure 9). The year 293, Heston suggested, would be another step
beyond that bloody Christian inheritance: Bruno's stake, witchcraft prosecutions, Christ crucified on the cross, the Inquisition,
the St. Bartholomew's Day massacre are all bundled together in
the darker half of the illustration under the ruins of superstition.
The daybreak of reason and science are on the distant horizon—a
prospect long delayed by the weight of Christian history. But even
if that new era of emancipating enlightenment appeared now on
the verge of fulfillment, unceasing vigilance was necessary: Uncle
Sam might rest complacently, as he did in "Some Snakes in the
Grass," in the graveyard of Puritanism with the tombstones of
Cotton Mather and Jonathan Edwards seeming to signify a safely
buried past (Figure 10). Yet, all kinds of threats—Catholic and
Protestant—remained coiled and hissing at his feet as Uncle Sam
slumbered. Heston always saw theocratic serpents nipping at the
heels of secular inevitability.

The freethought era that American infidels celebrated actually began far more definitively with Tom Paine than with Bruno.
For all practical purposes, Paine was a singular founding father
for American freethinkers and his *Age of Reason*, published in
two parts in 1794 and 1796, their originating manifesto. Paine was
seen as deserving laurels above any other founder—a perspective
made abundantly clear in Heston's 1895 tribute, in which Jefferson, Washington, and Franklin are all shown paying homage to
Paine as the great hero and patriot of American independence
(Figure 11). From the 1820s and 1830s onward, it would be toasts,
speeches, odes, and banquets honoring Paine that pulled infidels
together into fellowship and gave them a collective public presence. Heston captured that ritualistic import in his "A Memorial
to Thomas Paine" in 1887: the cartoon's appearance was timed to
the revolutionary deist's birthday on January 29—a visual token

Figure 9. Watson Heston, "The Past and the Future—The Old and the New Eras," *Truth Seeker*, 31 Dec. 1892, 833. Center for Research Libraries

FIGURE 10. Watson Heston, "Some Snakes in the Grass,"
Truth Seeker, 23 Nov. 1895, 737. Center for Research Libraries

FIGURE 11. Watson Heston, "In Memory of Thomas Paine,"
Truth Seeker, 1 June 1895, 337. Center for Research Libraries

added to the festivities freethinkers observed around that secular feast day (Figure 12). On the one side, Paine's political writings, posed as cannons, take aim at monarchic tyranny, while on the other the artillery of his religious writings, the *Age of Reason* most visibly, fire on Christian superstition. "What a happy thought those cannons are!" a woman in Touti, Illinois, rejoiced in this cartoon, hoping to get it enlarged and framed for display "where my neighbors could see it." The illustration, nesting one memorializing gesture upon another, carried beneath it a line from one of Ingersoll's orations venerating Paine and his legacy: "The doubter, the investigator, the Infidel, have been the saviors of liberty." Whatever Paine's manifold detractors might say about the swill and filth of his infidelity—and, even in the 1890s, his critics ran the gamut from fiery evangelists like Clark Braden to renowned politicians like Theodore Roosevelt—the freethinking guardians of his memory put him at the center of secularism's pantheon.[12]

If Paine served as the apotheosized founder, it was Ingersoll who stood as the living hero of American unbelief in the last quarter of the nineteenth century. Heston frequently juxtaposed an oversized Ingersoll with diminutive Christian opponents, as he did, for example, in "How the Orthodox Pigmies Hunt for the Freethought Giant" (Figure 13). Wielding various weapons, Ingersoll's miniaturized adversaries look fruitlessly for Ingersoll, who simply towers over them in a pose of untouchable sagacity. Heston repeatedly depicted Ingersoll as invincible; no David was going to be able to slay this Goliath; no evangelist's sermon was ever going to best one of Ingersoll's lectures. In "Our Champion—Set 'Em Up Again, Brethren," Heston drew Ingersoll as a strike-throwing bowler whose arguments knocked down every pin of Christian doctrine and practice (Figure 14). The pious were left to watch helplessly as the ball blasted through everything from miracles, eternal damnation, and biblical revelation to the "GOD MYTH." A Christian Endeavor banner and the bashed prayer pin recalled a recent kerfuffle in which that evangelical society had rallied three thousand members in Cleveland for a Thanksgiving campaign to pray for Ingersoll's conversion. This grand prayer initiative, widely

FIGURE 12. Watson Heston, "A Memorial to Thomas Paine,"
Truth Seeker, 29 Jan. 1887, 65. Center for Research Libraries

FIGURE 13. Watson Heston. "How the Orthodox Pigmies Hunt for the Freethought Giant,"
Truth Seeker, 26 March 1892, 193, Center for Research Libraries

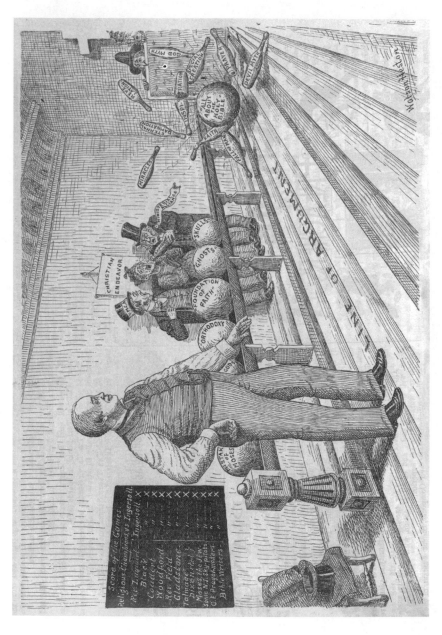

FIGURE 14. Watson Heston, "Our Champion—Set 'Em Up Again, Brethren!"
Truth Seeker, 21 Dec. 1895, 801. Center for Research Libraries

covered in the press, gave "Pagan Bob" another chance to dismiss the efficacy of the whole Protestant mission. "The prayers did not, so far as I know, do me the least injury or the least good," Ingersoll remarked to reporters. "I do not believe that a prayer was ever answered."[13] While freethinkers had a sizeable cadre of traveling lecturers for the cause, Ingersoll stood out as the most watched among them. His orations, so his admirers hoped, would prove the ruin of all those groups—from Christian Endeavor to the Young Men's Christian Association to the Woman's Christian Temperance Union—committed to asserting evangelical Protestantism's preeminent sway over American culture.

By idolizing Paine, the revolutionary pamphleteer, and Ingersoll, the stirring lecturer, freethinking secularists gave evidence of the homage they paid to the written and spoken word. Even in his own visual medium, Heston shared in that preoccupation; his images enshrined Paine's quill and Ingersoll's voice as the most exalted media of rational enlightenment. Even when Heston stepped back from that heroic plane, the printed and spoken word still dominated his picture of how freethinking unbelief was broadcast: his listing of a dozen secularist journals on the angel's wing in "The Modern Balaam" amply displayed his textual preoccupations. Perhaps no cartoon made that word-centered approach more apparent than Heston's picture of "A Sensible Santa Claus" (Figure 15). Kris Kringle's pack brims over with "FREETHOUGHT TRACTS, LECTURES, AND LITERATURE"—as if the only rational holiday presents were books and more books (especially those that recorded the stirring oratory of infidel lecturers like Ingersoll, John Remsburg, Helen Gardener, and W. F. Jamieson).[14] In point of fact, however, Heston's cartoons called into question the priority of the printed and spoken word for the advancement of liberal secularism. Their graphic force and comic immediacy prompted many of Macdonald's subscribers to reconsider what constituted the most powerful medium of progress and enlightenment. Heston's visual art suddenly threatened to surpass print and oratory as the favored vehicle for secularism's spread.

It was not long into Heston's run as the *Truth Seeker*'s go-to artist that testimonials proclaiming the superiority of the cartoonist's

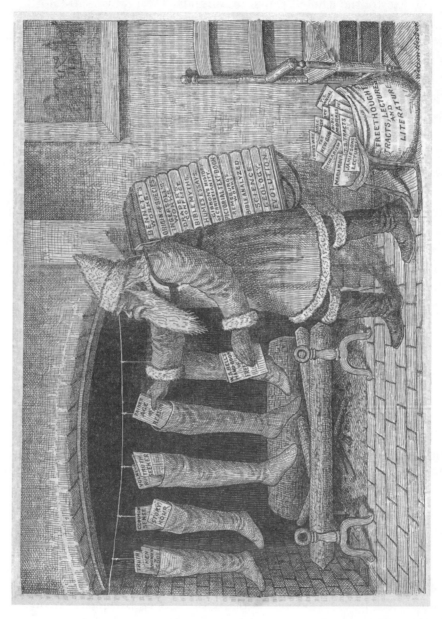

Figure 15. Watson Heston, "A Sensible Santa Claus; or Common-Sense Holiday Presents," *Truth Seeker*, 19 Dec. 1891, 801. Center for Research Libraries

visual medium began to pile up. "Those illustrations—well, they are simply grand," a physician from Belleville, Kansas, commented in a letter published in March 1886. "The conscious brain is reached through the eye far quicker than the ear, and usually the impression is more lasting." Printed and spoken words simply paled before the power and sway of these images, so one correspondent after another averred. "There is more force in one of your illustrations than in pages of printed matter or in thousands of speeches from the pulpit and platform," a Connecticut subscriber wrote in a letter to Macdonald that June. Another enamored correspondent thought that the cartoons, after only a year as a regular feature of the paper, were already "making more Liberals than all of our lecturers put together. Long live Heston!" Many subscribers readily admitted that they had come to value the paper more for the pictures than the articles. The cartoons were "the best part of the paper," one told Macdonald. The pictures are two-thirds of the paper," another claimed. The summary remark of Gustav H. Scheel of St. Louis in 1891 epitomized the drift of all this correspondence: "Pictures are more telling than words, and the effect is lasting, for 'seeing is believing.'" Or, perhaps more accurately in the case of Heston's cartoons, seeing was disbelieving.[15]

The visual medium was thought to have two decided advantages over print and speech: (1) the at-a-glance speed of its communication, and (2) its mnemonic potency. "This is a fast-going age, and America in particular is a fast-going country," said F. E. Sturgis of Danville, Indiana, explaining why he found Heston's cartoons so suited to the time. "The age of illustrations," Sturgis insisted, was "upon us"—one in which a single image effectively replaced "whole pages of printed ideas." Most people in this "fast age" of both abbreviated and accelerated communications no longer "take time to read," another fan of the cartoons insisted, but they would still look at Heston's pictures. And once they looked, no matter how swift their glance, these visual impressions were far more likely to last than those made by printed or spoken words. One testimonial from Elmina Slenker in Snowville, Virginia, captured this double power of Heston's cartoons—speed and indelibility—in remarking on the artist's "A Memorial to Thomas Paine." In condensing Paine's writings and achievements into a single frame, Slenker thought the picture was "more effective with most people than would be a volume of biographical information. There it is all at one glance; you see it and take it all in. It is daguerreotyped ineffaceably in the mind." Slenker's engagement with this one cartoon was indicative of her wider experience with Heston's illustrations. "I have all the pictures filed away," she went on to explain, "and a day or two ago I thought I'd look them over so as to impress them more fully in my mind, and I was astonished to find how familiar each one looked, thus proving what a hold they have on memory." Printed and spoken words "can easily be forgotten"; the striking cartoon was instantly and enduringly etched upon the mind's eye.[16]

Heston had not set out to usurp the tried-and-true media that Paine and Ingersoll so nobly represented as beacons of enlightened rationality, and yet his art offered a new secularist iconography that many American freethinkers found more compelling than their usual fare of essays and lectures. Part of the excitement was that a fully illustrated secularism felt long overdue. American Christians had seized upon the new visual media—from magic-lantern slides to chromolithography—to illustrate the religious life; their Bibles, Sunday-school literature, and parlor walls teemed with pictures to inspire devotion. Meanwhile, American infidels did not have much to show for themselves until Heston came along. Simeon Nixon, a freethinker in Butler, Pennsylvania, wrote to Macdonald in 1886 to lament how much "unnatural superstition" had been "fastened upon the minds of people by pictures." Protestant images were, Nixon thought, as ubiquitous as they were warping: "Our churches are full of them, our family Bibles are illustrated with them, and long before the child can read he has the flood, the lion's den, the fiery furnace, the crucifixion, and the resurrection all in his mind, and is scared so bad with the pictures of hell, and the ram with seven heads and ten horns, that he won't go to the kitchen alone in the dark to get a drink." It was with great relief and satisfaction that Nixon now

placed Heston's cartoons alongside those pious prints and made
his own jolly comparisons—how much more apt, for example, he
found Heston's depiction of Elijah than a rendering he had seen in
a series illustrating the "landmarks of biblical truth." For Nixon,
these irreverent cartoons created a crack in the visual edifice of
American Protestant culture; superstition began to crumble once
converse images of reason and ridicule took hold of the imagination. Nixon thus marked himself down as another subscriber who,
skimming over the "reading-matter," enjoyed "the pictures best
of all."[17]

Intending only to pay tribute to his own heroes, Paine and
Ingersoll, Heston had ended up sharing the stage with them. A
village atheist, dirt poor and tucked away in southwest Missouri,
he had become the artist-champion of the secularist cause. In 1887
Isaac Ivins, an eighty-one-year-old freethinker wrote from Middle-
bury, Indiana, of his own newfound hero: "Watson Heston is to-
day doing as much to free the mind from the old, rusty, galling
chains of mental slavery as any man in the United States. His
influence for good will as certainly reach down through all coming ages as will that of Pythagoras, Galileo, Copernicus, Newton,
Paine, or Ingersoll." That was extravagant praise—absurd in its
excess, but also telling. Other village infidels saw in Heston a pictorial standard-bearer, the like of whom they had never seen before. "I think that Watson Heston is the best artist on our globe,"
a freethinker in Grafton, North Dakota, effused in 1893. "We have
certainly two great men now living, and I don't know which has
done the most good—Col. R. G. Ingersoll and Watson Heston.
They have enlightened the world more than churches have ever
done in all their existence." The identification that widely dispersed and often isolated secularists came to share with Heston
was intense; he visualized—in bold and uncompromising terms—
their own unbelief and alienation. One admirer in Deming, New
Mexico, who felt "almost alone here" in his questioning of the
Christian God, wanted to make sure that the "inspiration" of Heston's illustrations was duly recognized: "Someday," he wrote, "we
will build him a monument higher than the church ever designed"

for its great evangelists. For freethinkers then invested in erecting the Bruno statue, it sounded like the perfect hero-exalting
ambition.[18]

———————◆———————

Heston's critique of Christianity was thoroughgoing. Its bedrock
was an anti-Catholicism of a formulaic variety. If Heston had
confined himself to antipapist imagery, it would have been hard
to distinguish his caricatures from those of Protestant nativists
who had already produced a rich visual repertoire depicting the
social, political, and sexual dangers of immigrant Catholics and
their leadership. In "The Spider and the Fly," he might as well
have been channeling Maria Monk's *Awful Disclosures of the Hotel
Dieu Nunnery* (1836), a sensationally popular exposé of the horrors of convent life—indeed, Maria Monk's work was among the
books in his sensible Santa's pack. The nun, in her all-enveloping
habit, pulls a young woman away from her idyllic country home
and lures her into a monastic prison-house: "ABANDON HOPE
ALL YE WHO ENTER HERE" (Figure 16). Elsewhere his debt
to Thomas Nast's antipapist cartoons for *Harper's Weekly* was
utterly transparent: Heston's "Our Undesirable Immigrants" from
1887, with its episcopal miters turned into crocodile mouths that
threatened public schoolchildren, was a direct echo of Nast's "The
American River Ganges" from 1871 (Figure 17). That Heston's
anti-Catholic cartoons drew on stock imagery made them no less
ferocious and sweeping. With American civil and religious liberties at stake, Roman Catholics could in no way be trusted. Secular
liberals feared Catholic power every bit as much as their Protestant counterparts did: "The Price of Popery Is Eternal Slavery" was a motto utterly interchangeable across the evangelical-
freethinker divide.[19]

     There was one crucial difference between Nast's anti-Catholic
cartoons and Heston's knock-offs: namely, Nast's aimed to protect middle-class Protestant culture from papal (and Irish) pre-
dations, while Heston's were but preliminaries for his attack on
the more proximate opponent—evangelical Protestantism itself.

FIGURE 16. Watson Heston, "The Spider and the Fly,"
Truth Seeker, 8 Sept. 1883, 561. Center for Research Libraries

FIGURE 17. Watson Heston, "Our Undesirable Immigrants,"
Truth Seeker, 10 Dec. 1887, 785. Center for Research Libraries

Unlike Nast, a German immigrant to New York City who left his natal Catholicism for the Episcopal church, Heston had little to no first-hand familiarity with Roman Catholic religious life (a Catholic parish was organized in Carthage in 1872, but it was a belated entry into a town already home to nearly a dozen Protestant churches). Nast knew the New York streets and had developed a visceral animosity toward the Irish gangs and roughs he encountered there; once he had met with artistic success, he would relocate with his wife and children to a New Jersey suburb at a safe remove. Heston's gut antagonisms were aimed instead at the ambient Protestantism of revival meetings, Sunday schools, religious tracts, family prayer, itinerant evangelists, Calvinist theological debate, blue laws, and Bible reading. It was not at all clear that he had ever met a Catholic priest, but Protestant preachers, along with their attacks on infidels, were part of his quotidian experience. Almost all of his named opponents—from evangelists Clark Braden, Dwight Moody, and Sam Jones to moral crusaders Anthony Comstock and Frances Willard—were evangelical Protestants; Catholics remained abstractions, undifferentiated embodiments of priestcraft from the pope on down.[20] Heston's freethinking battle with Christianity was a campaign aimed especially at the country's deep-seated Protestant mores.

No religious body more fully exemplified that ethos than the Methodists, then the nation's largest Protestant communion and a particular force across the Midwest from Ohio to Kansas. Camp meetings and revivals had long been staples of Methodist piety and practice; Heston lampooned such devout fervor in "The Revival and Its Prototype" turning parallel scenes of "THE HOWLING METHODIST" and "THE HOWLING MONKEY" into a Darwinian commentary on their primitive kinship (Figure 18). A freethinker in Riceville, Iowa, reported grasping hold of this cartoon for "a good comparison" when the Methodists in his "church-ridden town" got up their "revival meetings"—a time during which he, like other village atheists, was inevitably singled out for prayer and conversion.[21] Methodists were not the only ones Heston jabbed; Presbyterians and other Calvinists took their punches

FIGURE 18. Watson Heston, "The Revival and Its Prototype,"
Truth Seeker, 18 Feb. 1888, 97. Center for Research Libraries

as well. Freethinkers had a laundry list of Reformed doctrines that they found morally objectionable—from predestination to limited atonement—and Heston tarred them all with his brush. His attack on the doctrine of total depravity, for example, was unsparing. In "A Model Faith-Cure Establishment," the cartoonist pictures two ministers working together to force the doctrine's bitter pill down the mouth of a layman (Figure 19). "That picture represents ME in a most truthful and impressive manner," one former Presbyterian in Orange, New Jersey, wrote to Macdonald in 1886. "As soon as I saw that picture I said, 'How true to life in my case!'" Having spent more than twenty years highly active in the church, this New Jersey convert to freethought saw his belated disdain for Calvinist theology embodied in the "PIETY PILLS" of Heston's "GOSPEL DISPENSATORY." What better way, this erstwhile Presbyterian thought, of representing "that stupid doctrine of total depravity" than by "a huge pill"? The whole scene crystallized for him a mocking disregard for Calvinist theological subtleties: "You'll be damned if you do, and be damned if you don't."[22]

For all of the shots Heston took at Methodists, Presbyterians, and Catholics, his larger aim was to debunk religion across the board. The clamor of the different Christian sects was certainly bad enough, but Heston was intent on the grander skeptical project of dispelling any and all superstitions. Hence the whole array of truth claims being advanced by the various religions of the world came in for caricature. In "Who Has the Truth?" Heston suggested that the potential for noise and confusion reached cacophonous proportions once all the trumpets of revelation were sounded (Figure 20). Yet, amid this din of religious variety—Jew, Christian, Muslim, Mormon, Buddhist, and Hindu—the freethinker manages to sit serenely on the rock of rationalism above all religious factions and traditions. From that elevated vantage point the secularist was able to look down upon religions *in toto*, comfortable in the knowledge that the unique revelatory claims for the various holy books were effectively self-canceling. Protestant insistence on the plenary inspiration of the Bible, Heston suggested,

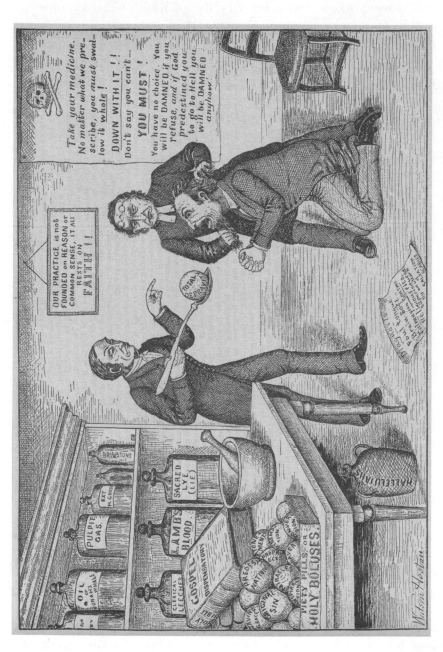

FIGURE 19. Watson Heston, "A Model Faith-Cure Establishment,"
Truth Seeker, 17 July 1886, 449. General Research Division, The New York Public Library,
Astor, Lenox and Tilden Foundations

FIGURE 20. Watson Heston, "Who Has the Truth?—Assertions Not Assuring Arguments," *Truth Seeker*, 18 Feb 1893, 97. Center for Research Libraries

sounded like tinkling cymbals when heard alongside Muslim or Mormon claims to have the true word of God.[23]

———————————◆———————————

Heston, like any good freethinker, hoped to advance a political program that would protect the state from religion's malign encroachments. Francis Ellingwood Abbot's Nine Demands of Liberalism (1872) had become the essential manifesto for American secularists, and Heston embraced Abbot's enumeration with the rest of his comrades. In "Bridging the Gulf," the artist depicted the Nine Demands as nine planks that, once hammered into place by the mallet of logic, would span "THE GULF OF SUPERSTITION AND IGNORANCE" and lead to a future of liberty, knowledge, prosperity, happiness, and peace (Figure 21). Secularism formed a bridge that kept the enlightened citizen safe from the chasm of religious persecution, violence, and irrationalism. Heston had other visual emblems for liberal secularism's protective powers as well; it was a constitutional wall, a shield, and a platform, all of which served to keep the hounds of popery and puritanism at bay. In "The Attitude of the Two Kinds of Jesuits," the cartoonist pictured secularism as a fence upon which cheerful agnostics, Unitarians, and other religious minorities could safely sit as Protestants and Catholics continued to fight one another (Figure 22). From one cartoon to the next, Heston visualized liberal secularism as a strong partition separating religion from the state—a fortification against the wolfish intrusion of Christianity into American public life, whether it came in the form of Bible devotions in the public schools or tax benefits for churches. His images effectively materialized the metaphors of strict separation in the secularist imagination.[24]

Heston was in the habit of picturing well-built fences and walls, but the Nine Demands were a secularist wish list, not a completed bridge or bulwark. The church-state world that freethinkers lived in was one of ceaseless entanglements, not impermeable barriers. What Heston pictured then were liberal ambitions for a fully secularized state, many of which went unrealized. The demand, for example, that state-funded chaplaincies be abolished never gained

FIGURE 21. Watson Heston, "Bridging the Gulf,"
Truth Seeker, 29 June 1895, 401. Center for Research Libraries

FIGURE 22. Watson Heston, "The Attitude of the Two Kinds of Jesuits," *Truth Seeker*, 7 July 1894, 417. Center for Research Libraries

traction, but that did not keep the cartoonist from hammering away on that point. In "A Long-Felt Want—Particularly Recommended to Congress," Heston imagined a "PRAYING MACHINE," a ministerial automaton that could offer cost-effective prayers and take the place of flesh-and-blood chaplains in Congress, state legislatures, and the military (Figure 23). Members of Congress could sit down on the "ANXIOUS SEAT," another of Heston's sardonic jabs at Protestant revival meetings, deposit a nickel, and hear the jack-in-the-box preacher deliver a prayer in "a solemn nasal drawl." Knowing that no one was actually stepping up to abolish chaplaincies, Heston switched gears in "If Not, Why Not?" with the proposal that liberals and infidels in the military should be supplied with their own freethinking, rationalist chaplains (Figure 24). "THE CHRISTIANS HAVE THEIR CHAPLAINS. NOW GIVE US OURS!" the secularist demands. President McKinley, a faithful Methodist layman, faints in the background upon seeing the unthinkable petition.[25]

A brash populist who frequently lent his artistic talent to the People's Party in the 1890s, Heston gave added bite to Abbot's Nine Demands by inflecting them with a fierce solidarity with labor and the dispossessed. The call to eliminate the tax exemption on church property was just one of the secularist planks that allowed Heston's populist indignation full expression. In "The Taxed Homes of the Poor and the Untaxed Temples of Superstition," he contrasted the opulence of a neo-Gothic church with the relative poverty of the miner's shanty, the pioneer's sod house, the Negro's cabin, and the mechanic's home (Figure 25). In the face of the everyday struggles of farmers and laborers, the government's indirect subsidizing of thriving religious institutions, which so often cosseted the plutocrats who underwrote these stately churches, seemed both ridiculous and unjust to Heston. The cartoonist's populist secularism extended to the demand to free Sunday from Sabbatarian restrictions that kept ordinary workingmen and women from enjoying a day of recreation free from both capitalist and ecclesial time disciplines. Like other freethinkers, Heston was disdainful of the nation's blue laws and the Protestant moralism they represented. Whether the Sunday

FIGURE 23. Watson Heston, "A Long-Felt Want—Particularly Recommended to Congress,"
Truth Seeker, 27 Feb. 1892, 129. Center for Research Libraries

FIGURE 24. Watson Heston, "If Not, Why Not?"
Truth Seeker, 3 Dec. 1898, 770. The New-York Historical Society

FIGURE 25. Watson Heston, "The Taxed Homes of the Poor and the Untaxed Temples of Superstition," *Truth Seeker*, 4 June 1892, 353. Center for Research Libraries

closing of museums, baseball parks, zoos, circuses, or fairs was at issue, the cartoonist took repeated aim at the "The Sabbatarian Scarecrow" (Figure 26).[26]

Heston's populist secularism was at its most defiant when pushing for government officials to stop turning religious festivals into state-endorsed observances. No Scrooge, Heston was not at war with the Christmas holiday season (which seemed, to most freethinkers, to be jovially pagan more than exclusively Christian). Why not use the increasingly commercialized celebration to market appropriately rational gifts? Instead, Heston's secularist campaign took aim at Thanksgiving. Incensed by presidential proclamations that enjoined a day of giving thanks to God, the cartoonist relished posing his own mock supplications in the guise of these official pronouncements. In "Thanksgiving Thoughts Concerning Grover and the God of Nations," Heston lampoons the "fat functionary" now in the White House and his catering to the wealthy—the "one percent of the rich"—and their god of Mammon (Figure 27). "THE DISINHERITED" look on forlornly from the background as President Cleveland acts as "THE MOUTH-PIECE OF GOD," a moneybag idol. The secularist objection to praying "according to the rules of the Civil Service" blended into a larger critique of the very theology of Thanksgiving—a populist theodicy aimed at Christian complacency and complicity. Quite familiar himself with the pinch of want at the holiday, Heston found the official piety of the occasion very much at odds with the experiences of the poor, the hungry, the sick, and the homeless. Disgusted with the civic celebration of plentitude, he felt compelled to offer his own holiday counter-proclamations: "O LORD, Let the millions of hungry beggars and tramps in this bountiful land be thankful that the dogs have not eaten all the crumbs that fall from the rich man's table.... Let the starving miners in Illinois and elsewhere be thankful that they have not yet been compelled to eat each other. Let the wretched sewing women in our large cities be thankful for the CHRISTIAN CHARITY that gives them 37½ cts per dozen for making shirts." It was a point Heston made with ritualized regularity: Thanksgiving, with its governmental sanction of a rosy picture of divine abundance, mocked those in

FIGURE 26. Watson Heston, "The Sabbatarian Scarecrow,"
Truth Seeker, 7 Aug. 1886, 497. General Research Division, The New York Public Library,
Astor, Lenox and Tilden Foundations

FIGURE 27. Watson Heston, "Thanksgiving Thoughts Concerning Grover and the God of Nations," *Truth Seeker*, 28 Nov. 1896, 753. Center for Research Libraries

want. And because of that, Heston made his own mockery of
Thanksgiving Day a near annual tradition.[27]

———————◆———————

The march of progress, freethinking secularists commonly imagined, was moving inevitably forward, and, as it did, religion
would disappear and science would reign supreme. That was the
rationalist's credo, and Heston regularly pictured that teleological
vision in all its supreme certitude. In "The Movement of the Clergy,"
a towering personification of freethought stands atop the globe;
carrying science's bright light and infidelity's honor roll, she drives
the ministers and priests into the dark oblivion they deserve (Figure 28). Secular triumphalism, though, was not so easy to sustain
in the face of religion's obvious persistence and power; that point
was made quite clearly in Heston's reverse image entitled "Christian Unity—What the Religious Bigots Would Like" (Figure 29).
In this instance Protestants and Catholics join forces to run freethinkers, spiritualists, Mormons, Jews, pagans, scientists, and
Muslims off the face of the earth. These mirrored cartoons highlighted a core tension within the culture of unbelief: Was history
headed inexorably toward secular enlightenment, or was religion
an unconquerable foe? Were those who wanted the United States
to be a fully secular republic finally on the verge of victory, or
would those who saw the country as a Christian nation succeed
in keeping unbelievers forever marginalized? Secular sanguinity
remained epidemic, but it was far from incurable. Anyone who
says that the cause is won, "that God is dead," activist Edwin C.
Walker wrote in 1899 in assessing secularism's future, is "optimistic to the verge of blindness." Freethought still faced "a terrible up-hill struggle," Walker warned; for all of the movement's
swagger, he considered it very likely that the bottom line for the
secularist cause in the nineteenth century was in "the debit column."[28]

Heston pondered in his cartoons the puzzle of whether the
United States should be seen as on a Christianizing or secularizing trajectory. Though he was certainly committed to the latter
storyline—the default liberal confidence in the progress of scientific

FIGURE 28. Watson Heston, "The Movement of the Clergy,"
Truth Seeker, 18 Aug. 1888, 513. Center for Research Libraries

FIGURE 29. Watson Heston, "Christian Unity—What the Religious Bigots Would Like,"
Truth Seeker, 7 Dec. 1895, 769. Center for Research Libraries

illumination—he remained more apprehensive than firmly convinced. Oftentimes Heston conceded that atheists, unbelievers, and skeptics looked more like a tiny, ostracized faction than a surging tide. In "The Infallible Judgment of the Majority—The Argument of Numbers," he pictured freethinkers as a despised minority, their "LARGE MINDS" endangered by the "LARGE MOBS" of believers (Figure 30). Those affirming God's existence constituted such a commanding majority as to make the atheist denial appear forlorn. In "The Kind of Government the Religionists Believe In," Heston provided the freethinker with two other minority allies, Jews and Adventists, but the power of Christian-nation Protestants pointed toward their joint disenfranchisement and exile (Figure 31). In these pictures the secularist cause looks beleaguered at best, borne by an enlightened few in the face of the believing multitudes. The unchurched appear hopelessly outnumbered and legally outmaneuvered; the nation's religiosity is pictured as simply overwhelming. Even when the issue was cast in more humorous than ominous terms—as it was in "A Suggestion to Those Who Are Trying to Get a 'Change of Heart'"—the numbers did not look good (Figure 32). The people, prostrating themselves before the ministers in the pulpit, yearn for an evangelical change of heart; an incarnated "REASON" offers "A CHANGE OF BRAINS," free to all, but attracts no takers.

Heston invariably regained his confidence and insisted that reason's advance was inexorable and that religion was in irredeemable decline. In "The Rising Tide of Skepticism," there was almost no place left for the religious figures to stand; they were being engulfed in the rising waters of doubt and unbelief (Figure 33). The Mormon man and his two wives are being swamped as surely as the Salvation Army trio clambering up the one remaining tree in the background. Skepticism, reason, and freethought were pictured as powerfully destructive forces that simply could not be stopped by any religious countermeasures. In "A Tottering Structure—The Great Christian Idol," a phalanx of freethinkers breaks through the walls of Christian superstition and violently brings down the triple-headed God, suggesting a complete secularist conquest of religion (Figure 34). All of this destruction led

FIGURE 30. Watson Heston, "The Infallible Judgment of the Majority—The Argument of Numbers," 12 July 1890, 433. Center for Research Libraries

FIGURE 31. Watson Heston, "The Kind of Government the Religionists Believe In," *Truth Seeker*, 28 July 1894, 465. Center for Research Libraries

FIGURE 32. Watson Heston, "A Suggestion to Those Who Are Trying to Get a 'Change of Heart,'" *Truth Seeker*, 29 March 1890, 193. Center for Research Libraries

FIGURE 33. Watson Heston. "The Rising Tide of Skepticism,"
Truth Seeker, 27 June 1891, 401. Center for Research Libraries

FIGURE 34. Watson Heston, "A Tottering Structure—The Great Christian Idol," *Truth Seeker*, 16 Dec. 1893, 785. Center for Research Libraries

not only to the demolition of the church and priestcraft, but also to the death of the gods and God. Heston and his fellow free-thinkers were sure that science and education were Jehovah's undertakers—that enlightened inquiry would explode the Rock of Ages to make way for the Highway of Progress. The train of secularist advance was simply unstoppable, no matter what ministers and their legislative allies threw in its way.[29]

Heston's secular triumphalism could never eliminate his qualms over unbelief's immediate prospects in American culture. How imminent or distant was the secularist golden age in which superstition would be toppled and science would reign? Was it reachable anytime soon amid the throng of believers? Would it be reached at all? Heston was as torn as the Protestant revivalists he disdained—only in reverse. Reading the signs of the times was no easy task for either side. Everything was going to hell in a handbasket, and yet the millennium was also just around the corner. The eschatologies of Protestant Christianity and liberal secularism played off one another in unpredictable ways. Liberal secularists were logically aligned with a kind of postmillennial progressivism in which the march forward was gradual but sure. Yet, they knew all too well the continuing vitality of religion despite all their predictions of its demise; they knew that the darkness and terror of the world persisted, unamenable to their optimism about science, technology, and secular learning. Dwight L. Moody, the era's most famous evangelist, believed the world was doomed to get darker and darker until the Lord's apocalyptic return: "I look on this world as a wrecked vessel," he once remarked. "God has given me a life-boat, and said to me, 'Moody, save all you can.'" In many ways, Heston and his fellow freethinkers also had only a life-boat—as was evident in "The Folly of Clinging to the Cross" (Figure 35). Exactly how many people they could save from the sharks of priestcraft was unclear. Their bark was small, the dark clouds of ecclesiasticism were forever foreboding, and there seemed no end to the popular desire to seek salvation through the cross rather than freethinking enlightenment. Heston's atheistic assurance of triumph often looked like its own kind of folly—a prophecy that had to be affirmed even as it kept failing to materialize. At

Figure 35. Watson Heston, "The Folly of Clinging to the Cross," *Truth Seeker*, 12 April 1890, 225. Center for Research Libraries

the originating moment of its visualization, American secularism looked more chimerical than triumphant; it was a lifeboat far more than an empire.[30]

———————◆———————

Freethinkers and infidels often saw themselves as an embattled minority under the majority rule of establishment-minded Protestants. In "The Kind of Government the Religionists Believe In," Heston suggested that the freethinker found solidarity in that status with at least two religious minorities, Jews and Seventh-day Adventists. Liberal secularists were engaged in a long campaign to ensure the equal liberty of atheists and infidels as citizens, but what about the wider politics of protecting minority rights and promoting civil equality? How much comradeship did Heston express for other religious minorities—Adventists, Mormons, and Jews—who were also very much outsiders to the prevailing Protestant ethos? How did he engage women and African Americans in their struggles for equality and enfranchisement? Heston's pictorial imagination proved vagrant and haphazard on these issues. He managed to express some solidarity in all of these instances, but rarely did so with any consistency. Frequently enough, his freethinking vision was just as blinkered as the Christian attitudes he attacked, his secularist projects of emancipation proving uneven and contradictory.

Heston's support for women's rights was certainly strong. If the question had been confined to the church's oppressive treatment of women, then Heston and his fellow anticlericals would have been unanimous champions of women's emancipation. That the Bible was a primal source of women's inequality stood out as an unswerving theme in Heston's work from his earliest days with the *Truth Seeker* through the tail end of his career with Etta Semple's *Freethought Ideal*. By the 1880s and 1890s, this scriptural critique had reached full expression in liberal secularist ranks, including the monumental labors of Elizabeth Cady Stanton in the production of the *Woman's Bible* in two volumes in 1895 and 1898. The caricaturist provided the visual emblems of that freethinking exegesis, blasting away at everything from the way in which the

Fall of Man had been blamed on Eve in the book of Genesis to Pauline strictures against women in the New Testament. "Think of it," Heston remarked of God's petty tyranny, "holding a grudge against a woman for eating an apple 6,000 years ago!!"[31] Along with Jehovah, the Apostle Paul came in for particular indictment as a cruel overlord. "Woman as St. Paul Would Hav[e] Her" provides "A SAINT'S CREED FOR WOMEN," a long list of subjections that the apostle enjoined upon women and to which Heston added his own commentary: "Verily, is an ox worthy of more regard than a woman?" (Figure 36). Paul gags the abject female figure who is bound in the chains the church has made for her; she carries a child on her back, a confirmation of Heston's mock creed in which the apostle tells women they must bear children or be damned. The churches, Protestant and Catholic, simply kept reiterating the same scriptural verses demeaning women. The road to emancipation, in Heston's view, was clear: "Woman's Path from Servitude to Freedom" entailed escaping the timeworn shackles of priestcraft and scaling the heights of freethought (Figure 37).

Taking shots at the Bible and Christianity on gender issues was easy for Heston, but putting those same questions to his fellow secularists proved a lot harder. While there were plenty of women in freethinking ranks—many of whom were leaders, including Helen Gardener, Elmina Slenker, Elizabeth Cady Stanton, and Katie Kehm Smith—the movement remained distinctly male-centered. Freethinkers, almost invariably, saw the churches as heavily feminized and feminizing, while their group was typically seen as heroically masculine, if not militantly so. For confirmation of that, one need look no further than Heston's "A Tottering Structure," in which a crowd of freethinking men are destroying the "Great Christian Idol," using as their weapon the phallus of reason. There was not a woman among that brigade (that they were also all white will bear notice shortly). Heston made these gender stereotypes—Christianity as weakly female, freethought as strongly male—crystal clear in "It Won't Work—Trying to Fit a Large Man to a Small Creed" (Figure 38). A miniature pastor tries to get an oversized freethinker to stick with his mother's Presbyterianism symbolized by a woman's dress. The absurdity

A SAINT'S CREED FOR WOMEN.
You must wear cheap clothing.
You must not braid your hair.
You must not wear jewels.
You must be silent.
You must not teach.
You must not have any authority.
You must not have any pleasure.
You must be grave and sober.
You must show double favors to the elders in the church.
You must be subject to your husband, that is, be his serf or slave.
You must bear children or be damned!! — St. Paul.
(See I Tim. ii. 9 to 15.— iii, 11.— V. 6. 17. 19.)
"Thou shalt not muzzle the ox," etc, —but put a muzzle and shackles on the woman! Verily, is an ox worthy of more regard than a woman???— W.H.
SILENCE
SLAVERY TO MAN
ORIGINAL SIN
OBEDIENCE TO PRIESTS
Watson Heston

FIGURE 36. Watson Heston, "Woman as St. Paul Would Hav[e] Her," *Truth Seeker*, 5 March 1892, 145. Center for Research Libraries

FIGURE 37. Watson Heston, "Woman's Path from Servitude to Freedom,"
Truth Seeker, 18 Jan. 1890, 33. Center for Research Libraries

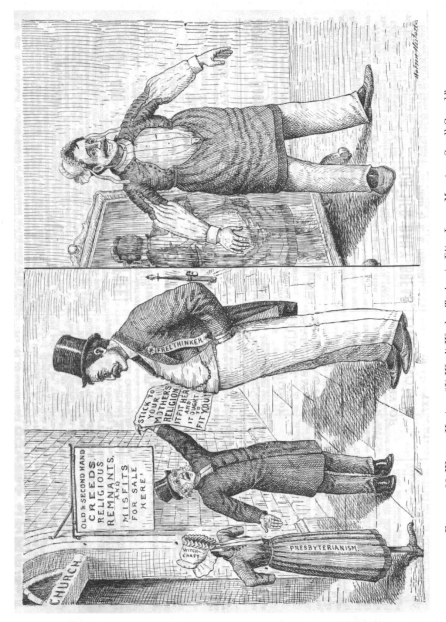

FIGURE 38. Watson Heston, "It Won't Work—Trying to Fit a Large Man to a Small Creed," *Truth Seeker*, 20 July 1895, 449. Center for Research Libraries

of that minister's exhortation is revealed in the paired frame: the
large freethinker dons his mother's attire—a cross-dressing scene
that makes apparent the absurd effeminacy of a man of reason
clothing himself in Christian piety.

Even as liberal secularists imagined themselves as having outgrown their maternal faith, it was not at all clear that they had
also set aside the corresponding notion that women were indeed
supposed to be good mothers above all else. Ingersoll repeatedly
echoed middle-class Protestant views of domesticity, and Heston's
work could certainly appear similarly redundant. His cartoon "A
Contrast," pitting a Catholic "Mother Superior" against the "Superior Mother," was a cultural tautology (Figure 39). The cartoon
might as well have been a Protestant icon of what constituted a
woman's proper maternal role (as opposed to the Catholic nun).
Heston had made the same differentiation in "The Spider and the
Fly"—depicting the prison-like convent versus the bucolic home
as the apron-wearing young woman's stark (and apparently only)
choices. Women might personify the abstracted ideals of reason,
science, or liberty in Heston's cartoons; they did not represent
the publicly visible infidel or atheist, who was almost invariably
pictured as a white man in the prime of maturity and vigor. Indeed, the only time Heston drew a specific female freethinker it
was Elmina Slenker prostrate on the ground, mute and helpless
after her arrest on obscenity charges. By contrast, when lecturer
C. B. Reynolds was indicted for blasphemy, Heston depicted him
erect and unbowed before his ignorant persecutors.[32]

Heston's real problem with women was that they were so
strongly wedded to the church. Their clinging to Christianity, despite the ways it oppressed them, was taken by Heston as a spe-
cies of false consciousness: "Orthodox Obstinacy—The Dangers of
Feminine Fanaticism" pictured a woman tenaciously holding onto
the Bible, even as the venomous snakes of shame, slavery, and deg-
radation were crawling out of it (Figure 40). Refusing to let go of
the scriptures, she turns away from the rope of reason that would
pull her out of the ecclesial quagmire. In Heston's view, women
propped up the church. They upheld it with their tithes, offerings,
and volunteer labor; and they provided unwavering support for

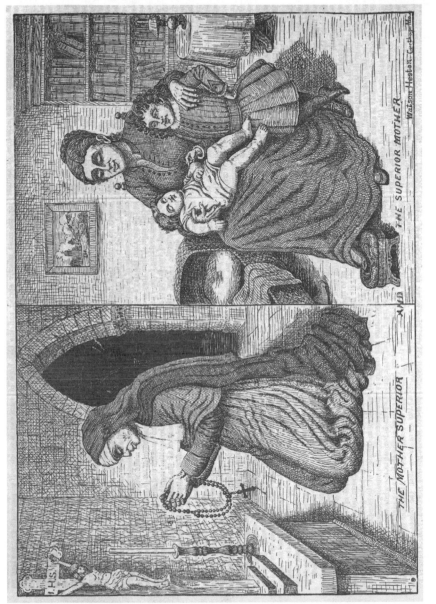

FIGURE 39. Watson Heston, "A Contrast,"
Truth Seeker, 11 June 1887, 369. Center for Research Libraries

FIGURE 40. Watson Heston, "Orthodox Obstinacy—The Dangers of Feminine Fanaticism," *Truth Seeker*, 20 Aug. 1892, 529. Center for Research Libraries

ministers and priests, so he complained in "The Preachers' Defenders" (Figure 41). No wonder then that Heston, despite his ostensible support for women's rights, had serious qualms about the implications of female suffrage. In "What May Happen—One View of the Woman Suffrage Question," Heston worried that women, overwhelmingly pious, would use the ballot box to disenfranchise infidels and embolden moral reformers like Anthony Comstock and Frances Willard (Figure 42). If evangelical women had Jesus for their king, did they really deserve to vote in American democratic elections? While the majority of freethinkers remained committed to a women's rights platform, the anxiety that giving the vote to all those church ladies would only make the country less amenable to liberal secularism was hard to assuage. Women's suffrage had been noticeably absent from the Nine Demands of Liberalism, and those voting rights long remained a contentious add-on plank to American secularism's founding agenda.[33]

Women's rights featured far more prominently in Heston's work than did racial politics, but race nonetheless remained inescapable. Ridiculing Christianity for the biblical foundations of proslavery arguments was commonplace among freethinkers: Ingersoll, Putnam, Lucy Colman, and Elizur Wright, to name four, all underlined the point. It was their standing conviction that the secular liberals of the late nineteenth century were the rightful heirs of the abolitionists and radical reformers of the antebellum era. Heston shared that line of thinking. In "A Biblical Custom, Lately Practiced by Christians and Defended by the Clergy," Heston shows a slave woman standing atop a large Bible, which serves as an auction block (Figure 43). The bidding proceeds, while a minister blesses the scene by reciting passages from the Old and New Testaments.

Heston rarely extended his commentary to the civil rights struggles of the post-Emancipation and post-Reconstruction eras, though he did see the growing reign of lynch mobs in the 1890s as a sure indicator of American Christianity's savage criminality. In "Moral Influence of Christianity," Satan himself is shocked by the depraved violence of a white Christian mob in Mississippi that burns a black man at the stake (Figure 44). In his anti-lynching

FIGURE 41. Watson Heston, "The Preachers' Defenders,"
Truth Seeker, 30 May 1891, 337. Center for Research Libraries

FIGURE 42. Watson Heston, "What May Happen—One View of the Woman Suffrage Question," *Truth Seeker*, 21 July 1894, 449. Center for Research Libraries

FIGURE 43. Watson Heston, "A Biblical Custom, Lately Practiced by Christians and Defended by the Clergy," *Truth Seeker*, 24 Dec. 1892, 817. Center for Research Libraries

FIGURE 44. Watson Heston, "Moral Influence of Christianity," *Truth Seeker*, 11 Nov. 1899, 705. Center for Research Libraries

cartoons Heston emphasized the barbarous depravity of God-fearing, relic-collecting mobs, even as he also assumed the guilt of the accused—the "COLORED FIEND" or "BLACK BRUTE." Invariably viewing lynching as more of a humiliation for Christianity than for the nation, Heston was good at pinpointing religious complicity in racial injustices, but had little to nothing to say about the state and the failures of its legal and political systems. Some freethinking secularists, including Ingersoll and Lucy Colman, displayed a robust civil-rights solidarity with African Americans and actively aligned themselves with Frederick Douglass as the leading spokesman of the cause, but Heston himself showed little inclination to question run-of-the-mill racial prejudices or to contest entrenched subjugations.[34]

In representing freethinkers—those who have reached the pinnacle of reason—exclusively as white men, Heston's cartoons both reflected and reinforced a social reality: namely, that the freethinking cause, as embodied in the National Liberal League and the American Secular Union, attracted few African Americans into its ranks and advanced none into its leadership. While the list of activist women in these circles was long, the comparable roll for African Americans was quite abbreviated. The one figure who managed to get noticed as a potential leader was David S. Cincore, an ex-slave and ex-preacher in Philadelphia, hailed variously in the mid-1880s and early 1890s as "the negro Infidel" and "the colored Bob Ingersoll." Cincore attended national freethought conventions, made it onto the platform at least once, and proclaimed his desire to enter the lecture field, especially to "work among my people in the South." His commitment to freethought was adamant: "One of Colonel Ingersoll's pamphlets is more to me than all the Bibles in this world," he averred in 1885, "and a line from Paine's 'Age of Reason,' is more than the Ten Commandments. I am an ex-slave, but I did not get my freedom from the church. The great truth that all men are by nature free was never told on Sinai's barren crags, nor by the lonely shores of Galilee." Cincore's anti-Christian animus attracted the ire of the primary organ of the African Methodist Episcopal Church, the *Christian Recorder*, which denounced his "infidel slime" in its pages in 1890, specifically a lecture he had recently given at a literary society in Philadelphia. Perhaps that hostility in his own community dissuaded him from venturing too far down the infidel path; by the turn of century, Cincore had moved on to a stage-acting career, dropped out of freethinking circles, and returned to the church. Now, as a tragedian, he played the part of Othello or Lear, not Ingersoll. In his transitory role as "the negro Infidel," Cincore complicated the whiteness of American secularism, though not enough to shake Heston's pictorial presumption about its essential color.[35]

Cincore had company as an African-American freethinker in this heyday of liberal secularist activism. A "colored brother" from San Francisco named Lord A. Nelson, for example, greeted Samuel Putnam's arrival on the Pacific coast with enthusiasm and wrote him a letter to cheer on the journal *Freethought.* "I am strictly secular; an Atheist of the olden type," Nelson reported in 1888, and then added: "'The woods is full' of us." Full was an optimistic estimate (for blacks and whites alike), but Nelson's irreligious profession made clear that open atheism very much crossed the color line—and long before that crossing became culturally pronounced in the Harlem Renaissance. After Cincore went back to the church, another African-American freethinker, R. S. King, assumed his mantle as "the negro Infidel," turning to the Truth Seeker Company as an outlet for the expression of his irreligion. King, like Cincore, remained enough of an anomaly that he could plausibly promote himself in 1904 as the "Only Negro Freethought Author in the United States." Within a decade, though, that cultural space was occupied more visibly by the Afro-Caribbean writer Hubert Harrison, who, like King, found a venue for his heretical views among the same Manhattan circle of freethinkers that had previously lifted Heston from obscurity to prominence.[36]

Despite the various inklings of African-American freethought (including elements of Frederick Douglass's own liberalized Protestantism), Heston left no hint of such developments in his prodigious imagining of secularism. The visual representation of the black freethinker, even more than the female atheist, was simply

inconceivable against the perdurability of the white male prototype. Like most of his compatriots, Heston proved incapable of
challenging the broad cultural suppositions that entwined race,
primitive supernaturalism, and crude emotionalism. If he wanted
a quick shorthand for the persistence of archaic beliefs, such as
witchcraft and "hoodooism," or for the ignorance of backwater
preachers, an African-American figure was frequently at hand,
but otherwise was rarely to be seen. As one freethought paper
concluded, "The black races are notorious for the manner in which
love, fear, hate, and all forms of superstition control their lives."
The invisibility of "the negro Infidel" was palpable in Heston's
white secularism.[37]

Heston's depictions of Jews possessed many of the same qualities as his renderings of African Americans. Ever keen to point
out Christian violence and persecution, Heston saw the viru-
lent anti-Judaism within Christianity as worthy of ridicule and
challenge. In "A Malicious Thief—How the Christian Served the
Jew," the cartoonist imagined the Christian stealing the God and
scriptures of Judaism and then compounding that robbery with
oppressive brutality (Figure 45). Cartoons deriding Christian pil-
fering and prejudice, of course, did not necessarily translate into
positive depictions of Jews or Judaism; debunking superstition
and idolatry, after all, remained Heston's guiding ambition whatever the religious tradition. Still, Heston's caricatures frequently
suggested a certain freethinking comradeship with Jews as a
scapegoated minority—as displayed, for example, in "The Kind
of Government the Religionists Believe In." That solidarity extended, in Heston's mind, to the 1899 Alfred Dreyfus affair, which
occasioned a sharp denunciation of French anti-Semitism from
the cartoonist.[38]

If only Heston had stuck with celebrated causes like the Dreyfus affair. In his gallery of racial, ethnic, and religious character
types, Heston's Hebraic portraits were as coarse, derogatory, and
predictable as any of them. And since comically illustrating the
scriptures was among his leading pursuits, the artist's clichéd
Semitic images also proved particularly numerous. One of these,
"A Few of the 'Good Old Patriarchs,'" can stand for the whole.

FIGURE 45. Watson Heston, "A Malicious Thief—How the Christian Served the Jew,"
Truth Seeker, 18 March 1893, 161. Center for Research Libraries

Providing ten portraits all in a single frame—from the hook-nosed Adam to the hook-nosed Elisha—the caricature arraigns the patriarchs for various crimes: drunkenness, polygamy, adultery, attempted murder, and the massacre of innocents (Figure 46). Heston's fierce economic populism also added another dimension to his anti-Jewish imagery. When cartooning for the People's Party, Heston personified East Coast banking interests through the figure of Shylock, a Jewish financial overlord bent on plutocratic exploitation of farmers, laborers, and the disinherited. That anti-Jewish canard did not feature in his freethinking productions for the *Truth Seeker*, but it was a standard part of his subsidiary career as a populist political cartoonist in the early-to-mid 1890s.

Heston's crude ethnic repertoire did not keep him from having Jewish admirers for his secularist cartoons. The *Hebrew Standard*, for example, expressed appreciation for the "honest bluntness" of his satires, even of Moses, and took positive note of the fact that the cartoonist presented Protestants and Catholics, not Jews, as the chief religious threats to American liberties. That Heston had not tarred Judaism with his anticlerical brush may have been, as the *Hebrew Standard* saw it, a "truthful compliment," but, if so, it was awfully oblique praise. Heston mostly saw Jews as primitive scriptural figures, responsible for the foundational superstitions and myths of the Hebrew Bible; and when his vision came forward in time, Jews were usually seen as harassed victims or greedy bankers. As was the case with African Americans, Heston never pictured a Jewish freethinker—no tribute to Ernestine Rose to match all the tributes to Paine and Ingersoll, no allusion to Felix Adler alongside Samuel Putnam. As Heston envisioned freethinking liberalism, there was no such thing as a secular Jew.[39]

The Mormon question was one of the all-consuming conflicts of the second half of the nineteenth century, and it enthralled Heston and his fellow freethinkers along with the rest of the country. The cartoonist was quite ready to enter the fray, especially to expose anew Protestant duplicity. That was evident in "Our Janus-Faced Religion," one of the earlier pieces Heston produced for the *Truth Seeker* (Figure 47). At the center of the cartoon is a two-faced Protestant minister. With one arm he wields a club against

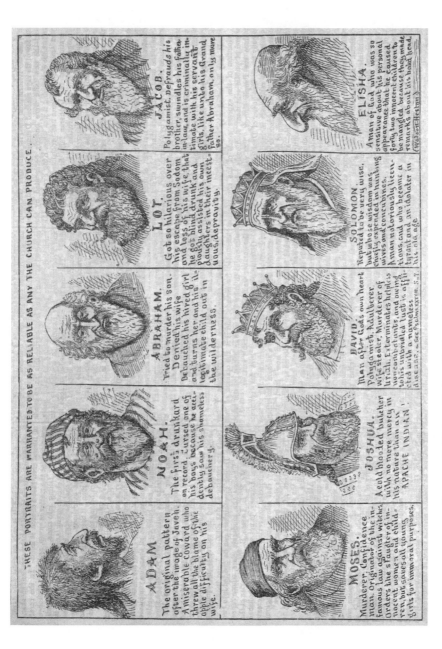

THESE PORTRAITS ARE WARRANTED TO BE AS RELIABLE AS ANY THE CHURCH CAN PRODUCE.

ADAM
The original pattern after the image of Javeh. A miserable coward who threw all the blame of the apple difficulty on his wife.

NOAH.
The first drunkard on record. Cursed one of his boys because he accidentally saw his shameless debauchery.

ABRAHAM.
Tried to murder his son. Denied his wife. Betrayed his hired girl and turns her and his illegitimate child out in the wilderness.

LOT.
Got so hilarious over his escape from Sodom and loss of his wife, that he got blind drunk and piously assisted his own daughters in their incestuous depravity.

JACOB.
Polygamist. Defrauds his brother, swindles his father-in-law, and is criminally intimate with his servant girls, like unto his Grand father Abraham, only more so.

MOSES.
Murderer. Confidence man. Originator of the infamous law against witches. Orders the slaughter of innocent women and children, but saves all young girls for immoral purposes.

JOSHUA.
A cold blooded butcher with no more mercy in his nature than an APACHE INDIAN

DAVID.
Man after Gods own heart. Polygamist. Adulterer Wife stealer. Murderer of Uriah. Exterminates helpless noncombatants and owing to his unbridled lust is afflicted with a nameless disease. See Psalms xxvii. 5, 7.

SOLOMON.
Reputed to be very wise, but whose wisdom was chiefly expended in humbug wives and concubines. A man notoriously licentious, and who became a tyrant and an idolater in his old age

ELISHA.
A man of God who was so sensitive about his personal appearance that he caused forty two innocent children to be mangled because they made remarks about his bald head.

(Watson Heston)

FIGURE 46 Watson Heston, "A Few of the 'Good Old Patriarchs,'" *Truth Seeker*, 19 July 1892, 449. Center for Research Libraries

FIGURE 47. Watson Heston, "Our Janus-Faced Religion,"
Truth Seeker, 5 June 1886, 353. General Research Division, The New York Public Library,
Astor, Lenox and Tilden Foundations

the Mormon leader John Taylor and his multiple wives, and with the other he offers a laurel wreath to Solomon who is surrounded by a sea of concubines. On the pulpit an open Bible underlines the scriptural sanction for polygamy, while a signboard mocks "Christian consistency": "FOR THE MORMON POLYGAMIST Curses, Persecution, Fines, Imprisonment, and Disenfranchisement. FOR SOLOMON the POLYGAMIST Love, Honor, Veneration, and Praise. The Subject of Sermons and Sunday School Lessons." If the Bible was the reference point, Heston suggested, the Latter-day Saints certainly looked to have the better part of this argument over plural marriage.

Beyond the opportunity to lampoon Protestant hypocrisy, Heston saw the Mormon question as a prime occasion to come to the defense of an ostracized religious minority. In "An Example of Christian Consistency," Heston juxtaposed the outrage of evangelical ministers over the Chinese persecution of Protestant missionaries with their indifference to Christian persecution of Mormon missionaries in the American South (Figure 48). The *Truth Seeker* habitually reported on incidents of violence against Mormons in southern states; indeed, the week before this cartoon appeared in August 1899, an article sardonically noted that Southern Methodists and Baptists in Carter County, Kentucky, accustomed to settling their vendettas through lynchings, had turned to threatening Mormon elders with the same fate. Latter-day Saints themselves took note of these sympathetic stands: a Mormon missionary magazine, *Southern Star*, reprinted Heston's "Example of Christian Consistency" for its own purposes in Chattanooga, Tennessee. It is hard to say what the freethinking cartoonist, had he known about this appropriation, would have made of it, but this much is clear: Heston had a strong sense that religious minorities—freethinkers, Jews, Seventh-day Adventists, and Mormons—needed to stand together against the tyranny of Christian-nation Protestantism and the mobbish intolerance of its enthusiasts.[40]

Like most secularists, though, Heston had a hard time remaining in sympathy with any religious group for very long, no matter how much political sense such an alliance might make. Jews, Adventists, and Mormons might experience similar kinds

Figure 48. Watson Heston, "An Example of Christian Consistency," *Truth Seeker*, 26 Aug. 1899, 529. Center for Research Libraries

of mistreatment and harassment, but, when all was said and done, atheists and unbelievers stood alone at the top, elevated above all religious phantasms. For Heston, Mormons ultimately shared the same lineage of superstition, imposture, and delusion as Protestants and Catholics. This was unmistakable in Heston's "Rising Tide of Skepticism": the Mormon polygamists in the background are being engulfed by the rationalistic deluge, just as much as the Protestant and Catholic figures in the foreground. It is safe to say that Heston's cartoons themselves were ambivalent and two-sided, even perhaps Janus-faced. His commitment to the skeptical unmasking of all religion repeatedly undercut his freethinking solidarity with religious minorities over civil liberties. How intent could he be on protecting the minority rights of those he thought doomed to disappear as science and skepticism progressed?

Toward the end of his career with the *Truth Seeker*, Heston's confused representations of Mormonism came back to bite him. The Mormon question had reached yet another crisis point in 1899 with the issue of whether polygamist B. H. Roberts should be seated in Congress as a duly elected representative from Utah. As the conflict boiled, Heston joined the fray with two anti-polygamy cartoons. In "The Situation with Roberts," the caricaturist employs a personification of decency and womanhood to declare a prison-garbed Roberts, with his three beastly wives, unfit for the halls of Congress (Figure 49). The next week Heston pictured the same three-headed monster confronting Uncle Sam and prostrating American womanhood; Roberts was shown hiding in the background in a skull-filled cave signifying a domestic hell for women. Even though the brouhaha over Roberts had reactivated much of the old alarm over polygamy's barbarity, it still made little sense for Heston to throw himself at this late point into the crusade. While the anti-polygamy campaign had gripped some leading freethinkers, including Ingersoll and Elizur Wright, it had not hitherto been Heston's cause.

That these two anti-Mormon cartoons created a hullabaloo was nothing new to the cartoonist. Heston's chosen art was designed to provoke controversy, and time and again his caricatures did just that. One outraged customer, on seeing a copy of Heston's collected

"You cannot come in here till you get rid of that beastly thing!"

U.S. CONGRESS.

B.H.ROBERTS.

POLYGAMY

THE AMERICAN WOMAN

UTAH

Watson Heston

FIGURE 49. Watson Heston, "The Situation with Roberts," *Truth Seeker*, 2 Dec. 1899, 753. Center for Research Libraries

cartoons at a cigar store in Los Angeles, had purchased the volume and then staged a book-burning in the streets. For a while in the mid-1890s, the *Truth Seeker* was banned from sale in Canada in large measure because of the perceived sacrilege of Heston's cartoons, and, on at least three separate occasions, Canadian customs officials seized copies of Heston's picture books and embargoed them as immoral and subversive. The National Reform Association, an American Protestant organization dedicated to the goal of building an explicitly Christian nation, repeatedly denounced Heston's artwork as diabolical; it was so "outrageously blasphemous in character, as to make its circulation a crime against the order of society." A speaker at one of the group's conventions in 1894 held a pair of Heston's cartoons aloft to make the case for the legal suppression of the *Truth Seeker*. But, it was not only religious and political opponents whom Heston provoked; fellow freethinkers were also ready to pounce when they found his cartoons mistaken or overly coarse. In the case of his anti-Roberts cartoons, the umbrage some secular liberals took was especially intense. The notoriously outspoken marriage reformer Edwin C. Walker blasted the *Truth Seeker* and its cartoonist at the Manhattan Liberal Club: "The Anti-Roberts cartoons of Watson Heston in the 'Truth Seeker' are a disgrace to Liberalism, reflecting alike upon its justice and its common sense."[41]

Walker thought Heston had completely misjudged the Roberts case. Emphasizing individual rights and personal autonomy in sexual matters, Walker very much believed in getting both governmental and religious bodies out of the business of imposing monogamy as a prescriptive social institution. It was extremely foolish, he thought, for freethinkers "to assist in trampling down" constitutional guarantees of "civil and religious freedom by joining hands with the aggressive and stronger party in an acrimonious sectarian quarrel." Walker was incensed that Heston would play into the hands of Protestant "majorityism" against Roberts, whom Walker considered a wholly reasonable and dignified figure in this festering controversy. As Walker saw the case, much more was at stake than "a battle between two systems of marriage"; "deep down," he said, it was "a conflict between compulsory marriage

itself and sexual freedom." Freethinkers should be rallying behind Roberts; the equal rights of minorities, including those of
secularists themselves, and the forwarding of individual liberties,
particularly in the domains of marriage and sexuality, depended
on liberals seeing Roberts's cause as their cause too.[42]

Walker's diatribe against Heston's anti-polygamy cartoons almost seemed reserved compared to some of the blowback Macdonald received. The angry letter from Kansan S. R. Shepherd
was a case in point: "Having taken The Truth Seeker ever since
its birth," he wrote, "and always finding it on the side of liberty—
even defending the Adventists against the legal invasion of their
natural rights—I was surprised to see Heston allowed its use to
help the hell-spawned mob of clerical birds and . . . puritan inquisitors who are hurling the missiles of death at that poor devil
Roberts." After raking Heston over the coals for artistic malfea-
sance, Shepherd arrived at his antinomian bottom line: "Let the
people mate and unmate to suit themselves. . . . Everybody mind
their own business." The criticism was so strong that Macdonald issued an editorial admission that the anti-Roberts cartoons
amounted to an "aberration of Mr. Heston's pencil"; conceding the
debate to those defending Roberts, Macdonald openly distanced
himself from Heston. The cartoonist's long and illustrious career
at the *Truth Seeker* may have already been winding down—the
editor and the cartoonist had various financial grievances with
one another by this point—but the Roberts controversy certainly
accelerated the breakup. Heston's illustrations had been a major
marketing tool for the journal for more than a decade, and his
picture books were consistent bestsellers for the Truth Seeker
Company. Nonetheless, Macdonald unceremoniously dropped the
artist's cartoons from the front page in January 1900, a month
after the anti-Roberts cartoons had appeared, and then eliminated them entirely that April.[43]

◆

The ruckus over the anti-Roberts cartoons pointed to a strong un-
dercurrent of disapproval in the reception of Heston's secularist
artwork. For all the excitement his caricatures generated among

freethinkers, notes of criticism were often sounded as well. Heston's admirers among readers of the *Truth Seeker* were always in a commanding majority, but his detractors complained often enough about his take-no-prisoners approach to Christianity to create a long-simmering debate among secular liberals about the relative merits of ridicule and civility for advancing the cause.[44] Was caricature really the medium through which unbelievers wanted to engage their religious neighbors and relatives? Did the heartfelt convictions of the devout not deserve more temperate and respectful criticism? Was the cartoonist's confrontational posture courageous and tough-minded or offensive and counterproductive? Were infidels and atheists to defer to the feelings of the devout, or were they to make a point of expressing themselves freely, daring Christians to invoke blasphemy as a gag on their free speech? Heston's work produced all kinds of controversy, but it was this debate about mockery and courtesy that dogged his cartoons time and again.

By the summer of 1896, readers of the *Truth Seeker* had been debating the benefits and drawbacks of Heston's incivility for over a decade. The quarrel had gotten so out of hand that the cartoonist decided it was time for some reflexive commentary on the controversy. That August Heston thus produced a cartoon criticizing the critics of his cartoons (Figure 50). In the first panel a nattily dressed man tells the artist-soldier who brandishes a rifle labeled "CARTOON GUN" to hold his fire. Marching toward the battlements is an army that musters under a flag emblazoned with the motto, "DEATH TO FREE-THOUGHT." In the second panel another gentlemanly figure orders the posters for three liberal lecturers—the triumvirate of Ingersoll, Putnam, and John Remsburg—torn down, lest "our dear Christian friends" be shocked. Next another appeaser blocks the way of the artist-soldier, now carrying an ostentatiously phallic sword marked "CARTOON," who is again told to stand down. And finally, as the tiger of RELIGION mauls the goddess of FREETHOUGHT, the obviously naïve protestor waves off the gun-toting cartoonist one last time, blows into a tiny horn, and says there is no need to hurt the beast since he can "charm it with my little bazoo." On

FIGURE 50. Watson Heston, "A Criticism of the Critics,"
Truth Seeker, 1 Aug. 1896, 481. Center for Research Libraries

a signboard in this last scene, Heston mocks the mealy-mouthed criticism of his work: "I am a Freethinker provided perhaps that is if nobody gets shocked. I'd sooner hit a brother Liberal than shock a dear Christian bigot."

At one level this was an in-house debate about tactics. Secularists wanted to combat Christianity—its theological claims, moral reforms, and political functions—but was that best done through Heston's militant ridicule or through well-mannered persuasion? Heston's critics were quite sure that his cartoons repelled more people than they attracted, and that the visual prominence of his artwork in the journal complicated the missionary work of freethought. One reader from Union, Missouri, wrote to Macdonald in March 1886 to say that he used to be able to lend his copy of the *Truth Seeker* to his Christian neighbors, but now with Heston's "childish" cartoons on the cover he felt "ashamed" to do so. "I am an Infidel, and also a Liberal," he explained, "and I know, and every Infidel should know, that we can only change a church-member to an Infidel by using kind and liberal arguments, and not by insulting him." Texas freethinker J. D. Shaw, editor of the *Independent Pulpit* in Waco, expressed similar reservations about the illustrations. "Ridicule and contempt may serve to gratify the minds of the extremely prejudiced," Shaw argued, "but rarely accomplish anything in an argument.... If we would convince Christian people we must reason with them and not scandalize what they deem sacred and dear." The religiously cosmopolitan editor of *Open Court*, Paul Carus, agreed with Shaw: Heston's "grotesque pictures" might make "the iconoclast laugh, but the believer will turn from them in disgust"; wrongheaded in conception, they would necessarily win "few converts." Heston's cartoons, his critics insisted, were actually a serious hindrance to advancing secularism.[45]

Heston and his many admirers dismissed polite persuasion and courtesy as inadequate in the struggle with Christianity; instead, the most effective weapon was "the cartoon method of propaganda." "It must not be thought the victory will be won by throwing cotton balls," a reader in Clarksville, Iowa, averred in 1890. "If the pictures disturb the equanimity of the Christian, so much the better." John Peck, known in secularist circles as the Learned Blacksmith, scorned those "tender-footed brother Liberals" who expressed qualms about the cartoonist's bare-knuckle approach to Christianity. "Is it our duty to handle such holy nonsense gingerly and touch it only with velvet?" Peck asked sarcastically. For Peck and other Heston fans, the caricaturist's ability to produce hearty laughter at the Bible, the church, and the ministry was crucially important for loosening the hold of Christianity on the populace. "The church has perpetuated her power and influence by demanding solemnity," the wayfaring lecturer W. F. Jamieson claimed. "God does not like laughter." Or, as H. B. Milks wrote to Macdonald from a ranch near Beaumont, Kansas, in 1886, the cartoonist had done exactly the right thing in exposing the Christian faith to side-splitting humor: "A big laugh over the Bible kills it; mirthfulness and Christian sanctity are strangers." The desacralizing potential of Heston's medium made his admirers utterly ebullient. When Mark Twain, himself a subscriber to the *Truth Seeker*, quipped in his private notebook in 1888 that "no god and no religion can survive ridicule," it could have served as the motto for Heston's enthusiasts.[46]

At another level, the in-house debate about Heston's artwork was about class, refinement, and respectability. The minority of readers who expressed disapproval of the cartoons usually did so on the grounds that they appeared coarse, rough, or vulgar. Shaw, in registering his concerns about Heston's illustrations, had called attention to the reputable standing of the *Truth Seeker* and suggested that "ridiculous caricature was rather beneath its high sphere of action." One subscriber, who admired Heston's pictures on the whole, nonetheless suggested that the artist should work harder to make them look "more genteel." Another correspondent, however, found Heston's cartoons entirely unsalvageable; they were "vile, horrible, and most shocking to any refined or sensitive person." In their sheer "vulgarity," New Yorker Frederick W. Peabody complained summarily, the cartoons were "utterly repellent to the refined and cultivated"; he threatened to stop his subscription on account of them. Heston, a hardscrabble populist with a common-school education, acknowledged that his art did not measure up to such cultured aesthetic standards. "Never having had any artistic training, I know my work is crude and lacking in finish," he acknowledged in a letter of reply to his critics in May 1897. The Missourian's putative lack of refinement had even prompted Macdonald to invite the cartoonist to New York to attend "art school and improve his touch," but Heston had apparently bristled at the notion that the "coarseness" of his work required softening. His rough edges, after all, were precisely what had made Heston so popular in the first place—one village atheist in artistic communion with a bunch of other village atheists scattered across the country from Maine to New Mexico.[47]

The debate, above all, was about whether atheists and Christians should work toward civility with one another or commit themselves to the uncompromising battle of sworn enemies. From the point of view of Heston and his supporters, the struggle had no middle ground. Between Christianity and freethought, superstition and science, ecclesiastical tyranny and civil liberty, "there never has been and never can be a compromise." All the varieties of religious liberalism—from Horace Bushnell's Congregationalism to Theodore Parker's Unitarianism to Lucretia Mott's Quakerism—were cast into the shadows, leaving a simple and stark contrast. "There can be no wider difference between two classes of men," the Learned Blacksmith insisted in defending Heston's pictures, "than exists between Christians and Liberals. . . . I tell you there is no half-way house where Liberals and Christians can meet and indorse each other's plans. The attempt is just as foolish as to try to weld a piece of cast steel to an icicle." In light of this irresolvable conflict, Peck was dumbfounded at the notion that freethinkers should "carry on the Liberal work in a sort of pious way so as not to offend Christians." Such a wishy-washy disposition was all the more absurd because the godly held nothing back in attacking atheists and infidels. "Even a careless perusal of the Christian papers of the country," Peck insisted, "ought to satisfy any mind that [Christians] observe no honorable rule of warfare, but lie in wait for us like a beast of prey." Viewing

Christianity and freethinking secularism as occupying enemy camps, Peck could make no sense of the "squeamishness" that some of his fellow liberals expressed about the cartoons.[48]

That the feelings of the pious deserved special protection from rancorous words and rough images struck more aggressive infidels like Heston and Peck as a ludicrous double standard. In "The Cry of Collared Christians—'Don't Hurt Our Feelings,'" Heston depicts a Christian pleading with a freethinker not to offend him, even as the pious soul wields a whip of persecution, malice, and slander against the unbeliever (Figure 51). The notice in the background makes the entreaty: "LIBERALS AND INFIDELS, PLEASE DON'T HURT OUR FEELINGS!! BY REQUEST OF THE CHRISTIANS." The notion that Heston should pull his punches out of deference to Christian feelings ignited fury in his admirers; they did not hesitate to tell Macdonald that they very much *wanted* the cartoonist to give offense. As a freethinker from Maine scolded the fainthearted in 1886, "Talk about wounding the feelings of Christians! Damn it. They have wounded our feelings for nearly two thousand years, and we have had to grin and bear it. And now allow me to say to Mr. Heston, return the compliment with double compound interest, and let them grin and bear it awhile and see how well they like it." His defenders did not want Heston to be courteous and civil; they wanted him to be scurrilous, combative, and insulting; they wanted the vicarious satisfaction of his boldness. "I wish I could paint, or write, or talk," a Heston fan wrote from Iowa, "so as to make Christians hate me like poison."[49]

The case Heston made for ridicule and incivility left many of his fellow secularists unconvinced. The cartoons, these peacemakers thought, exuded an intolerant spirit at odds with liberal ideals of individual freedom and charitable broad-mindedness. "I am an avowed Agnostic or Infidel. This has been my creed for the last ten years," a reader in Indian Grove, Missouri, explained in 1888. "However, I don't think much of those cartoons. I am opposed to intolerance, Secular as well as orthodox. I stand on the broadest Liberal platform, and am willing to accord others the same privileges claimed for myself." Even Heston's fans sometimes wanted

FIGURE 51. Watson Heston, "The Cry o' Collared Christians—'Don't Hurt Our Feelings,'" *Truth Seeker*, 5 May 1888, 273. Center for Research Libraries

him to seek more of a balance. Charles Bursee of Benwood, West Virginia, had enjoyed many a laugh over Heston's comic sketches, but nonetheless hoped that the cartoonist would not be too hard on religious folks and their sincerely held beliefs. "While I am well aware that those Christians who respect the rights and feelings of Liberals are few and far between," Bursee elaborated, "yet I believe it is better to do unto them as we would be done by than to do unto them as they do by us." Those wary of Heston's cartoons also questioned the dualistic division that placed Christians and secular liberals at inevitable loggerheads. "While I may radically differ with the views promulgated by the church," a freethinker named J. Tompkins from western New York wrote, "I believe and know there are many of its ministers and lay members who are earnest and honest, and are endeavoring to do good and make the people better." The American religious world was no orthodox monolith, Tompkins reminded freethinkers; its liberal currents were pronounced; indeed, it was now "moving in the right direction fully as fast as we can expect." Out of fairness and civility Tompkins advised secularists to give Christians—such as Henry Ward Beecher and his considerable following—"credit for being as liberal as they are." Heston's way of "throwing mud" refused evenhanded consideration to the views of his opponents and failed at useful alliance-building. No good would come of such blatant incivility.[50]

Heston saw any call for more charitable relations with Christians as a sign of weakness and cowardice. In "'To Be or Not to Be'—A Hint to the Timid," Heston lampooned how quickly the bravery of some freethinkers turned to fright once confronted with the wrath of their Christian neighbors (Figure 52). Three scarecrows—the first representing the Christian boycott of infidel businesses, the second the threat of social ostracism and diminished public reputation, and the third the power of religious excommunication—send the infidel brigade into rapid retreat. When one freethinker, Ohioan H. C. Gill, wrote to stop his subscription because Heston's cartoons had created such discord for him with Christian friends, he set himself up for the charge of spineless capitulation to these very scarecrows. "Being that Christianity is

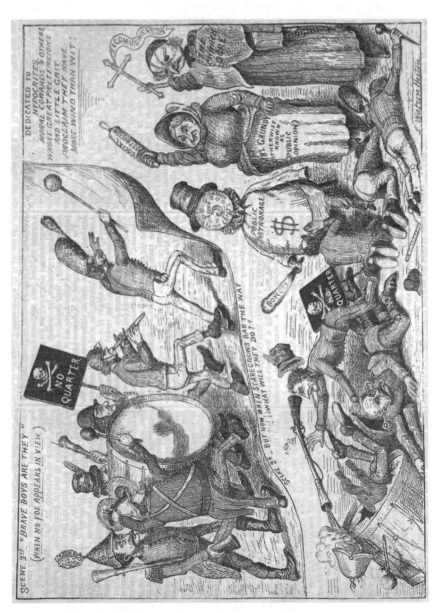

FIGURE 52. Watson Heston, "To Be or Not to Be'—A Hint to the Timid,"
Truth Seeker, 15 Oct. 1887, 657. Center for Research Libraries

a part of the great fabric under which we live," Gill explained, "the less we punch it the less liable we are to get wet by having a damp blanket thrown over our prospects, our social standing, our business relations with one and another. Let us be charitable with each other if we do not believe just alike." Gill's rationalization set off Macdonald who rallied to Heston's defense and urged such "terrified Infidels" to "get up off their knees, wipe the tears from their cheeks, stand erect, and claim their rights." In order to salvage his local respectability, Macdonald charged, Gill had lost all self-respect. If so, Gill was hardly alone. A liberal-minded schoolmaster "out west" wrote in anonymously to confess that "the Christian boycott" against heterodox teachers was so strong in his community that he found it impossible to speak his mind for fear of losing his job: "Openly I smile benevolently on the sentiment that takes my manhood from me, but loathe in my heart the tyrannic souls of these ultra-Puritanic guardians of education." He enjoyed teaching above any other profession, but the religious dissembling it entailed made him feel emasculated.[51]

Heston's bellicosity—his very lack of tact and compromising charity—allowed socially vulnerable freethinkers to envisage their own masculinity through the cartoonist's resolute and unyielding posture. Gill was attacked as a sniveling coward; the peace he sought with his Christian neighbors was depicted as without honor; like the schoolteacher's dissimulation, Gill's prudence was seen as "a sacrifice of manhood." In "A Poor Way to Tame the Tiger," Heston openly derided the sugar-plum approach to Christianity as effeminizing: Granny Good wants to offer "love and sweet things" to the faithful and thus waves off the well-armed cartoonist with his weapons of caricature, ridicule, and cold facts (Figure 53). The predictable result: Granny Good ends up being devoured, another victim of Christian intolerance. Liberal charitableness wears an apron and a bonnet; atheist derision comes dressed as a soldier. "Those who object to the pictures," William E. Renwick wrote from Hammond, Indiana, "may call themselves 'Liberals,' but their wives and children go to church and Sunday-school while they sit straddle the fence and blow hot and cold. Any true Atheist can detect them in an instant." Time

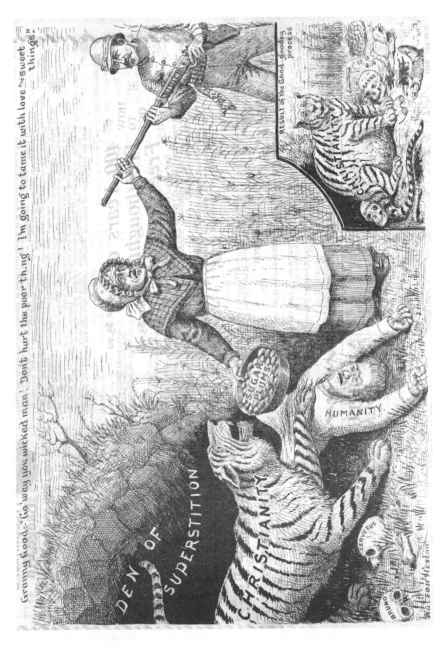

FIGURE 53. Watson Heston, "A Poor Way to Tame the Tiger,"
Truth Seeker, 28 March 1896. 193. Center for Research Libraries

and again, Heston facilitated the manly bravado of the unequivo-
cal infidel. A freethinker in Elsinore, California, wrote to praise
one of the cartoonist's pieces and to say it was just the thing to
hang in his office window while a Methodist revival was in progress in town: "I shall be abused and preached about and cursed,
but, brethren, I am with you always when it comes to doing what
I think is right." Heston enabled his often-beleaguered admirers
to imagine themselves enacting his fearlessly aggressive pose in
their own locales.[52]

Perhaps the Elsinore freethinker proudly displayed the cartoon right in the teeth of a town revival and worried not, as Gill
and the schoolmaster would have, about the impact of that gesture on his employment and public reputation. Perhaps, but, in so
strongly identifying with Heston's jeering ridicule, village atheists were also trying to convince themselves that they had the
mettle to broadcast their irreligion in the face of churchgoing expectations and ostracizing social pressures. Candor was not easy;
Gill and the schoolteacher were surely right about that; there
were good reasons for caution and reticence. As one small-town
infidel admitted in 1884, "We have quite a number of Freethinkers here, but very few dare come out and state their honest opinions, for fear of wounding the feelings of Christian friends and
injuring their own business. You can't blame those who depend on
their living on the public for keeping their belief to themselves, for
they have wives and children to support." An unbeliever in Dal-
ton, Georgia, put himself on the side of Heston's audacity before
acknowledging how hard it was to buck "the orthodox pastime
of persecuting and proscribing infidels. There are a few Liberals
in this country, but most of them have not backbone enough to
avow their sentiments for fear of church influence." Heston's de-
fiance served as vicarious atonement for all those times isolated
infidels found themselves surrendering to the social and religious
demands of their local communities. "I live in a small village;" an
out-of-the-way Heston fan in Mount Alton, Pennsylvania, wrote
in 1887, "the people are all, or nearly all, of the old superstitious
class. Those who would like to be Freethinkers dare not for fear
it will not suit their neighbors." A model for courageous confron-

tation, Heston's abrasive humor was also a palliative for social isolation and dissembling, a proxy for an outspokenness that was too costly to perform. Heston was an embodiment of the village atheist that Van Wyck Brooks wanted Mark Twain to be—an uncensored freethinker openly at odds with the American piety that religion itself was a good and indispensable thing: no deferrals, no equivocation, no qualms about offending the feelings of the devout, just bare-knuckle ridicule of the gods and their acolytes.[53]

———————◆———————

Heston had a stellar run at the *Truth Seeker*. No other artist came close to having his stature in the freethinking secularist cause. His weekly cartoons, along with the picture books that were compiled from them, became the leading emblems of American secularism and unbelief. "Watson Heston's name should be written with a red-hot poker on every church door and schoolhouse from Maine to Oregon as one of the greatest reformers of the nineteenth century," an admirer wrote from Schuyler, Nebraska, in 1892. Along with Ingersoll's, Heston's very name became a way for freethinkers to show their identification with infidelity—not by branding it on church doors, but instead by choosing it for a child. "Tell Mr. Heston I have a boy two weeks old named for him," a fan of the cartoonist reported from McDonald's Mill, Georgia, in 1889. "I admire his illustrations very much." For the christening of an infant freethinker, Heston's name could have almost talismanic import—as if it marked a child as beyond the reach of the church. One father wrote in to report that he had named his newborn son "Heston" despite the protests of the baby's Christian mother and grandmother. For a village atheist in southwestern Missouri, Heston had worked his way into some elite company. One couple, for example, chose to honor four illustrious infidels—Voltaire, Volney, Ingersoll, and Heston—in the first and middle names they picked for their two sons.[54]

None of this success and admiration lifted Heston out of hardship. When he had initially approached the *Truth Seeker* in 1884, he was financially strapped and in poor health. That was essentially the same situation he and his wife, Lottie, found themselves in 1900, when Macdonald pushed him aside at the *Truth Seeker*. Macdonald could never afford to pay Heston more than "an ordinary mechanic's wages" and was forever complaining about the costs associated with illustrating the journal, even as he was using the cartoons as his chief tool for promoting subscriptions. The Truth Seeker Company had sold at least fifteen to twenty thousand copies of Heston's stand-alone picture books by 1900, but those sales seemed to have benefited the artist very little. By the end of his tenure working with Macdonald, the artist felt bilked out of nearly a thousand dollars by the editor's "false promises and treachery"; Charles Chilton Moore, editor of the *Blue Grass Blade*, agreed that Heston had been robbed of money rightly his, but the protests came to naught. That financial betrayal left the Hestons forlorn; they lost almost all their personal property, including their small home, to creditors. The couple's prospects may have been especially grim after 1900, but in fact their fortunes had never felt particularly secure. Plagued by bad health, Heston had become nomadic again after 1893, as he searched for more salubrious climes as well as a better situation for himself as an artist. Over the course of a decade he and Lottie had moved from Missouri to San Diego, California, to Morristown, Tennessee, to Kokomo, Indiana, to Pemberton, Ohio, only to settle again in Carthage, despite knowing that their options there were severely limited. An oversupply of doctor's bills and an ill-chosen profession meant that Heston spent a good part of his life on the edge of destitution and even vagrancy.[55]

Heston never recovered from his dismissal from the *Truth Seeker*. He eked out what work he could, producing some cartoons for the *Freethought Ideal* and the *Blue Grass Blade* as well as advertising his services as a portrait painter. His health steadily worsened, and, as a result, he was able to work less and less; by late 1903, he was reportedly too sick "to do anything." Lottie had no resources to hire a nurse, let alone to hospitalize him. With her husband "perfectly helpless—nothing but a living skeleton," as one friend wrote in December 1904, Lottie had little time of her own to bring in income as a seamstress and dressmaker. As word spread about Heston's bleak situation, some of his sympathetic ad-

mirers rallied to raise a relief fund, while some of his unforgiving
opponents ventured that the atheistic cartoonist was suffering the
fate he deserved. "The orthodox people," one Indiana paper reported, "say that he is reaping the whirlwind, and that God is now
punishing him for his work." The infidel deathbed was mythically
contested—this Heston well knew, as evidenced in a cartoon he
had produced years earlier entitled "The Unclean Things Which
Annoy the Dying Freethinker" (Figure 54). That infidels suffered
horrible deaths and called desperately upon Jesus to save them
was a tried-and-true motif of Protestant tracts and sermons. Voltaire and Paine were long the imaginative hubs for stories about
the infidel's macabre death scene, but every expiring freethinker
was potential fodder. Heston's supporters, including Lottie, were
quick to get the jump on any "lying ministers" who dared suggest
that the cartoonist had wavered at the last. He died peacefully on
Friday afternoon, January 27, 1905, so Lottie reported, without
a particle of struggle and definitely with no parsons on hand.
"It was hard for me to have to give him up," she wrote, "for I
lost a lovely companion." Lottie also made sure to carry out her
husband's "last wishes" for a godless funeral. He was "laid away
nicely," with "no preacher to preamble over his body."[56]

Heston was not expecting an afterlife and did not have much
of one. The British blasphemer J. W. Gott kept Heston's images
in recurrent circulation for another decade in his publishing
enterprises—postcard commonplaces for derisive secularist expression. Queen Silver, a notorious young evangelist for atheism
in the 1920s, and her socialist mother, Grace, were familiar with
Heston's work and cultivated a visual repertory similar to his in
Queen Silver's Magazine; indeed, a cover of theirs in 1929 recycled
one of his old cartoons. The street-preaching Silver was enough
of a cultural sideshow in Los Angeles to attract the attention of
Cecil B. DeMille who produced a movie, *The Godless Girl* (1928),
loosely based on her provocations, especially her role in promoting junior-atheist clubs. In researching the ominous threat godlessness posed to American youth and what atheist propaganda
of the 1920s looked like, the studio came upon one of Heston's cartoons in a recent freethought pamphlet, reproduced by an upstart

FIGURE 54. Watson Heston, "The Unclean Things Which Annoy the Dying Freethinker," *Truth Seeker*, 17 March 1894, 161. Center for Research Libraries

secularist group known as the American Association for the Advancement of Atheism. For their visual effect, irreligious cartoons would loom large in the film, serving as a particular provocation in an opening brawl between Christian and atheist students—a fitting tribute perhaps to Heston's visualization of a bellicose secularism a generation earlier. Though the gesture did not make its way into the final film, the shooting script even called for a Christian youth, amid the mayhem, to stuff a "Blasphemous cartoon" down the throat of one of his atheist counterparts—an indication of the visceral power DeMille and company accorded such God-defying images.[57]

That the filmmaker imagined "terrible cartoons" like Heston's giving riotous offense to Christians is telling. Not that DeMille wanted to be seen as endorsing that violent response—the overheated Fundamentalist reaction, he cautioned in one exposition of the script, was every bit as wrongheaded as atheist sacrilege: after all, in a free country, atheists "have a perfect right to hold a meeting" and give expression to their unbelief. Still, the cartoons were blasphemous and subversive, and DeMille's *Godless Girl* made it seem perfectly intelligible that a school's Christian youth would want to rip them down from the walls as an offense against God and country. That the cartoonist's art can serve as a potent flashpoint in stand-offs over blasphemy and free speech has become freshly obvious in recent years. The outrage produced by cartoons of the Prophet Muhammad in the Danish newspaper *Jyllands-Posten* and in the French magazine *Charlie Hebdo* makes it far easier to see another kind of afterlife for Heston's artwork. A granddaddy of the more recent cartoon wars, Heston stoked debates about caricature and religious insult, blasphemy and free expression, combative atheism and liberal accommodation in ways that remain strikingly familiar. His visible incivility provided a trial run for secularists to debate at length the contours and implications of their irreligious animus: Was ridicule to be a major part of the atheist repertoire? Was the cartoonist's art—in all its offensiveness to religious sensibilities—to be embraced or eschewed? Was the publication of such impudent satire a fundamental right to be protected, or was it so incendiary that public order required its careful policing?[58]

At the heart of the controversies Heston engendered were such questions about civil liberties, tolerance, blasphemy, and free expression. Heston himself got off pretty easy, especially compared to his British counterparts George W. Foote and J. W. Gott, both of whom went to prison for their irreverence—indeed, specifically for publishing sacrilegious cartoons. Certainly, some American Christians thought that Heston should be held legally accountable for his "shocking pictures" and that his horrid caricatures should be "promptly suppressed." While Canadian customs officials embargoed Heston's cartoons from time to time, the artist himself was never arrested for his derisive work or formally charged with blasphemy or indecency. An affronted soul might occasionally declare that the cartoonist deserved rough justice: "That man Heston ought to have his throat cut," one of the offended exclaimed. "He ought to be hanged." But, Heston was never mobbed or run out of Carthage or Kokomo. He certainly had plenty of arguments with local preachers and laypeople; even if uncivil in tone, they were nonetheless debates, not gunfights. Heston's art and photography business never flourished, perhaps because his Christian neighbors intentionally steered clear of him. All the same, he kept his modest trade going for over two decades. Despite his lurid incivility and godlessness, he received a certain amount of forbearance from the Christians of Carthage and elsewhere. Still, the question of the equal rights and civil liberties of unbelievers was far from settled—Heston brushed up against impediments at several points. The infidel lecturer C. B. Reynolds would find out in much more pressing ways the threats and constraints under which freethinking secularists labored, and Heston would be more than ready to cartoon the blasphemer's travails at the hands of New Jersey's Christians.[59]

CHAPTER 3

THE BLASPHEMER

◆

OR, THE RIDDLE OF
IRRELIGIOUS FREEDOM

THAT HIS NAME WOULD BE SPLASHED IN NEWSPAPER HEAD-lines across the country in 1886 and 1887 as "Blasphemer Reynolds" seemed quite improbable. Just a few years earlier Charles B. Reynolds had been a devoted and long-serving preacher in the Seventh-day Adventist Church. An 1880 photograph shows him at a camp meeting in western New York, one among a couple dozen heralds of the Adventist movement, fully at ease in a group portrait that includes the church's visionary leader, Ellen G. White. Long after his burst of public notoriety had subsided, warm memories of his ministry circulated among the faithful. "C. B. Reynolds pitched a tent near us," E. T. Russell recalled in 1901 of his conversion twenty-two years earlier, "and I embraced the truth then." Yet, in Boonton, New Jersey, in late July 1886, Reynolds had erected another tent, his "good cotton cathedral," and held forth as "a Freethought evangelist." Conflict with local Protestants and Catholics had arisen immediately, and by the night of his second lecture a noisy mob was poised to run him out of town. Reynolds cut his performance short and sought protection from authorities in order to proceed with his tent meetings the next night; instead, he was arrested and charged with blasphemy—with "contumaciously reproaching the being and existence of God" as well as "the scriptures as contained in the books of the Old and New Testament." That accusation set off ten months of legal maneuvering and culminated in a high-profile trial in May 1887, with Robert Ingersoll himself serving as defense lawyer. Ingersoll made

FIGURE 55. C. B. Reynolds, from Samuel P. Putnam, *400 Years of Freethought*
(New York: Truth Seeker Co., 1894), plate at p. 540. Author's Collection

a riveting and much publicized closing argument, but his client was nonetheless convicted and fined. Elder Reynolds had become Blasphemer Reynolds, "a dime museum monstrosity," in the eyes of the *Brooklyn Daily Eagle* and much of the national media.[1]

The trial of C. B. Reynolds, in its infamy as "JERSEY'S HERESY CASE," has occupied a place of some prominence in histories of blasphemy, free speech, and religious liberty. On the one hand, it is invoked to show the vigor and durability of Christian-inflected jurisprudence—the sharp limits on freedom of expression and religion that prevail within a Protestant-dominated moral and legal order. It stands as a cautionary tale of just how coercive church-state entanglements have been, notwithstanding the American mythos of exceptional religious liberty. On the other hand, Reynolds's case is also called to mind, much like the Scopes trial, in triumphant narratives of liberal secularism in which the brilliant unbeliever (Ingersoll rather than Clarence Darrow in this case) shows up the religious bumpkins as living anachronisms. From that perspective, Reynolds's conviction was at best a Pyrrhic victory for the pious; Ingersoll's grandiloquent defense was simply so compelling that blasphemy jurisprudence was henceforward embarrassed into irrelevance. Caught between those counterpoised narratives—the enduring weight of Christian authoritarianism versus the forward march of liberal secularism—Reynolds's tale has been narrowed to fit one plotline or the other. In actuality, Elder Reynolds and Blasphemer Reynolds shared more than either would have cared to admit—certainly far more than any neat division between a Christian nation and a secular republic suggests. C. B. Reynolds became a village atheist, but the persistently religious textures of his secularism remained as important as his infamous disavowals. The sinuous complexity of Reynolds's story has not been well served by the competing myths of Protestant hegemony and ascendant secular liberality.[2]

As the most colorful and consequential episode in his life, Reynolds's blasphemy trial has understandably cast the rest of his career into the shadows. This chapter does not lose sight of that central event, but it places Reynolds's local New Jersey skirmish within the broader context of the long-running debate about the rights and liberties of unbelievers—the persistent riddle of ir-religious freedom. The question of enforcing blasphemy laws was only one part of a much larger dispute about whether atheism and infidelity should be actively restricted, and, if so, how that was to be done. Reynolds, after all, could have been hauled in for any number of other offenses against public peace and order. The blasphemy allegation certainly helped sensationalize the case, but it was also a bit of a red herring. As the *New York Times* editorialized:

> Where public decency is offended it is the right and duty of the public to suppress the offender. Obscene literature and blasphemous literature stand upon the same footing. Both are to be suppressed, and the promoters of both to be punished for a violation of public decency.... It is well that there should be some means of suppressing a noisy and offensive blackguard like REYNOLDS, and whether he be suppressed as a blasphemer or merely a plain blackguard is a matter of very minor consequence.

The indictment for blasphemy, in other words, was only a fraction of what Reynolds found himself fighting against; his infidelity was cast as an offense against moral decency, good order, and public peace. As a freethinking unbeliever, Reynolds faced a broad array of legal impediments and social suspicions. It remained an open question whether the irreligious possessed the same civic capacities, rights, and protections as the godly.[3]

J. H. Burnham, a Methodist minister turned freethinking lecturer, showed a certain weariness on this point just a few months before Reynolds arrived in Boonton. "This government, in its gracious liberality, has extended its protective covering to all kinds of religions and religious practices," he vented in the pages of the *Truth Seeker*, "but, for some unaccountable reason, it never thought that there might be citizens of this nation *without religion*, who, in fact, might need the same kind of toleration granted to these religionists, especially when we remember how intolerant these devotees have been through all history. We have had enough religious toleration specialized—let us have a little for the men and women who are so unfortunate—or fortunate, as the case may be—to have no religion at all." Burnham had a list of grievances on this score, starting with the use of religious oaths in court-rooms and the disqualification of atheists as competent witnesses. In Burnham's view, belief and unbelief should have no bearing whatsoever on the rights and liberties of citizens. It was high time for the special elevation of "this *divine thing, religion*" to give way to the civic equality of the godly and the godless—there should be no separate privileges for the religious, no exclusive penalties for the irreligious. Reynolds's career goes to the heart of these issues: What were the prospects for the equal rights and liberties of the irreligious—or even simply for their toleration? Was it possible to nurture a liberal democratic society, as freethinking secularists hoped, in which there would be "no legal, political, or social dis-abilities, discriminations, or ostracisms on account of religious belief, or of any absence of such belief"?[4]

◆

Born to immigrant parents in New York City in 1832, Reynolds was orphaned at age five and "left to fight life's battle without kith or kindred." How he made his way after that is not known. One story has him being raised by a troupe of traveling actors, but there is little to no reliable record of his life until the late 1860s.[5] By then, in his mid-thirties, he had become a dedicated evangelist in the Seventh-day Adventist movement, keenly hopeful about the Lord's imminent return. As he traveled from one place to an-other, he faced the same "fierce opposition" that other Adventist preachers did to their proclamation that Christians were required to observe the Sabbath on Saturday rather than Sunday. In a Protestant culture intent on legally enforcing Sunday as a day of rest and devotion, that teaching marked the Adventists out as su-premely different, if not dangerous. Reynolds, like other Advent-ist emissaries, counted his success as a roving preacher in terms of how many he convinced in any given community to observe the Saturday Sabbath in the face of often withering disapproval. "One year ago, there was but one Sabbath-keeper near here, and he was in a badly backslidden condition," Reynolds wrote of a village he visited in 1877. "Last Sabbath, twenty-eight were present, and twenty-six soul-stirring testimonies were given."[6]

Promoting a Saturday Sabbath proved a surprisingly good preparation for Reynolds's emergence as a liberal freethinker. It was often a forlorn prospect in the small towns of western New York (and elsewhere) to worship on a different weekly rhythm than all the folks in the neighboring Protestant churches. A piece in the *Adventist Review and Sabbath Herald* in 1876 was addressed "To the Lonely Ones," those who found themselves isolated from others of like faith and practice: "Does it seem hard that you alone, in your community, should hold up God's down-trodden and despised truth? . . . Take courage; God is with you." To be a village Adventist, like being a village atheist, was to be a very distinct minority, especially on a Sunday. Habituated to attacking conventional Protestant Sabbatarianism through a dozen years of justifying the seventh-day alternative, Reynolds found it easy enough to recycle Adventist exegesis for secularist purposes. One of his first forays into freethinking polemics for the *Truth Seeker* was a two-part essay, published in May 1883, attacking the biblical basis for keeping Sunday as the Sabbath. "It is no less strange than true that in this age of bibles very few know what the Bible contains," he observed. His case in point: "There is no text, no word in the Bible, in regard to any change of the Sabbath from the seventh day to first day, or Sunday." Seventh-day Adventists and liberal secularists shared an alienation from the majoritarian demands of Protestant timekeeping. Reynolds was able to glide from the one oppositional posture to the other.[7]

Reynolds's devoted embrace of the Saturday Sabbath also prepared him for direct engagement, on secular terms, in disputes over church-state separation. Adventists were on the frontline of religious liberty debates in the late nineteenth century; the group's right to observe a seventh-day Sabbath and to breach Sunday blue laws was fiercely contested. Reynolds, thoroughly schooled in Adventist advocacy of strict church-state separation, carried with him into liberal freethinking circles a vehemence on this point born of his immediate knowledge of legal harassment and community hostility. In 1891, long after he had left the church, he still took personal offense when he thought a fellow secularist had insulted the Adventists, whom he saw as allies in the cause of "the entire and complete divorce of church and state." He informed freethinking readers of the *Boston Investigator* that his old church was the "most fearless, able and consistent opponent" of everything from Sunday laws to religious devotions in the public schools and had distributed far more literature on such questions than secularists had yet managed to do. In turn, the Adventist journal the *American Sentinel*, showing no qualms over Reynolds's apostasy, picked up his robust defense of the church and happily ran it for its religious audience. When Reynolds became active in the National Liberal League in the early 1880s and started promoting its vision of fully disentangling church and state, his new secular platform required—on these issues—no departure from his Adventist roots.[8]

The Adventists, while possessing a distinct sectarian identity, nonetheless continued to share much with the evangelical culture that had birthed the movement in the 1840s. This was especially evident in the prominent place the church accorded camp meetings and tent revivals in its evangelistic work. Reynolds, like any other Adventist preacher worth his salt, was a practiced hand in this arena: "Eld. C. B. Reynolds is now holding tent meetings both afternoons and evenings," a report from Ogdensburg, New York, indicated in 1879. "The tent is so crowded that many have to stand outside. We are well suited with Bro. Reynolds. He completely holds the attention of a large audience. Our hopes are high that many will accept the truth." For Reynolds, tent preaching was what he knew; he had pursued it summer-in, summer-out for over a decade; he saw it as the best way to draw a crowd and advance a cause; it was how "missionary work" was done. Thus when he became a freethinker, he almost immediately began promoting that evangelistic technique as the key to advancing the agenda of the National Liberal League. "No other means devised can so popularize Secularism, so effectively make the people know our aims and objects, and the principles which actuate us," Reynolds exhorted would-be contributors to his "Tent Fund" in 1885. "No other means will so quickly develop backbone in the mollusks.

When they see every afternoon and evening immense crowds flocking to the tent, they will so rapidly gain vertebrae that they will declare they were always heart and soul in the good work." Enough of Reynolds's liberal compatriots agreed with him that he soon raised the $500 necessary to afford the appurtenances of summer revival meetings for his new freethinking ministry (Figure 56).[9]

Reynolds's labors as an Adventist evangelist imbued him with a salvific urgency. "There is no half-way heaven, to reward half-hearted service," Reynolds had prodded the Adventist faithful, and with the same all-out ardor he approached the spread of liberal secularism. Chiding the fainthearted and the fitfully devoted, he exuded a wide-awake, soul-winning intensity as much for the one cause as for the other. One freethinker, noting how much Reynolds's enthusiasm for liberalism mirrored his previous earnestness for the gospel, remarked dryly in early 1886: "It is a wonder he did not bring the world to an end when he was an advent preacher." Reynolds readily translated the Christian rhetoric of salvation into a religious diction for secularism. "To work out our salvation is indeed the momentous business that should occupy us; it should call forth our greatest care and exertions," he preached in typical fashion in his Adventist days. A few years later at a Freethinkers' Convention in 1884, now an avatar of unbelief, he dubbed his lecture "Salvation" and proceeded to explain that liberal secularism was "a means to an end, and that end is salvation—salvation from error, bigotry, fanaticism, and ignorance, insuring a more useful, better, nobler, and consequently happier life." Liberal salvation, he proclaimed, was to replace "Christian salvation," which was "mythical, visionary, absurd," but liberal salvation was still salvation—a conversion into a world of secular education, science, and progress. Reynolds's vision for the triumph of enlightened rationality shared an eschatological imperative with the evangelistic world he had ostensibly renounced.[10]

Reynolds shared Samuel Putnam's assurance that conversion to liberal secularism was a wholesale transformation, a movement out of the darkness of superstition into the light of reason, without religious remainder. No doubt much about Reynolds's world

FIGURE 56. "C. B. Reynolds' Tent," *Truth Seeker Annual and Freethinkers' Almanac for 1886*
(New York: Truth Seeker Co., 1886), 106. WHi-12006. Wisconsin Historical Society

was profoundly altered as he exited the faith, as he exchanged an evangelical apocalypse for a secular millennium, Christian salvation for its liberal counterpart. But so much remained unchanged. From his years as an Adventist, Reynolds knew in his bones that tobacco and liquor were ruinous substances inimical to godliness and health. Sure enough, as a freethinker, he sounded every bit the stern moralist on such matters: "Of all the evil habits ever inflicted upon society," he informed the readers of the *Truth Seeker*, "smoking, chewing, and snuffing are the most detestable, disgusting, and demoralizing." Shame on those "Agnostics [who] blow a cloud," he scolded. Likewise when, as an ex-minister, he conducted a fellow unbeliever's funeral service "without hymn, prayer, or any religious ceremonies," he summed up the man's life under this heading: "FUNERAL OF JAMES BEVERIDGE, THIRTY YEARS A DEVOUT PRESBYTERIAN, AND HABITUAL USER OF INTOXICANTS—FORTY-ONE YEARS A CONSISTENT INFIDEL, AND STRICT TEMPERANCE MAN." The habits of moral discipline were the same; Reynolds's religion of humanity appeared, on these points, little more than an echo of his gospel of holiness.[11]

The resonances between Reynolds's twin forms of evangelism did not end with the reform of bad personal habits but reverberated more deeply. In deserting the church, Reynolds disclaimed his "faith in Jesus or any other mediator, savior, or redeemer," and yet he insisted that secularists still needed to experience "real, genuine, bona fide repentance." Freethinkers, too, were sinners, and not only because they indulged in tobacco or strong drink. When they failed "to love justice and mercy," when they neglected opportunities "to remove prejudice and awaken honest inquiry," when they betrayed the weak and the unfortunate, they needed to repent and turn back from wrongdoing. "Strange, but true," Reynolds, the reborn freethinker, proclaimed, "Christ says not one word of what did you believe, but 'What did you do?'" And then he directly glossed Matthew 25:35–45: "Did you feed the hungry? give drink to the thirsty? help the needy? clothe the naked? minister to the sick? visit the prisoners?" As a secular liberal, Reynolds came to disdain "the slang of the meeting-house," but he remained very much in the grip of its scriptural cadences. He imagined his two identities—the Christian and the freethinker —as successive and sharply oppositional, but, in all kinds of ways, he lived in a gray area between them. For Reynolds, the bright line separating the believer and the unbeliever turned out to be a penumbra. He may not have switched into and out of the church the way Putnam did, or have explored new spiritual terrains as George Chainey and Albert Leighton Rawson had, but the righteousness of Christ's Kingdom nonetheless continued to haunt his secularism. Within the liberal credo of compassion, love, and benevolence—whether articulated in Protestant or post-Protestant terms—Jesus and Ingersoll had too much in common to keep American secularism neatly secular. That blurring enraged purists like Heston and John Peck, but their denigration of compromise and courtesy did not eliminate the frequent smudging of liberal Protestant and secular identities.[12]

How exactly Reynolds fell away from the Adventist faith is hard to piece together, but, like other Christian wayfarers, he well knew Satan's snares of worldly temptation and sinful unbelief, hazards that were only intensified for those living "amid the closing scenes of earth's history." In October 1879, Reynolds published a meditation in the *Adventist Review and Sabbath Herald*. It was called "Drifting Away," and it worried over the devil's powers of deception—"to allure us from God, from the truth, from eternal life." His despair was utterly familiar: too many of the faithful were "drifting away, giving heed to seducing spirits, growing lukewarm, wearying of the struggle, yielding to the fatal fascinations and allurements of the world"; surely, "we have reached the trying, testing time." At this point Reynolds appeared unconcerned that he himself might become a backslider; he was simply doing what God had called him to do, exhorting the faithful to hold steadfast in the perilous end times that were at hand. That he would soon become a "traitor within the citadel"—that "Drifting Away" was somehow self-admonition—hardly seemed in view in the autumn of 1879.[13]

The first clear indication that Reynolds had drifted away from the Adventist church came in December 1882 when he showed up at a memorial meeting in Rochester for D. M. Bennett, the founding editor of the *Truth Seeker* and a free-speech activist with a hero's reputation for his battles with Anthony Comstock. The gathering was held in the home of Elias Gault, a freethinker of local prominence in that part of New York. Speaking at Gault's invitation, Reynolds was presented as a minister who had "outgrown the narrow grooves of his church" through his budding familiarity with the *Truth Seeker* over the last year. His recent association with Gault's circle and his sampling of secularist literature had been enough to prime him for eulogizing Bennett who had died earlier that month. In setting up a contrast between "Liberal love" and "stingy sectarian love" (Bennett was seen as a shining embodiment of the former), Reynolds hardly sounded like a flaming infidel. Instead, he emphasized gentleness and forbearance as necessary virtues for freethinking liberals in their relations with honest-hearted Christians and with each other. The memorial speech was written up approvingly in the *Truth Seeker* with the hope that Reynolds, a minister courageous enough to speak his mind "regardless of bread and butter," would soon be heard from again on "the Liberal platform."[14]

Pastor Reynolds moved quickly to capitalize on that introduction and establish his new identity as a credible freethinker. About a month after that memorial meeting, he penned his first essay for the *Truth Seeker* on the subject of "Scandal." No doubt his coming out as an admirer of Bennett had set tongues wagging, but it was unclear exactly whose backbiting defamation he had in mind—his own, Bennett's, or that of infidels in general. He certainly bewailed "the hideous caw, caw" of gossip in tones that suggested his vexation was personal, that his very character had been called into question by his new flirtation with freethought.[15] Soon enough he developed a thicker skin and a stronger voice. Reynolds made frequent contributions to the *Truth Seeker* over the course of 1883, and, in the summer of that year, he got an important break that propelled him into national prominence in liberal ranks. Freethinkers and secularists were planning to hold a major convention in Rochester that August; Reynolds threw himself into its promotion and won a keynote position on the program. He was still intent on eulogizing Bennett, but he was now hailing Paine and Ingersoll as well and taking the three together as "the noble and heroic trinity of Freethought." He also openly embraced the infidel label with "just pride," for infidelity was the way of "honest truth seekers," of those who dared to question the authority of the Bible and insist on their right to express their irreligious findings. The orthodox, Reynolds avowed, would do all they could to crush such "noble souls"; they would trump up charges of blasphemy and obscenity, turning an inquisitorial wrath upon infidel editors and orators. Freethinkers, Reynolds proclaimed, would not quake before such bigotry, calumny, and persecution. The Rochester convention sealed Reynolds's new career: secular liberals had found another orator for the cause, a lecturer who was very eager to get out on the circuit.[16]

Like the movement's other roving lecturers, including Putnam and Ingersoll, Reynolds soon developed a repertoire of speeches on a range of liberal themes: among them, "Secularization through Organization," "What Liberalism Teaches," "The Bible the Enemy of Women," "Salvation—Secular or Christian, Which?" and "Why I Left the Pulpit." His base of operation remained North Parma, New York, a small town outside Rochester, but his early lecture tours took him across Pennsylvania and into Canada, from Toronto to Montreal. He then turned to tent meetings, pitching his new tent first in Kalamazoo, Michigan, in May 1885, and closing the season that October in Alliance, Ohio. Another round of tent evangelism was planned for the next summer; in the meantime, Reynolds took the show indoors and used a stereopticon to illustrate his lectures (he promised pictures of the Holy Land that would "show it up in a manner highly detrimental to its reputation"). All of this activity was indicative of just how fast Reynolds's star was rising within secular ranks; his lectures were attracting much attention from one place to another, and he had climbed into the top leadership of the National Liberal League. An excited report from Frackville, Pennsylvania, about Reynolds's appearance there in February 1885, said that the town was in "a perfect ferment" after his lecture. The curiosity to see the "Ex-Rev. C. B. Reynolds" had been intense. After all, "next to Colonel Ingersoll," the correspondent hyperbolized, Reynolds was "the greatest secular gun in America."[17]

◆

Before Reynolds arrived in Boonton, New Jersey, in July 1886, he had encountered only limited trouble as an itinerant lecturer. The most portentous episode had taken place in Montezuma, New York, a village of about four hundred people, which had seen both Reynolds and another prominent freethinking lecturer, John Remsburg, descend upon it together in January 1885. The four local churches—Methodist, Baptist, Free Methodist, and Catholic—mobilized against the irreligious lecturers and against a merchant, Edward Ross, who had encouraged them to come and had secured a hall for their use. Threatened with "the destruction of his business" and "the death of all political influence," Ross had dug in his heels. The faithful responded by calling in their own itinerant evangelist to take on the infidels, and soon emotions in town were at "fever heat." Remsburg and Reynolds looked gentlemanly enough, but rumors that they possessed diabolical appendages were whispered through the village; another report briefly buzzed that the hall where the infidels were to speak was on fire and that the flames were the Lord's judgment. Still, the debate went off, with the itinerant evangelist challenging the visiting infidels face-to-face. "The hot zeal and frantic hate and wild excitement" left one reporter on the scene breathless, wondering whether the crowd would "commit violence on Remsburg and Reynolds." The good people of Montezuma did not resort to mobbish force, but the antagonism was sufficiently intense that Remsburg remarked he had never seen such animosity in his four years as a traveling lecturer.[18]

The charged scene in Montezuma perhaps augured the conflict to come in Boonton, but even here, amid the feverish tension, the religious and irreligious strove for civility rather than Heston-like confrontation. Among the best indications of the courtesy, even graciousness, the pious and the freethinking were ready to extend one another is what happened next in Montezuma. Only a week or so later, merchant Edward Ross's six-month-old infant died after a brief and sudden illness. Some in town were quick to fling an "I told you so" in his face, declaring the child's death "the just judgment of God" for his part in bringing the Bible-flouting lecturers to town. Sick with grief but undaunted, Ross telegraphed Reynolds to invite him to conduct the funeral, a gesture that seemed guaranteed to reignite the conflict. But Ross and his wife were known to be good and generous members of the community; they had the respect of many in the village despite their rejection of Christianity; and most of their neighbors felt for them in their loss and sorrow. The question necessarily arose—where to hold the baby's funeral?—since, after all, there was no infidel congregation in town. Tellingly, the Baptist church decided to open its doors for the service and to allow Reynolds, at the family's request, to officiate. The church choir, volunteering to take part, selected pieces to sing that were in harmony with the liberal sentiments of the Rosses. Reynolds himself readily acknowledged that the church and its choir deserved "the highest encomiums for their brave and kindly action." Standing in a pulpit once again, "Infidel Reynolds" took the opportunity to toll the bells of liberal universalism and compassion in the presence of an infant's death: "[W]e are all travelers on the same journey. Oh! how much we all need each other's tender, pitying love. . . . Friends, let us no longer feel unkindly to each other on account of creeds." Instead of worsening tensions, the "somewhat unusual funeral service" that Reynolds and the Baptists performed together was the catharsis the town needed. When the infidel returned for another round of lectures in Montezuma the next year, he was greeted with almost uniform warmth and courtesy.[19]

The initial hostility that Reynolds experienced in Montezuma left him unmarked by trepidation. When asked a few months later, in April 1885, if he worried about Christians vandalizing or destroying his tent, Reynolds appealed to his experience as an Adventist evangelist. Despite the bitter opposition he had encountered from "saints and rough sinners" alike, he had never in ten years of revival preaching had a tent "injured one dollar's worth."

The law was bound, he said, "to protect our cotton meeting-house as much as the most stately cathedral." His summary estimate: "There is no danger." If that sounded just a tad Pollyannish, it was. In a tiny village in Michigan, a mere four months later, he had to hire an armed watchman to protect the tent at night; the one minister in town, a Methodist, had been exhorting folks to drive Reynolds out and to do away with "this accursed Tent." The threats felt real enough that the infidel lecturer despaired for his safety, fearing that "some stealthy assassin" would crack his skull with a rock or club as he walked in the dark from the tent to his hotel. Again, though, the ruffians had more bark than bite. Reynolds finished out his six-day tent campaign without violence and with a measure of satisfaction at how many had braved the minister's wrath to attend his lectures.[20]

Reynolds had already visited Boonton once before, a town of about two thousand five hundred people that had struggled to regain its footing after the collapse the previous decade of its main industry, the New Jersey Iron Company. He had lectured there without disturbance in February 1886, and so had his wife, Frances C. Reynolds, who began joining him on the platform with an offering of "A Woman's Reasons for the Gospel of Humanity."[21] These were "the first Liberal lectures" the town had ever hosted, and they generated enough enthusiasm that a few locals—sixteen in all—organized a club they called the Boonton Secular Union, a beachhead for freethinking liberalism amid the town's thriving Methodist, Reformed, Presbyterian, and Catholic congregations. The group began inviting other irreligious speakers to town, and this raised the hackles of some churchgoers who did not like seeing a revolving cast of freethinking infidels coming through the village. "The province of Liberalism is to turn the attention of the men and women away from the gods, to turn men and women from an imaginary world to a world of reality," explained Florence Hennion, Secretary of the Boonton Secular Union, in an April 1886 report on two other speakers the group had recently hosted. She saw meanness and aggression lurking in the hearts of her Christian neighbors; "the more orthodox the people are, the more liable they are to commit a crime," Hennion claimed. She also anticipated getting Reynolds back to wake Boonton up again with his fervid rationalism and to goad local ministers in their own den. By puffing the club's activities in this way, Hennion certainly made it sound as if confrontation was already in the air.[22]

Reynolds was more than a month into his second season of tent evangelism when he arrived in Boonton at the end of July 1886 for a weeklong campaign. The first lecture on Monday evening the 26th went reasonably well, though there were already "premonitions" of trouble—stones were thrown onto the roof of the tent and one rope was damaged. The opening night had piqued enough curiosity that the tent filled up the next evening; but an unruly crowd of "some two hundred fifty roughs" also collected around outside. The mob howled so loudly when Reynolds began to speak that he had to break off his address and dismiss the audience; more stones were hurled at the tent, and two more ropes were cut. Reynolds, aware of who the ringleaders of the opposition were, entered a legal complaint against five of them on Wednesday morning; he sought the protective aid of a local judge and of the town's mayor and marshal. That evening, as he started to light the tent's lamps in preparation for his third lecture, the marshal arrived, but only to arrest Reynolds on a charge of blasphemy and haul him off to face the local justice of the peace. A rabble trailed behind the officer and the offender hooting its approval. Instead of locking Reynolds up for the night, the judge released him on $300 in bail.[23]

Angry and defiant, Reynolds returned to the tent determined to give his Wednesday night lecture. The marshal, the mayor, and the town council all washed their hands of providing security for him, and that necessarily emboldened the hooligans, who quickly took over the scene. Worried for the safety of his audience and himself, Reynolds aborted his lecture and made a hasty retreat with the help of a prominent local family. His "beloved tabernacle," left in the hands of the mob, was flattened, "an almost total wreck." Everyone agreed Reynolds was lucky to have escaped unharmed—without being tarred and feathered or dunked in the nearby canal, or worse. As one local paper reported on the furor, "All that was lacking was someone to say 'go'; and I doubt if the word had been given, that Reynolds or any of his clique would ever undertake to tell the people of Boonton again that there was no God and that their religion was a farce."[24]

———————◆———————

Thursday morning Reynolds and the town of Boonton awoke to a legal mess. Reynolds was ready to sue the town for damages, and, for its part, the town council called a special meeting to pass a resolution prohibiting Reynolds from ever holding "his so-called Liberal but unlawful meetings" within Boonton's corporate limits again. Incensed by the uproar the infidel's presence in town had created, the council had decided to forbid the preaching of liberal secularism—or, at least, Reynolds's tent-style version of it. No longer banking much on civility and tolerance, Reynolds shot back that the council's resolution "exhibited the most monumental asinine stupidity on record." There was going to be no repeat of the reconciliation in Montezuma.[25]

Two days later, on Saturday July 31, the justice of the peace, a stalwart Methodist, held the hearing on the blasphemy charge against Reynolds. A coal dealer, who was a member of the Reformed Church and the Young Men's Christian Association, swore that Reynolds had cast aspersions upon God and mocked the scriptures in his Tuesday lecture. A handful of phrases had stuck in the man's mind as particularly blasphemous. He remembered Reynolds's reference to God as "the Old Man"; his comment upon Eve's creation from Adam's rib, "Who believes any such nonsense"; and the lecturer's jesting remark about not knowing whether God used "Ether or Chloroform" to put Adam to sleep before performing that rib-removing operation. A second witness offered less detail but confirmed that Reynolds had made fun of the Bible. The prosecuting attorney—his law office sported a large Prohibition Party banner in its front window with the motto, "For God and Home and Native Land"—was the village Comstock and took the charges with dead seriousness. Reynolds, serving as his own counsel, was feeling equally combative. He sat at the table with a copy of the *Truth Seeker* in hand, angering many onlookers once again by flaunting Heston's cartoons satirizing Christianity and the Bible. But even if Reynolds had opted for a more peaceable demeanor, it would most likely not have helped. The deck was stacked against him. The judge readily sided with the prosecutor and agreed to pass the case along to the grand jury in Morristown for indictment. By contrast, the rioters were never charged, and Reynolds's hope to collect damages from the town proved vain.[26]

This initial hearing already showed that the legal difficulties Reynolds faced went well beyond the blasphemy accusation. The swearing of witnesses made that reality especially plain. The two the prosecutor called sailed through the oath to give their damning testimony. But then, when the defendant called a fellow freethinker, John Cramer, who had been at the Tuesday lecture and was ready to dispute the blasphemy complaint, the prosecuting attorney immediately challenged his competency. He peppered Cramer with questions: "Do you believe there is a God?" "Do you believe the Bible is true?" "Do you believe any punishment will be inflicted upon you by almighty God if you swear Falsely?" "What effect would it have upon you with God if you told a lie?" To which the freethinker replied in order: "Yes," "No," "I don't know," and again "I don't know." The judge, in his turn, pressed Cramer further on his ideas about "the Character & Attributes of God," by which time the witness declared himself "an Agnostic" with "no views" on the religious subjects under discussion. Theological questions like these were posed often enough in American courtrooms to create a serious problem for freethinking secularists. Though it remained a losing cause in many places (including yet another legislative defeat in Massachusetts in May 1886, just two months before Reynolds's hearing), abolishing such religious tests was a signature issue of liberal activism. Like other states, New Jersey allowed witnesses who had pious scruples against oath-taking (Quakers, for example) to offer a solemn affirmation of truth-telling without the "So help me God" phrasing and without swearing upon a Bible, but the prosecutor argued that atheists and agnostics did not fall within the allowance made for religious conscience: "The laws of New Jersey say you *must* believe something. New Jersey rules out infidels." The judge agreed with the prosecutor, and Cramer was thus disqualified as a witness. Few things made the civil inequality of unbelievers more apparent than the religious application of judicial oaths.[27]

By some accounts, the defendant was also deemed incompetent to testify at his own hearing. One report claimed that when Reynolds was asked to make a statement under oath, he had refused to swear on the Bible. His tone when answering the questions put to him was said to have been derisive, and his atheism manifest. To the question, "Do you believe in God?" he had replied that he and "the old fellow" were strangers, "not on intimate terms." To the question about eternal punishments, he had scoffed about it being hot enough for him already in New Jersey. The *Truth Seeker*, which was the most attentive recorder of the whole affair, did not report this banter, but at least two other papers did. This much is clear: neither Reynolds nor Cramer got the chance to offer testimony contesting the prosecution's description of events. Reynolds, in particular, was ready to show that his accusers had mistaken bona fide biblical references, unflattering though they might be, for sacrilegious parodies of scripture: was the mere recital of biblical stories blasphemous? Like the handful of other evangelical ministers who became freethinking lecturers, Reynolds had at least one thing going for him: namely, "an uncanny knowledge of scriptural texts and [an] ability to locate them." If the hearing had come down to who was more adept at citing the Bible chapter and verse, Reynolds almost certainly would have shown up the witnesses against him. His scriptural savvy was, after all, as integral to his freethinking critique of Christianity as it had been to his Adventist evangelism. Ingersoll would play out this gambit in his defense of Reynolds, arguing that his client had "simply repeated what is in the Bible," but the defendant never got a court hearing on that point himself. As an infidel, Reynolds was necessarily a witness of dubious veracity.[28]

Out on bail awaiting news from the grand jury, Reynolds resumed his lecture itinerary—*sans* tent. He did not let Boonton slip long from his sights, though. He was back less than two weeks later with hundreds of copies of a pamphlet arguing that New Jersey's hoary blasphemy law was inconsistent with the state's constitutional protections of freedom of speech and religion. The tract also made the secular argument against religious tests for witness competency: "Criminals in New Jersey may freely testify, but upright and conscientious Freethinkers may not. Great is New Jersey, and the kingdom of God shall be hers!" Reynolds blanketed the town with the leaflet and made a point of handing one personally to the judge who had presided at his hearing. Reappearing there so soon looked like a martyr's move, and, even though "no violence was offered" him this time, his audacity kept the temperature rising. The same week Robert Ingersoll announced that he was prepared to serve as Reynolds's defense lawyer, and his oratorical fame instantly raised the case's profile. The artist Thomas Nast—who, as a resident of Morristown, had the drama playing out in his own backyard—satirized the news that Ingersoll was on the case; his *Harper's Weekly* cartoon showed the freethinking orator laying his hand on the shoulder of a prison-striped devil and remarking: "Any time one of your followers is on trial you can count on me for the defence" (Figure 57). With Ingersoll involved and with cultural watchmen like Nast eyeing it, Reynolds's legal predicament suddenly had the makings of a *cause célèbre*.[29]

Ever peripatetic, Reynolds was back in New Jersey in mid-September, this time leafleting Morristown, where the grand jury was soon to meet, and circulating copies of a recent issue of the *Truth Seeker* that sported a Heston cartoon on its cover: "Casting Pearls before Swine—C. B. Reynolds in New Jersey." Heston's caricature drew its inspiration from a *Truth Seeker* report that specified "Catholic and Methodist roughs" as having been primarily responsible for the assault on Reynolds in Boonton. The cartoonist turned that detail into a mockery of "METHODIST SLOP" and "CATHOLIC SWILL" and the porcine followers of both churches (Figure 58). Reynolds then doubled down on the insult and produced his own pamphlet in early October entitled *Blasphemy and the Bible*, which featured the cartoon prominently as a two-page insert. He immediately headed to Boonton and Morristown with fifteen hundred copies for "gratuitous circulation," and that foray sparked renewed outrage in both places. Within days, the grand jury delivered its indictment, but with new ammunition. Instead of focusing on what Reynolds had said

FIGURE 57. Thomas Nast, "The Being That He Really Believes In,"
Harper's Weekly, 18 Sept, 1886, 600. Washington University in St. Louis

FIGURE 58. Watson Heston, "Casting Pearls before Swine—C. B. Reynolds in New Jersey," *Truth Seeker*, 4 Sept. 1886, 561. General Research Division, The New York Public Library, Astor, Lenox and Tilden Foundations

in Boonton in late July, the inquest shifted attention to this latest outrage—the distribution of this "scandalous, impious, and blasphemous" pamphlet, filled with insults of God and the scriptures, not to mention verbal and pictorial sneers at New Jersey's rioting Christians. "Was it to the honor and glory of Jehovah to wreck my Tent," Reynolds had pressed, "in the hope to thus prevent my destroying the Bible God?" Surely, he argued, the scriptures themselves were the real sacrilege. They were laced with such violent, absurd, and contradictory depictions of God that it was a wonder "even a New Jersey Christian" could "believe such stuff." Whatever "Liberal love" Reynolds had once expounded was fast giving way to uncompromising secular combat. The polarizing ridicule cut in both directions: Reynolds had been demonized as the devil; his religious opponents dehumanized as pigs.[30]

The trial date was set for October 27, and it looked for a moment as if Reynolds would have to face the court without Ingersoll as his lawyer. Throat surgery had temporarily sidelined the agnostic lecturer, his voice reduced to a whisper, and the judge ordered Reynolds to find new counsel. When it became clear that Reynolds was unable to do that on such short notice, the judge relented and granted Ingersoll's motion for postponement of the trial until January. That disappointed the train-car of witnesses who had come to Morristown from Boonton ready to testify against Reynolds, and who were eager to see him sentenced and led off to jail. For Reynolds and Ingersoll, the delay bought them some time to let the battle play out as a referendum on free speech and the wisdom of enforcing blasphemy laws. It also gave Reynolds time to burnish his latest discourse for the lecture circuit, "Religious Persecutions of the Nineteenth Century."[31]

As fall rolled into winter, emotions cooled, and there began to be some doubt as to whether Morris County authorities actually wanted to try the case. In January the court postponed the trial again, setting it down for May. The prosecution may well have been having second thoughts; certainly, many citizens of Boonton and Morristown were; all the publicity appeared to be doing orthodoxy as much harm as good. The leading local papers now went on record wishing the case would be postponed indefinitely.

"No possible good can come from the trial," the *Jerseyman* advised in early February 1887, "and in whatever way it terminates its principal effect will be to give Reynolds more notoriety and more power for mischief than he now possesses. The whole legal proceedings in the case have been a mistake." For Reynolds's part, the second delay allowed him time for another lecture tour through Ohio, Michigan, and Indiana, now with the added frisson of blasphemy following him.[32]

Regret did not get the horse back in the barn. The case was called before the Court of Common Pleas on Thursday May 19, with no further delay. The atmosphere in Morristown was circus-like with many people pouring into town to see what would happen. The courtroom itself was "filled to suffocation" with both the friends and foes of Reynolds, and a throng of spectators lingered outside the building, turned away for lack of space. There were three judges; presiding was Francis Child, a justice who made his antipathy toward the defendant apparent from the outset. He allowed Ingersoll only six challenges to prospective jurors, which were soon spent, and that left the defense with a jury of a noticeably Christian bent. The district attorney called about a dozen witnesses, all of whom confirmed that Reynolds had energetically distributed his "blasphemous and impious pamphlet." That procession of witnesses ate up the first session; after a brief recess, the floor belonged to Ingersoll. The defense had no witnesses to call. Possibly Ingersoll did not want a repeat of the prior oath-taking debacle, but it was also indisputable that Reynolds had published *Blasphemy and the Bible* and had handed it out in bulk in both Boonton and Morristown. Back-and-forth testimony about what Reynolds had actually said last July was no longer relevant; his dashed-off pamphlet, readily produced as material evidence, was what had to be defended as protected expression.[33]

For Ingersoll, the fine points of Reynolds's defense were almost incidental to his rhetorical objectives. Ingersoll was there to speak with orotund solemnity about free speech and mental liberty and to excoriate the benighted inquisitors who stood against those principles. Casting Reynolds into the shadows, Ingersoll held forth for the rest of Thursday's session and then continued where he left off Friday morning. "I deny the right of any man, of any number of men, of any church, of any State," Ingersoll exhorted, "to put a padlock on the lips—to make the tongue a convict. I passionately deny the right of the Herod of authority to kill the children of the brain." Those who would enforce blasphemy laws were the direct heirs of those who thought it right "to burn heretics and tie Quakers to the end of a cart"; they still regarded "the thumbscrew as an instrument of progress." Ingersoll did make a sustained effort to vindicate Reynolds's pamphlet and the questions it raised about the biblical God, the Patriarchs, and the Incarnation; he did not see a word of blasphemy in it, only honest questioning. More often, though, Ingersoll fell back on oratorical flourishes that had little to do with the specifics of the case: "Blasphemy is what an old mistake says of a new discovered truth. Blasphemy is what a withered last year's leaf says to a this year's bud." It was a spellbinder—great theater more than a well-crafted defense. As the New York *Sun* observed, "The jurymen began to feel as he talked that they were not sitting in judgment upon the attempt of annoyed citizens to relieve themselves of a pestilent disturber, but were called upon to decide great principles. The stuffy little court room enlarged into a world where freedom and free speech were at stake." Captivating, hortatory, and aphoristic, Ingersoll's oration played well with many of the spectators and journalists, but it was certainly not the most precise piece of legal reasoning.[34]

The district attorney did not try to compete with Ingersoll's eloquence. Ingersoll had gone on for over three hours, but the prosecutor spoke for only ten to fifteen minutes after the defense sat down. Judge Child seemed almost offended by the district attorney's lack of prosecutorial zeal and so took it upon himself in his instructions to the jury to make plain the legal stakes involved. Reynolds's heterodoxy, Child said, was not on trial; the state was not in the business of enforcing any "standard of faith" or "form of worship." There is "no offense to our laws as heresy or nonconformity." But "blasphemous libel" was another matter; that offense hinged, as Child described it, on the "scoffing and railing manner" in which it was performed; an abuse of liberty, its intent was "to wound the feelings of the Christian community" through vilifying God, Jesus Christ, or the Holy Bible. Child returned to Judge James Kent's time-honored reasoning in *The People v. Ruggles* (1811), a case in which the defendant had loudly proclaimed in the presence of many "good and Christian people" that "Jesus Christ was a bastard, and his mother must be a whore." Kent affirmed that "free and decent discussions on any religious subject" were protected, but not the "profane ridicule" or "reviling" of Christianity displayed by the likes of John Ruggles. That distinction meant the prosecution of blasphemy very much hinged on how irreverence was expressed—the vulgarity of its social performance, the audacity of its affront to "decency and good order." By that measure, Ingersoll's defense had not done enough to address Reynolds's scandalous manner, his malicious disruption of the Christian mores of the community. Ever attentive to his own reputation for virtue and civility, Ingersoll had conceded that there were many things in the pamphlet that he himself would "not have said at all" and acknowledged the particular insult Heston's cartoon had given. In not tackling the legal precedent in *Ruggles*, Ingersoll had left Judge Child the opportunity to spell it out clearly on his terms.[35]

Child also dismissed Ingersoll's contention that New Jersey's blasphemy law was an antiquated throwback without contemporary relevance. Ingersoll tried to cast the Morristown case as a freakish rarity; it was unlike anything the country had seen since Abner Kneeland's conviction for blasphemy a half century earlier. To be sure, pairing Kneeland and Reynolds worked for Ingersoll in that they were both infidel defendants who embraced the free-speech fight, but the suggestion that the two somehow constituted the sum total of nineteenth-century blasphemy jurisprudence was entirely mistaken. Blasphemy charges were fairly common in the early decades of the nineteenth century, part and parcel of the wider maintenance of public peace and order on Christian terms. Even after mid-century, the crime came up often enough: annual jail statistics for Connecticut counties in the 1870s, for example, regularly showed a handful of convicts locked up for blasphemy—two in 1877, three in 1878, and four in New Haven County alone in 1879. A Delaware grand jury, in 1881, had very seriously considered indicting Ingersoll himself for blasphemy after a lecture he gave in Wilmington; a year later in Paterson, New Jersey, "a wholesale notion dealer" was charged with blasphemy for "abusing the mother of Christ" with "improper names"; and, as late as 1919, a Lithuanian freethinker, Michael Mockus, was found guilty of blasphemy in Maine (he had already been arrested and tried for the same crime in Connecticut in 1916). So, Child was correct in saying that blasphemy laws were far from obsolete—certainly, they were a lot less archaic than Ingersoll's rhetoric suggested. If anything, in the 1870s and 1880s, the offense had been given new traction through toughened obscenity laws, which many liberal critics rightly took to be "blasphemy laws revived under a new name." Once again then, Child got the better of Ingersoll on the legal point, instructing the jury that the question was not whether the blasphemy law was passé, but whether Reynolds had broken it.[36]

With Child's detailed instructions finished and with a copy of *Blasphemy and the Bible* in hand, the jurymen filed out at 11:00 am on Friday morning. They reached a verdict in just over an hour, and, when asked for it, the foreman announced, "Guilty." Judge Child, satisfied with the conviction, softened his tone when passing his sentence, perhaps under pressure from his two colleagues on the bench, who seemed to have no interest in imposing "the full penalty of the law," which allowed for up to a year in prison and a $200 fine. Together the three justices settled on "a light fine" of $25, plus court costs. A convicted blasphemer, Reynolds had nonetheless escaped the penitentiary. As the *Truth Seeker* cheerily concluded, "Mr. Reynolds is now free from the toils of New Jersey savagery, and will resume his labors for intellectual liberty."[37]

Reynolds went back to the lecture circuit and soon turned his eyes westward. Not long after his arrest a hearty liberal in Greeley, Colorado, had written the *Truth Seeker* to invite the infidel lecturer to "the glorious West, where a man can think for himself, and speak his honest convictions, without hindrance." In the late summer of 1887, just three months after his conviction, Reynolds heeded that advice and launched an extensive "Western Tour." As he made his way across the country, his recent travails in New Jersey seemed to garner him more curiosity and esteem than hostility. In Kewanee, Illinois, for example, he reported that some "came quite long distances" to hear his lectures and "shake the hand of the Jersey blasphemer." Nearly everywhere he went fellow liberals clamored for a copy of Ingersoll's "blasphemy-defense speech," which became a popular infidel tract in its own right. That was true in Bethany, Missouri, where Reynolds's faithful competed with a "Methodist revival in full blast" and "a baptism of converts at the river"; he filled the lecture hall there with 250 freethinking enthusiasts and exhausted his supply of books and pamphlets. By the next summer he had edged his way through Colorado, New Mexico, Arizona, Southern California, and up the coast through Oregon and Washington. Enamored with the last two environs especially, he vowed to return the next year with his wife and children and make a new home there.[38]

Reynolds finished out his career in the Pacific Northwest, a leader of the Washington Secular Union. He fought the good fight for freethinking liberalism in Walla Walla, Seattle, Tacoma, Portland, and elsewhere, taking particular aim at religious exercises in the public schools and at Sunday closing laws. His tried-and-true secular causes remained divisive, but Reynolds never again experienced anything like the blasphemy brouhaha in New Jersey. Perhaps some dim shade of the old conflict could be seen in one of his campaigns in 1892, when the son of a fellow freethinker was expelled from a Washington public school for saying that "he did not believe in the Bible God." Not surprisingly, Reynolds rushed to help the infidel youth, whose teacher had allegedly told him, "We won't allow such blasphemy in our school; we love our God!" Reynolds filed at least two formal protests and was sure he would triumph over the teacher whom he labeled a "fanatical despot." Whether he did or not went unreported; the school board, at least, sustained the expulsion. That episode, along with the arrest of a barber and some clothing merchants for doing business on Sunday, was about as much inquisitorial heat as Washington afforded him. Reynolds died in Seattle at the end of July 1896, ten years after the riot in Boonton; the cause of death was a head injury he had sustained in a fall from a swing in McMinnville, Oregon, where he had gone to conduct the funeral service of another "old-time Liberal."[39]

———————◆———————

The twofold career of "Elder Reynolds" and "Blasphemer Reynolds" was played out in the up-for-grabs space between a Christian nation and a secular republic. Ingersoll and other freethinkers were quick to spin Reynolds's conviction, in spite of appearances, as "a great victory for free speech"—a death blow to blasphemy jurisprudence and a harbinger of liberal secularism's triumph. The "religious jackasses" who were responsible for the case had been shamed in the court of public opinion, so Ingersoll told anyone who would listen. That was hardly the message, though, that papers as diverse as the *Brooklyn Daily Eagle*, *New York Times*, *Atlanta Constitution*, Chicago's *Western Rural*, or the Methodists' *Christian Advocate* took from Reynolds's trial, all of which saw the jury's guilty verdict as fully warranted. Reynolds was a public nuisance—an "indecent blasphemer" and a "vulgar-mouthed person"; he deserved to be convicted, even if the sentence had been largely symbolic. Perhaps, the *New York Times* suggested, the suppression of blasphemy would have to be recast in less obviously religious terms as a clampdown on indecency and disorderly conduct, but letting a blackguard like Reynolds get away with this kind of community intrusion was out of the question. To say that the regulatory ambitions of Protestant moral reformers were unfazed by the trial is an understatement. No secular republic was in the offing.[40]

But, then again, no Christian nation was either. Ingersoll was right about this much: Reynolds's conviction was hardly an unqualified victory for Protestant censors against pesky secularists. Numerous Christians actually cheered for the defense and were dismayed at the outcome. One Presbyterian minister, rushing up to Ingersoll after his courtroom speech, exclaimed his agreement: "I must say that was the noblest speech in defence of liberty I ever heard! Your hand, sir; your hand." Just as Abner Kneeland had possessed his share of religious supporters—William Ellery Channing and Theodore Parker, among them—Reynolds did too. As one liberal Protestant pastor wrote the New York *World*, "I am a Christian minister, but in my opinion if God and the Christian religion cannot take care of themselves without resort to courts of human law, both are in a bad way.... I venture the opinion that there are many Christians in New Jersey who are ashamed of the Reynolds trial and conviction, as I certainly am." The relationship between Protestant Christianity and freethinking secularism—in Reynolds's own life as in the broader culture—was fraught, a jumble of antagonisms and affinities. When, for example, Francis Ellingwood Abbot launched his secularist campaign into national prominence at the country's centennial a decade earlier in 1876, he had been careful to secure the blessing of key liberal ministers, even as he excoriated Christian-amendment campaigners among evangelicals. Reynolds's case hardly cut through those larger antipathies and alliances; it was instead a creature of those unresolved conflicts.[41]

In some ways, Reynolds's career as a freethinking lecturer was remarkable for how much forbearance he experienced. His wayfaring generated plenty of spirited debate and prayerful opposition, but almost no violence. Over the course of thirteen years, he lectured over a thousand times in hundreds of different places, but only once did things get really ugly. Boonton was the exception. By and large, Reynolds criticized Christianity and applauded liberal secularism from one community to another before curious and civil audiences. The same pattern held for other infidel lecturers of the period, including the ever-traveling Samuel Putnam, who was courteously received most places he went. That routine civility was captured in the good-natured reception that the Secular Pilgrim met with in Salt Lake City in 1886 for his lecture on "The Glory of Infidelity." "Mormons, Episcopalians, Congregationalists, and Methodists, together with Liberals" shared afterward in an "animated and most cordial discussion" of Putnam's address: "All had an opportunity to say their say." On another occasion when an orthodox clergyman could not restrain himself from publicly interrupting one of Putnam's lectures, the minister leaped on the stage afterwards to apologize for his rudeness and even "moved for a vote of thanks" for Putnam's discourse. In most instances, freethinkers were given ample allowance to speak their mind; far more often than not, the sharp differences of religious opinion subsisting between infidels and Christians led not to a violent stand-off but to civil debate. That intellectual liberality flowed, in fair measure, from shared principles—that freedom of conscience was a hallowed right and that religious belief should not be coerced. Most American Christians had imbibed enough of Jefferson, Madison, and their allied Baptist dissenters to agree with Ingersoll and company on this basic point: "Christianity will never reap any honor, will never reap any profit, from persecution."[42]

The toleration that Reynolds usually experienced was a product not only of shared principles, but also of practical considerations. A roving gadfly, he achieved forbearance through careful groundwork and preparation. Almost anywhere he went, it was at the invitation of a prominent local freethinker or a small league of them. That Reynolds first pitched his tent in Kalamazoo was hardly a random choice; his freethinking patrons, the Gaults, had recently moved there from Rochester. Even in Boonton, when push came to shove, Reynolds could rely on a well-known family in town to provide him refuge. His itineraries meshed closely with a network of freethinking liberals, joined together through local auxiliaries of the National Liberal League and American Secular Union, as well as through secularist weeklies like the *Truth Seeker* and *Boston Investigator*. When, for example, Reynolds showed up in Oxford, Iowa, he was welcomed by a liberal "banner-bearer," a seventy-five-year-old army veteran known in town as Uncle Thomas Sherlock. "Everyone in the village, old and young," Reynolds reported, "always greets him with kind smiles and cheering words, although he is such a dreadful infidel." Upstanding village freethinkers, like Sherlock, paved the way for Reynolds and were often crucial for securing a venue for his lectures—an opera house, a Unitarian church, or a parcel of land for the tent. None of those advance arrangements necessarily prevented strong religious opposition from arising against the ex-minister, but it meant that Reynolds usually had respectable local allies—as in Montezuma, New York—who buffered him from the worst of it. Toleration, in other words, was a result of vigilance and planning.[43]

Forbearance was also a posture born of pragmatic calculation on the part of the infidel's Christian opponents: namely, a reluctant acknowledgment that attempts to stop Reynolds or other freethinking lecturers would only draw more attention to them. That was why Morristown's leading paper, the *Jerseyman*, wound up regretting the whole episode; it had only served to publicize the infidel views of both Reynolds and Ingersoll. Another New Jersey paper, the Mount Holly *Mirror*, turned this realization into blanket advice: "Any effort to interfere" with infidel lecturers like Reynolds "can only work to their advantage by offending the love of Americans for freedom of speech and fair play, and by giving them a chance to pose as martyrs, and thus advertise themselves and their lectures. They should be 'left severely alone.'" Ingersoll himself pointed out how "almost idiotic" it was to try to suppress Reynolds by legal action. If the folks of Boonton and Morristown "had just kept still," Reynolds's lectures and pamphlets would have echoed all of "a few thousand feet." Now the trial was being reported "all over the United States," affording "Mr. Reynolds a congregation of fifty millions of people." Tolerance, under these circumstances, was simply more prudent than intolerance. Most towns, when Reynolds appeared, operated accordingly; Boonton and Morristown learned the lesson the hard way. Infidels and freethinkers wanted to establish the legal principle that religious freedom applied equally to the irreligious; what they frequently had to settle for was a practical forbearance.[44]

Sometimes they would have been quite happy to achieve that much. That Reynolds did not get mobbed ninety-nine-point-nine times out of a hundred was all good and well, but the one time he did made the hazards the irreligious faced all too apparent. The Boonton affair disclosed any number of social and legal impediments that infidels and atheists confronted. It raised serious doubts about the unbeliever's equal protection under the law; it showed the tenacity of religious tests in determining witness competency; it revealed the varied legal strata that could be applied to godless utterances—blasphemy, libel, profane swearing, obscenity, indecency, and public disturbance; it made manifest the social ostracism that unbelievers frequently experienced; and it demonstrated the double standard to which freethinkers so often attested—that Christians were free to ridicule infidels all they wanted, but the "same liberty" did not work in reverse. Similar lessons could be gleaned from the lone instance in which Samuel Putnam encountered serious violence in his ceaseless itinerancy. That came in May 1887, in Ukiah, California, when an enraged layman stood up to denounce the Secular Pilgrim as a scoundrel before hurling a kerosene lamp at Putnam's head. He missed, but, as others in the crowd moved to subdue him, the assailant shouted "Damn him, kill him!" and launched another "blazing weapon" at the infidel—again missing his target. Freethinkers were left all the more indignant when the perpetrator was acquitted of any wrongdoing by "a jury of twelve Christian men." Among the jurors was a Methodist exhorter who reportedly gloated: "I thank God for the opportunity being offered me to strike a blow for religion." The satisfaction of justice was, in this instance, as remote a possibility for Putnam as it had been for Reynolds against the mob.[45]

Reynolds and Putnam were mostly tolerated, but being mostly tolerated was only modest consolation for the absence of redress in the Boonton and Ukiah episodes. The same could be said of the experience of lecturer B. F. Underwood. Already in 1877, after a tour through Michigan, he had noted one vexation in particular: namely, that Odd Fellows and other fraternal groups made belief in a Supreme Being a membership requirement and thereby often kept avowed infidels from joining. The case of an atheist expelled from the Lodge of Odd Fellows in Hudson, Michigan, especially attracted his protest: "Is it not about time these benevolent organizations ceased to be instruments in the hands of narrow-minded bigots for persecuting honest men on account of their religious views?" A wayfaring lecturer whose travels took him across the country, Underwood was used to spirited debate—whether with Campbellite elders, Methodist preachers, or "Orthodox" Odd Fellows. He was accustomed as well, though, to having good-sized audiences for his discourses, with plenty of "warm-hearted Liberal friends" on hand. Like Reynolds and Putnam, Underwood discovered that an otherwise well-planned lecture could go badly awry. When he stopped to lecture in Irwin Station, Pennsylvania, in early 1879, he was arrested for using the schoolhouse for "immoral purposes"—in this instance, for giving a lecture on "Science versus Theology." Confident of quick vindication, Underwood instead became enmeshed in legal wrangling for almost a year and a half; eventually convicted, he was fined $500, including court costs. The judge determined that Underwood's public derogation of religion—the "Atheistical Earthquake" he had produced in town—violated the state's common-law protection of Christianity from such insult. Underwood's problem was not hooting ruffians, but the lack of equal freedom accorded his infidelity.[46]

It was not only the occasional travails of highly visible public lecturers like Reynolds, Putnam, and Underwood that revealed the shaky ground under the rights and liberties of unbelievers. Less bombastic freethinkers often experienced the same hit-and-miss uncertainties. In an article entitled "No Atheist Need Apply," published just a couple weeks after the Boonton clash, another infidel writer, S. H. Preston, ticked off a series of outrages as complements to Reynolds being "rioted out of town." A vigilant civil-liberties watchdog, Preston began his piece with a recent naturalization case in which an immigrant named Carl Robitscheck had refused to swear his oath of allegiance on the Bible and had announced that he was an atheist. He was thereupon denied citizenship, with the notation: "This applicant declaring that he is an atheist . . . was refused." (Upon legal challenge the denial was later reversed.) Another episode Preston recalled went back a decade to J. William Thorne's expulsion from the North Carolina legislature on the grounds that he was an atheist. The charge was false but nonetheless effective: Thorne was actually a radical Quaker whose real problem, as the *Boston Investigator* saw it, was that he "disbelieved the God of the South." Preston had still more cases close to hand—another atheist immigrant temporarily denied citizenship; a pair of freethinking witnesses barred from testifying in court; and a newspaper editor imprisoned for being "a naughty talking Infidel." All these instances of mistreatment and discrimination left Preston incensed with the "bullying bigotry" aimed at unbelievers and secularists. "Is it not a startling fact," he asked incredulously, "that American citizens are to day refused political privileges, and denied their legal and constitutional rights wholly on the ground of their being Infidels?"[47]

Having provided that long litany of incidents, Preston did not even need to mention two especially flagrant cases of intolerance, both of which became infamous in freethinking circles. The first involved Ingersoll. A rising star in the firmament of Republican politics in the early-to-mid 1870s, Ingersoll was effectively excluded from holding any office of public trust once his irreligious views became a matter of national notoriety. When word got out in 1877, for example, that President Rutherford B. Hayes was on the verge of putting Ingersoll's name forward as ambassador to Germany, the religious hue and cry against him was so intense that the nomination went nowhere. "Only think of committing this whole Christian Republic to the deep, deep disgrace," one New York correspondent reported aghast, "of being represented in the German Empire by a clever, loud, contemptuous scoffer at the Christian religion and the Bible!" Liberal secularists, including Francis Ellingwood Abbot at the *Index*, took the Ingersoll debacle as a dramatic indication that open unbelievers were essentially barred from public office-holding through de facto religious tests. As the *Boston Investigator* fumed upon hearing the news that Ingersoll had been snubbed for the Berlin mission, "Our politics are governed this day almost as much by religion as if we had a nationally established church and creed." The lesson appeared obvious: no matter how qualified, "an avowed Atheist or Infidel" stood little chance of being elected (or even appointed) to a position of civic trust.[48]

Even more outrageous, however, than Ingersoll's political rebuff was the ordeal of L. J. Russell, a freethinking physician in Bell County, Texas. By gathering together a local society of infidels and Liberal-League secularists in 1875—the first such association in Texas—Russell had left himself exposed to community ire. One Saturday night in early October 1877, a party of four men took the doctor hostage at gunpoint, bound his hands, and brutally beat him. "You are an Infidel—you don't believe in the Bible, and you are leading weak-minded souls to hell," they told him in explaining why they had to give him "a good whipping." The vigilantes released him "on condition that he would not lecture or debate on infidelity any more in this county"; should he fail to take heed, they assured him that next time they would kill him. "We are going to put down Infidelity, God being our helper," one of the abductors told the doctor before joining in the flogging. Soon thereafter, Russell's enemies posted a public notice threatening similar violence upon anyone else in the "infidel club" who dared to take the physician's place: "We will burn you out of house and home, and hang you until you are dead." The lynch-law aggression against Russell was bloody confirmation of just how fanatical the prejudice against atheists and infidels could be. "The Texas Infamy" made any forbearance and toleration that Reynolds and company gained look like a considerable accomplishment.[49]

C. B. Reynolds, Adventist evangelist turned public atheist, found himself a player in a larger cultural drama that pitted liberal secularist principles against Protestant-suffused statecraft. Was Reynolds a blasphemer or a free-speech martyr, a mobbed victim of religious intolerance or a pestilent disturber of the public peace? Did infidels and atheists enjoy the rights, liberties, and protections of citizenship on equal terms with their religious counterparts? All the commotion Reynolds generated in New Jersey looked as if it had been designed to play out those elemental Christian-secularist tensions, and yet those lurid battlelines hardly circumscribed Reynolds's story. On a closer look, the familiar oppositions appeared far more unsettled, the back-and-forth exchange between Reynolds's Christianity and his secularism far more pronounced. The Baptist-freethinker funeral in Montezuma and Reynolds's tent-style evangelism for liberal salvation were as much an index of his infidel career as the Boonton riot and the Morristown trial. Harassment and even violence sometimes greeted Reynolds and other freethinkers in their wayfaring, but for every lecture that met with disruption—with howling protest, clanging noise, or evangelistic

confrontation—dozens went off without a hitch. Civility, toleration, and forbearance were certainly not the full story, but they
remained crucial elements of Reynolds's tale.

Before the packed courtroom in Morristown, Ingersoll had
made a plea for the liberal secularist ideal of fairness and equality for those without religious belief. "A man does not wish to
belong to any church," Ingersoll had hypothesized. "How are you
going to judge him? Judge him by the way he treats his wife, his
children, his neighbors. Does he pay his debts? Does he tell the
truth? Does he help the poor? Has he got a heart that melts when
he hears grief's story? That is the way to judge him." Sometimes it
seemed as if the objectives of Ingersoll's appeal were within reach.
One man, living just outside Arenzville, Illinois, reported in 1889
that all the people in town "know that I am Infidel, yet I have as
many friends as any man in the neighborhood" and "no enemies."
Folks did not let his irreligion get in the way of judging his character fairly. But Ingersoll's hope for the acceptance of unbelievers
still went unrealized much of the time. He well knew, from count-
less aspersions upon his own integrity, that many churchgoers
still found it impossible to overlook a person's lack of faith—that
moral reputation and religious adherence remained thoroughly
interwoven. "Being an outspoken Liberal, I am considered the
wickedest man in town," a village atheist in Palmyra, New York,
wrote in despair in 1890. His Christian neighbors refused to pa-
tronize his business or give him any work, "although they can find
nothing against me only that I am an unbeliever." The Arenzville infidel met with cordial trust, and the Palmyra liberal with
a Christian boycott; their dual fates epitomize how uneven the
social terrain for atheists and unbelievers proved to be. Occasionally it was smoothed out with courtesy and evenhandedness, but
just as frequently it was potholed with prejudice and conflict.
Reynolds's own career suggested the same patchiness of tolerant
acceptance and community proscription. Irreligious freedom remained a cultural riddle with no clear resolution at hand.[50]

Fairness, liberty, and equal rights for the blasphemous freethinker—that was a cause Ingersoll was ready to take up with all
the eloquence at his command, but what about the accused pur-

veyor of obscene literature? Ingersoll wanted to keep a safe distance from the impurities associated with the indecent infidel, even as the vulnerability of freethinking publishers to obscenity charges mounted. Blasphemer Reynolds walked out of the Morristown courtroom with a small fine; several of his fellow freethinkers arraigned for circulating obscene literature fared far worse. Ingersoll expressed grave concern about the ways in which freethought materials were getting caught in the net of the Comstock laws, but he remained as outraged as any Protestant moralist about "manifestly obscene" books and pictures. "Burn them up," he said. "The Liberals of this country believe in purity." He strongly warned freethinking secularists against sullying their cause by attempting a wholesale repeal of the Comstock laws and thus associating the movement with the defense of obscene literature and other bawdy materials. Ingersoll's strategy, though, left all too many infidels exposed to arrest and prosecution. The travails of the atheist marriage reformer Elmina Drake Slenker and her sundry companions would make those dangers plain.[51]

CHAPTER 4

THE OBSCENE ATHEIST

OR, THE SEXUAL POLITICS OF INFIDELITY

EVEN AS THE BLASPHEMY TRIAL OF C. B. REYNOLDS WAS coming to a close in May 1887, the next big legal battle for freethinkers was already looming. Just three weeks before the Morristown verdict was reached, a United States marshal, acting on evidence provided by agents of Anthony Comstock's New York Society for the Suppression of Vice, had shown up in the very little town of Snowville, Virginia, to arrest one of the country's most notorious atheists, an ex-Quaker and displaced Yankee named Elmina Drake Slenker. Comstock's far-flung inspectors had been keeping a watchful eye on Slenker for several years. They knew that she had been carrying on a vast correspondence about marriage and sexuality with various editors, physicians, amateur investigators, and advice seekers. They also knew that Slenker, nearing age sixty, was an infidel of long standing—one who relished her forthright identification as an atheist and who seemed to take particular pleasure in instilling children with her godless principles. As the *New York Times* rightly observed at the time of her arrest, there was "no newspaper office of a free thinking or infidel character in which her signature was not a familiar sight." In the eyes of Comstock and company, it was hard to say which made Slenker more threatening—her brazen unbelief or her uncensored candor about marriage, sexuality, and the body. To those going after her, her blasphemy and obscenity were utterly entangled; her shameful irreligion and her "immoral sentiments" about sex were all part of the same witch's brew.[1]

FIGURE 59. Elmina Drake Slenker. Photograph from the Ralph
Ginzburg Papers. WHi-120178. Wisconsin Historical Society

The marshal had hauled Slenker off to jail in Lynchburg, where she awaited a preliminary hearing the next day. That initial court appearance only served to highlight her double offenses of blasphemy and obscenity. The hearing got off to a predictably bad start when Slenker challenged the usual religious oath. As the *Times* reported incredulously, Slenker had refused "to be sworn on the Bible, as she was a Materialist and didn't believe in the Bible, Christianity, God, heaven, hell, devils, angels, or ghosts. She believed that when she died she would merely return to dust and that would be the end of it." Slenker then went on to say that none of the writings about marriage and sexuality that she circulated should be considered "obscene"; indeed, she predicted that people would soon come to view such physiological leaflets "in the same light as they would articles on medicine or surgery." None of this went over well. Her case was summarily referred to the federal district court in Abingdon; in the meantime, she was locked up again, "cribbed, cabined, and confined like a common felon," sharing a rat-infested cell with a town pauper. Bail had been set prohibitively high at $2,000. Though Slenker's husband, Isaac, had long been supportive of his wife's freethinking mission, he was now "wild with grief and shame" over the obscenity charge and initially refused to help bail Elmina out. As if it had not been dicey enough for his public reputation and his woolen mill business to be married to a self-declared atheist, the obscenity epithet now made his wife's infidelity seem also libertine and whorish. So Isaac left Elmina to stew in jail—a decision, she reported cheerfully in a letter from prison, that must be for "some good purpose."[2]

Slenker eventually made bail and appeared in federal court in mid-July. By then, Isaac had come around. As his wife of thirty-one years was formally indicted for mailing obscene literature, he stood visibly supportive of her in her courtroom face-off with Comstock's inspectors. Already a household name among freethinking liberals well before this dust-up, Slenker had numerous friends and admirers who rallied to raise a defense fund to pay for her legal fees. Spearheading those efforts was the National Defense Association, a civil-liberties group based in Manhattan that had grown up in the late 1870s as a liberal counterweight to Comstock's Vice Society. Among its leadership was physician Edward Bliss Foote, who himself had been convicted eleven years earlier of violating the obscenity laws and fined steeply for sending a marital-advice pamphlet through the mails. Since then, Foote (as well as his son Edward Bond Foote) had been in the forefront of fundraising for the defense of Comstock's liberal targets, and among the lawyers whom the Footes had enlisted in their free-speech campaign was New Yorker Edward W. Chamberlain. A tenacious civil-liberties advocate, Chamberlain would travel to Abingdon to lead Slenker's legal team. He and fellow members of the Manhattan Liberal Club had come to see her case as another crucial battle in defense of free expression and another chance to expose the overreach of Comstock's crusade. Watson Heston, too, immediately injected himself into the fray, picturing Slenker under the tyrannical boot of religious superstition and the postal laws, her right to free speech seemingly extinguished (Figure 60). As one alarmed veteran of the obscenity wars declared about the Vice Society's orchestration of Slenker's arrest, "How the unfeeling brute and blood hound of the New York Society of Bigots must gloat over this last triumph over a woman! ... It is only a question of time when Ingersoll, Remsb[u]rg, Jamieson and every other freethought speaker and writer will fall at the hands of the Comstock gang."[3]

It was with the free-speech battle cry that Slenker's fellow secularists most often greeted her legal predicament. Obscenity, however, remained an endlessly touchy subject, even for freethinkers. The architect of liberal secularism's Nine Demands, Francis Ellingwood Abbot himself, had refused to back the campaign to repeal the Comstock laws for fear of being besmirched as a supporter of lewdness and indecency. Many of Abbot's colleagues joined him in drawing the same line, concerned that open discussion of sexual physiology, even for medical or marital-advice purposes, could all too easily become entangled with obscene literature. Only the most unbuttoned radicals were ready to defend obscenity per se: "We do not care to dispute about definitions of obscenity," the freethinking editor of the *Winsted Press* opined in

FIGURE 60. Watson Heston, "A New Coat of Arms Suggested for Virginia," *Truth Seeker*, 25 June 1887, 401. Center for Research Libraries

the lead-up to Slenker's trial. "We insist that it is just as much our right to be obscene as it is our right to swear." Few of Slenker's defenders were ready to make that leap; instead, they maintained that her correspondence and leaflets about sex and marriage did not fall into the obscene category. "On no account would we defend obscenity in any one," the *Boston Investigator* insisted, even as it upheld Slenker's moral character and physiological investigations. She had been a contributor to the *Boston Investigator* for thirty years at this point; the paper staunchly supported her, but not the "foul, filthy, offensive and disgusting" literature it associated with obscenity.[4]

The *Boston Investigator* had good grounds for presuming Slenker's innocence. Even as she had broadened her interests to include the study of "sex, hygiene, and morality," Slenker had appeared the perfect ascetic among the freethinking physicians and social radicals long associated with sex reform. Recommending continence within marriage as a way of taming the husbandly abuses that attended unbridled lust, Slenker clothed sex with an aura of exquisite rarity. Intercourse was to be solely reserved for procreative purposes within monogamous marriages—a position known in these wider reform circles as Alphaism. Slenker had made plain those commitments in a series of articles on "Sexual Intemperance" in the *Truth Seeker* in the early 1880s, as well as in frequent contributions to Caroline B. Winslow's journal of marital and moral redemption entitled *Alpha*, the namesake journal for Alphaism. Like other Alphites, Slenker was invested in extending the cause of temperance—its battle against the animal sensuality and familial destructiveness of strong drink—into sexual relations, especially as a means to subdue the brutish and violent passions of men. "Woman must be queen of the great realm of sex," she remarked in the pages of the *Alpha* in 1883. Once that reign was inaugurated, lust would be vanquished; venereal diseases, unplanned pregnancies, and prostitution would disappear; and "true love" would lift husbands and wives, now ideally kept to separate beds, beyond the carnal. It was that side of Slenker's writings that made her defenders so confident that her pursuit of sexual physiology was in keeping with the strictest demands of moral purity. As "a Christian friend" wrote in her defense, "Mrs. Slenker is not a free lover, in thought or deed. She is a monogamist—is intelligent, thoughtful, upright, honest, virtuous." Slenker might be "a Freethinker of the most radical type," but she was still, this defender swore, "a good and a pure woman."[5]

The problem for Slenker's defenders, especially those who were certain about her chasteness of expression, was that most of them were unaware of the extent of the evidence that the postal inspectors had piled up against her. Comstock's agents had been monitoring her correspondence for over a year and had also successfully decoyed her into sending them other incriminating material. As the case wound its way to trial, news of what they had found in her private correspondence and in her favored leaflets began to leak out. For some marriage reformers—Ezra Heywood, Angela Heywood, and Henry M. Parkhurst were among the most adamant in this regard—frankness of sexual expression was seen as critical for cutting through the silences and euphemisms that they thought abetted prim ignorance and domestic exploitation. One way to demonstrate that fearless candor was to embrace "vulgar" English terms and use them freely in discussions of human sexuality—even including such four-letter standbys as "cock," "cunt," and "fuck." It was especially through her correspondence with Parkhurst, a successful inventor and astronomer who had belatedly turned his attention to sex questions, that Slenker had moved in that direction. When reading the leaflets he sent her, she reported being at first "disgusted, shocked, and amazed at his free use" of such crude terms: "I protested, argued, and objected, only to be converted and convinced at every point." Weary of "false prudery" and longing for "plain speech" on unmentionable subjects, Slenker embraced such "short, emphatic, clear" words for the discussion of "the sexual organs and their functions." The wisdom of that decision was lost on almost everyone, even most liberals. As the *Truth Seeker* opined, "The English language is rich enough and flexible enough to convey all shades of meaning without borrowing from the vocabulary of the abandoned class."[6]

Slenker's four-letter-word problem was bad enough, but then there was the route she had taken, along with several of her fellow correspondents and investigators, into issues of deformed births, idiocy, contraception, and heredity. These preoccupations certainly had a reform-minded thrust to them—raising issues such as how to have fewer and healthier children—but they also lent themselves to explorations of misbegotten sex acts. Slenker and her coworkers swapped tales of monstrous births and speculated on their causes and possible prevention. Among the questions that piqued Slenker's curiosity was how bestiality and the risk of animal-human hybrids could be woven into such discussions. Fascinations of this ilk were described only in circumlocutions in published reports, but one piece of direct evidence had slipped its way into print a year earlier in Ezra Heywood's *Word*. "I'm getting a host of stories (truths) about women so starved sexually," Slenker wrote in a letter to Heywood, "as to use their dogs for relief, and finally I have come to the belief that a CLEAN dog is better than a drinking, tobacco-smelling, venereally diseased man is!" Slenker swore that she never intended for Heywood to publish this missive: that letter, like the rest of the correspondence the postal inspectors had seized, was supposed to have remained a private exchange within a circle of like-minded inquirers into the "forbidden fruits" of sexual knowledge. At this point, though, Slenker could not get the dog back into the kennel. In the formal indictment against her, only one leaflet was given a name, "The Girl and the Dog." Once the whispers turned to her inquiries into bestiality, most freethinking associates wanted to keep a safe distance. "Mrs. Slenker has circulated that which we can in no wise defend, even when clothed with the title of 'scientific research,'" the *Truth Seeker* editorialized. Claiming that "ninety of every hundred Freethinkers" condemned her sex reform work, the paper dismissed her as "verging upon insanity" in her reckless fixations. As in the case of Samuel Putnam's scandalous demise, reputation-minded secularists—including Putnam's nemesis H. L. Green—were intent on walling off libertinism's taint: Slenker was "a crank" and guilty as charged.[7]

The National Defense Association, particularly Edward Chamberlain and the Footes, did not waver, however. In its appeal to freethinkers to stand by her, the group admitted Slenker had become "so much absorbed in this search for facts in the domain of heredity, human experiences in sexology, and instances of vagaries or perversions in the domain of sexual pathology" that she had lost a sense of just how shocking such investigations would seem to those beyond the circle of physicians and amateur inquirers who were gathering such data. Was it so bad that she approached sex like a "zoological student," or that the evidence she collected made vivid "the terrible results of natural propensities unnaturally repressed"? Plenty of her correspondents, after all, were ready to testify to the good her candid advice on marital relations had done for them. Most importantly, though, Chamberlain and his colleagues urged freethinking secularists to remain committed to the fight for free expression: "The tribe of Comstockian post-office detectives" had plotted a "foul conspiracy" against Slenker, a multilayered scheme of surveillance and entrapment that highlighted the broader threat to American liberties posed by these "sneaking bloodhounds" of Christian morality. Now was not the time to be spooked by the obscenity bugbear and cringe from liberal principles.[8]

Slenker's trial in Abingdon began on the last day of October in 1887. The courtroom was packed. Elmina and Isaac sat together, along with her three lawyers, including Chamberlain as head counsel. The jury impaneled, the prosecution's leading witnesses—the pair of vice-fighting postal inspectors—laid out the considerable evidence they had compiled against Slenker: her use of vulgar nomenclature, her leaflets on marital intimacy and restraint, and her data-filled correspondence describing "all kinds of sexual experiences," including "the dog letters." Her defense attorneys, for their part, argued that sealed private correspondence was protected from inspection and did not fall into the category of obscene publications. They lambasted the treachery of Comstock's agents in using aliases and decoy letters to ensnare an overly trusting old woman (they played up Slenker's grandmotherly virtuousness and plainspoken honesty). They had also brought along their own pair of expert witnesses who vouched for the importance of Slenker's work to the new science of sexology, including Henry Parkhurst himself, but the court excluded that expert testimony. (Parkhurst still made the most of his trip from New York: an accomplished stenographer, he recorded the trial in detail for the *Truth Seeker*.) When on the third day of the trial Slenker herself was called to the stand, the prosecutor initially tried to make a public display of her infidelity by inquiring into her religious belief, but the judge blocked that line of questioning as unnecessary. She was allowed to testify by affirmation, not by religious oath, and took advantage of the opportunity to explain how and why she had come to study "sexual intemperance." Chamberlain described her testimony as eloquent and spellbinding, if ultimately forlorn: "The superb old woman . . . told her simple story to a judge who did not, to an audience who could not, and to a prosecution who would not understand her."[9]

Chamberlain thought that Slenker's affecting presence on the stand had "softened" the prosecutorial edge in the courtroom, but not enough to change the judge's charge to the jury. The critical question was: had the defendant circulated writings of "an obscene, lewd, and lascivious character"? The test for obscenity that the judge enunciated derived from a British case in 1868 and was known as the Hicklin standard: did the materials in question have a tendency to corrupt innocent minds, excite lustful thoughts, or deprave morals? If so, the obscenity label applied. The professed motives of the defendant—whatever high-sounding scientific or reform purposes she might invoke—were in no way exonerating. Likewise, the surreptitious means by which the evidence against her was collected was irrelevant: the detection of crime often demanded subterfuge. The jury, so charged, retired to deliberate; they returned in all of ten minutes with a guilty verdict. Chamberlain was now left to raise a series of technicalities by which he hoped to have the judgment against her set aside without formal sentencing. The court reconvened on Friday November 4, and the judge granted Chamberlain's motion, agreeing that the original indictment was flawed in claiming Slenker had *knowingly* deposited obscene writings in the mail. Much to the consternation of the prosecution, the judge had decided to avoid the spectacle of sentencing Slenker to more jail time. Found guilty of obscenity, she nonetheless went home to Snowville, a village atheist relieved by this sudden reversal of fortune.[10]

Chamberlain happily wired news of Slenker's release back to New York, but the National Defense Association was hardly in a position to do a victory dance. Too many other freethinking marriage reformers were then in legal jeopardy—Edwin C. Walker and Moses Harman most imminently—for anyone to imagine that Slenker's escape on a technicality portended a significant turning point in the obscenity battles with Comstock and his associates. The New York Society for the Suppression of Vice had made an express mission of stamping out the conjoined work of "free-lovers and free-thinkers," the "blasphemy and filth" that so promiscuously "commingled" in these circles. In the wake of Slenker's trial, secular liberals considered that conspiracy against them to be as ominous as ever. "How many Anthony Comstocks do you think it would take," one infidel asked the week following Slenker's release, "to kill out or imprison all the Freethinkers in this free country of ours?" Obscenity jurisprudence was, in the view of many secularists, a newly potent mechanism for suppressing outspoken atheists and unbelievers. Slenker herself strongly suspected that she had been singled out for particular surveillance in her circle of physiological inquirers because of her long-standing attacks on the Bible and Christianity. When the activist Lucy Colman heard of her coworker's arrest for obscenity, she immediately asked: "Who does not know that such a charge is an 'entering wedge' . . . to get works of Free Thought excluded from the public eye?" Slenker's imbroglio brought the supercharged sexual politics of infidelity into clear view. Her own illustrious career as "a woman-Atheist" illumined a broader religious and legal landscape in which obscenity was fast becoming a more effective prosecutorial tool than blasphemy. That portentous development would bedevil the lives of a significant cadre of freethinkers and infidels and raise new doubts about the equal protection of their civil liberties. Frequently enough, the obscene atheist would end up a jailbird.[11]

———————◆———————

Elizabeth "Elmina" Drake had come by her irreligion initially through her father, Thomas Drake, a farmer. He and his wife, Eliza Pinkham Drake, had joined the Oswego Meeting of Friends—just outside Poughkeepsie, New York—in April 1829, when Elmina, their firstborn, was sixteen months old; they had necessarily brought their daughter into the fold with them. As the family grew (Elmina would eventually have five sisters and two brothers), Thomas and Eliza kept very much involved in local Quaker circles. The Oswego Meeting duly recorded the birth of each of their children—as well as the death of one daughter—but Thomas began to show up in the records in more singular ways. A vociferous contributor to the meeting, Thomas increasingly looked like a Friend with a little "too much light." By the time Elmina was in her late teens, her father had become openly disaffected; and after a series of quarrels with fellow members of the Oswego Meeting in 1847 and 1848, he was disowned for his disruptive religious views. The society's records left unspecified the content of Thomas's dissent—other than to observe that his repeatedly expressed opinions were undermining "the solemnity of our religious meetings." Elmina later suggested that her father's problems stemmed from his growing attraction to radical reformers, the ultraists on everything from abolition to women's rights to diet and temperance to free inquiry. Just how far Thomas had gone down an infidel path at the time of his expulsion is unclear, but this much is evident: his ejection from the meeting as a troublemaker effectively unraveled the family's kinship with the Religious Society of Friends. Elmina entered her twenties newly disconnected from the faith in which she had been raised.[12]

Religiously adrift in the early 1850s, she taught school, read voraciously, and looked for a husband. Worrying at age twenty-seven that she was in danger of becoming an "old maid," she decided in 1855 to place a marriage advertisement in the pages of the *Water-Cure Journal*. In doing so, she joined hundreds of others in looking for a companion through the paper's popular section of "Matrimonial Correspondence." Elmina succeeded in attracting dozens of potential suitors and ultimately settled on Pennsylvanian Isaac Slenker as a man of "kindred mind" and "loving heart." They were married in a simple ceremony at her parents' home in Lagrange, New York, in June 1856. From there, she would follow her husband's business ventures—first to Flemington, Pennsylvania; then to Elizabethton, Tennessee; and finally in the early 1870s to Snowville, Virginia. Isaac had no public visibility to speak of in freethought circles, but Elmina always presented him as a camp follower among godless liberals. If they ultimately came to disagree about her involvement in sex reform, they nonetheless shared all along a sense of themselves as estranged outsiders among church folks, a pair of "awful Infidels" who evoked a mixture of fear and curiosity from their neighbors. Throughout their marriage Elmina poured time and money into freethinking enterprises—sink-hole publishing ventures, legal defense funds for arrested radicals like Moses Harman, pecuniary relief for aged and ailing reformers like Jeremiah Hacker, postage costs for huge piles of correspondence. "All my work was a financial loss," she remarked at her trial. "It has been a loss to me all my life." Isaac, with his woolen mill, served as a tacit partner in her tireless and unprofitable infidelity.[13]

Isaac certainly knew what he was getting into when he married Elmina in June 1856. The previous month she had publicized her atheism for the first time in a letter to the *Boston Investigator* defending the women's rights exponent and antislavery activist Ernestine Rose. "I have been an openly avowed Atheist for seven or eight years," Elmina claimed, which marked her irreligious awakening as roughly coeval with her family's exit from the Quakers. Her doubts, she claimed, had first arisen in her early teens after her mother offered her a dollar if she would "read the Bible through." Instead of having the intended devotional effect, her plunge into holy writ left her "bewildered with its contradictions and improbabilities" and highly skeptical that such a book "could be an emanation from an all-wise Being." Her scriptural misgivings found resonance with her father's growing heterodoxy. Once expelled from the Society of Friends, Thomas had turned the family's homestead on Pious Hill into "a general rendezvous for all Liberal lecturers that came that way," a sanctuary for "free meetings" independent of any particular denominational affiliation. Among the notables Thomas hosted, the most fateful for his eldest daughter's future was the émigré infidel Ernestine Rose, a dauntless reformer who had moved into the top rank of women's rights activists since her arrival in New York two decades earlier. Slenker knew as well of the prior labors of Frances Wright, a much calumniated freethinker and equal rights advocate, but it was Rose especially whom she reverenced as an immediate inspiration. The infidel daughter of a rabbi, Rose had made her own way as a radical lecturer and open unbeliever; she provided an almost singular paragon for the young Slenker—a model for the development of her own public persona as "a woman-Atheist."[14]

In the spring of 1856, when Slenker came to her defense in the *Boston Investigator*, Rose was just coming off her winter showdown with the Reverend G. B. Little of Bangor, Maine. The Congregational minister and his allies had stirred the pot of religious controversy with their widely publicized claim that Rose, as "a *female Atheist*," was more loathsome than the "vilest strumpet." Rose managed to turn the Bangor confrontation to her advantage with a pair of packed lectures, but her embarrassment of Little did not procure a ceasefire in the polemics aimed against her. It was an intervening blast at Rose from the pious editor of the *Buffalo Morning Express* that had caught Slenker's eye and hastened her to come out as "a woman-Atheist." Who was this Mrs. Rose, the editor queried, who dared to argue so forcefully for women's rights and against the authority of the Bible? "A woman Infidel," this newspaperman announced, was a "moral impossibility." Few women would ever sink so low, he consoled himself, as to dishonor marriage, motherhood, home, and religious faith with brazen unbelief. "What a hell upon earth this world would be" if Rose proved anything but a freakish aberration.[15]

The Buffalo editor's rhetoric quickly became overheated in its depiction of Rose as a sexual abomination, its acrimony indicative of the supercharged cultural space in which the young Slenker was inserting herself to craft her own outré identity:

> A woman *an Infidel*! It is monstrous, she must be a moral *lusus naturæ*, a deformed, dwarfed, blighted, blasted creature. . . . Thank God, there are but few women who are Infidels; there are but few, no, not one but Ernestine L. Rose, who is so bold, so defiant of all regard for public opinion, such a dog in the forehead, as openly to proclaim her disbelief in the Divine authority of the Bible. What a calamity such a woman would be at home, if she can ever have a place so sacred as home! What a race of monstrosities such women would bring up for the duties and responsibilities of citizenship!

Reading this "dastardly attack" upon a "free-minded woman" whom she admired, Slenker rushed to declare her concurrence with Rose's "theological opinions." For good measure, she then signed her own letter "A 'Woman Atheist.'"[16]

In coming out publicly as a woman atheist in 1856, at age twenty-eight, Slenker was declaring her identification with the unimaginable and repulsive. "Well do I remember the day when the truth first dawned upon my mind that I was an Atheist!" she wrote in another letter to the *Boston Investigator* two months later in 1856. "I fairly trembled with *fear*. A woman-Atheist! It would never do; people would scorn, shun, and despise me." Told by friends and relatives that she would have to hide her irreligious opinions if she ever hoped to find a husband—"no man would marry an Infidel woman," they said—Slenker delighted in reporting that she had found a like-minded companion in Isaac and expressed optimism that, as infidelity spread, the stigmatizing of atheists would rapidly decline. Christian enemies of progress and reform would soon yield the field, she prophesied, to "us Infidels and Atheists." Her youthful secularist assurance predictably did not square well with the persistent public antagonism toward atheism, particularly any infidelity associated with women. The specter of the female atheist was, indeed, a perdurable fright, "a very Succuba" of the religious imagination. As the *Times-Picayune* editorialized in 1839 in presenting unbelief as a fundamental violation of the "submissive modesty" required of women, "There is something extremely revolting to every well regulated mind, in the idea of a female infidel." Or, as the poet Ella Wheeler Wilcox would remark in 1901, "To me the most repellent object on earth is a woman infidel. She is as unnatural as a flower which breathes poison instead of perfume." Self-reliance and open-road individuality were the prevailing pieties of misfit reformers like Slenker, but to adopt the moniker of the woman atheist required a particular perversity, if not obscenity. Embracing the marker screamed transgression—of the divine order and woman's pious nature. Through and against the menacing anomalies of the female infidel, Slenker fashioned both her own atheist identity and her sexual politics.[17]

Slenker had projected an optimistic air about infidelity's robust future in announcing herself an atheist in mid-1856, but only a year later there were already signs that her hopes had been brought down to earth. Having moved with Isaac to Flemington, Pennsylvania, bereft of her family of lapsed Quakers, Slenker observed that it was "very easy for Infidels to say, 'Avow your principles, live out your doctrine in the face of public opinion.'" Small-town Pennsylvania was proving a particularly unamenable place for such pronouncements. "Just fancy yourself 'a woman Atheist' alone, amid a bigoted set of sectarians," Slenker urged in a letter she penned to the *Boston Investigator* in the summer of 1857. Social intercourse for women especially, she claimed, depended on their willingness to play the part of the "beautiful saint," weak and timid, resting gently on Jesus's "*imaginary* breast." When encircled by such pious expectations, was it really "so easy *then* to 'be bold' and 'dare to stand alone?'" Slenker asked in an almost desperate tone. Ostensibly she was writing to offer encouragement to "my sister Infidels" who felt the same isolation and to say that she was going to keep circulating "Liberal books and papers," no matter the disgust that those efforts provoked locally. But, in point of fact, being identified as "the only Infidel woman in town" amid "a crowd of opposers" had turned out to be quite unpleasant and difficult. It was an experience that Slenker would have serially over the course of her life. As she remarked three decades later from Snowville, Virginia, she was the "first woman Atheist" anyone had ever seen "in any place where I have ever lived."[18]

Lonely peculiarity was a leitmotif of Slenker's career. Occasionally, later in life, she would wax enthusiastic about how plentiful women atheists had become since she had first charted this course for herself, but most of the time female infidels still seemed fugitive and hard to come by, especially in comparison to their male counterparts. The experience of one of Slenker's admirers—M.C.G. Reed of Burnside, Pennsylvania—resonated with a note of heterodox isolation quite familiar to Slenker. The daughter of a Methodist preacher, Reed had married an infidel and had ended up traveling that godless path with him. Living in "a little village of about two hundred inhabitants," she found herself entirely ostracized. "During the last three years," she wrote in September 1878, "there has not [been] a woman of the village or the surrounding country paid me a single visit, all on account of my religious belief (or theirs)." No wonder she found herself so closely identifying with Slenker in their shared marginality: "I believe I really love her." Reed's felt-experience of singularity stood out in the story she told of an eighty-year-old freethinker who, living at some distance from her, had sent word that "he was coming to see me, as he had never seen a woman who was an Atheist in the course of [a] long life." Together Reed and her husband ran a small drugstore, and she knew that their business often suffered on account of their irreligion. One customer, quite sure that even the way her husband talked about his goldfish disrespected the Bible and Jesus Christ, had tried (unsuccessfully) to invoke the charge of blasphemy against him. Despite all of this, Reed and her husband were not giving up the ship, for they believed there was "fairer sailing just a little ahead." Being a village atheist invited cold shoulders; being a female village atheist doubly so.[19]

Slenker built her public career around a conspicuous attentiveness to "sister Infidels" like Reed. At the heart of her vocation were distinctly gendered projects that defined and fortified her particular identity as a *woman* atheist. These labors often had a mitigating quality—as if the best way to secure her public role as a freethought exponent was to allay concerns about her unwomanliness. She devoted much of her energy, for example, to producing didactic materials for the young, including motherly instructions on rearing inquisitive, freethinking children. For many years she edited the "Children's Department" of the *Boston Investigator* and eventually launched her own small (and ever-struggling) journal entitled the *Little Freethinker*. Her sundry pedagogic efforts were encapsulated in *Little Lessons for Little Folks*, a collection that appeared in two distinct versions, the first in 1884 and the second in 1887, the latter the same year as her arrest for obscenity. Her modules, short and didactic, offered children digestible tidbits of Darwinian naturalism and sensible rationality: "No God was needed to create it," she remarked in her mini-essay on protoplasm; reports of ghosts and angels were the products of diseased imaginations and sensory illusions, she noted sternly in her lesson on the nerves. Her childrearing advice often drew on her own experiences as a mother: Elmina and Isaac had two children, a daughter named Lillie, who died at age four, and a son named Oscar, whose marriage would provide the couple with three grandchildren. Often gesturing toward her own domestic life, Slenker reassured her readers as to her wifely and maternal qualities, including her housekeeping and flower-gardening skills. At her trial she would instinctively invoke her lifelong domesticity, soothingly informing the court that she had always done "my own housework, and never neglected home for anything else." For all her "self-sacrificing" efforts on behalf of children and family, her fellow freethinkers would regularly sing her praise: a woman atheist, she was at least partially domesticated as dear old "Aunt Elmina," the "Mother of Liberalism."[20]

Slenker's focus on children's literature—her promotion of "Liberal books for Liberal children"—was complemented by her dedication to domestic fiction aimed especially at young women. Believing that what the secular cause really needed was a whole series of novels and short stories in which "the heroes or heroines" were all "Infidels or Atheists," Slenker turned her hand to fiction to make her mark as a freethinker. She began with a handful of original stories for the *Boston Investigator* in the early 1870s, her plotlines often featuring the successful searches of youthful infidel heroines for liberal-minded husbands who would treat women as equals and scorn religious bygones. Slenker liked to pair these emancipated young women with unfortunates who had not been able to free themselves from church and Sabbath school and were thus prey to seducing ministers and deceitful deacons. In "The Infidel and the Christian; or, The Two Friends," serialized in five parts in 1871, Slenker matched Mary, "a pious little Methodist," with Ella, "a confirmed and openly avowed Infidel." Mary worries much about Ella's soul and prays earnestly for her friend to see the error of her ways; Ella counters with a gift of her personally annotated Bible, the marginalia intended to help Mary "out of the mists and fogs of superstition." Spanning a decade in their friendship, the story dwells on Mary's growing disillusionment with church hypocrites, her familial losses, and her eventual conversion to atheistic infidelity. "I am now a FREE woman, and a happier one than I have ever been before in all my life," she exclaims. For Ella's part, she moves to the "sunny South," just as Slenker herself did, and there finds a hostile reception for her "family of unbelievers, Infidels, and Atheists." Stared at as curiosities and damned from the pulpit, Ella and her husband are initially shunned, and their children taunted and abused at school. Inevitably, Slenker gives the last word to Ella's "Infidel Family." They set moral, educational, and horticultural standards that begin to civilize the townspeople and ameliorate the baneful effects of religious ignorance.[21]

Slenker's domestic romances were born of a core tension. She strove to depict strong, atheistic women who were quite capable of persuading anyone they might encounter to exchange threadbare theology for scientific rationality. She was also intent, though, on presenting the female infidel as a paragon of homemaking, domestic economy, and familial devotion. Take, for example, her bright young atheist protagonists, Susan and Fanny Proctor, in *John's Way: A Domestic Radical Story* (1877). They are adept at prompting irreligious awakenings in the minister's daughter, Olive Newton, and the deacon's wife, Abby Slocum; Susan is especially practiced at debunking scriptural passages that malign and

constrain women; and both girls have learned all about dress reform and spousal equality from their infidel parents. At the same
time, Slenker makes plain how much Susan and Fanny know about
cooking, knitting, flower gardens, neatness, and the affections of
home life, especially as modeled by their kindly and ever indus-
trious mother. Similarly, in "The 'Experience' of Mrs. Holmes; or,
Religion and Infidelity," Slenker presents the strained relationship
between the pious Mrs. Holmes and her infidel daughter-in-law,
Minnie. Mrs. Holmes is certain that her son has squandered any
hope of a "pleasant family fireside" by marrying a "bold and un-
womanly" atheistic lecturer. Only two years into the marriage,
however, Minnie wins over her mother-in-law. Tenderly nursing
Mrs. Holmes during a feverish illness, Minnie completely dispels
the presumption that infidel women make "wretched housekeep-
ers" and neglectful mothers. In the face of Minnie's exemplary
household skills, Mrs. Holmes begs her daughter-in-law's forgive-
ness. Like most of Slenker's heroines, Minnie manages to redress
the transgressive dangers of the woman atheist through her con-
summate domesticity.[22]

In her fiction Slenker sought to normalize infidels, to bring them
within the pale of social trust, and this she did by situating them
snugly within loving and well-ordered home circles. Her most substantial novel, *The Darwins: A Domestic Radical Romance* (1879),
mixed autobiographical elements into her account of a Yankee
family struggling to gain acceptance in a small village in Virginia
(the infidel father operates a woolen mill and the atheist mother
is an erstwhile Quaker). The novel opens with some of the young
women of the town contemplating a visit to the Darwins just to
see "how real Infidels looked, talked, and acted in their homes."
One remarks that she is sure that they must be "terrible folks"
who "quarrel and fight among themselves like cats and dogs,
and drink liquor and blaspheme and swear all the time." Soon
enough, two of the girls do call upon these strange neighbors,
and both are immediately impressed with Mrs. Darwin, "so motherly and kind," and with her two "ladylike" daughters. The Darwins in their openness and hospitality especially make inroads
with one of their inquisitive young visitors named Myra. Infidels

are "as harmless, gentle, humane, and kind as any other class of people," Myra discovers; it is a "wicked shame" the way preachers defame their character. Indeed, she soon sees that the town's resident infidels are far better than many Christians she has long known, including Deacon Conway, a violently abusive husband and father, who stands in sharp contrast with Mr. Darwin, who waxes eloquent about the evils of the corporal punishment of children as well as the need for strict temperance. The warmly familial atheism of the Darwins spurs Myra's awakening to free-thinking investigation—to reading Tom Paine's *Age of Reason* and D. M. Bennett's *Truth Seeker*. In turn, her defection from the church ripples outward as other young women in town also lose their religion, often mixing their "girlish excitement" over beaus with an equal enthusiasm for sloughing off outworn myths, creeds, and gods. In *The Darwins*, as in other stories, Slenker suggested that young infidel women could have it all: equal rights, a model husband, a very happy home, as well as the social acceptance of their unbelief.[23]

Slenker could only make the woman atheist so homey, however. The young women in *The Darwins*, born anew into infidelity, occasionally come to see cracks in the domestic edifice they so often romanticize. "Sometimes I think it would be well for our sex if there was less marrying done," Myra remarks after hearing of a Methodist preacher's desertion of a young woman he had seduced, impregnated, and promised to marry; "less weight given to love and domestic ties, and girls would strive to become something more than wives and mothers." Jennie Martin, another young woman in this circle of liberal converts, particularly displays the limits that Slenker placed on the "holy, natural, and happifying" blessings of marriage and domesticity. Realizing that all her "girlish aims" need not be directed at "winning a companion for life," Jennie chooses never to marry—a decision from which Slenker draws this moral: "The great world has need of something more from woman than the mere duty of making a happy home for some man and rearing his children. The female element is needed throughout all social, moral, intellectual, and governmental departments of our land." Toward the close of the novel, Jennie's experience as an infidel parallels most closely the vocational turn that Slenker was in the process of making herself. It is Jennie who asserts the importance of promoting marriage reform, studying sexual physiology, and giving reproductive control to women. And it is Jennie who rails against Comstock as a pious sneak, claims not to fear him or his supporters, and pledges to keep up her reform work even if she is arrested and imprisoned. Most of Slenker's female characters are consumed, notwithstanding their triumphant infidelity, by romance and household affairs, but in her depiction of Jennie's social and religious radicalism Slenker finally refused that domestication.[24]

That refusal was impossible for Slenker to sustain in her own life as a public-minded atheist. "Why should you of all others elect to do this dangerous work?" she imagined skeptics asking about her decision to get involved in sex reform. "I answer because a woman was needed," she wrote from jail in 1887. "A clean, pure, happy, married woman; a wife and mother; and one who had filled the role of woman's duties as a true home maker and home lover." She could never part with her carefully crafted image as the "Mother of Liberalism," an "Infidel woman" always solicitous of children and ever committed to doing her own housework. That persona was both too useful and too integral to her self-understanding. Elmina Slenker could not be Jennie Martin, but she could imagine her—the female freethinker who need not constantly enclose herself in home and family. But no matter how much energy Slenker devoted to domesticating the woman atheist, she was still unable to elude the smear of obscenity.[25]

———————◆———————

The Darwins, Slenker's third and last domestic novel, had been serialized in the *Truth Seeker* in 1878, the same year that one of her Manhattan associates, Dr. Sara B. Chase, was first arrested by Anthony Comstock for selling contraceptive devices and for publishing a reform journal called *The Physiologist and Family Physician*. Chase dodged conviction that time and kept her journal going, a publishing enterprise that Slenker would join as an assistant editor in mid-1880. As her formal connections to Chase solidified and her articles on "Sexual Intemperance" for the *Truth Seeker* proliferated, Slenker's infidelity became inextricably entwined with sex reform—and, in turn, with legal rulings on obscenity. These growing entanglements only served to underscore her social and religious transgressions—the woman atheist mutating into the obscene atheist, a character virtually guaranteed concentrated scrutiny from the New York Society for the Suppression of Vice and its allied agents. Comstock's targets were manifold: lottery operators, bohemian artists, lewd photographers, risqué impresarios, birth-control providers, and bellydancers, to name a few. One amalgamation, though, had proven especially potent—the fearful combination of freethinker and free lover. At that intersection Comstock and his fellow agents ensnared Slenker, along with many of her compatriots from Chase to D. M. Bennett to Moses Harman. The legal suppression of atheists and infidels at the end of the nineteenth century was no easy task—as the struggle to silence blasphemer C. B. Reynolds suggested. Comstock's regulation of obscenity offered the best chance for successfully prosecuting freethinking offenders and for making public atheists think twice about the literature they were circulating.

When Comstock got to work in earnest in 1871, he began keeping a detailed ledger of the offenders his Vice Society arrested and prosecuted—noting their particular crimes, their ages and occupations, their legal fate. He also had a column for recording the religion of each wrongdoer. Unsurprisingly, given the nation's Christian imprint, most of the culprits Comstock dealt with were Catholics and Protestants, but he logged a significant minority as Jews, and also a small yet noticeable fraction as unaffiliated: "Not Any" or "None in particular." Most of the time Comstock's religious identifiers did not seem to count for much: the Methodist brothers, William and Charles Barkley, fined and imprisoned for selling obscene books; the Episcopalian exhibitionist, William A. Van Wagner, discharged on grounds of insanity for "indecently exposing himself entirely nude at [a] window for an hour at a time"; or Martin Hoffman, a Jew who "sometimes attends Mission Chapel on Bowery," arrested for mailing black-market contraceptives, among other misdeeds. That Comstock was content to gloss the

religion column for George Livingston, proprietor of an anatomi-
cal museum, with nothing more than a question mark made perfect sense. Livingston's crime was materially demonstrable: he
was displaying full-size wax figures of nude women, as well as a
vast array of phallic objects. As with most of the Vice Society's
cases, the religion column in Comstock's ledger was incidental to
the criminal proceedings against Livingston.[26]

A devout evangelical, with particular ties to the Young Men's
Christian Association, Comstock was quite familiar with the nation's denominational terrain, but that did not guarantee the pre-
cision of his ledger on religious matters. His identifiers could be
perfunctory, even sloppy. For example, he listed Edward Bliss
Foote as Protestant, though the physician was conspicuous among
Manhattan liberals and freethinkers. (Raised Presbyterian, Foote
had become a post-Christian Unitarian and then an agnostic.)
Likewise, Comstock recorded the notorious freethinker, spiritualist, and sexologist Ida C. Craddock once as a Protestant and
once as a question mark, while also noting in another column
that she was the self-proclaimed "Pastor of [the] Church of Yoga."
Predictably, Comstock was also loose with the category of "heathen," using it as a catchall for both the Chinese gamblers and
the "Turkish Hip Dancers" whom he arrested. The "none to
speak of" or "none worth mentioning" categories were likewise
roomy, vague markers of religious indifference and ecclesial disregard. Sometimes, to be sure, Comstock attached a strong dose
of judgment to such identifiers: for example, he described "blackguard" John O'Brien's religion as "None of any description except to serve the Devil." But, as a rule, the vice fighter found it
unnecessary to record his disdain for the unchurched. His ledger
was usually as matter of fact about the religiously unaffiliated
as it was about Protestants, Catholics, and Jews. In certain irreligious and heretical categories, though, Comstock remained
highly invested: namely, infidel, atheist, freethinker, blasphemer,
"Free-Love Spiritualist," and "Blatherskite Liberal." He used
such labels infrequently—for little more than two dozen offenders
between 1872 and 1910—but when he did, they usually signaled
especially contentious cases. Unlike the more routine notations

of "Protestant," "Catholic," "Jew," or "Not Any," these religious indicators sizzled with controversy. Comstock was paying close attention when he used them, and the labels mattered materially to how and why he pursued such wrongdoers.[27]

The religious dissidents who first caught Comstock's attention were free lovers and spiritualists, especially the sisters Victoria Woodhull and Tennessee Claflin, both of whom the Vice Society pursued in late 1872. Woodhull and Claflin were infamous—as women's rights advocates, clairvoyants, radical publishers, and scandalmongering critics of Henry Ward Beecher. Even as Comstock marked them down as spiritualists rather than infidels, the line between their free-love heterodoxy and freethinking irreligion was anything but clear. That was quite evident in the wayfaring figure of George Francis Train, whom Comstock arrested the month following his apprehension of Woodhull and Claflin. Dedicated to advancing free-love principles and women's suffrage, as well as to overthrowing the scriptures, Train had come to the sisters' defense immediately. To goad Comstock further he had also published "obscene" extracts from the Bible under blaring headlines of patriarchal turpitude in his short-lived paper known as the *Train Ligue*. With a copy of that scriptural satire in hand, Comstock obtained an indictment against Train, who was then sent to the Tombs to await trial. Gleefully insisting on his own guilt for circulating such terribly obscene literature, Train was flamboyant and determined in the courtroom, a self-declared pagan in the hands of craven Christians. "There is no law against infidelity, free speech, or free thought in the Constitution," he told a reporter who visited him in prison while he awaited trial. "My quotations are *verbatim* from the Bible, and Christianity goes down with my sentence," he predicted. It is hard to say whether Comstock or Train got the better of this spectacle. For his antics, Train had his sanity roundly questioned, and the judge was prepared to consign him to a state lunatic asylum in Utica; already weary after several months in prison, Train eluded further institutionalization by fleeing the country for Europe. Throughout the affair, however, freethinkers chortled over the way Train had managed to obtain an obscenity indictment for a collection of Bible quotations.[28]

Train's case was a harbinger of things to come for the obscene infidel, but it fell to editor John A. Lant to be the first to experience the full weight of the Vice Society's combined campaign against marriage reformers and freethinkers. At the time of his arrest in late July 1875, the thirty-year-old Lant garnered a heterodox trifecta in Comstock's ledger: "Spiritualist Infidel & Blasphemer." Lant had first run afoul of the censors two years earlier as a newspaper editor in Ohio through his publication of the Toledo *Sun*, damned out of the gate as "an outspoken Freethought paper" offering a heady blend of sex reform and irreligion. Forced to close up shop in Ohio, Lant decided to move his paper to Manhattan, where he restarted his weekly in the very face of Comstock's direct warnings. Within two months he was confined to Ludlow Street jail; the Vice Society had seized his entire inventory, padlocked his office, and shut down his "filthy" publication. Beyond bearding the lion in his den, Lant's sins were many. He had embraced George Francis Train and amplified his voice in the *Sun*; he had hawked a reprint of Robert Ingersoll's "Oration on the Gods"; he had published a physician's letter that used objectionable medical terms relating to sexual physiology (apparently "penis" and "semen"); and he had reprinted a mock supplication attributed to Henry Ward Beecher called "The Adulterer's Prayer." Lant's defenders admitted that his radical paper was spicy and tactless, but surely he had not thereby forfeited his freedom of expression. The support of fellow freethinkers made little difference: when Lant's case came to trial five months later, the trial was "short and severe." Convicted of mailing obscene literature (Comstock had decoyed Lant into sending him several issues of the Toledo *Sun*), Lant was fined $500 and sentenced to eighteen months at hard labor in the state penitentiary in Albany. Left destitute, his wife and three small children survived on the charity of sympathizers while Lant served the next fifteen months in prison. Though pardoned by President Ulysses S. Grant three months early on account of failing health and continued liberal petitioning, Lant never recovered his footing as a freethought editor.[29]

D. M. Bennett's coverage in the *Truth Seeker* saw Lant's case as especially portentous in its sleight-of-hand: namely, the Ohio editor had been tried "ostensibly for obscenity, but really for blasphemy." The paper pushed hard on this point. What doomed Lant was his anti-orthodoxy, not the "insignificant" traces of obscenity to be found in the Toledo *Sun*: "Lant presumed to write and publish his honest belief that the Christian religion is untrue, and for this reason the charge of obscenity was trumped up against him." In the eyes of Bennett and his comrades, Comstock's Vice Society had alighted upon a grand new strategy for suppressing atheism and infidelity, and Lant's fate was a leading exhibit of it. "Obscenity is merely a subterfuge or pretense," Bennett editorialized, "under which Freethought and Liberalists are to be punished and suppressed." On this point Bennett's rhetoric often became hyperbolic, but the summary notation Comstock made about Lant's case in his ledger suggests that this liberal contention nonetheless had merit. Lant was, Comstock wrote, "a most irrepressible scamp. His paper is full of the most horrid blasphemy." Not obscenity, blasphemy. Also, in one face-to-face confrontation, Lant claimed that Comstock had told him directly that he found the paper "blasphemous" and that he was empowered to prosecute the editor accordingly. To be sure, free-love spiritualism, free-thinking infidelity, obscenity, and sacrilege were all a jumble of wrongdoing for Comstock and his colleagues, but this much was clear: the charge of "sending obscene papers through the mails" provided an expansive web for catching infidels, blasphemers, and marriage reformers as much as pornographers. Lant's case presented an important bellwether for the legal clampdown on infidelity as obscenity.[30]

While Lant languished in prison in 1876, Comstock kept up the attack. In January of that year, he arrested the esteemed free-thinking physician Edward Bliss Foote for mailing a pamphlet entitled *Words in Pearl for the Married*. That run-in with Comstock turned Foote into an indispensable bankroller of liberal causes, especially ones aimed at thwarting enforcement of the obscenity laws (hence his visibility, along with his son, in setting up Slenker's defense fund). Later that same year, in November 1876, Comstock also caught up with the infidel free lover Joseph Treat. One of Slenker's early associates, Treat had recently sent ripples through the liberal press when a Philadelphia judge debarred him as a trial witness after he proclaimed himself an atheist (and a scientist). A veteran infidel orator, Treat exhibited a fiery devotion to unbelief. In a discourse on "God, Religion, and Immortality," delivered at a commemoration of Tom Paine's birthday in 1860, Treat had thundered that he came to supersede Paine's deism with clearheaded atheism: "THERE IS NO GOD! God is the first, great, eternal mistake of the Age of Reason! God is the grand, pivotal mistake of all systems! God is the great central Superstition, round which all other Superstitions cling! God is the sole foundation of Bibles, Sabbaths, Churches, Priesthoods, Religions, Resurrections, Judgments, Heavens, Hells, Spirits, Spirit-Worlds, all! I strike home at this root!" Treat was also one of the original founders, in 1857, of the "Free Love Farm" in Berlin Heights, Ohio, and he had more recently developed a fraught allegiance to Victoria Woodhull. That association, along with its quite public undoing, had brought Treat into Comstock's sights in 1876. Free-love spiritualism and free-love infidelity—that was not a distinction Comstock bothered to parse. Victoria Woodhull, Ezra Heywood, Joseph Treat, John Lant, and Sara B. Chase—he marked them all down together on a spiritualist-infidel-libertine-blasphemer-liberal continuum.[31]

In fuming about Comstock's Vice Society, especially the treatment of Lant and Foote, D. M. Bennett was well aware that, as the contrarian publisher of the *Truth Seeker*, he too could become a target. His turn came in November 1877, seven months after Lant's release from prison. Bennett's case, above all, would reveal the deep interconnection between suppressing obscenity and suppressing freethought. Comstock made this convergence very apparent in his ledger at the time of Bennett's initial arrest. For the editor's occupation, he listed "Publisher of Blasphemous and Infidel Works," and, for religion, he used the single tag of "Infidel." In the "Remarks" column he unleashed further invective in describing Bennett's activities: "Publishes most horrible & obscene blasphemies. Also indecent tracts that purport to be scientific. Also quack medical works. He also publishes 'The Truth Seeker.' He is everything vile in Blasphemy & Infidelism." The freethinking Bennett, a harsh and voluble critic of Comstock's activities, made the vice crusader seethe with indignation. The works he published were "not only obscene, but so blasphemous that they almost make one's blood run cold." Bennett's infidel smut provoked Comstock's utter disgust. Here was an offender who defied "all laws of man, state or God."[32]

Comstock had arrived, along with a U.S. deputy marshal, at Bennett's office with a warrant for the editor's arrest. It was for the usual offense—sending obscene materials through the mail. When Bennett asked what the offending matter was, Comstock produced two pamphlets, one a scientific tract on the propagation of marsupials, which Bennett had mischievously published to highlight the absurdity of prohibiting any and all discussions of sexual physiology. The other was a piece from Bennett's own pen, *An Open Letter to Jesus Christ*, which even Slenker admitted on first reading "shocked me by its irreverence." It took the form of a long series of mock "interrogatories" addressed to "His Excellency, IMMANUEL J. CHRIST." Page after page the questions dripped with sarcasm:

> Did you ever fall in love with any girls of your age, and if so, did anything serious come of it? . . . Upon mature reflection, do you still think you were right and reasonable when you got angry at the fig-tree and cursed it because it did not bear figs at an untimely season of the year? . . . Does blood actually appease your Father's anger? . . . As God, or as man, are you, or were you ever acquainted with what are called the Sciences?

The ridicule contained in Bennett's *Open Letter* could hardly be counted lewd and lascivious, but it could certainly be deemed disparaging of Christianity and the Bible. Hauling Bennett away, Comstock also seized the remaining inventory of the marsupial tract and the *Open Letter*. With liberal supporters working what political connections they had, Bennett eluded conviction on the first go-round, but Comstock swore he would "get the old Infidel into prison" yet. Rearrested a year later, this time for promoting one of Ezra Heywood's free-love pamphlets, Bennett was convicted in May 1879, fined $300, and sent to the Albany State

Penitentiary for thirteen months. Comstock had finally snared Bennett, an obscene infidel *par excellence*.[33]

Comstock and his allies were clearly invested in making it harder for freethinkers to circulate their irreligious views, and the most effective means of doing that was to catch them in a dalliance with marriage reform and sexology. Bennett provided that hook with the tract on the propagation of marsupials and with his connection to the Heywoods; Train, Lant, Treat, Foote, and Slenker all offered that same opportune target. The hook, though, did not always have to be sex. "Infidel" Louis Post and "Atheist" Joseph Hart, publishers of "a Blackguard sheet," were arrested three times in 1880 and 1881 for advertising a lottery—certainly a form of gambling the Vice Society wanted to squash. But, it could hardly have helped that Post, the chief editor of the offending paper, was known as "a splendid Infidel" among Manhattan freethinkers and frequently had his "Sunday Sermons" consisting of satirical biblical commentary reprinted in the pages of the *Truth Seeker*. Nor could it have helped that Post's "Blackguard sheet" had also been editorializing against Comstock and in defense of several of his liberal targets. Two decades later, though Post had by then softened his own atheistic edge, he was still denouncing Comstock's postal censorship and defending the free-love editor Moses Harman. If not a lottery imbroglio, then libel might prove a useful charge—as it did when Comstock had the "Blatherskite Liberal" Montague R. Leverrow arrested for that offense in 1896 (he was acquitted, much to Comstock's amazement, despite the aspersions he had cast on the vice reformer's character). Still, cases like Post's and Leverrow's were exceptions. The chief problems that infidels and atheists faced before the Comstock laws inevitably revolved around sex and obscenity.[34]

In October 1888, a year after Slenker's case reached its conclusion, Comstock arrested the New York physician Theodore R. Kinget, another long-standing "Infidel," for advertising items to prevent conception. Like Slenker, Kinget was a hoary presence in the secularist cause, sixty-five years old at the time of his arrest. Part of the atheist vanguard of the 1850s, along with Ernestine Rose and Joseph Treat, Kinget had been commissioned in 1860 as one of two traveling lecturers for the Infidel Association of America, a tiny group constituting the public debate wing of the *Boston Investigator*. The maelstrom of the Civil War had derailed Kinget's inchoate ambitions to form a whole "staff of lecturers" for the infidel cause, but by 1866 he was at it again, resolving to create an Independent Order of Secularists, a secret society for atheists and unbelievers. Three lodges were formed—one in New York and two in Minnesota—each pledged to the diffusion of "enlightened Secularism" and "the overthrow of superstition." Kinget's order lasted all of four or five years before its remaining energies were absorbed into other freethought efforts at organization, including those of Francis Ellingwood Abbot. By the 1880s, the Manhattan Liberal Club and the National Defense Association served as Kinget's principal outlets for his freethinking views, and the *Truth Seeker* provided him a hospitable place to advertise his book, *Medical Good Sense and Private Reading for Married People, Embracing Sexual Philosophy and Physiological Marriage*. The well-illustrated tome, Kinget boasted, "unfolds some of the deepest mysteries of human nature in the generation and development of life, sexual relationship, marriage, parentage, and offspring, all viewed from a secular standpoint." This turn to overtly publicizing his views on sexual physiology finally allowed Comstock to arrest Kinget, whom the vice fighter labeled "an old offender," notorious among the "Free-love" and "Infidel" elements. The physician was fined $250 and sentenced to three months in jail.[35]

Comstock's prosecution of freethinkers as "free-lusters" continued into the next decade. Some cases were carryovers, among them the Vice Society's long-running battle with the Kansas liberal and sex radical Moses Harman, who was in and out of prison several times over a two-decade span. Other cases were fresh, including the two-year sentence imposed in December of 1892 on the Chicago bookstore owner and publisher George E. Wilson, known for retailing the works of Paine and Ingersoll along with "obscene" translations of French literature. (Like Slenker, Wilson was made the target of Comstock's western agent, R. M. McAfee, who found the young bookman "quite conspicuous" as the proprietor of "The Only Agnostic Publishing House in Chicago.") Wilson himself was hardly a huge catch, but several others were genuinely small fry—a seventy-three-year-old "Freethinker" in Freehold, New Jersey, charged with vending obscene medical books; an "Agnostic" street peddler, convicted of selling lewd "Art Studies"; or an "Atheist" tobacconist, arrested for displaying risqué pictures and obscene cigarette holders in his shop. Well into the first decade of the next century, Comstock found occasion to pursue this prosecutorial conjunction: Edmund McLoughlin, "Atheist" and all around "bad egg," arrested for mailing obscene matter or Rudolphe Mielke, "Freethinker" and physician, convicted for giving away an obscene book. Even in these smaller cases, which offered none of the secular celebrity accorded Lant, Bennett, and Slenker, the melding of irreligion and sexual indecency remained vivid. As Comstock remarked salaciously in his *Frauds Exposed*, "infidelity and obscenity occupy the same bed."[36]

The Comstockian prosecution of the obscene infidel often teetered between the absurd and the tragic. On the more farcical side was the case of a one-armed village atheist in Industry, Kansas, named Jacob B. Wise. A peddler of freethought literature, including Heston's picture books, Wise liked to argue with people about the Bible, even though he found all too many Christians ready to denounce him as "a blackguard and a blasphemer" for speaking "the honest truth" about the scriptures. Already by the fall of 1892 he had had several run-ins with Reverend H. B. Vennum, "a very portly and God-fearing sky-pilot in our village who preaches for the evangelical flock." Vennum had been sermonizing on a routine basis about the evils of infidelity, and Wise felt compelled to challenge him from one week to the next. The back-and-forth continued for months. When Wise helped orchestrate a series of secularist lectures in town by Missourian Mattie Krekel, he made sure to invite the minister. Vennum ignored the invitation but wondered out loud in the pulpit "why the good Lord let such a fellow as [Wise] live," a noxious colporteur of "Infidel trash." By the spring of 1894, the pastor was at wit's end after his irreverent antagonist sent him a postcard with a single Bible verse on it, Isaiah 12:36, an Assyrian taunt of the besieged people of Judah:

"But Rabshakeh said, 'Hath my master sent me to thy master and to thee to speak these words? Hath he not sent me to the men that sit upon the wall, that they may eat their own dung, and drink their own piss with you?'" In a move reminiscent of George Francis Train's imbroglio over lewd Bible stories, Vennum decided to invoke Comstock's postal laws against Wise—in effect, labeling this scatological scriptural reference indecent and obscene. Thus, the mailing of it, Vennum maintained, was a prosecutable offense.[37]

That gambit appeared ludicrous to Wise's liberal comrades—at least, until a sheriff from Topeka arrived in mid-June 1894 to haul the maimed freethinker off to jail in Leavenworth. Indicted by a federal grand jury, Wise had a hard time posting bail, so he spent almost a month in prison before the National Defense Association and other sympathizers came to his rescue. While outraged over Wise's arrest and imprisonment, secularists were nonetheless giddy at the prospect of the case going to trial, for it would afford a golden opportunity to impugn "the moral quality and character" of the Bible, its human imperfections and vulgarities. On the other side, Wise's unamused opponents were eager to see justice done. In August 1894, while the village infidel awaited trial, the *Atlanta Constitution* editorialized:

> It strikes us that when a man with evil intentions makes improper use of a portion of the scriptures in a manner that is calculated to injure public morals he commits a crime and should be punished. . . . The man who deliberately picks out single sentences from the Bible that will suggest impure thoughts and then makes them public is an enemy to society, morality, and religion. There should be a heavy penalty for such offenders, and it is to be hoped that Mr. Wise will not escape. No good citizen—no Christian—ever hunted up certain peculiar passages in the Old Testament and published them without context. This should be the test.

That it was Vennum, not Wise, who had turned a small piece of private correspondence into a much-noticed public controversy, was lost in the newspaper's remonstrance. Still, the editorial suggested the cultural force of the Comstockian vantage point—that wanton acts of infidelity, even of postcard size, warranted legal suppression as threats to public order and decency.[38]

The case, initially set down for October 1894, got pushed back until the next April. The *Truth Seeker* continued to monitor closely Wise's legal predicament, wondering as the trial neared why "the ponderous machinery of the national courts should be set in operation to crush a man whose only offense is that he faithfully transcribed a passage from the book which is declared to be from the hand of God." Freethinkers saw the whole case as tantamount to admitting that the Holy Bible was "an obscene book," though clearly to Vennum and company the critical issue was Wise's subversive and contumacious disposition toward the scriptures and not the coarseness of the particular verse he had highlighted. Attorney Adolph Bierck, who journeyed from New York to defend Wise, made a strong case that the offending passage was technically not obscene by the prevailing legal standards—nothing about it could be said to excite libidinous thoughts. The corollary of convicting Wise, Bierck argued, would be the exclusion of all Bibles from the mails—a ridiculous notion. Everything about the prosecution, Bierck protested, was an "intense absurdity"; the case should never have crossed "the threshold of the grand jury room." For his part, the U.S. attorney mostly let the facts speak for themselves. Wise had sent what he had sent, and that proved to be enough for the judge and jury. The conclusion: Christians could mail the scriptures on a religious errand, but not an infidel like Wise who did so for irreligious purposes. Fined $50, the old freethinker was left with his lawyer's hope that an appeal to the U.S. Supreme Court would gain traction. It did not, and Wise's conviction stood—a small-town unbeliever rebuked for blasphemy under the guise of Comstock's obscenity laws.[39]

The almost farcical prosecution of Wise had the company of far more ruinous and tragic cases. That was particularly evident in the travails of Slenker's long-time colleague Sara B. Chase, who, having escaped conviction in 1878, found herself again under arrest in 1893. This time in his ledger Comstock marked Chase's religion as "Infidel" and her occupation as "Abortionist." Comstock's feud with Chase was a marathon. Moving her medical practice from Cleveland to New York in the mid-1870s, Chase had begun almost immediately to stage public lectures on sexual physiology and to vend advice on preventing pregnancy. In April 1878 she launched the *Physiologist and Family Physician*, a journal devoted especially to women's health, family hygiene, and reproductive control. Intent on suppressing the *Physiologist* and her wider medical ventures, Comstock kept Chase forever on the defensive and made it especially difficult for her to sustain her editorial labors. He finally ran her paper aground, but only after it had managed a solid run of about five years. Much like Edward Bliss Foote's *Health Monthly*, Chase's *Physiologist* became a civil-liberties organ out of the exigencies of the Vice Society's continual harassment.

A former Presbyterian, Chase had left the church after coming to New York and sought out alliances with Manhattan's sundry freethinkers and free-love spiritualists, linking arms with the *Truth Seeker* cadre especially. Though she herself rarely dove into irreligious critique (except of Comstock himself), several of her closest associates, including Slenker and atheist activist S. H. Preston, were routinely outspoken in their unbelief. As with Foote and Bennett, the vice crusader abhorred Chase for her multilayered advocacy and remained ever on the alert to end her career. Of course, it did not help matters that Chase had attempted a countersuit against Comstock, or that she had renamed one of her women's health devices after him, the "Comstock Syringe," and bravely marketed it under that label. Comstock's opportunity came when one of Chase's patients died, evidently from complications stemming from a clandestine abortion procedure. Chase claimed that she was only attending to the young woman after a midwife had already performed the fatal operation—but to no avail. Convicted of manslaughter from medical malpractice, Chase was sentenced in June 1893 to nine years, eight months in the Auburn State Penitentiary, the longest prison term Comstock secured for any of the obscene infidels he pursued.[40]

Chase's penalty exemplified the harshness of Comstock's protracted crusade to destroy the liberal combine of obscenity and infidelity. Certain that marriage reformers and freethinkers had forged an alliance hell-bent on sullying the nation's "old-fashioned religion" and "pure Christian character," Comstock had come to see "Liberal Traps," "Infidel Traps," and "Free-Love Traps" as all constructed from the same bawdy and blasphemous materials. "Oh, Infidelity and Liberalism," Comstock wailed in prophetic tones, "ye great defenders of obscenity and crime! Ye are mighty in your own conceit, in attempting to defame the mighty God." In casting "the infidel of to-day" not only as an enemy of God, Jesus, and the Bible, but also as a vendor of obscenity, a trafficker in lewd and lascivious publications, Comstock was able to craft a distinct legal brief against unbelief with the statutory teeth to give his arrests bite in the courtroom. The long campaign against the obscene atheist that the Comstock laws authorized was certainly effective, at least to a fair degree: It destroyed several careers and redirected others; it wrecked the health of some of the incarcerated; and it interrupted and shortened the span of a number of freethinking papers, especially those that ventured into sexual physiology. Still, the attacks often only emboldened those who were targeted. Bennett, for example, wrote a two-volume history of the gods and religions debunking the whole lot of them, Christianity right along with the rest, while in prison in Albany. Slenker went back to Snowville and took up where she left off—a woman atheist with a mission to educate Americans about equal rights, freethinking secularism, and improved marital relations. Wise, too, wasted no time going back to business as usual after 1895. He continued peddling his infidel wares in and around Industry, Kansas, and imparting his low opinion of Christianity and the Bible, much as he had before the postcard fray. Comstock and his allied agents won a lot of individual battles, but they most certainly did not win the war against the obscene infidel.[41]

———————◆———————

Slenker was a frequent contributor to Chase's *Physiologist and Family Physician* from its inception and soon even joined Chase as an editor of the journal. In embracing the work of this controversial monthly, Slenker played a role that she had already carefully rehearsed—that of the freethinking mother who offered cheerful advice about floriculture and home life. But that was hardly the sum of her contributions. Chase's journal also gave Slenker free rein to express fully her views on women's equality: "We want women to have an equal voice in all things," she wrote in 1881. "Let them hold an equal proportion of the offices in all our societies, in temperance lodges, masonic halls, in churches, in benevolent institutions, in jails, in schools, in law, medicine, and government." The *Physiologist* gave her space as well to admit that the sexual continence she championed was not without limits; it remained the ideal, but clearly not everyone could achieve that level of purity and self-control. She argued accordingly: "We plead for the right to search out a scientific, healthful preventive of conception, and the right to make it known to all and free to all. We ask that its use shall be lawful and without let or hindrance." The paper also allowed Slenker to indulge her recurring "revelation" that women were actually superior to men (a view she shared with the freethinking sociologist Lester Frank Ward, among others). Ultimately, Slenker predicted, the social order would reflect the elevation of the feminine over the masculine, and it would be much improved thereby. "Woman being the supreme incarnation of love," she prophesied, "is destined to be the world's last greatest and most effectual saviour." In contrast to the male editorial leadership controlling the *Boston Investigator* and the *Truth Seeker*, two of her other favored venues, Slenker delighted in the *Physiologist* as "a real woman's paper."[42]

Male privilege and masculine presumption always remained prominent features of the infidel landscape that Slenker inhabited. In her own secular eschatology she was hopeful that the world was turning slowly but surely "towards womanhood and motherhood" as beacons of social and political transformation, but there was frequently little evidence of that reorientation even among her closest associates in atheist ranks. She often found herself needing to remind her fellow freethinkers about the importance of including women equally in their proceedings. Of one "Forum" published by the *Truth Seeker* in 1888, she remarked: "I am forcibly struck with the masculinity of the whole thing. Here and there is a reference to a woman, but nearly all the persons

mentioned are men, and the things done are done by men." Why
were liberal women and "the mothers of reform"—from Ernestine Rose to Matilda Joslyn Gage—left entirely unnoticed? How
could the journal compile a list of "Scholars of Infidel Color," she
asked at another point, and fail to include a single woman of intellect and learning? Or, why when C. B. Reynolds displayed portraits of heroic infidels at his lectures did he settle on the trinity of Paine, Ingersoll, and Bennett and not think to hang the
portraits of "noble women" alongside these men? "Will Liberals
never cease following in the footsteps of the church," she asked
pointedly, in "ignoring woman and her labors?" Not one to leave
these critical observations as rhetorical questions, Slenker went
on to write a whole series of articles for the *Truth Seeker* on "Eminent Women" from Harriet Martineau to Lucretia Mott. She was
intent on making the infidel woman more than a curiosity to all
those freethinkers so often committed—like those who reveled
in Heston's cartoons—to staging their own manly bravado. Leve-
ling this particular playing field was an almost impossible task;
the hyper-masculinity of the atheist assault on pious femininity
was baked into the movement. Still, Slenker always throve on the
challenges posed by her anomalous unconventionality—within as
much as beyond secularist ranks. "Unscrew the locks from the
doors! / Unscrew the doors from the jambs!" she exclaimed with
her beloved Walt Whitman.[43]

In a moment of ebullience in 1891, four years after her obscenity trial, Slenker expressed excitement about how many "Atheist women" she could now count as correspondents. "The mother
molds the race," she pronounced, "and very, very glad am I to find
so many Atheist mothers." That moment of enthusiasm may well
have been short-lived—Slenker also continued to bemoan, in her
role as epistolary matchmaker, how hard it was to find enough liberal women to pair up as correspondents with freethinking men.
Her prolific literary career began to taper off not long thereafter,
though she lived on in Snowville until 1908. Dependent toward the
end of her life on the charity of old-time freethinkers who remembered her sundry contributions to the secularist cause, she died
in early February of that year, within two weeks of her erstwhile

associates at the Abingdon trial, lawyer Edward Chamberlain and sexologist Henry Parkhurst. "A Free Speech Trio Drop Out Almost Hand in Hand," the headline in the *Truth Seeker* announced.[44]

If as death approached Slenker had scanned the horizon for the promised "Atheist women" who would yet bring her vision to fruition, she might have alighted on a few emissaries—freethinking activists Voltairine de Cleyre, Josephine Henry, Emma Goldman, and Marilla Ricker especially. In the next decade, she would have had the birth-control pioneer Margaret Sanger to consider, whose own Comstock-targeted paper, the *Woman Rebel*, rallied under the banner "No Gods, No Masters." She would have had, too, the example of Mary Antin, whose celebrated memoir, *The Promised Land* (1912), recounted her passage from her Russian Jewish roots to an American secularist identity. "Wasn't I a Jew?" a Boston classmate had demanded in urging her to observe Passover. No, Antin replied, "I was a Freethinker.... I didn't believe in God." As a circle of fellow students "pressed me with questions, and mocked me, and threatened me with hell flames," Antin stood her ground, indignant that "a crowd of Free Americans were disputing the right of a Fellow Citizen to have any kind of God she chose." Another generation or two later, Slenker would also have had the determined secularist campaigners Vashti McCollum and Madalyn Murray O'Hair to ponder. Both were cast as "Atheist mothers" intent on transforming American public life on liberal, godless terms by de-Christianizing the nation's schools. Purposeful actors in their own courtroom dramas, these freethinking women—along with other plaintiffs—would decisively reorient the legal terrain for atheists and nonbelievers.[45]

EPILOGUE

◆

THE NONBELIEVER IS ENTITLED
TO GO HIS OWN WAY

WHEN THE SOCIOLOGIST WILL HERBERG SURVEYED THE
nation's tri-faith landscape in the early 1950s in his classic study,
Protestant-Catholic-Jew, he emphasized "the extraordinary per-
vasiveness of religious identification among present-day Americans." Almost everyone, it seemed, gladly claimed fellowship with
one of the country's three primary religious groups. Amidst this
high tide of religious affiliation, Herberg surmised that "the old-
time 'village atheist'" had become "a thing of the past, a folk curiosity like the town crier," having disappeared without leaving
a successor:

> The present generation can hardly understand the vast excite-
> ment stirred up in their day by the "atheists" and "iconoclasts"
> who vied for public attention less than a half century ago, or
> imagine the brash militancy of the "rationalist" movements
> and publications now almost all extinct. Religion has become
> part of the ethos of American life to such a degree that overt
> anti-religion is all but inconceivable.

Herberg took it as axiomatic that the country had changed vastly
since the 1890s when infidels like Robert Ingersoll roamed the
land "defying God" with their irreligious oratory, and even since
the 1920s when literary sophisticates like Sinclair Lewis made ridicule of Babbittry and the Bible Belt de rigueur. In the grip of the
Cold War struggle against godless communism, the United States
had become—more resoundingly than ever before, the sociologist

249

averred—a nation "under God" (the phrase was added to the Pledge of Allegiance in 1954, the year before Herberg published his banner work). The country's long-standing distrust and abhorrence of atheists was at a floodtide. Nonbelievers had become utterly anathema to an American Way of Life in which citizenship and religious profession were manifestly interwoven.[1]

The twentieth-century fate of the village atheist was not, however, quite as bleak as Herberg imagined it when he pictured the "militant secularist" fading haplessly into inconspicuousness and inconsequence. If anything, freethinkers had gained renewed vigor in the 1920s and 1930s, evident especially in the combative theatrics of the American Association for the Advancement of Atheism, founded in 1925 and led by the uncompromising Charles Lee Smith. That group had the ample company of other freethinking dissidents and humanistic inquirers, including Clarence Darrow and Emanuel Haldeman-Julius, who pressed the claims of nonbelievers in American public life with a panache quite equal to that of their late-nineteenth-century predecessors. These interwar agitations, in turn, came to full flower after World War II. Even as Herberg was writing atheism's Cold War epitaph, nonbelievers were making demonstrable inroads through the courts—the victory of Vashti McCollum in 1948 was an important bellwether. By the early-to-mid 1960s, the success of liberal secularist challenges —on religious tests for public office, on school prayer and Bible reading, on conscientious objection—was full-blown. If the postwar era was the axial moment for making palpable the country's civic theism—Congress adopted "In God We Trust" as the national motto in 1956—it was also the period in which freethinkers, humanists, and atheists gained critical legal vindication through the Supreme Court. These secularist victories were the flipside of all the "Back to God" movements that the era generated and that the nation's political leaders eagerly embraced. The rights and liberties of nonbelievers were, in short, given fresh reconsideration at the very moment when social and political pressures to privilege religion over irreligion reached a new peak of intensity.

American freethought looked like an extended funeral procession after Robert Ingersoll's death in 1899—at least, it often felt that way to those foot soldiers watching the passage of infidelity's old standard-bearers. When editor Singleton Waters Davis launched the *Humanitarian Review* in Los Angeles in 1903, he certainly had not planned it to be a necrology of nineteenth-century liberal secularism. Yet, the obituaries kept piling up. Toward the close of the first volume, Davis published a letter from James L. York, an aged warhorse himself at this point, about the death of H. L. Green, long-time activist and publisher in the cause. (Green, who had worked sedulously to expose Samuel Putnam and May Collins after their scandalous demise together, also perished— ironically enough—by asphyxiation from a gas leak, he and his wife dying in concert and thereby prompting rumors all their own of a double suicide.) "One by one our editors and lecturers are passing away," York observed, "with few young men disposed to take up and carry the increasing burden of Freethought." The obituaries were not only for people: with Green's passing so ended his *Free Thought Magazine*, and the next year Davis lamented the close of T. B. Wakeman's *Torch of Reason* as well as the *Boston Investigator*, the oldest of the infidel papers, in publication since blasphemer Abner Kneeland had first instigated it in 1831. By 1906 Davis's death notices had come to include Watson Heston, Charles Chilton Moore, Edward Bliss Foote, the British secularists George Jacob Holyoake and Charles Watts, as well as York himself. A few years later, when Davis was forced to halt his own review for lack of financial support, it was absorbed into another small secularist journal, one with a fittingly backward-looking title, the *Ingersoll Memorial Beacon*.[2]

Over the next few decades, village atheists were almost consumed by a wave of nostalgia. The loss of their contrarian, nonconformist spirit was grievous—at least in the literary imaginings of Van Wyck Brooks, Sinclair Lewis, George Seibel, and company. Singleton Davis had anticipated that wistfulness when he included a warmly reminiscent piece on "The Village Infidel" in the pages of his *Humanitarian Review* in 1906, one more glance backward "thirty or forty years ago" to a time when "almost every village had a studious, worthy citizen, scornfully epithetted 'the infidel.'" Intractably noncompliant, "this derelict on the sea of salvation" was the sworn enemy of ecclesiastical norms and conventions. Even when subject to "social, political, and commercial boycotting," the village atheist simply refused to accede to "hamlet theologies." Such nostalgic representations soon congealed into a tried-and-true romance of the heroic nineteenth-century freethinker, the small-town heretic who had "absolutely lived the life" of irreligious candor in the face of concerted ostracism. "The Village Atheist never marched with the crowd," so one paean went. "Single-handed and alone he withstood the bigoted ignorance and treacherous hypocrisy of the religionists." The village infidel as an embodiment of intellectual independence athwart pious constraint and sanctimony—it was that wistful rearward projection that made Van Wyck Brooks's improbably large claim in 1920 somehow conceivable: "There is no type in our social history more significant than that ubiquitous figure, the 'village atheist.'"[3]

The nostalgic temptation to burnish an Ingersollian golden age never let up; indeed, it remains a regular feature of the stories American secularists tell themselves about their own past. The funereal lament over a vanishing world of dissent should not be taken at face value, however. It was being voiced, in the early decades of the twentieth century, by journalists, literary figures, and legal gadflies who themselves were carrying the torch for freethinking secularism against a newly dubbed foe, Protestant Fundamentalism. Nostalgia for the village atheist was less about the disappearance of militant unbelief or the decline of this-worldly humanism as it was a call to keep up the fight. If forlorn village infidels stood up for themselves in two-bit towns in Kansas or Kentucky in the 1870s and 1880s, then surely enlightened cosmopolites a half-century later could come to the rescue of embattled rationalists in places like Dayton, Tennessee. Clarence Darrow, for one, very much struck that secularist pose in doing battle with William Jennings Bryan at the Scopes trial in the summer of 1925;

after which, he cheerfully compiled an anthology of freethinking skepticism, *Infidels and Heretics*, to help open the "obstinately closed" minds of "the religionaries" who still refused to embrace the idea of biological evolution. The Darrow-Bryan showdown was but one headline in the veritable spate of rambunctious unbelief that the decade witnessed. Perhaps no episode better encapsulated this than Sinclair Lewis's sensational gesture less than a year later: climbing into a church pulpit in Kansas City, the novelist defied God to strike him dead then and there for his faithlessness. Lewis set his watch down on the pulpit and gave God ten minutes to act. It was the perfect way to call attention to his forthcoming novel *Elmer Gantry*, a scathing indictment of evangelistic duplicity and Fundamentalist aggression. Directly invoking Ingersoll's oratory, the novel even featured "Village Atheist" Lem Staples, "a jovial horse-doctor" and aficionado of the *Truth Seeker*. Nostalgia had its purposes—but one of them was not historical verisimilitude. Freethinking infidelity was alive and well long after Ingersoll's death.[4]

No group was more prepared to keep up the secularist fight than the American Association for the Advancement of Atheism (4A). Chartered in New York in November 1925 in the heaving wake of the Scopes trial, the 4A heralded itself as the first American group to fly the atheist banner with such unflinching explicitness—no flaccid invocation of liberalism, humanism, or agnosticism sufficed. Its virile appeal was nearly total: one survey of its membership from 1930 returned a result of 93 percent male (its racial composition was even more homogenous—99 percent white). Heir to Heston's confrontational belligerency, the association relished controversy and disdained compromise. "The 4A is a militant foe of the Church and Clergy," the group proclaimed. "Our strategy is to storm the forts of the enemy in a direct frontal assault."[5]

Pugnacity was the 4A's trademark, but one episode stands as especially emblematic: namely, the effort by Charles Lee Smith, the group's president, to bring atheism and evolution to Little Rock, Arkansas, in the fall of 1928. Smith had honed his irreligious skills in New York City, writing for the *Truth Seeker*, but he was born in Arkansas, grew up in Oklahoma, and knew his Protestant opposition intimately. Arriving in Little Rock, he proceeded to set up an atheist headquarters on Main Street. In a large show-window, he planted a placard that read: "EVOLUTION IS TRUE. THE BIBLE'S A LIE. GOD'S A GHOST." That Smith failed to save "Darkest Arkansas" from evangelical Protestantism goes without saying. Instead, he was arrested twice—first for disturbing the public peace and then for blasphemy. Barred from the witness stand, he was found guilty on both charges and imprisoned for sixteen days when he refused to pay a fine. His atheist shop was pillaged, his tracts confiscated, and the chief of police refused him any security: "I would not give protection to a house of prostitution or a bootlegging joint and I don't see why I should protect you," he had reportedly informed Smith in tones reminiscent of the way Boonton authorities had treated C. B. Reynolds forty years earlier. A ham-fisted assault on conservative Protestantism, Smith's blitz and the disturbance it provoked gained national media attention—much as Darrow's excursion to Tennessee had. An undersized venture, like most freethought groups, Smith's 4A nonetheless managed to make plain that America's distinct brand of combative secularism was not going to fade gently away.[6]

The 4A gleefully thrust itself into the clamor of religious controversy in the mid-to-late 1920s. One of its chief ambitions was to create satellite chapters on college campuses, and it achieved a publicity coup when it undertook to inaugurate a club at the University of Rochester in early March 1926. A small group of students (eleven men and two women) answered the atheist call at the Baptist-affiliated campus and dubbed their new fellowship the Society of Damned Souls. Latched onto by the local papers and then by the Associated Press, the Damned Souls quickly garnered notice in *Time* magazine—in back-to-back weeks. What had started mostly as lighthearted collegiate rebellion was widely recast as a disturbing trend of the times. Ministers condemned the students from the pulpit—one labeled them "perverts"; alumni were enraged over the "unwholesome publicity"; and the student leader, Salvatore Russo, was taunted in the streets and eventually assaulted. Soon Clarence Darrow and the nascent American Civil Liberties Union (ACLU), along with the 4A, were offering support to the students, but the Society of Damned Souls had largely been cowed. Most of the collegians peeled away, and a supportive philosophy professor eventually convinced the remaining members to drop the "Damned" from their name and just be called "The Souls." The school's president, Rush Rhees, was quick to reassure his nervous constituents that "never before have young people, as a whole, been so overwhelmingly religious." To underline the restoration of Protestant order, Rhees invited Shailer Mathews, the Divinity School Dean at the University of Chicago, to give that year's commencement address.[7]

The local fate of Rochester's Damned Souls certainly counted as one more defeat of freethinking unbelief at the hands of the Protestant establishment, but the 4A nonetheless managed to run with the publicity and capitalize on it nationally. Indeed, the squashing of this one student group seemed only to embolden youth elsewhere. Within the next year the 4A was proudly claiming chapters on twenty college campuses—from Brown University to the University of Kansas to the University of California. At Yale "a group of daring young radicals" emulated the Rochester cabal, banding together, the *New York Times* reported incredulously, on "the platform that the old religion is bunk, that God is a figment of the diseased mind, and Heaven a luscious frankfurter held out on the end of a stick to keep the anthropoid rabble working like the trained dog in a circus." As was the case with *Time* magazine's coverage, the *New York Times* did not consider this new collegiate atheism "much of a menace to Christianity"; yet, ironically, the reporter also went on to complain that these groups of young freethinkers were receiving an unjustified amount of press attention. That media notice was precisely the success the 4A gained through its campaign to organize "a junior atheist movement" in American colleges and high schools. The clubs were generally tiny and fleeting, but they nonetheless managed time and again to gain news coverage out of all proportion to their membership.[8]

The grandest indication of the visibility that the 4A had attained through its junior-atheist clubs came in 1928 with the release of Cecil B. DeMille's spectacular melodrama, *The Godless Girl*. An Episcopalian, who credited his father's commitment to family

Bible reading each evening with having shaped both his movie-making and his lifelong faith, DeMille already had such scriptural epics as *The Ten Commandments* and *The King of Kings* under his belt. Looking for another morality tale, he found it in the sinister efforts of the 4A, particularly the group's rumored recruitment efforts at nearby Hollywood High School. *The Godless Girl* centers on a young rebel named Judy, played by Lina Basquette, who organizes a Godless Society, much to the chagrin of both her school's leaders and her Christian classmates. (One of the 4A's junior-atheist groups had actually taken the name "Society of the Godless," a little sharper-edged than the clubs calling themselves "Truth Seekers" or "God's Black Sheep," and a lot pithier than the one hailing itself "The Hedonic Host of Hell-bent Heathens.") The film's opening title card sets the stage for the disturbing story to follow: "There are Atheist Societies using the schools of the country as their battle-ground—attacking through the Youth of the Nation, the beliefs that are sacred to most of the people."[9]

After that ominous pronouncement, the film cuts to a printing press multiplying hundreds of leaflets that carry the invitation: "Join the Godless Society. Kill the Bible." Immediately the school's principal rallies the faithful against the scourge, denouncing the Godless Society as a bunch of "little rebels [who] blow spit-balls at the Rock of Ages." (In the shooting script he holds the atheist pamphlets and trembles with alarm: "Do you know this [literature] is striking at the root of the nation?") Despite all the distress they have created, the young atheists persist, beckoning new members to take an oath with their hands solemnly placed on a monkey's head: "Swear that you don't believe in the Bible—the Church—or God!" Unsurprisingly, things do not go well for these youthful agitators for unbelief. An egg-throwing, vegetable-heaving mob of Christian students is soon raised against the club—an overheated reaction, DeMille suggested, but one that nonetheless seemed understandable in the face of "unlawful" atheist propaganda and agitation. Amid the mayhem a young woman falls over an upper-floor balustrade, and, as she lies dying, Judy helplessly leans over her without being able to offer a word of religious solace. Both the godless Judy and the Christian ringleader, Bob (who also plays the role of Judy's budding love-interest), are then locked away in a reformatory where they are treated brutally. Imprisoned, the youthful atheist eventually comes to her religious senses and re-affirms God's existence (in one especially grim scene, she even has the sign of the cross burned into her hands by an electrified fence). Resisting the prison's sadistic guards, she and Bob eventu-ally regain their freedom when the reformatory is consumed in an inferno. As in the University of Rochester episode, DeMille's film moves toward the seemingly inevitable Christian reclamation of a youthful malcontent. Judy realizes, especially through her bloom-ing passion for Bob, that God is love and love is God.[10]

DeMille's religious verities notwithstanding, *The Godless Girl* provided the 4A's atheistic campaign with big-screen, mass-culture exposure that made the notices in *Time* magazine look small bore. For all of the director's dire warnings about atheistic prop-aganda poisoning American youth, the 4A understood the film's release in a different light: it proved that they had picked the right target. "About one in three college students are Atheists," a 4A spokesman confidently asserted. "Colleges are a fruitful field for us—for this is where the young people begin to think." For the 4A, the attention *The Godless Girl* focused on their college and school clubs, no matter how alarmist, was promotional pay dirt. Overmatching Judy's newfound God—one version of the script had her chirp about the "Big Friend that loves us all"—was a task the 4A relished. Was her lightweight conversion going to change the minds of the 188 atheist students at Dartmouth College that the 4A claimed to have identified through a questionnaire? Or the mind of one of the 4A's favorite godless girls, eighteen-year-old Christine Walker, former secretary of the Christian Endeavor Society in her hometown, who happily explained to an obliging media how she overcame her youthful religious folly: "Plain horse sense tells us there is no God." Smith liked to complain about DeMille's use of motion pictures "to sustain religion and blacken the character of Atheists," but there was little doubt that *The Godless Girl* was a godsend for the 4A.[11]

That Christine Walker had defected from Christian Endeavor, an evangelical youth organization, to take a leadership role in the

4A's junior-atheist movement was exactly the message Charles Lee Smith wanted to send. Much as Watson Heston had done with his cartoons, the 4A offered a studied parody of the country's prevailing Protestant culture. "Help us Atheize America in this generation," one plea from the 4A beckoned—in direct imitation of the Student Volunteer Movement for Foreign Missions, which rallied the faithful under the banner of evangelizing the world in this generation. The 4A also promoted the notion of an American Anti-Bible Society, an explicit counterthrust to the American Bible Society, and pledged to make "a laughing-stock of the Christian fetish book." Similarly, when the 4A distilled its own credo, it called the statement "The Five Fundamentals of Atheism" (materialism, sense-based empiricism, biological evolution, the inexplicability of evil and suffering, and here-and-now happiness). It was no coincidence that conservative Protestants had already condensed their faith into the "Five Fundamentals," line-in-the-sand doctrines against modernist dilutions of orthodoxy (biblical inerrancy, the genuineness of Christ's miracles, the bodily resurrection of Jesus, the virgin birth, and Christ's atoning sacrifice). As these paired lists of fundamentals suggest, atheist activists gathered energy in close tandem with their conservative evangelical sparring partners.[12]

Nothing suggests the back-and-forth theatrics of atheists and Fundamentalists more clearly than the public debates in which 4A leaders and prominent evangelists engaged. By the end of its first year in 1926, the 4A boasted thirty-four speakers ready to debate Christians on any number of questions: "Is Religion Essential to Progress?" "Is There a God in the Universe?" "Are Miracles Possible?" (When the 4A could not goad a believer into a face-to-face debate, its members sometimes settled for debating each other—in one case on the blithe question: "Which is Worse, the Old or the New Testament?") Often those willing to take up the 4A's challenge were traveling evangelists who well knew the persuasive force of good oratory as well as the publicity benefits of old-fashioned showmanship. The Mississippi Baptist revivalist T. T. Martin, for example, first clashed with 4A-backed lawyer Howell S. England in Charlotte, North Carolina, in 1926. Not long thereafter Martin, who headed the Anti-Evolution League of America and was known for such fiery pamphlets as *Hell and the High Schools: Christ or Evolution, Which?* (1923), agreed to take on Charles Lee Smith himself in three evenings of debate in Louisville, Kentucky.[13]

Martin and Smith quickly became a road show, with debates in Indiana, Arkansas, and Texas. Not surprisingly, Smith rarely fared well with the crowds that gathered to hear him and Martin square off. One of these Martin-Smith debates in West Virginia, for example, was actually cancelled when local officials and clergy intervened to keep Smith from speaking at all. The ACLU protested this denial of free speech and open debate, but to no avail. Even if Smith had somehow gotten a platform in West Virginia, there was little doubt what the debate's outcome would have been. "The audiences of the Bible belt overwhelmingly voted against Atheism and Evolution," the 4A happily admitted of the Smith-Martin debates. Likewise, when Smith later faced the evangelist Aimee Semple McPherson in yet another atheist versus Fundamentalist debate, the crowd once again decided "overwhelmingly for Sister McPherson." Smith, in short, was a fall guy; he was setting himself up to lose—but to lose spectacularly. In doing so, he was not scoring many points for atheism, but was instead hoping to tarnish the public image of Christianity, showing it to be a hayseed faith of Fundamentalist bumpkins and "pious hill-billies." Giving atheism a good name remained a lost cause; giving religion a bad name by linking it to regional backwardness, willful ignorance, and unreasoning emotion had half a chance of succeeding.[14]

Smith and his companions in the 4A had four principal lines of attack in tarring the nation's persistent religiosity. The first was to press the warfare view of the relationship between science and religion—indeed, three of the five fundamentals emphasized this divide (the avowal of materialism, sense-based knowledge, and evolutionary biology). Theism was dissolved in the combined naturalism of these three essentials, but the focal conflict—the one that energized the 4A's campaign against Christianity—was "godless evolution." Spurred on by the fanfare surrounding the Scopes trial, the group made the defense of evolution a secularist badge. The group's speakers and pamphleteers were certainly capable of going on at some length about Darwinism—about the process of natural selection and the survival of the fittest, about the descent of man from anthropoid apes—but they were particularly fond of telegraphic dicta. One leaflet proclaimed in bold print: "Evolution is true. There is no God. Darwin disproved the Supernatural. Evolution means Materialism." It possessed the verbal economy of advertising jingles or billboard slogans. The 4A boiled science and religion down to irreconcilable difference, and the agitation over anti-evolution laws provided the occasion for making that larger point repeatedly. When Smith headed back to his natal state of Arkansas to save its public schools from backwardness, he was drawn there by the need to combat a new "Monkey law." "Fundamentalists will not be checked by pussyfooters," he proclaimed, and, certainly when it came to such blatant disregard for science's authority, Smith was no milquetoast compromiser. For secularists of the 1920s nothing less was at stake than saving the nation from a Fundamentalist return to the Dark Ages of ignorance and inquisition.[15]

The second line of attack the 4A pursued was the association of religion with prudery and censorship. Among the five fundamentals of the group's atheism was "hedonism," the here-and-now pursuit of human happiness long dear to freethinkers from Tom Paine to Samuel Putnam. Such earthy sensuality necessarily stood in contrast with religious repression—an insistent juxtaposition made especially vivid by setting Christianity's "insane sex ideas" against the bodily freedoms secularism promised. Promulgating the new sciences of sexology and Freudian psychoanalysis, the 4A saw its hedonism as crucially informed by the wider cultural "Revolt against Sex Taboos." By the 1920s, the overtly irreligious had largely jettisoned any nervousness about the marriage-reform strands within nineteenth-century freethought and reached wide agreement on the need to secularize sex right along with the state—that is, to free the human body of puritanical denials and regulations of the flesh. To that end, the 4A presented birth control, sex education, liberalized divorce laws, and free literary expression as axiomatic atheist causes. The modern secular logic seemed utterly irrefutable to this freethinking cohort: "The Bible rules for sex are as out of date as its rules for healing. To the clerical imperative, 'Thou shalt not,' the rising generation asks, 'Why not?' There is no rational reply."[16]

On matters hedonic and sexual, it proved all too easy for members of the 4A to bait their Christian opponents. One of Charles Lee Smith's favorite foils was the Manhattan preacher and Fundamentalist champion John Roach Straton, and the targeting was necessarily mutual (the 4A's Ingersoll Forum met right across the street from Straton's Calvary Baptist Church, so the barbs did not have to fly far in either direction). The 4A had already been hassling Straton with charges of violating child-labor laws by employing the "girl evangelist" Uldine Utley at revival meetings, but the group took particular pleasure in goading him with mailings of its literature, including a piece on birth control and another that contained a ribald joke about the Holy Ghost. Smith considered everything about the 4A obscene and turned instinctively for help to John Sumner, the heir of Anthony Comstock's mantle at the New York Society for the Suppression of Vice. Soon summoned to face charges of violating the reigning postal laws, Smith found—just as D. M. Bennett and Elmina Drake Slenker had before him—that the Vice Society and its allies were hard to overcome in court. Smith was fined $100, and Sumner duly noted the conviction in the old ledgers that Comstock had begun keeping more than a half century earlier—Charles Lee Smith, "atheist," guilty of circulating offensive and harassing "propaganda." Straton rejoiced that the 4A's "sensuous and un-American infamies" had been rebuked in court; perhaps the modern Babylon with all its "rouge pots" and "petting parties" would yet take heed of his prophesying: "This country cannot endure half infidel and half Christian."[17]

Straton's hopes of dousing the 4A by prosecuting its firebrand president proved fleeting. The court imbroglio only allowed Smith and company to guffaw once again over the humorless prudery of evangelical Protestantism and to amplify through gleeful repetition "The Holy Ghost Joke" with its casual sexual references:

A very pious young lady had died and had gained admittance into heaven. Saint Peter took her around and presented her to

God, Christ, and various other notables. Being left alone, she strolled about and admired the scenery, but noticed she was being followed by a very small, mean looking fellow, who kept bowing to her and was evidently trying to "pick her up." Much alarmed, she ran back to St. Peter, told him what had happened, and asked him who this little fellow could be. Looking up and seeing who it was, Peter replied: "Oh, that's the Holy Ghost, but we don't introduce him to the ladies since he had that little affair with the Virgin Mary."

Not exactly a battle over Walt Whitman or D. H. Lawrence, but the Smith-Straton dust-up over "The Holy Ghost Joke" did suggest how intent the 4A was on portraying the sexual propriety of conservative Protestantism as fussy and sanctimonious. Straton might have learned something from the regret of those who had prosecuted C. B. Reynolds decades earlier. The faithful usually fared better when they left such atheist provocateurs alone.[18]

The 4A's third line of attack revolved around theodicy. The problem of evil, the group maintained, made a lie of Christian notions of a loving and all-powerful deity. Among the association's five fundamentals of atheism was the following: "THE EXISTENCE OF EVIL—The patent fact that renders irrational the belief in a beneficent, omnipotent being who cares for man." The leaders of the 4A found it absurd to praise God for blessings bestowed, while according him no blame when things went terribly wrong, as they so often did—earthquakes, floods, cyclones, droughts, and pestilences. Almost as a matter of course, the group revisited one of Watson Heston's favored themes: namely, that presidential proclamations for Thanksgiving were grievous political and theological errors. When President Herbert Hoover predictably ignored the 4A's call to desist from the "irrational act" of "a public Thanksgiving to God," the group puckishly lobbied for equal time, proposing a new national holiday to be known as Blamegiving Day. "Shall we credit God with good and not charge him with evil? That would be dishonest bookkeeping," leaflets of the 4A announced. "Cropless farmers" and "jobless workers"—all "the victims of Divine Negligence"—deserved better than such civic religious platitudes, especially as the Great Depression deepened. The 4A was not inclined toward philosophical or theological subtlety. Their polemics on the problem of evil displayed instead the sardonic, antireligious populism long palpable among the nation's village infidels.[19]

The fourth major area of concern for the 4A—and the one that would prove of most consequence in the decades to follow—was promoting the strict separation of church and state. That secularist principle underpinned the group's entire operation. The church-state issues the 4A highlighted were a direct inheritance of the Nine Demands around which the National Liberal League and the American Secular Union had coalesced in the last quarter of the nineteenth century. Among the causes the 4A embraced as its own were: the elimination of the tax exemption on church property; the combatting of any laws, including Sabbath protections, that underwrote the notion of the United States as a Christian nation; and the erasure of commonplace markers of the nation's civic theism (such as the "In God We Trust" motto on American coinage). Underpinning the group's entire list of demands were two long-standing secularist principles: (1) religion was not to be legally favored over irreligion; and (2) freethinkers and atheists were to enjoy the same rights, liberties, and protections under the law as believers did. For Smith, convicted in Arkansas on charges of both public disturbance and blasphemy, as well as in New York on grounds of mailing objectionable literature, the vindication of those legal principles remained all too pertinent. Arkansas was among a handful of states that retained a constitutional ban on atheists holding offices of public trust, and Little Rock's municipal court had used Smith's atheism to disqualify him as a witness in his own defense. Smith, a trained lawyer, wanted to mount a challenge in the federal courts to state "anti-Atheist laws" and ultimately to find a constitutional remedy through the United States Supreme Court.[20]

The Fourteenth Amendment was the key to Smith's legal strategy, as it would be for other secularist plaintiffs. Adopted in the wake of the Civil War to compel the former Confederate states to recognize emancipated slaves as full citizens and accord them equal protection under the law, the Fourteenth Amendment also became the avenue by which the religion clauses of the First Amendment were made binding at state and local levels. In late 1931, New York authorities arrested Smith again, this time for not having a permit when he started expounding his atheistic views on the city's streets and in public parks. That Smith had been singled out because of his irreligious oratory seemed obvious; police left two other unlicensed speakers at the same location alone. After much legal maneuvering, the New York Court of Appeals upheld his conviction in 1934 on the grounds that such public attacks on religion were likely to occasion so much "passion, rancor, and malice" as "to justify especial supervision over those who would conduct such meetings on the public streets." This left Smith and the freethinking lawyer Frank Swancara incredulous: surely, the onus was on religious believers not to form "violent mobs" and "manhandle" atheist speakers who offended them. To Swancara, a tireless advocate for the civil liberties of nonbelievers, it seemed transparently clear that Smith was not being accorded equal protection under the law and that the state of New York had violated his rights to free speech and free religious expression. Smith appealed again, this time to the United States Supreme Court, hopeful that his case would provide the occasion for making plain the applicability of the Fourteenth Amendment in protecting the constitutional rights of the First Amendment at the state level. His appeal was summarily dismissed "for want of a substantial federal question," leaving Swancara to shake his head at yet another injustice done to Smith, whom he grandiloquently dubbed "Rationalism's Dred Scott" after the slave whose case for citizenship and freedom was infamously rejected by the Supreme Court in 1857.[21]

With the banner free-exercise and establishment cases of the 1940s still on the horizon, the salvos of Smith and the rest of the 4A were usually hard for anyone beyond freethinking ranks to take seriously. Seen as almost comically litigious, Smith and company filed a lawsuit "to oust the chaplains from the halls of Congress and from the Army and Navy." They gained no traction with that challenge. They looked also for plaintiffs with "sufficient courage" to launch cases against "the bootlegging of religion into the public schools," particularly against Bible reading, prayer, and release time for catechetic instruction. They threatened repeal campaigns on religious tests for public office, not only in Arkansas, but also in Maryland, Mississippi, Texas, Pennsylvania, Tennessee, and the Carolinas. With the ACLU, the 4A took on a New Jersey case in 1931 defending the right of atheists to testify in court without taking a religious oath: "The conscience of an atheist should be as much respected in law as the religious scruples of a Quaker." Likewise, the 4A rushed to the defense of garden-variety blasphemers such as the German laborer in Reading, Pennsylvania, who—in refusing to swear on the Bible—had exclaimed instead "To hell with that" and was then indicted for profaning the scriptures. However frivolous or forlorn the 4A's lawsuits seemed in the 1920s and 1930s, a generation later no one was laughing. By 1965 a string of Supreme Court decisions had vindicated a number of secularist, atheist, and humanistic plaintiffs. The 4A's view of the country's "godless Federal Constitution"—its indignation over "the foul and unlawful cohabitation of Church and State" had come to appear far less quixotic by that point.[22]

The efflorescence of the 4A was brief—at most, it managed a decade of conspicuous controversy after its founding in 1925 before dribbling away as Charles Lee Smith turned his energies back to the *Truth Seeker*. Still, in that window of time, the 4A was not entirely mistaken to see itself as the "visible part" of "a huge iceberg"—a "submerged mountain" of religious disaffection and misgiving upon which the group staged its bumptious and histrionic brand of unbelief. With Fundamentalists waxing in influence, a growing number of liberal Protestants began to suspect that they had more in common with secularists than with their conservative kin. As one embattled Congregational minister remarked, "If my church forced me to believe in the infallibility of the Bible, the second coming of Jesus in person, the bodily resurrection, the damnation of those who refuse to believe in a certain creed, the hell-fire theory, and the virgin birth, I would choose to be numbered among the Atheists, Infidels, and Agnostics." If the choice came down to John Roach Straton's ascetic

Fundamentalism or John Dewey's liberal humanism, Billy Sunday's revivalism or H. L. Mencken's wit, American modernists—Protestant and otherwise—knew which side they would take. When the literary lion Carl Van Doren took his stand with the ungodly in 1926, he did so with panache, confident that the "wolves for conformity" had been defanged and that a more worldly sensibility had been set loose. "In this little breathing-spell of toleration," he remarked from his perch at Columbia University, "even an unbeliever may speak out."[23]

———————◆———————

Charles Lee Smith was far from alone as a gadfly for the rights of atheists and for strict church-state separation. Among his most tenacious comrades was Joseph Lewis, the son of a Jewish merchant in Selma, Alabama. The family had made its way to New York City just after the turn of the century, and young Lewis left school to work for his father. An autodidact, he had absorbed the works of Paine and Ingersoll while carrying on a successful trade as a men's clothier. In 1921 he launched his own Freethought Press Association to broadcast his atheistic views as well as his sharply secularist perspective on the nation's founding fathers. That venture allowed him to fire off one title after another—from *The Tyranny of God* to *Jefferson, the Freethinker* to *The Bible Unmasked*. His publishing enterprise was but preparation for his primary preoccupation, the litigation of church-state cases in order to "get God out of public institutions." He challenged prayers at city board meetings, the recitation of the Ten Commandments in the public schools, and the expenditure of public funds to transport students to parochial institutions. Eventually, he would even challenge the addition of the "under God" phrase to the Pledge of Allegiance, the building of airport chapels, and the use of public firehouses for religious meetings. A self-avowed "Enemy of God" who worked to organize freethinkers into a national society, Lewis made it his perennial mission to question religion's persistent entwining with the country's public institutions. Even though most of his suits were quickly dismissed—"Legalistically Freethinker Lewis hardly ever wins a battle," *Time* magazine smirked in 1935—he nonetheless managed to keep such secularist provocations in the national news from one year to the next. Lewis even gained some well-placed admirers along the way—Clarence Darrow for sure, but also Unitarian John Haynes Holmes and journalist Heywood Broun, who editorialized in the pages of the New York *World* in 1926 on behalf of this "small minority" of atheists and freethinkers against a "stampeding" Christian majority.[24]

Highly visible agitators like Smith and Lewis had the company of equally committed, if more local and obscure, comrades. A prime example was Arthur G. Cromwell, an architect from Rochester, New York. Raised in a staunch Presbyterian family (his father was an elder in the church), Cromwell had been a doubter of the faith since boyhood and renounced Christianity entirely after his violently disillusioning experience in the army during World War I. Disabled, he spent three years in and out of army hospitals, then devoted much of the next decade to digesting the works of religion's critics—from Voltaire to Ingersoll. By the 1930s, Cromwell had organized his own local society of freethinkers in Rochester and was serving as the group's president (it was an affiliate branch of Joseph Lewis's bare bones national organization). Soon, the usual skeptical inquiries into God and revelation spilled over into familiar forms of secularist activism. Joining Lewis in his fight against religion's role in the public schools of New York, Cromwell bombarded local newspapers with letters to the editor explaining the educational harm of everything from Bible reading to Christmas pageants. In 1940, he produced a fiery sixteen-page pamphlet on *Rationalism vs. Religious Instruction in the Public Schools*, just one more squib in the ongoing legal battles that Smith, Lewis, and company had been pursuing for the last fifteen years. It would have been an unremarkable contribution except for one thing: five years later, in 1945, one of Cromwell's daughters, Vashti McCollum, would file suit against the release-time program operative in the schools of Champaign, Illinois—an action that set the stage for the first major Supreme Court victory, in 1948, for an avowedly secularist plaintiff. Arthur Cromwell, acerbic local freethinker, would have his moment in the national spotlight thanks to his ungodly daughter. He would see his tiny Rochester pamphlet brandished in an Illinois court as an illustration of the atheistic militancy and familial delinquency behind McCollum's challenge. Called to the stand himself, Cromwell would send a gasp through the courtroom when he flatly denied God's existence and announced he was proud to be an atheist.[25]

The public schools of Champaign, Illinois, had started a program of religious instruction in 1940 in which Protestant, Catholic, and Jewish children learned from representatives of their respective faiths about their own tradition. The program, dominated by a palpable Protestant majority, was conducted in school classrooms on a release-time basis, for a half-hour each week. Like her father, Vashti McCollum was a humanistic freethinker and so was her husband, John, a professor of horticulture at the nearby University of Illinois. The couple was disturbed at the prospect of their three sons being incorporated into Champaign's "voluntary" program of religious instruction. When their oldest son James Terry entered fourth grade, the level at which the religious curriculum began, Vashti took the lead in getting him excused. Placed by himself in the hallway or in a music room, Jim was stigmatized by his classmates for not participating in the program, further steeling McCollum's resolve to have religious instruction removed from the public schools. With the support of a local Unitarian minister, Philip Schug, and a civil-liberties group in Chicago, McCollum filed suit against the school board. The case went to trial in September 1945, garnering national media attention, much of which was scornful of McCollum, an "Anti-Bible Mother," with a finger-pointing atheist for a father and "a young Voltaire" for a ten-year-old son. In January 1946, a three-judge panel of the Sixth Illinois Circuit Court denied her petition, seeing no constitutional or statutory violations stemming from Champaign's system of religious education. She appealed to the Supreme Court of Illinois, which upheld the Circuit Court's verdict; she and her lawyers then turned to the Supreme Court of the United States, which agreed to review the case and heard oral arguments in December 1947.[26]

Ten months earlier, in February 1947, the Supreme Court had decided another crucial Establishment-Clause case, *Everson v. Board of Education*, in which it narrowly upheld a New Jersey

school district's use of public funds to transport students to parochial schools. Though the school's policy was vindicated, Justice
Hugo Black made plain in his majority opinion that the First
Amendment's prohibition of any law respecting "an establishment of religion" was indeed applicable through the Fourteenth
Amendment to state and local governments. So, even as the court
decided that in this instance there was no breach of the First
Amendment, Black and his fellow justices (including those who,
in dissent, did see a clear breach) pledged the nation's highest
court to a new vigilance against religious establishments broadly
construed. Rehearsing the founding principles of Jefferson and
Madison, Black made a sweeping separationist argument:

> The "establishment of religion" clause of the First Amendment
> means at least this: neither a state nor the Federal Government
> can set up a church. . . . No person can be punished for enter-
> taining or professing religious beliefs or disbeliefs, for church
> attendance or non-attendance. . . . In the words of Jefferson, the
> clause against establishment of religion by law was intended to
> erect "a wall of separation between Church and State."

All citizens—whether "Catholics, Lutherans, Mohammedans, Baptists, Jews, Methodists, Nonbelievers, Presbyterians, or the members of any other faith," in Black's compendious listing—were to
share equally in the rights and liberties of the First Amendment.
The state was required to be studiously "neutral in its relations"
with "religious believers and nonbelievers" alike. With those
words Black, an Alabama Southern Baptist turned humanistic
Unitarian, gave McCollum hope. The religious and irreligious had
equal standing under the Bill of Rights, and those protections were
enforceable on the states through the Fourteenth Amendment.[27]

The backlash against the McCollum family had been severe
after Vashti initiated her suit in 1945 and then continued to press
it despite the Illinois court rulings. To her opponents, McCollum's
challenge to religious instruction was not so much a First Amendment case as it was "an attack on God" and "the moral basis of
our society." She perversely exalted her own minority views on
atheism and rationalism at the expense of the nation's welfare and

the majority's religious rights. Those who viewed the McCollums as the tools of "Godless Communists" felt that reprisals were warranted. University officials were lobbied to fire John McCollum from the Illinois faculty and institute a blanket rule never to employ an atheist; that effort failed, but Vashti's part-time teaching of physical education classes was terminated. The bullying of Jim intensified, and school officials painted him as a troubled child who had never been able to make friends among his peers. By the time the case made its way to the U.S. Supreme Court, the parents had felt compelled to withdraw him from the Champaign schools and send him to live with his grandparents in Rochester, where he enrolled in a private school at a safe remove from the fray. While McCollum won a number of important allies along the way, she felt much of the time "disliked and despised all around," especially in Champaign itself. One Halloween a group of locals heaved tomatoes at her when she answered the door thinking it was trick-or-treaters; they stayed long enough to sing "Onward, Christian Soldiers," to hiss her as an atheist, and to heap trash on the family's doorstep. Hate mail poured in from around the country, including from one writer who enclosed a newspaper clipping of her picture disfigured with devil's horns and a tail. Another correspondent scribbled over her face, "Lost going to hell"; still another jotted, "You are a disgrace to our nation . . . and should be driven out of this country at once"; finally, one letter writer hazarded loose sexuality and a violent remedy: "You probably had your child before you married if you are married. What you need is someone to beat the hell out of you."[28]

Given his strong predilection to protect minority rights, Justice Black certainly had that kind of case before him when he wrote the majority opinion in *McCollum v. Board of Education*, an 8-1 decision in favor of the appellant, announced on March 8, 1948. Invoking the same language as he had used in the *Everson* case, Black found this time that the breach of the First Amendment's Establishment Clause was "beyond all question." The city of Champaign was clearly using "the tax-established and tax-supported public school system to aid religious groups to spread their faith," an encroachment on the Jeffersonian wall of separation that *Everson* had elevated. As Black saw it, the state's use of the "compulsory public school machinery" for "the dissemination of religious doctrines" was simply incompatible with a "high and impregnable" wall separating church and state. Justice Robert H. Jackson joined the majority, but in a concurring opinion warned that the court appeared to be sustaining "the plaintiff's complaint without exception." As an "avowed atheist," which, Jackson emphasized, "she has every right to be," McCollum had advanced a position that extended well beyond the release-time plan to encompass "every form of teaching which suggests or recognizes that there is a God." She would apparently ban, for example, "all teaching of the Scriptures," including biblical recitations. Where did that leave the Psalms, the Lord's Prayer, or the Ten Commandments? Was all religious instruction to be "cast out of secular education"? Were lessons on sacred music or the Bible's influence on English literature to be omitted? Jackson rightly warned that the sweep of the *McCollum* decision left the door wide open to further secularist challenges and that it offered very little guidance on "where the secular ends and the sectarian begins in education." Jackson predicted that *McCollum* would make Jefferson's wall "serpentine," and it did. In those judicial windings, as one Establishment-Clause case after another made its way through the courts, atheistic and humanistic plaintiffs would find themselves on both the winning and losing sides of the snaking wall that *Everson* and *McCollum* built.[29]

No case more fully demonstrated the judicial twisting over the Establishment Clause than *Zorach v. Clauson*, a 6-3 decision four years after *McCollum* in April 1952. Faced with another release-time program, this one in New York City, in which public school children were taken to religious centers off school grounds for catechetic instruction, the court decided that there was no violation of the First Amendment. The crucial difference for Justice William O. Douglas, who wrote the majority opinion, was that this program took place off school property and that all costs were borne by religious organizations. But, he also took the opportunity to soften Black's more vigorous language about an impregnable wall, arguing that the First Amendment "does not say that in every and all respects there shall be a separation of Church and State."

> Otherwise the state and religion would be aliens to each other—hostile, suspicious, and even unfriendly.... Prayers in our legislative halls; the appeals to the Almighty in the messages of the Chief Executive; the proclamations making Thanksgiving Day a holiday; "so help me God" in our courtroom oaths—these and all other references to the Almighty that run through our laws, our public rituals, our ceremonies would be flouting the First Amendment. A fastidious atheist or agnostic could even object to the supplication with which the Court opens each session: "God save the United States and this Honorable Court."

Douglas punctuated his jab at the "fastidious atheist" with a classic Cold War formulation of American citizenship that suggested the irreligious were not up to its basic demands: "We are a religious people whose institutions presuppose a Supreme Being." Or, as Will Herberg captured this entwining two years later: "Not to be—that is, not to identify oneself and be identified as—either a Protestant, a Catholic, or a Jew is somehow not to be an American." Needless to say, Vashti McCollum's victory had left unresolved the public standing of the nation's nonbelieving minority.[30]

Douglas wanted the state to be friendly, not hostile, to religious belief, but Black saw the reverse side of this claim and articulated it very clearly in his dissenting opinion reaffirming the "fundamental philosophy" of *Everson* and *McCollum*. Conjuring up a colonial bloodbath of "fighting sects" in which those branded as "heretics" or "atheists" were under recurrent threat, Black suggested that it was precisely *because* Americans were such a religious people that complete church-state separation was necessary—otherwise that kind of sectarian violence could rear its head again. Now, as in the eighteenth century, he argued, it was "only by wholly isolating the state from the religious sphere and compelling it to be completely neutral" that the freedom of believers and nonbelievers would be equally maintained. *Zorach* represented an abandonment of that neutrality—a loss that was, as Black put it, "all the more dangerous to liberty because of the Court's legal exaltation of the ortho-

dox and its derogation of unbelievers." Writing as if the majority opinion was inventing this religious preferment rather than
affirming a commonplace of American public life, Black noted
darkly the inequities the decision exposed:

> Before today, our judicial opinions have refrained from draw-
> ing invidious distinctions between those who believe in no reli-
> gion and those who do believe. The First Amendment has lost
> much if the religious follower and the atheist are no longer to
> be judicially regarded as entitled to equal justice under law.

Black won over his colleague Robert Jackson, who this time worried in dissent not about vindicating the expansive claims of fastidious atheists (like Charles Smith, Joseph Lewis, or Vashti Mc-
Collum), but about the way the decision openly marginalized such
dissenters. "The day this country ceases to be free for irreligion
it will be cease to be free for religion," Jackson wrote in stinging
reply to the "warped and twisted" opinion of the majority.[31]

The dissents of Black and Jackson in *Zorach*, soaring rhetori-
cally well beyond the reaches of a specific release-time program,
were remarkable rebukes of the "compulsory godliness" of the
1950s. Registering *Zorach* as a dangerous step backward from *Mc-
Collum*, they vigorously reemphasized secularist aspirations in
the teeth of the Cold War: namely, the rights and liberties of nonbelievers were to be wholly equal to those of believers. The very
next month, in May 1952, it looked as if the ascent of that principle
was back on track. The Court delivered its opinion in *Burstyn v.
Wilson*, a unanimous decision declaring unconstitutional a New
York statute that allowed the banning of motion pictures on the
grounds of sacrilege. In 1951 a New York board had prohibited
the further exhibition of a "sacrilegious" Italian film entitled *The
Miracle*, and the film's distributor had appealed the action as a violation of both the free speech and the religion clauses of the First
Amendment. The film, directed by Roberto Rossellini, had won
critical acclaim in the New York arts community, but had also
been met with outrage, especially from the National Legion of
Decency, a Catholic organization that considered it blasphemous
for its depiction of a poor young woman who conceives a child by

a stranger she imagines to be Saint Joseph. That perceived mockery of the virgin birth raised the old specter of John Ruggles who, in his ridiculing of the Virgin Mary as a whore and Jesus as a bastard, had helped set the defining precedent for American blasphemy jurisprudence in 1811. Even if Rossellini's artsy film was not to be conflated with Ruggles's ribald outburst, both nonetheless raised the same critical question: was the state to protect Christians from offense and Christianity from derision?[32]

In delivering the opinion of the Court, Justice Tom Clark observed that New York's Court of Appeals had treated the statutory provision forbidding sacrilege as clear and comprehensive in meaning: "That no religion, as that word is understood by the ordinary, reasonable person, shall be treated with contempt, mockery, scorn and ridicule." Under that expansive definition—which saw religion across the board as protected against insult—the ban on sacrilege may have sounded nonsectarian enough, but Clark argued that the enforcement of this standard of censorship would actually end up being quite parochial. It would be governed by "the most vocal and powerful orthodoxies" at the expense of the "unpopular sentiments" of religious (and irreligious) minorities. The "sacrilegious" test, Clark suggested, ran afoul of church-state separation, but it failed most obviously on the grounds of freedom of speech and the press: "The state has no legitimate interest in protecting any or all religions from views distasteful to them," certainly no interest sufficient to justify abridging the free expression of those views. "It is not the business of government in our nation," Clark sweepingly concluded, "to suppress real or imagined attacks upon a particular religious doctrine, whether they appear in publications, speeches, or motion pictures." In his concurring opinion, Justice Felix Frankfurter openly disclaimed blasphemy as a "chameleon phrase" used to enforce the "ruling authority" of whatever religious orthodoxy reigns at the moment. Sacrilege and blasphemy—as much as apostasy and heresy—were crimes peculiar to "the realm of religious dogma"; they could not be squared with the First Amendment. While legal disputes over obscenity and pornography continued apace in the 1950s and 1960s (and beyond), *Burstyn v. Wilson* marked an important turning point on the religious front. The policing of sacrilege and blasphemy—protecting aggrieved Christians from the "distasteful" opinions of those who offended them—was counted stultifying censorship.[33]

Lessening the immediate sting of *Zorach*, *Burstyn* pointed ahead to several other crucial victories for secular activists over the next decade or so. On religious tests and public office-holding, the case of Roy Torcaso, a Maryland atheist and the manager of a construction business, proved especially momentous. To become a notary public in the state required taking a solemn oath pledging faithful allegiance, "in the presence of Almighty God," to the constitutions of both Maryland and the United States; it also required a distinct declaration of belief in God's existence. Torcaso wanted to make an affirmation in lieu of the religious oath and declaration, but the Circuit Court of Montgomery County denied that petition in 1959, as did the Maryland Court of Appeals the next year. The Appeals Court pointed to the state's constitution, which made a declaration of belief in God a prerequisite to holding any office of public trust and to serving as a witness or juror in Maryland courtrooms. It also pointed to Douglas's majority opinion in *Zorach*, highlighting the dependence of American institutions on a belief in a Supreme Being, before coming to this forthright conclusion:

> It seems clear that under our Constitution disbelief in a Supreme Being, and the denial of any moral accountability for conduct, not only renders a person incompetent to hold public office, but to give testimony, or serve as a juror. The historical record makes it clear that religious toleration, in which this State has taken pride, was never thought to encompass the ungodly.

As a historical judgment, that appraisal fairly captured the long-reigning majoritian view that lifted believers above unbelievers in American public life. It failed, though, to recognize the equally tenacious challenge American secularists had been mounting to such invidious legal distinctions for well over a century. The Maryland court counted the limits placed on irreligious freedom a settled question in the nation's history when, in fact, that issue had been in dispute from the beginning. The *Torcaso* case promised to bring some resolution to those endlessly smoldering debates.[34]

With the backing of both the ACLU and the American Jewish Congress, Torcaso took his case to the Supreme Court in 1961. Once again, Justice Hugo Black delivered the Court's opinion, this time unanimous in favor of the appellant. Torcaso's lawyers— among them Leo Pfeffer, a front-rank defender of religious liberties who had also helped fight the *Burstyn* case—had argued that Maryland's oath requirements violated Article VI of the Federal Constitution, which expressly forbids religious tests for public office, as well as the First and Fourteenth Amendments as in-terpreted in *Everson* and *McCollum*. Skirting the Article VI ar-gument and its bearing on the states, Black instead presented the Supreme Court's reversal of the Appeals Court as another exemplary Establishment-Clause case. Neither the state nor the federal government, Black insisted, "can constitutionally pass laws or impose requirements which aid all religions as against non-believers"; neither can offer special aid to those who pro-fess a belief in God over those who do not. *Torcaso v. Watkins*, in its unanimity, was the legal vindication for which atheists and secular-ists had long been waiting. Theistic qualifications for public office-holding, court testimony, and jury service had been rendered un-constitutional; beyond Maryland, that judgment had direct im-plications for state provisions in Arkansas, Mississippi, North Carolina, Pennsylvania, South Carolina, Tennessee, and Texas. The liberties and protections of the First and Fourteenth Amend-ments were not for theists alone; they applied equally to atheists and nonbelievers. Finally, the Supreme Court had untangled some of the toughest legal knots in the nation's long-snarled debate over irreligious freedom.[35]

Torcaso hardly meant, though, that such issues were settled in the court of public opinion. Sharp disagreement was evident in a pair of counterpoised essays the *Saturday Evening Post* ran in the wake of the decision. The first by Robert Bendiner, sometime-editor at the *Nation*, was entitled "Our Right Not to Believe," and the second by Billy Graham, ubiquitous Cold War evangelist, was headlined "Our Right to Require Belief." While encouraged by Torcaso's victory, Bendiner still saw conventional wisdom running very much against unbelievers entering public life on equal terms. He recalled Richard Nixon's "gesture of generosity" toward John F. Kennedy, his Democratic and Roman Catholic rival, in the presidential election of 1960: "There is only one way that I can visualize religion being a legitimate issue in an American political campaign," Nixon had said. "That would be if one of the candidates for the Presidency had *no* religious belief." Bendiner took Nixon's statement as emblematic of the culture's prevailing norms, no matter what the Supreme Court said about Roy Torcaso's rights. In these "timid days," Bendiner concluded, atheists and freethinkers were still "casually put beyond the pale, as though the Constitution sanctioned their exclusion and national tradition hallowed it."

Billy Graham replied the next week with a ringing affirmation of the very tradition of exclusion that Bendiner lamented. Scorning the "tiny minority" who would "take the traditional concept of God out of our national life," Graham launched into a full-throated defense of the nation's essential religiosity. This was a country, the evangelist averred, "forged in the fire of a burning faith in God"; American freedom and democracy rested on those "religious foundations." Already widely seen by the early 1960s as the spiritual counselor to the nation's presidents, Graham was not at all sure that unbelievers could be trusted with the reins of government. If atheists and agnostics were in public office, would they defend the Bill of Rights, resist the communist threat, and work to preserve American civilization? The preacher was doubtful. Citizens had every right to expect of their public leaders "a deep, personal faith" in God, for how else would the nation endure and prosper? As the paired perspectives of Bendiner and Graham made plain, the *Torcaso* decision had only raised the cultural stakes involved in upholding the rights and equal citizenship of the nonbeliever.[36]

Those stakes appeared all the more pronounced as the battles over prayer and Bible reading in the public schools crested over the next two years. *Engel v. Vitale* (1962) struck down a one-sentence, state-authorized school prayer in New York; *Abington v. Schempp* (1963) decided against the daily reading of ten Bible verses and the recitation of the Lord's Prayer in Pennsylvania schools; and *Murray v. Curlett* (1963), which was folded into the *Schempp* decision, rendered unconstitutional similar practices in Baltimore's schools. In all three cases humanist and atheist plaintiffs loomed large (in *Engel*, two Jewish appellants joined a cohort of five challengers who included a Unitarian, an atheist, and an ethical humanist). The strict separationist logic of *Everson* and *McCollum* reached its apogee in those cases and occasioned a new storm of outrage. The Court had moved, in the eyes of its critics, from friendliness through neutrality to overt hostility toward religion. Much like the McCollums fifteen years earlier, the Schempps, a humanistic Unitarian family, as well as the five plaintiffs in the New York lawsuit came under venomous attack—a mixture of anti-atheist, anti-communist, and anti-Jewish rants. (Lawrence Roth, the atheist among the *Engel* litigants, had his home picketed and received death threats; a cross of gasoline-drenched rags was burned in his driveway by a group of teenagers who went unprosecuted.) Only the Baltimore litigant, Madalyn Murray (O'Hair), reviled as "the most hated woman in America" for her particularly brash atheism, seemed to thrive on the infamy of the moment. The heat of the ongoing conflicts even convinced Justice William O. Douglas, the author of the majority opinion in *Zorach* with its snide attack on the fastidious atheist, to move over to Hugo Black's view of the need to protect irreligious nonconformity from harrying religious coercions. The philosophy of the First Amendment, Douglas now wrote in his concurring opinion in *Engel v. Vitale*, is that "the atheist or agnostic—the nonbeliever —is entitled to go his own way."[37]

With that pronouncement Douglas wrote the lore of the village atheist into church-state jurisprudence. (Mark Twain, after all, had described Judge York Driscoll, the small-town infidel in *Pudd'nhead Wilson*, as someone who ventures "to go his own way and follow out his own notions.") Between *McCollum* in 1948 and *Schempp* in 1963, the contrarian freethinker had secured a measure of vindication. As Paul Blanshard, another high-profile secularist, wrote in the wake of the *Torcaso* decision, "Religious liberty in a nation is as real as the liberty of its least popular religious minority." For the United States, Blanshard said, the proper gauge was whether that freedom was accorded atheists and nonbelievers. Far from a sell-out to communist Russia and its atheistic state, this judicial course—according equal rights, liberties, and protections to a quintessentially despised minority—was, Blanshard suggested, exactly what separated the United States from totalitarian regimes. One hardly had to embrace Blanshard's secularist vision to recognize the legal shifts that had taken place. Even the lone dissenter in the combined *Schempp* and *Murray* decisions, Justice Potter Stewart, was pointed in his defense of the "governmental neutrality" demanded by the First and Fourteenth Amendments—"the extension of evenhanded treatment to all who believe, doubt, or disbelieve." He only suggested remanding the cases for the collection of additional evidence on whether the school boards had failed to meet that constitutional standard. Indeed, Stewart closed his dissent with a marked validation of the country's varied nonbelievers: "What our Constitution indispensably protects is the freedom of each of us, be he Jew or Agnostic, Christian or Atheist, Buddhist or Freethinker, to believe or disbelieve, to worship or not worship, to pray or keep silent, according to his own conscience, uncoerced and unrestrained by government." Through a long drawn-out process of secularist activism, a tiny minority of atheists, agnostics, and freethinkers had managed to gain explicit judicial acknowledgment alongside three of the world's major faiths.[38]

By the mid-1960s, the era of required godliness that Herberg described in *Protestant-Catholic-Jew* was fast unraveling. Amid growing struggles over the Vietnam War and civil rights, citizenship and patriotism were no longer so effortlessly merged with religious belief and identification. Among the activists slain in 1963, for example, was the lone postman Bill Moore, a white atheist on a civil-rights trek to Jackson, Mississippi, shot in the head in Alabama for his inflammatory views on both race and religion. Moore, an ex-Marine and a close associate of Madalyn Murray, was eulogized as a saintly hero of the cause by sympathetic politicians and clergy alike. His atheist involvement did not prevent his recognition as one among the movement's martyrs. Two years later in 1965 Daniel Seeger, a conscientious objector who espoused "a purely ethical creed" and openly expressed his skepticism as to God's existence, won his case before the Supreme Court. Despite Seeger's failure to declare on his Selective Service System form his belief in a Supreme Being, the Court decided that his nontheistic moral rationales were functionally equivalent to the beliefs of those who sought conscientious objector status on conventionally recognized religious grounds. *Seeger* looked like a tortured piece of theological reasoning—the plaintiff's agnostic principles were turned into veiled theistic expressions—but the upshot was clear: the conscience of the ethical humanist counted as much as the conscience of a peaceable Christian. By the next year, in April 1966, *Time* magazine could plausibly run its famous cover story with its perfectly sincere query about the country's theological mood: "Is God Dead?" Atheism, existentialism, and humanistic secularism had become serious countercultural alternatives by the mid-1960s.[39]

The Cold War forces of reaction continued unabated, of course, and no one whose experience extended beyond the most rarified intellectual enclaves could have reasonably concluded that Nietzschean ruminations on the death of God captured the tenacious religious realities of American life. As *Time* opined in the very cover story announcing the advent of "the new atheism" of the 1960s, the United States remained "a country where public faith in God seems to be as secure as it was in medieval France." Atheists were still hated by all too many Americans, no matter how often Hugo Black and his fellow mid-century justices stressed the fundamental equality of believers and nonbelievers. The animosity and harassment aimed at the McCollums, Roths, Schempps, and Murrays provided bountiful evidence of that. Long after the *Torcaso* decision, none of the affected states showed any inclination to remove the dead-letter bans on atheists from holding public office, leaving them in place as "an obsolete but lingering insult" to nonbelievers. As late as 1991, South Carolina tried to enforce its provision of atheist exclusion against Herb Silverman, a mathematics professor at the College of Charleston. Applying to be a notary public but refusing to acknowledge God, Silverman had his application denied, the only rejection out of 33,471 applicants. It took him six years of legal wrangling until the South Carolina Supreme Court, against the express opposition of the state's governor, affirmed the constitutionally obvious: that South Carolina could not deny Silverman a notary commission simply because he was "an open atheist." The mid-century court battles had done little to ameliorate the widespread social distrust of atheists or to lighten the God talk expected of political candidates. If anything, those legal successes seemed only to deepen antagonisms toward a small minority that was seen as subverting the nation's covenantal conventions. A well-respected public theologian, Richard John Neuhaus, could still ask with all due seriousness in 1991: "Can Atheists Be Good Citizens?" He found it a question difficult to answer in the affirmative. A decade later, in the first gleamings of George W. Bush's faith-imbued presidency, Natalie Angier could yet despair in a *New York Times* piece entitled "Confessions of a Lonely Atheist": "Nothing seems as despised, illicit and un-American as atheism."[40]

Angier registered her feelings of isolation in early 2001, eight months before 9/11. The terrorist attacks on the World Trade Center and the Pentagon would have innumerable aftershocks in American culture, among them the renewed energy that the hijackings gave to religion's critics: "Science flies you to the moon; religion flies you into buildings," so bumper-stickers, T-shirts, and posters proclaimed as the "New Atheism" took form. If the geopolitics of the Cold War had made American godliness a civic requirement, the new war on terrorism suggested a potential reversal of the equation. America's secular political order, it seemed, now confronted a global surplus of religious radicalism and violence that desperately required the promotion of Jeffersonian enlightenment. That international threat had its domestic corollary for freethinking secularists in President George W. Bush's coziness with the Religious Right—a confluence that only redoubled the liberal imperative to defend and revive secularism. By the end of Bush's second term, a whole host of bestsellers had made this latest secularist campaign—in the guise of the "New Atheism"—a media sensation of immense proportions: Sam Harris, Richard Dawkins, Christopher Hitchens, Susan Jacoby, and Bill Maher were among its most visible proponents. Concurrent with the luxuriant growth of atheist and secularist literature, sociologists began to flag the rapid growth of the "Nones," those Americans claiming to have no religious identification at all, a significant portion of whom openly identified as atheists and agnostics. That mounting survey data would provide the demographic underpinning for all the attention accorded the New Atheists in the decade-plus following 9/11.

Perhaps the New Atheists and the Nones offer intimations of secularism's belated advance in American culture. But, that story—the mainstreaming of open unbelief—is hardly the sum of the matter. Controversies over the standing of atheists in American public life have continued to boil as hotly as ever in the last two decades, especially in the courts. Justice Antonin Scalia's "atavistic" approach to the Establishment Clause set the tone, evident in his sharp attack on "the supposed principle of neutrality between religion and irreligion." Forcefully calling into question the wall-of-separation views that Black especially had advanced in the mid-twentieth century, Scalia defended a common-ground monotheism as the nation's shared inheritance. In a 2005 dissent supporting the display of the Ten Commandments in Kentucky courtrooms, he wrote: "With respect to public acknowledgment of religious belief, it is entirely clear from our Nation's historical practices that the Establishment Clause permits . . . the disregard of devout atheists." When it comes to conflicts between theists and atheists—whether over legislative prayers or the "under God" phrase in the Pledge of Allegiance—the notion of neutrality is, for those holding Scalia's conservative views, a mistaken constitutional interpretation. Both the nation's religious history and its original political framing are on the side of God against the ungodly. That reasoning has gathered substantial traction in recent years; certainly, the logic by which municipally sponsored Christian prayers were vindicated in *Town of Greece v. Galloway* (2014) offers a strong indication of its influence. At minimum, *Greece v.*

Galloway points to the continuing minority status of atheists and nonbelievers in a country that remains almost reflexively theistic and instinctively hostile to those who would challenge the country's God-invoking conventions.[41]

Jessica Ahlquist, a sixteen-year-old high school student in Rhode Island, quickly discovered the staying power of those animosities when, in 2011, she challenged a religious display on the wall of her school's auditorium. A banner, eight feet in height, exhibited a prayer invoking "Our Heavenly Father" for moral strength and character; it had been placed in the auditorium in 1963 as a direct reproach to the Supreme Court's rulings removing prayer and Bible reading from the public schools. Ahlquist, though baptized Catholic, had come to see herself as a convinced atheist and found the prayer exclusionary: "It seemed like it was saying, every time I saw it, 'You don't belong here.'" With the help of the ACLU, Ahlquist filed a lawsuit to have the prayer banner taken down. That legal challenge immediately made her the object of hate-filled threats and ugly cyberbullying to the point that a police escort was required to ensure her safety at school. One man railed against her on social media, "May you rot in Hell for your sin[,] atheist. You are a scourge to this country and un-American." When a federal judge decided the case in Ahlquist's favor in January 2012, her own state representative denounced her on talk radio as "an evil little thing." Enraging many in (and beyond) her local community, while simultaneously attracting the praise of secularists and religious liberals for her brave stance on behalf of minority rights, Ahlquist played out a cultural role by now deeply familiar. The village atheist was a lonely and despised freethinker, an abominated sinner in the midst of the country's endless revival meeting—and also a vaunted dissenter from the majoritarian demands for a Christian-favoring state. That twofold image of the village infidel—of stigmatized marginality and gutsy nonconformity—yet retains its allusive force for America's nonbelievers as they continue to make their way in a godly nation.[42]

NOTES

PREFACE

1. See William Cummings, "The One Group Still Excluded from the Boy Scouts—Atheists," *USA Today*, 29 July 2015, (accessed Aug. 26, 2015), http://www.religion news.com/2015/07/29/boy-scouts-atheists-race/; Hemant Mehta, "Boy Scouts of America Finally Ends Ban on Gay Leaders, but Atheists Are Still Not Welcome," 27 July 2015, (accessed Aug. 26, 2015), http://www.patheos.com/blogs/friendlyatheist/2015/07/27/ boy-scouts-of-america-finally-ends-ban-on-gay-leaders-but-atheists-are-still-not-wel come/.
2. Kimberly Winston, "Atheist Coalition Wants You to Know They Are 'Openly Secular,'" Religion News Service, 24 Sept. 2014, (accessed Aug. 21, 2015), http://www.religion news.com/2014/09/24/atheist-coalition-wants-know-openly-secular/; Pew Research Center, May 2014, "For 2016 Hopefuls, Washington Experience Could Do More Harm than Good," (accessed Aug. 26, 2015), http://www.people-press.org/files/legacy -pdf/5-19-14%20Presidential%20Traits%20Release.pdf; Tim Keown, "The Confession of Arian Foster," 6 Aug. 2015, (accessed Aug. 26, 2015), http://espn.go.com/nfl/story/_/ id/13369076/houston-texans-arian-foster-goes-public-not-believing-god; Cort McMurray, "Arian Foster Is an Atheist. So What," *Houston Chronicle*, 14 Aug. 2015, (accessed Aug. 26, 2015), http://www.houstonchronicle.com/local/gray-matters/article/Arian-Fos ter-is-an-atheist-So-what-6445048.php. There was, of course, some hostility toward Foster on social media, but most news coverage was civil, even ecumenical, in tone. See, for example, David Ramsey, "Arian Foster, Football's Atheist, Inspires Precious Conversations about Faith," *Colorado Springs Gazette*, 11 Aug. 2015, (accessed Aug. 27, 2015), http://gazette.com/ramsey-arian-foster-footballs-atheist-inspires-pre cious-conversations-about-faith/article/1557164.

INTRODUCTION:
THE MAKING OF THE VILLAGE ATHEIST

1. "Freedom of Unbelief Denied," *Truth Seeker*, 23 April 1904, 260. One of the orthographic quirks of the *Truth Seeker*, especially in its early years, was the editorial policy of shortening some words by leaving the "e" off the end (for example, "have" frequently became "hav" or "live" became "liv"). I have corrected those spellings in quoted material without bracketing the added "e" in order to make the text clearer and less cluttered. In article titles and cartoon captions, however, I have duly noted the peculiarity by using brackets.
2. Van Wyck Brooks, *The Ordeal of Mark Twain* (New York: Dutton, 1920), 64, 69, 184–85, 254. For a more nuanced examination of Twain's caution in publicly identifying with freethinkers, including the way he indicted himself for lacking candor on religious subjects, see Thomas D. Schwartz, "Mark Twain and Robert Ingersoll: The Freethought Connection," *American Literature* 48 (1976): 183–93. For a full-orbed discussion of Twain's religious views, including his attraction to the liberal Protestantism of his ministerial companion Joe Twichell, see Harold K. Bush, Jr.,

Mark Twain and the Spiritual Crisis of His Age (Tuscaloosa: University of Alabama Press, 2007).

3. Mark Twain, *Pudd'nhead Wilson*, ed. Malcolm Bradbury (1894; New York: Penguin, 2004), 52.

4. John Locke, *A Letter Concerning Toleration and Other Writings*, ed. Mark Goldie (Indianapolis: Liberty Fund, 2010), 52–53, 132. The Latin edition of Locke's letter had appeared in 1685, the better-known English translation in 1689. Locke's refusal of toleration for atheists has attracted much debate and commentary. For a particularly helpful parsing of its religious grounding, see Jeremy Waldron, *God, Locke, and Equality: Christian Foundations in John Locke's Political Thought* (Cambridge: Cambridge University Press, 2002), 217–43. On the Aikenhead case, see Michael Hunter, "'Aikenhead the Atheist': The Context and Consequences of Articulate Irreligion in the Late Seventeenth Century," in Michael Hunter and David Wootton, eds., *Atheism from the Reformation to the Enlightenment* (Oxford: Clarendon Press, 1992), 221–54.

5. See Susan Juster, "Heretics, Blasphemers, and Sabbath Breakers: The Prosecution of Religious Crime in Early America," in Chris Beneke and Christopher S. Grenda, eds., *The First Prejudice: Religious Tolerance and Intolerance in Early America* (Philadelphia: University of Pennsylvania Press, 2011), 122–42 (with Sawser case discussed on pp. 133–34).

6. David Thomas Konig, ed., *Plymouth Court Records, 1686–1859*, 16 vols. (Wilmington, DE: Glazier, 1978–1981), 3: 219. See also the repeated judicial charges to protect public morals from such irreligious offenses in Stanton D. Krauss, ed., *Gentlemen of the Grand Jury: The Surviving Grand Jury Charges from Colonial, State, and Lower Federal Courts before 1801*, 2 vols. (Durham: Carolina Academic Press, 2012), 1: 315–18, 341–43, 525–28.

7. Philip Dormer Stanhope, Earl of Chesterfield, *The Life of the Late Earl of Chesterfield; or, The Man of the World* (Philadelphia: Sparhawk, 1775), 270–71.

8. Thomas Paine, *The Age of Reason*, ed. Philip S. Foner (1794; Secaucus, NJ: Citadel, 1998), 50–51. For a recent examination of Paine's shifting reputation through the withering assault on his irreligion, see Amanda Porterfield, *Conceived in Doubt: Religion and Politics in the New American Nation* (Chicago: University of Chicago Press, 2012), 18–30, 46–47.

9. Alexis de Tocqueville, *Democracy in America*, 2 vols., trans. Henry Reeve and ed. Phillips Bradley (New York: Vintage, 1945), 1: 314–16, 324; *New-Hampshire Gazette* (Portsmouth, NH), 25 March 1834, 4. On the persistent suspicion that infidels could not be trustworthy citizens, see Christopher Grasso, "The Boundaries of Toleration and Tolerance: Religious Infidelity in the Early American Republic," in Beneke and Grenda, eds., *First Prejudice*, 286–302; Albert Post, *Popular Freethought in America, 1825–1850* (New York: Columbia University Press, 1943), 211–15. On how the witness competency issue unfolded in the new republic, see Ronald P. Formisano and Stephen Pickering, "The Christian Nation Debate and Witness Competency," *Journal of the Early Republic* 29 (2009): 219–48.

10. *Middlesex Gazette* (Middletown, CT), 11 Nov. 1826, 2; *American Mercury* (Hartford, CT), 29 Aug. 1826, 3; *American Mercury* (Hartford, CT), 15 Sept. 1829, 2; *Norwich Courier* (Norwich, CT), 30 June 1830, 1; *Connecticut Courant* (Hartford, CT), 6 June 1836, 2. The state constitutions are compiled in Benjamin Perley Poore, *The Federal and State Constitutions, Colonial Charters, and Other Organic Laws of the United States*, 2 vols. (Washington, DC: Government Printing Office, 1878). Much of the

debate about irreligious expression centered on what counted as civil intellectual disagreement with Christianity and what amounted to gross infidelity dangerous to public order and civic virtue. On this point, see Eric R. Schlereth, *An Age of Infidels: The Politics of Religious Controversy in the Early United States* (Philadelphia: University of Pennsylvania Press, 2013), esp. pp. 31–44, 234–35.

11. Thomas Jefferson, *The Autobiography of Thomas Jefferson, 1743–1790*, ed. Paul Leicester Ford (Philadelphia: University of Pennsylvania Press, 2005), 71; John Locke, *A Letter Concerning Toleration* (Windsor, VT: Spooner, 1788), with omission at p. 57.

12. Thomas Jefferson, *Notes on the State of Virginia* (Philadelphia: Carey, 1794), 231.

13. John Mitchell Mason, *The Voice of Warning, to Christians, on the Ensuing Election of a President of the United States* (New York: Hopkins, 1800), 19.

14. "The Legal Oppression of Infidels, &c.; No. VI," *Boston Investigator,* 21 Oct. 1857, n.p. For a Jeffersonian Baptist use of the same argument, see John Leland, *The Rights of Conscience Inalienable, and Therefore Religious Opinions Not Cognizable by Law* (New London, CT: Green, 1791), 13.

15. "Mrs. Rose and the *Bangor Mercury*," *Boston Investigator*, 12 Dec. 1855, n.p.; "Mrs. Rose and the *Bangor Mercury*," *Boston Investigator*, 19 Dec. 1855, n.p.; W. B., "A Letter from Bangor," *Boston Investigator*, 26 Dec. 1855, n.p.; Ernestine L. Rose, "A Defence of Atheism," *Boston Investigator*, 8 May 1861, 18.

16. "Atheism," *Boston Investigator*, 14 Nov. 1860, 237; Robert Baird, *Religion in America; or, An Account of the Origin, Progress, Relation to the State, and Present Condition of the Evangelical Churches in the United States* (New York: Harper and Brothers, 1844), 125, 318. Granting infidels the right to assemble and express their opinions, Baird nonetheless considered existing legal restraints on blasphemy, profane swearing, and the court testimony of atheists as still fully warranted. Orestes Brownson, a pilgrim himself out of skepticism into Roman Catholicism, was among those who encouraged Christians to treat infidels with civility as honest inquirers rather than social pariahs. See Christopher Grasso, "Skepticism and American Faith: Infidels, Converts, and Religious Doubt in the Early Nineteenth Century," *Journal of the Early Republic* 22 (2002): 491.

17. "The Bible Discussion," *Boston Investigator*, 29 June 1853, n.p.; "The Paine Celebration," *Boston Investigator*, 16 Feb. 1859, n.p; Ida Husted Harper, *The Life and Work of Susan B. Anthony, Including Public Addresses, Her Own Letters, and Many from Her Contemporaries during Fifty Years*, 2 vols. (Indianapolis: Hollenbeck Press, 1898), 1: 121; 2: 631, 853–54. Much of Rose's work has been expertly anthologized in Paula Doress-Worters, ed., *Mistress of Herself: Speeches and Letters of Ernestine Rose, Early Women's Rights Leader* (New York: Feminist Press of the City University of New York, 2008). The Massachusetts debate over allowing atheists to testify was particularly marked in the 1850s, but those who wanted to see the test abandoned lost in their efforts to get legislation passed. See "Atheists, as Witnesses," *Boston Investigator,* 4 March 1857, n.p.; "The Testimony of Atheists," *Boston Investigator*, 29 June 1859, 77. The result was the same the previous decade in Maine. See "Competency of Atheists as Witnesses," *Boston Investigator*, 12 Aug. 1846, n.p. On the divisions between freethinkers and Christians in the women's rights movement, see especially Kathi Kern, *Mrs. Stanton's Bible* (Ithaca: Cornell University Press, 2001), 63–68, 195–98.

18. "The Infidel Convention," *Boston Investigator*, 7 Nov. 1860, 226–27. On deist clubs and publishing activities in the early republic and the alarm that such infidelity

generated among Protestants, see especially Schlereth, *Age of Infidels*. The two "authorized" lecturers noted in 1860 were Thomas Curtis and Theodore R. Kinget. See "Commission to Lecture," *Boston Investigator*, 22 Feb. 1860, 351; "Commission to Lecture," *Boston Investigator*, 8 Aug. 1860, 127.

19. "Colonel Ingersoll's Lecture," *Sacramento Daily Union*, 5 June 1877, clipping in "The Papers of Robert Green Ingersoll," microfilm reel 26, Manuscript Division, Library of Congress, Washington, DC. Ingersoll has received generous biographical attention, exemplified most recently by Susan Jacoby, *The Great Agnostic: Robert Ingersoll and American Freethought* (New Haven: Yale University Press, 2013).

20. *Minutes of the Infidel Convention, Held in the City of Philadelphia, September 7th & 8th, 1857* (Philadelphia: n.p., 1857), 13–15, 29–32; "Minutes of the Proceedings of the Infidel Convention," *Boston Investigator*, 26 Oct. 1859, 210; John R. Kelso, "In Union There Is Strength," *Truth Seeker*, 4 Oct. 1884, 636; George Seibel, "Atheism Succumbs to Doubt," *American Mercury* 30 (1933): 428. These small infidel conventions, promoted in the pages of the *Boston Investigator*, began the previous decade, the first one assembling in New York City in May 1845; already the question of what to call themselves was ripe for discussion: "infidel," "materialist," "liberal," "rationalist," "unbeliever," "naturalist," and "universal philanthropist," each was mentioned, but the group stuck with "infidel." See "Infidel Convention," *Boston Investigator*, 14 May 1845, n.p.; "Infidel Convention (Continued)," *Boston Investigator*, 21 May 1845, n.p.

21. "Is a Secularist an Atheist?" *Boston Investigator*, 4 Jan. 1882, 5. The correspondent had noticed that certain London freethinkers continued to lift up the name "secularist" over "atheist." The Boston paper liked the latter term just fine—"atheist" was seen as the more decisive appellation—but the journal saw no reason not to accept "secularist" as well. American freethinkers who expressed a preference for the secularist designation often did so because they thought the strict separation of church and state was the defining issue; those who preferred "liberal" usually considered it the more comprehensive term with a clearer reach beyond the domains of law and politics. See, for example, Samuel P. Putnam's parsing of the terms in "'Secular' or 'Liberal'—Which?" *Boston Investigator*, 22 Aug. 1888, 3. These naming issues very much persist in contemporary discussions of secularism. Jacques Berlinerblau, for example, is at pains to define secularism as a political philosophy and divide it from the anti-metaphysical certitude of the New Atheists. See Jacques Berlinerblau, *How to Be Secular: A Call to Arms for Religious Freedom* (Boston: Houghton Mifflin Harcourt, 2012), esp. pp. 53–68.

22. "Crabbe's *Poems*," *Monthly Review; or, Literary Journal Enlarged* 56 (1808): 176; George Crabbe, *Poems* (New York: Innskeep and Bradford, 1808), 57–58; Henry A. Beers, *An Outline Sketch of American Literature* (New York: Chautauqua Press, 1887), 65. See also Henry A. Beers, *Initial Studies in American Letters* (New York: Chautauqua Press, 1891), 52–53.

23. Ralph Waldo Emerson, "The Divinity School Address" (1838), in David M. Robinson, ed., *The Spiritual Emerson: Essential Writings* (Boston: Beacon, 2003), 76; William Channing Gannett, "The Present Constructive Tendencies in Religion," *Proceedings at the Eighth Annual Meeting of the Free Religious Association* (Boston: Cochrane and Sampson, 1875), 20–21; Minot J. Savage, "Who Are Infidels?" *Index*, 6 Sept. 1877, 422–23; Minot J. Savage, "The Village 'Infidel,'" in his *Poems* (Boston: Ellis, 1882), 134–36; Harry Leon Wilson, *The Seeker* (New York: Doubleday, Page, and Co., 1904), xvi, 5, 35.

24. Edgar Lee Masters, *Spoon River Anthology* (New York: Macmillan, 1916), 250; Herbert S. Bigelow, *The Religion of Revolution* (Cincinnati: Daniel Kiefer, 1916), 37–40;

Twain's letter cited in Eva Ingersoll Wakefield, ed., *The Letters of Robert G. Ingersoll* (New York: Philosophical Library, 1951), 64; Brooks, *Ordeal*, 184, 236, 251.

25. Seibel, "Atheism Succumbs to Doubt," 424–31; George Seibel, "There Were Giants in Those Days," *Truth Seeker*, 1 Sept. 1923, 586–87.

26. For Emanuel Haldeman-Julius's spirited embrace of the "village atheist" as a type in preference to "the cultured atmosphere of universities" with its highbrow critics, see his Little Blue Book entitled *The Age-Old Follies of Man* (Girard, KS: Haldeman-Julius, 1930), 40–63. Lewis's *Elmer Gantry* in its harsh anti-Fundamentalism paints a chilling picture of the violent dangers that atheists and infidels faced from witch-hunting Christians of the 1920s. One suspected atheist, the lapsed liberal Protestant minister Frank Shallard, is brutally beaten by vigilantes when he takes on anti-evolutionists in one town. See Sinclair Lewis, *Elmer Gantry*, ed. Jason Stevens (1927; New York: Signet, 2007), 419–25. In *Babbitt* Lewis stresses the banal conventionality of the title character's Presbyterian churchgoing; his religious mores are part and parcel of the mindless conformity Lewis was satirizing; a village atheist could only provide a needed jolt to such hackneyed orthodoxy. See Sinclair Lewis, *Babbitt* (New York: Collier, 1922), 204–207.

27. "Come In, Gents," *Time*, 1 March 1943, 78.

28. The still classic studies in this regard are Michael J. Buckley, *At the Origins of Modern Atheism* (New Haven: Yale University Press, 1987), and James Turner, *Without God, Without Creed: The Origins of Unbelief in America* (Baltimore: Johns Hopkins University Press, 1985). Turner crisply remarks on Protestant Christianity's primary accountability for its own atheistic negation: if anyone were "to be arraigned for deicide," it was "not the godless Robert Ingersoll but the godly Beecher family" (p. xiii). With France as his focus, Buckley is instead concerned with the gradual bankruptcy of Catholic theology. Turner and Buckley are usefully joined to Charles Taylor's more recent *A Secular Age* (Cambridge, MA: Harvard University Press, 2007). Offering a philosophical diagnosis of the rise of "exclusive humanism" as an all-encompassing "social imaginary" over the last half millennium—the ways in which "secularity" comes to define European modernity against its medieval Catholic past—Taylor flies over the landscape at a very high altitude. Safe to say, the ground-level world of the village atheist does not come into focus, all the more because the fate of Christian belief remains both the point of departure and the nucleus of concern. For all the attention Taylor's work has received, it is well worth returning to Turner and Buckley for acute intellectual histories addressing the question: "How did the practically universal assumption of God disappear?" (Turner, p. xiii). For an earlier study that made the Protestant uses of freethought the historical measure of infidelity's consequence, see Martin Marty, *The Infidel: Freethought and American Religion* (Cleveland, OH: World Publishing, 1961). That religious index—viewing atheists as primarily useful figments of the American Protestant imagination—remains in play in more recent historiography. See Charles Mathewes and Christopher McKnight Nichols, eds., *Prophesies of Godlessness: Predictions of America's Imminent Secularization from the Puritans to the Present Day* (New York: Oxford University Press, 2008). For a reworking of the secularization literature that shifts attention away from Christian sources of unbelief to antireligious activism, particularly among intellectuals who promoted secularism for their own ends and purposes, see Christian Smith, ed., *The Secular Revolution: Power, Interests, and Conflict in the Secularization of American Public Life* (Berkeley: University of California Press, 2003), esp. Smith's "Introduction," 19–20, 32–53. For a

heroic rendering of the nation's secularist insurgents, see Susan Jacoby, *Freethinkers: A History of American Secularism* (New York: Henry Holt, 2004). While Jacoby offered a call to action for atheists, agnostics, and nonbelievers amid George W. Bush's faith-imbued presidency, she also provided an engaging survey of American freethought, a tradition that had been largely neglected in the historiography since a vital handful of works a half-century and more earlier. See Stow Persons, *Free Religion: An American Faith* (New Haven: Yale University Press, 1947); Post, *Popular Freethought*; Herbert M. Morais, *Deism in Eighteenth-Century America* (New York: Columbia University Press, 1934); and Sidney Warren, *American Freethought, 1860–1914* (New York: Columbia University Press, 1943). In recent years that historical neglect has given way to a more robust engagement, as evidenced by the already cited works of Christopher Grasso, Amanda Porterfield, and Eric Schlereth. Beyond the historical literature, the study of secularism has also increased substantially through the attention paid to it by anthropologists and critical theorists, notably from the generative influence of Talal Asad's *Formations of the Secular: Christianity, Islam, Modernity* (Stanford: Stanford University Press, 2003). Asad's discursive analysis of secularism and religion as embedded categories, the structures of knowledge and power that their underlying formations contain, has been extended to the study of American religion and literature as well, often in order to reveal the hidden ideological congruence of Protestantism and secularism. See especially John Lardas Modern, *Secularism in Antebellum America* (Chicago: University of Chicago Press, 2011), and Tracy Fessenden, *Culture and Redemption: Religion, the Secular, and American Literature* (Princeton: Princeton University Press, 2007).

29. Barry A. Kosmin and Ariela Keysar, *American Nones: The Profile of the No Religion Population: A Report Based on the American Religious Identification Survey 2008* (Hartford: ISSSC, 2009); "'Nones' on the Rise," Pew Research Center, 9 Oct. 2012, (accessed Feb. 4, 2014), http://www.pewforum.org/2012/10/09/nones-on-the-rise/; "America's Changing Religious Landscape," Pew Research Center, (accessed May 20, 2015), http://www.pewforum.org/2015/05/12/americas-changing-religious-landscape/.

30. "Barack Obama's Inaugural Address," *New York Times,* 20 Jan. 2009, (accessed Feb. 4, 2014), http://www.nytimes.com/2009/01/20/us/politics/20text-obama.html.

31. *Zorach v. Clauson*, 343 US 306 (1952). Scalia's disregard for "devout atheists" was expressed with particular clarity in his dissenting opinion in *McCreary County v. American Civil Liberties Union of Ky.*, 545 US 844 (2005), a case involving public display of the Ten Commandments. These larger church-state conflicts are examined at some length in the epilogue.

32. Penny Edgell, Joseph Gerteis, and Douglas Hartmann, "Atheists as 'Other': Moral Boundaries and Cultural Membership in American Society," *American Sociological Review* 71 (2006): 218; Ryan T. Cragun, Barry Kosmin, Ariela Keysar, Joseph H. Hammer, and Michael Nielsen, "On the Receiving End: Discrimination toward the Non-Religious in the United States," *Journal of Contemporary Religion* 27 (2012): 114–15. A direct extension of the 2006 study is in the works; drawn from a 2014 survey, it suggests that "anti-atheist sentiment" has remained "strong and persistent" over the last decade despite the growing visibility of the New Atheists and the Nones; disapproval of atheists remains at roughly the same level as in the prior study, though Muslims have now edged ahead as the most distrusted group. See Penny Edgell, Douglas Hartmann, Evan Stewart, and Joseph Gerteis, "Atheists and Other Cultural Outsiders: Symbolic Boundaries and the Non-Religious in the United States," Working Paper, Boundaries in the American Mosaic Project, Sociology De-

partment, University of Minnesota. See also Will M. Gervais, Azim F. Shariff, and Ara Norenzayan, "Do You Believe in Atheists? Distrust Is Central to Anti-Atheist Prejudice," *Journal of Personality and Social Psychology* 101 (2011): 1189–1206. Labeling makes a big difference. When sociologists conduct polling for attitudes toward the "nonreligious" rather than toward "atheists" and "agnostics," they find significantly higher levels of social acceptance, though social trust still skews toward the "religious" over the "nonreligious." See Robert D. Putnam and David E. Campbell, *American Grace: How Religion Divides and Unites Us* (New York: Simon and Schuster, 2010), 460–61, 506–508.

33. David A. Hollinger is especially shrewd at capturing the two-sidedness of the Christianization-secularization question, arguing that attention to how de-Christianization has been furthered must be paired with consideration of how Christianity has maintained such a tenacious hold on American culture. See particularly David A. Hollinger, *Science, Jews, and Secular Culture: Studies in Mid-Twentieth-Century American Intellectual History* (Princeton: Princeton University Press, 1996), 17, 21.

34. H. K. Carroll, *The Religious Forces of the United States Enumerated, Classified, and Described on the Basis of the Government Census of 1890* (New York: Christian Literature Co., 1893), xxxiv–xxxvi. When Carroll offered a revised edition of this work in 1912 with updated data, the nonreligious population had risen to just over 10 percent, but his Protestant optimism remained the same. Rates of religious disaffection were uneven; in some areas and enclaves, 8–10 percent would have been a severe underestimation. In Chicago, for example, Bruce C. Nelson puts the number of those "indifferent or hostile to religion" as "more than a third" in the 1880s; among the city's Czech population, the irreligious actually outnumbered the religious at "a ratio of six-to-one." See Bruce C. Nelson, "Revival and Upheaval: Religion, Irreligion, and Chicago's Working Class in 1886," *Journal of Social History* 25 (1991): 233–35, 240. For an international overview of recent statistics on atheism and nonbelief, see Phil Zuckerman, "Atheism: Contemporary Numbers and Patterns," in Michael Martin, ed., *The Cambridge Companion to Atheism* (Cambridge: Cambridge University Press, 2007), 47–65. For a long-range perspective on religious adherence rates in the United States—one that charts an upward trajectory from the Revolution through the 1950s—see Roger Finke and Rodney Stark, *The Churching of America, 1776–1990: Winners and Losers in Our Religious Economy* (New Brunswick, NJ: Rutgers University Press, 1992). For another examination of the demographics of freethinkers, see Evelyn A. Kirkley, *Rational Mothers and Infidel Gentlemen: Gender and American Atheism, 1865–1915* (Syracuse: Syracuse University Press, 2000), 16–19.

35. O. B. Frothingham, *Attitudes of Unbelief* (New York: G. P. Putnam's Sons, 1878), 185–86; O. B. Frothingham, *Beliefs of the Unbelievers and Other Discourses* (New York: G. P. Putnam's Sons, 1876).

36. W.H.H. to Editor, *Boston Investigator*, 24 May 1854, n.p.

37. Frank Swancara, *Have We Religious Freedom?* (Girard, KS: Haldeman Julius Publications, n.d.), 6.

CHAPTER 1. THE SECULAR PILGRIM;
OR, THE HERE WITHOUT THE HEREAFTER

1. "Samuel P. Putnam," *Freethinkers' Magazine* 12 (1894): 130–33; Samuel P. Putnam, *My Religious Experience* (New York: Truth Seeker Co., 1891), 6–7. The former portrait

was written in the third person, but Putnam himself had drafted this "life sketch." See the editorial note in H. L. Green, "Samuel P. Putnam—May L. Collins—Obituary Notices—A Discordant Voice," *Free Thought Magazine* 15 (1897): 48. The best biographical sketch is in *Union and Federation: Memorial Volume to Samuel P. Putnam and May L. Collins* (New York: Truth Seeker Co., 1897), 67–77. It was prepared by Putnam's long-time collaborator George E. Macdonald. The sketch appeared anonymously, but Macdonald noted his authorship of it in George E. Macdonald, *Fifty Years of Freethought*, 2 vols. (New York: Truth Seeker Co., 1929), 1: 295.

2. Putnam, *My Religious Experience*, 8, 20; "Samuel P. Putnam," 133; Samuel P. Putnam, "News and Notes," *Truth Seeker*, 17 Sept. 1887, 596; Samuel P. Putnam, "News and Notes," *Truth Seeker*, 12 June 1886, 372. Putnam dubbed himself "the Secular Pilgrim" in accounts of his lecture tours, and by the end of his life it was his commonly recognized moniker. See *Memorial Volume*, 106; "From the 'Investigator,'" *Truth Seeker*, 26 Dec. 1896, 828; Macdonald, *Fifty Years*, 1: 516.

3. Putnam, *My Religious Experience*, 6.

4. Samuel P. Putnam, "News and Notes," *Truth Seeker*, 7 Aug. 1886, 501.

5. Putnam, *My Religious Experience*, 6–8.

6. Putnam, *My Religious Experience*, 8–11.

7. Putnam, *My Religious Experience*, 9–15; "Samuel P. Putnam," 131.

8. Putnam, *My Religious Experience*, 14–15.

9. Putnam, *My Religious Experience*, 16–18. Brief portraits of Putnam's war service can be found in Hyland C. Kirk, *Heavy Guns and Light: A History of the Fourth New York Heavy Artillery* (New York: Dillingham, 1890), 652; *Memorial Volume*, 68–69.

10. Putnam, *My Religious Experience*, 19–24.

11. Putnam, *My Religious Experience*, 21, 32–35.

12. Putnam, *My Religious Experience*, 37–39.

13. Putnam, *My Religious Experience*, 39–41. Bushnell, a lionized American theologian, has been amply studied. I have relied here especially on E. Brooks Holifield's summary assessment in *Theology in America: Christian Thought from the Age of the Puritans to the Civil War* (New Haven: Yale University Press, 2003), 452–66.

14. Putnam, *My Religious Experience*, 41–42.

15. Putnam, *My Religious Experience*, 43, 46, 77.

16. Putnam, *My Religious Experience*, 47–51.

17. Putnam, *My Religious Experience*, 51–54. For Putnam's cultivation of his Unitarian churchmanship and his ties to Bellows, see Samuel P. Putnam, "The Problem of Life," *Liberal Christian*, 9 Nov. 1872, 1; Samuel P. Putnam, "The Divinity of Christ," *Liberal Christian*, 8 Feb. 1873, 1; Samuel P. Putnam, "How to Find a Parish," *Liberal Christian*, 1 March 1873, 1; Samuel P. Putnam, "The Skepticism of Orthodoxy," *Liberal Christian*, 29 March 1873, 1; Samuel P. Putnam, "Preaching Christ," *Liberal Christian*, 24 May 1873, 1; Samuel P. Putnam, "The Spirit of the Unitarian Missionary," *Liberal Christian*, 12 July 1873, 1; Samuel P. Putnam, "The Purpose and Method of Liberal Christianity," *Liberal Christian*, 27 Feb. 1875, 4.

18. Putnam, *My Religious Experience*, 53–54; "Faith the Ground of Theism," *Index*, 11 Sept. 1873, 351–52. See also S. P. Putnam, "A Plea for Faith as the Foundation of Theism," *Index*, 15 Jan. 1874, 29; S. P. Putnam, "The Ground of Theism: A Dialogue," *Index*, 7 May 1874, 224; S. P. Putnam, "The 'Scientific Method' Not the Sole Authority in Religion," *Index*, 17 May 1877, 236 (with Abbot's reply on p. 235); S. P. Putnam, "Feeling a Truth-Discoverer," *Index*, 26 July 1877, 356 (with Abbot's reply on p. 354); S. P. Putnam, "The Intellect and Sentiment," *Index*, 15 Nov. 1877, 547 (with Abbot's

reply on p. 546). On the rise of the Free Religious Association and Abbot's band of post-Unitarians, see Stow Persons, *Free Religion: An American Faith* (New Haven: Yale University Press, 1947).

19. "Organize!" *Index*, 4 Jan. 1873, 1. For Putnam's investment in the Nine Demands, see S. P. Putnam, "A Protest, with an Addition," *Index*, 4 Feb. 1875, 57; S. P. Putnam, "The Catholic Conspiracy," *Index*, 26 Aug. 1875, 404; S. P. Putnam, "The Function of Government," *Index*, 11 Nov. 1875, 530. For the National Liberal League membership figure, see "National Liberal League," *Boston Investigator*, 2 Sept. 1885, 3. For Abbot's biography, including an account of his secularist campaign, see Sydney Ahlstrom and Robert Bruce Mullin, *The Scientific Theist: A Life of Francis Ellingwood Abbot* (Macon, GA: Mercer University Press, 1987), esp. pp. 101–111. For the larger legal context of Abbot's secularist program, see Philip Hamburger, *Separation of Church and State* (Cambridge, MA: Harvard University Press, 2002), 287–338.

20. Putnam, *My Religious Experience*, 57–59; "Radical Lectures," *Index*, 7 Jan. 1875, 12; "Glimpses," *Index*, 27 May 1875, 241; Samuel P. Putnam, "Charles Bright," *Boston Investigator*, 14 June 1882, 6; "Notes and Comments," *Index*, 10 June 1875, 26. For Putnam's speech at the Free Religious Association, see *Proceedings at the Eighth Annual Meeting of the Free Religious Association, Held in Boston, May 27 and 28, 1875* (Boston: Cochrane and Sampson, 1875), 67–72. For his part, Bellows expressed disappointment over Putnam's decision to leave the Unitarian ministry but honored his sincerity and integrity, so much so that it was clear he would be happy to have him back. See "Signs of the Times," *Liberal Christian*, 12 June 1875, 1. For some indication of Putnam's anguish over whether to leave the ministry or not, see S. P. Putnam, "The Real Question," *Index*, 17 Dec. 1874, 608.

21. "The Hand of Welcome," *Truth Seeker*, 15 June 1875, 8; S. P. Putnam, "Manliness and Godliness," *Truth Seeker*, 1 Oct. 1875, 3; "A Letter from S. P. Putnam," *Truth Seeker*, 15 Oct. 1875, 13. Bennett also issued at this time one of Putnam's poems as a *Truth Seeker* tract under the title *The True Saint*, which extolled the mundane ethical action of a humble minstrel over the "useless life" of an intensely pious hermit. See the advertisement in *Truth Seeker*, 1 Nov. 1875, 16. It was then bundled into a collection of *Truth Seeker Tracts* (New York: Bennett, 1876), tract number 20.

22. "Rev. Mr. S. P. Putnam," *Boston Investigator*, 28 June 1876, 4; Putnam, *My Religious Experience*, 59–66; S. P. Putnam, "Living for Humanity," *Truth Seeker*, 1 Aug. 1875, 3.

23. Putnam, *My Religious Experience*, 70–72. Poetry became a popular medium for Putnam in the mid-1870s. In *My Religious Experience* he cited a number of his own poems from the period as indicative of his spiritual yearnings at this point in his life.

24. Putnam, *My Religious Experience*, 75, 80–84.

25. Putnam, *My Religious Experience*, 83; "A Case in Point," *Index*, 27 March 1879, 150. For one of the very few sources that makes mention of his family (including his children's names and birth dates), see Horace Stuart Cummings, *Dartmouth College: Sketches of the Class of 1862* (Washington, DC: Rothrock, 1884), 106–107. Macdonald's sketch in the *Memorial Volume* also mentioned Putnam's marriage but put it one year earlier (1867); it acknowledged the two children as well but skated over the couple's separation as a result of "religious and temperamental differences" (p. 70). A ministerial committee investigating the scandal cleared Putnam's name of the more sensational rumors about his womanizing—"grosser immoralities"—and stressed that his guilt consisted in his repeatedly visiting one young woman in his flock and announcing his desire that they "might always live together." See "Case in Point,"

150. For the more scandalous version of Putnam's "astounding rascalities" and multiple "inamoratas," see the untitled report in *New Hampshire Sentinel* (Keene, NH), 16 Jan. 1879, 2.

26. "A Statement by S. P. Putnam," *Index*, 24 April 1879, 201; "Case in Point," 150–51; "A Retrograde Ideal," *Index*, 24 April 1879, 198. Putnam made his case for broadly extending (and enacting) the right of private conscience "in all the affairs of life" in Samuel P. Putnam, "The Two Fundamental Ideas of the New Religious Movement," *Truth Seeker*, 15 March 1879, 166.

27. "Case in Point," 150–51; Putnam, "Two Fundamental Ideas," 166.

28. At least one of Putnam's sermons in Vincennes survives (from December 1879), and it suggests that he was still very much entwined with his ministerial role and its required theistic professions, despite the thorough-going atheistic awakening at the end of his Northfield pastorate that he described in *My Religious Experience*. See Samuel P. Putnam, *The Old and the New* (Vincennes, IN: Vincennes Commercial Press, 1879). A critical report on that sermon, making light of Putnam's lingering theism, appeared in the *Boston Investigator*, 14 Jan. 1880, 4. It urged Putnam to turn to the bigger question of whether God exists at all and to find his way toward a more forthright form of unbelief. Another excerpt from one of his sermons at this time, urging the deconsecration of marriage and the promotion of contraceptives, appeared as "Marriage, Prevention of Conception, Etc.," *Physiologist and Family Physician* 3 (Sept. 1880): 21. The date and place of the sermon were unreported, but it has the tenor of his Northfield revolt.

29. "Mr. Putnam's Lectures," *Truth Seeker*, 10 July 1880, 442; George E. Macdonald, "Memories of Putnam," *Truth Seeker*, 30 Jan. 1897, 69; Putnam, *My Religious Experience*, 85–87; "Letters from Friends," *Truth Seeker*, 26 Nov. 1881, 764; "Stalwart Liberalism," *Truth Seeker*, 18 Nov. 1882, 727.

30. Putnam, *My Religious Experience*, 85–90; "A Farewell Meeting," *Truth Seeker*, 30 July 1881, 484; "The Banquet Reception—Concluded," *Truth Seeker*, 26 Aug. 1882, 536; "First Boston Ethical Society," *Boston Investigator*, 9 May 1883, 6; S. P. Putnam, "Charles Watts's Lectures," *Boston Investigator*, 28 May 1883, 3.

31. Putnam, *My Religious Experience*, 92–93; "Talmage and Ingersoll," *New York Times*, 23 Jan. 1882, 2; "Col. R. G. Ingersoll's Lecture in New York," *Boston Investigator*, 19 April 1882, 6; "Col. Ingersoll's Lectures," *Boston Investigator*, 3 May 1882, 6; "The Great Infidels," *Boston Investigator*, 11 May 1881, 3. Meeting Ingersoll could have happened early in Putnam's relocation to New York, but he did not position it there in his narrative. The encounter is mentioned only after several other incidents, but Putnam knew Ingersoll's work already and its influence on him became increasingly evident from 1880 on. See Samuel P. Putnam, "Atheism and Morality," *Boston Investigator*, 9 June 1880, 1.

32. Putnam, *My Religious Experience*, 92–93, 95–96, 99. For further exposition of his atheistic turn after 1880, see Samuel P. Putnam, *The Problem of the Universe, and Its Scientific Solution* (New York: Truth Seeker Co., [1883]), esp. pp. 35–39.

33. Samuel P. Putnam, *Ingersoll and Jesus* (New York: Truth Seeker Co., [1882]), 4–10. The poem had first appeared in *Truth Seeker*, 18 Feb. 1882, 103.

34. "The Golden Throne," *Truth Seeker*, 24 March 1883, 190. Putnam produced another book of poetry in these years. See Samuel P. Putnam, *Why Don't He Lend a Hand? And Other Agnostic Poems* (New York: Truth Seeker Co., [1885]).

35. Samuel P. Putnam, *Golden Throne: A Romance* (Boston: Chainey, [1883]), 47, 55–62; Samuel P. Putnam, *Waifs and Wanderings: A Novel* (New York: Truth Seeker

Co., 1884), 174–77. Putnam's experience as a captain of an African-American infantry unit during the war, along with his abolitionist background, informed his sympathetic portrait of Columbus as a protagonist in *Waifs and Wanderings*. Putnam makes the ambiguous racial identity of the fair-skinned Amy part of his twisting plot. At the very end of the novel she turns out to have been born to white parents but to have landed in slavery via a shipwreck; thus, Putnam deprived his narrative at the last moment of an African-American atheist and wound up underlining the whiteness of his secularist cause. For more on the complex racial politics of postbellum freethought, see chapter 2.

36. Samuel P. Putnam, *400 Years of Freethought* (New York: Truth Seeker Co., 1894), 788–89; "The Eighth Annual Congress," *Truth Seeker*, 20 Sept. 1884, 596; Samuel P. Putnam, "News and Notes," *Truth Seeker*, 7 Aug. 1886, 501; "Watts and Putnam's Engagements," *Truth Seeker*, 10 Jan. 1885, 25; "Messrs. Watts and Putnam," *Boston Investigator*, 22 April 1885, 6; Samuel P. Putnam, "News and Notes from the Lecture Field," *Boston Investigator*, 20 May 1885, 3.

37. Putnam, *400 Years*, 554–55, 788–89; *Memorial Volume*, 73–76; Samuel P. Putnam, "To the Members of the Secular Union," *Boston Investigator*, 15 Aug. 1888, 3; Samuel P. Putnam, "News and Notes," *Truth Seeker*, 17 Sept. 1892, 597; John R. Charlesworth, "The Freethought Federation of America," *Truth Seeker*, 17 Sept. 1892, 598; Samuel P. Putnam, "Liberal Political Organization," *Truth Seeker*, 17 Sept. 1892, 599–000; Samuel P. Putnam, "The Situation at Washington," *Boston Investigator*, 4 Jan. 1893, 2; Samuel P. Putnam, "The Constitution and Holy Days and Holidays," *Boston Investigator*, 25 Jan. 1893, 3; Samuel P. Putnam, "The Museums in the Park," *Truth Seeker*, 13 March 1886, 162–64.

38. Samuel P. Putnam, *Religion a Curse, Religion a Disease, Religion a Lie* (New York: Truth Seeker Co., 1893), 23, 35, 38–44; Putnam, *My Religious Experience*, 99–101.

39. S. P. Putnam, "Four Hundred Years of Freethought," *Boston Investigator*, 21 April 1894, 2.

40. Putnam, *400 Years*, 15, 683–85.

41. "Book Reviews," *Freethinkers' Magazine* 12 (1894): 646–47; "Book Notice," *Boston Investigator*, 10 Nov. 1894, 6. On Putnam's feuding with York over lecture style, see "The Burlesque Method," *Freethought*, 4 Aug. 1888, 373–75. For an admiring portrait of York's career, see F. E. Sturgis, "Life-Sketch of Dr. York," *Humanitarian Review* 4 (1906): 352–57. On Rawson, see Roderick Bradford, *D. M. Bennett: The Truth Seeker* (Amherst, NY: Prometheus, 2006), 133–35, 315–17; Susan Nance, *How the Arabian Nights Inspired the American Dream, 1790–1935* (Chapel Hill: University of North Carolina Press, 2009), 92–97; John Patrick Deveney, "Nobles of the Secret Mosque: Albert L. Rawson, Abd al-Kader, George H. Felt, and the Mystic Shrine," *Theosophical History* 8 (2002): 250–61. Bennett himself had spiritualist and theosophical ties (not least through Rawson) but had been far too prominent as a freethinker for Putnam to downplay. In *Religion a Curse*, Putnam had said he could make peace with "the Secular Spiritualist" but explicitly excluded cooperation with "the religious or godly Spiritualist" (p. 5); it was a distinction that was hard to parse, let alone maintain. Another illustrious wayfarer the second reviewer found missing was Moncure Daniel Conway. A Virginian Methodist itinerant who had turned into an abolitionist Unitarian minister in the mid-1850s, Conway went to London after the Civil War, where he led a Universalist chapel that eventually became a leading center for the Ethical Culture Society. Meanwhile, Conway had also come to idolize both Robert Ingersoll and Thomas Paine (he produced a monumental two-volume

biography of the latter in 1892). Even as Conway steeped himself in freethought, he remained religiously cosmopolitan. His last work was entitled *My Pilgrimage to the Wise Men of the East* (1906), which contained sympathetic sketches of Buddhists, Jains, Hindus, and Muslims. Putnam had no more room for Conway's multiplicity than he did for Rawson's. Another heralded freethinker whom Putnam noticeably banished was the editor John A. Lant whose case is discussed in chapter 4. Lant mixed his freethought initially with spiritualism and later with Islam.

42. Putnam, *My Religious Experience*, 90–91; George Chainey, *From the Methodist Pulpit to the Freethought Platform; or, Why I Left the Church* ([Sydney]: n.p., [1886]); "Paine Hall Lectures," *Truth Seeker*, 9 April 1881, 228; Charles Watts, *American Freethinkers: Sketches of Colonel Ingersoll, T. B. Wakeman, B. F. Underwood, and George Chainey* (London: Watts and Co., [1883]), 12–15. Chainey's little memoir of his religious experience was also published under the revised heading of *How and Why I Became a Spiritualist*.

43. "The Convention," *Truth Seeker*, 13 Sept. 1884, 584–85; "Editorial Notes," *Truth Seeker*, 25 July 1885, 473; "Editorial Notes," *Truth Seeker*, 12 Jan. 1889, 25; "Notes and Clippings," *Truth Seeker*, 23 March 1889, 177; "George Chainey's New Fad," *Truth Seeker*, 30 Nov. 1889, 757; "Rather Severe upon George Chainey," *Truth Seeker*, 4 Jan. 1890, 5; Putnam, *400 Years*, 658.

44. Putnam, *400 Years*, 685–89. For Adams's own account of his religious experience, see Robert C. Adams, *Travels in Faith from Tradition to Reason* (New York: G. P. Putnam's Sons, 1884), esp. pp. 1–69.

45. "May L. Collins," *Truth Seeker*, 19 Dec. 1896, 809; Samuel P. Putnam, "The Last of 'News and Notes,'" *Truth Seeker*, 19 Dec. 1896, 809; *Memorial Volume*, 111–29.

46. "The Double Tragedy," *Truth Seeker*, 19 Dec. 1896, 804; "Death of S. P. Putnam," *Truth Seeker*, 19 Dec. 1896, 808; "The Facts Re-Stated," *Truth Seeker*, 23 Jan. 1897, 52; E. C. Walker, "Additional Notes on Our Double Bereavement," *Lucifer the Light Bearer*, 6 Jan. 1897, 5; "Collins-Putnam," *Minneapolis Journal*, 31 Dec. 1896, 7.

47. Green, "Discordant Voice," 50–51, 59.

48. Green, "Discordant Voice," 46, 50–52; E. B. Foote, Sr., "The Great Affliction," *Free Thought Magazine* 15 (1897): 37. For the tract, see *I Am Afraid There Is a God! Founded on Fact* (Boston: Ford and Damrell Temperance Press, 1833). For an example of how the drunken infidel stories worked in popular preaching, especially in regard to Paine, see E. M. Bohall to Editor, *Truth Seeker*, 6 June 1885, 363.

49. Green, "Discordant Voice," 47, 51, 53–55.

50. Green, "Discordant Voice," 55–56, 58–59. Green also took note of how much posthumous support Putnam was receiving from *Lucifer the Light Bearer*. That included a glowing tribute from Lillian Harman's partner, E. C. Walker, in "The Funeral of Samuel Putnam," *Lucifer the Light Bearer*, 25 Dec. 1896, 1. As Green kept up the attack, Moses Harman also issued a vigorous defense and rebuttal. See Moses Harman, "The Tragedy at Boston—Samuel P. Putnam and May L. Collins," *Lucifer the Light Bearer*, 19 May 1897, 153–55, 157. For a full account of the Edwin Walker-Lillian Harman relationship and the legal battles surrounding the couple, see Hal D. Sears, *The Sex Radicals: Free Love in High Victorian America* (Lawrence: Regents Press of Kansas, 1977), 81–96.

51. Foote, "Great Affliction," 37; Green, "Discordant Voice," 61; Moncure D. Conway, *My Pilgrimage to the Wise Men of the East* (London: Constable, 1906), 23 (on the Ingersoll encounter with Whitman); D. K. Tenney, "Hon. D. K. Tenney on the Boston Tragedy," *Free Thought Magazine* 15 (1897): 91. For an indication of the intensity

of debate the scandal occasioned about the sexual politics of secularism, see Orford Northcote, *Ruled by the Tomb: A Discussion of Free Thought and Free Love* (Chicago: M. Harman, 1898). B. F. Underwood, taking Green's side in this debate, claimed to have long judged Putnam an unacceptable leader on the grounds of his free-love principles and practices. That division suggests another reason Putnam might have had for leaving the Underwoods out of *400 Years*. See B. F. Underwood, "Underwood's Endorsement," *Free Thought Magazine* 15 (1897): 121. In *400 Years* Putnam was noticeably inclusive of those who embraced radical ideas about marriage and sexuality as part of their freethinking secularist labors. That included very favorable remarks on the Heywoods, the Footes, the Harmans, and Edwin C. Walker.

52. J.H.A. Lacher to H. L. Green, *Free Thought Magazine* 15 (1897): 108; *Memorial Volume*, 70–71, 102; Macdonald, *Fifty Years*, 2: 134; Putnam, *My Religious Experience*, 60.

53. Joseph Treat, "Not Religion, but Infidelity," *Boston Investigator*, 8 June 1859, n.p.

54. *Chronicles of Simon Christianus and His Manifold and Wondrous Adventures in the Land of Cosmos* (New York: Bennett, 1878), 28, 67, 80. The *Chronicles* were published anonymously as a discovery of I. N. Fidel.

55. See Heston's "A Choice for the Children—An Old Allegory Remodeled," *Truth Seeker*, 6 July 1889, 417, and also his "Trying to Coax Christian Cripples Out of the Mire," *Truth Seeker*, 14 Feb. 1891, 97.

CHAPTER 2. THE CARTOONIST;
OR, THE VISIBLE INCIVILITY OF SECULARISM

1. Details about Heston's life before 1884 are scarce. I have relied on the United States Federal Census Records for locating him in 1850, 1870, and 1880. For a brief biographical sketch, see "Watson Heston," *Free Thought Journal* 15 (1897): 489–91. See also "Death of Watson Heston," *Truth Seeker*, 4 March 1905, 132–33. The *Truth Seeker*, when taking note of his mother's death, claimed she had shared her son's irreligious views. See "Mrs. Leutilia Heston," *Truth Seeker*, 1 June 1889, 344. Heston appears to have grown up with little to no formal connection to the church. The biographical sketch cited above claimed that Heston "never belonged to any church" and that he had steered clear of preachers and Sunday schools "even when a boy." But that distance hardly eliminated his routine exposure to the ambient Protestantism of prayer, Bible reading, preaching, and revivalism—as his cartoons make manifest repeatedly. For events surrounding the local Liberal League in Carthage, see "W. F. Jamieson," *Truth Seeker*, 23 March 1878, 185; Eber Budlong to Editor, *Truth Seeker*, 31 Aug. 1878, 557; "Request for a Charter," *Truth Seeker*, 21 Dec. 1878, 807; "National Liberal League," *Truth Seeker*, 6 March 1880, 155; G. C. Kellogg to Editor, *Truth Seeker*, 17 Nov. 1883, 731; J. T. Kennedy to Editor, *Truth Seeker*, 6 Sept. 1884, 571; W. F. Jamieson, "Liberal Lecturing," *Truth Seeker*, 8 May 1886, 292. Heston has been little noticed in the secondary literature on secularism and freethought, though his cartoons have frequently enough been used in isolation from his biography as illustrations. For one brief treatment of Heston, including the reprinting of several of his cartoons, see Fred Whitehead and Verle Muhrer, eds., *Freethought on the American Frontier* (Buffalo: Prometheus, 1992), 124–41.

2. Watson Heston to Editor, *Truth Seeker*, 9 Aug. 1884, 507. On the National Liberal League's embrace of the new secular calendar at its 1882 convention, see Samuel P.

Putnam, *400 Years of Freethought* (New York: Truth Seeker Co., 1894), 532–33. For American support of the Bruno monument, see "The Bruno Statue at Rome," *Truth Seeker*, 4 May 1889, 277–78; H. L. Green, ed., *Giordano Bruno: His Life, Works, Worth, Martyrdom, Portrait and Monument, with a Complete List of the American Subscribers to the Fund for Its Erection, and Other Interesting Matter* (Buffalo: Green, 1889). Heston was listed among the donors. He also made much of Bruno and the freethought calendar in his cartoons. See his cover cartoons for *Truth Seeker*, 1 Jan. 1887; 20 July 1889; 16 Nov. 1889; 31 Dec. 1892.

3. Heston to Editor, *Truth Seeker*, 9 Aug. 1884.

4. Watson Heston to Editor, *Truth Seeker*, 13 Dec. 1884, 795; L. C. Tidball to Editor, *Truth Seeker*, 14 Feb. 1885, 107.

5. Tidball to Editor, *Truth Seeker*, 14 Feb. 1885; Watson Heston to Editor, *Truth Seeker*, 18 April 1885, 251; Michael Bakounine, *God and the State*, trans. Benjamin Tucker (Boston: Tucker, 1883), 17. On Bakunin's spirited reception after the appearance of Tucker's translation, see "God and the State," *Truth Seeker*, 29 Sept. 1883, 616–17; "The Liberal Club," *Truth Seeker*, 24 Nov. 1883, 740–41.

6. Heston to Editor, *Truth Seeker*, 18 April 1885. Liberal, Missouri, became a lightning rod, and Braden was among its chief antagonists. See Clark Braden, *A Dream and Its Fulfillment: An Exposé of the Late Infidel Would-Be Paradise, Liberal, Barton County, Missouri* (New York: Braden, [1887]). For more favorable descriptions, see the untitled notice in *Truth Seeker*, 9 Aug. 1884, 505, and "The Godless Town of Liberal," *Boston Investigator*, 26 Nov. 1884, 2.

7. G. W. Biddle to Editor and S. E. Brewer to Editor, *Truth Seeker*, May 16, 1885, 315; J. H. Wood to Editor, 20 June 1885, 395; G. Beebee to Editor, *Truth Seeker*, 4 July 1885, 426; Sarah C. Hilton to Editor, *Truth Seeker*, 1 Aug. 1885, 491; A. L. Frisbee to Editor, *Truth Seeker*, 23 May 1885, 330; H. Gilmore to Editor, *Truth Seeker*, 30 May 1885, 347; W. O. Davies to Editor, *Truth Seeker*, 6 June 1885, 362; George H. Gibson to Editor, *Truth Seeker*, 8 Aug. 1885, 507; "Those Impressiv[e] Pictures," *Truth Seeker*, 25 July 1885, 475; "The Modern Balaam," *Truth Seeker*, 30 May 1885, 344.

8. "A New Picture," *Truth Seeker*, 11 July 1885, 436. See also "The Lesson for Christians," *Truth Seeker*, 25 July 1885, 469; "The Short Lesson," *Truth Seeker*, 18 July 1885, 456.

9. "Compliments from Over the Water," *Truth Seeker*, 27 June 1885, 409; "The Picture," *Truth Seeker*, 1 Aug. 1885, 485; "Pictures that Speak Volumes," *Truth Seeker*, 1 Aug. 1885, 489; "Editorial Notes," *Truth Seeker*, 13 June 1885, 377; "A Short Lesson in History" and "The Modern Balaam," Advertisements, 29 Aug. 1885, 557; Watson Heston, "Our Artist Uses His Pen," *Truth Seeker*, 5 Sept. 1885, 566.

10. J.K.B. Baker to Editor, *Truth Seeker*, 10 July 1886, 442; "Books and Magazines," *Boston Investigator*, 24 Sept. 1890, 6. For Heston as a prodigy, see *Truth Seeker*, 10 April 1886, 234; as a brick, see *Truth Seeker*, 27 March 1886, 203 and 5 Jan. 1889, 10; as a Gatling gun, see *Truth Seeker*, 12 Nov. 1887, 730; as a jewel, see *Truth Seeker*, 11 June 1887, 378; as a grand artist, see *Truth Seeker*, 17 April 1886, 251; as a Hogarth, see *Truth Seeker*, 4 Jan. 1890, 11 and 18 Feb. 1893, 107; as the equal of Nast, see *Truth Seeker*, 27 March 1886, 203; 31 March 1888, 202; and 8 April 1899, 213; as a second Voltaire, see *Truth Seeker*, 3 May 1890, 283. The work that Joseph Keppler had done for *Puck* and *Frank Leslie's Budget of Fun*, along with the work that Thomas Nast had done for *Harper's Weekly*, were standing reference points for political and religious cartooning of the era. Heston's work was compared to *Puck*'s program broadly and to Nast's labors specifically. Both Nast and Keppler were pointed satirists of papal

authority, clericalism, and Mormonism, but neither pursued the wholesale critique of religion that Heston would bring to his work for the *Truth Seeker*. See Richard Samuel West, *Satire on Stone: The Political Cartoons of Joseph Keppler* (Urbana: University of Illinois Press, 1988), esp. pp. 90–93, 116–18, 140–53, 180–81; Fiona Deans Halloran, *Thomas Nast: The Father of Modern Political Cartoons* (Chapel Hill: University of North Carolina Press, 2012), esp. pp. 202–205. The comic Bible sketches that were being run by Foote's *Freethinker* as of 1881 were also a possible source of influence, perhaps especially on Macdonald's decision to start illustrating the *Truth Seeker*. It is unlikely, though, that Heston himself had access to the British publication; soon it was evident that the flow of influence was actually moving very strongly in the other direction. Foote's *Freethinker* frequently published unacknowledged knock-offs of Heston's cartoons, so often in fact that Macdonald urged that credit be given where credit was due. See Macdonald's editorial note in *Truth Seeker*, 26 Jan. 1889, 62. For three examples, see the cover pairings of *Truth Seeker*, 30 June 1888 and *Freethinker*, 7 Oct. 1888; *Truth Seeker*, 9 July 1887 and *Freethinker*, 5 Feb. 1888; *Truth Seeker*, 17 Nov. 1888 and *Freethinker*, 30 Dec. 1888. On Foote's use of cartoons, see especially David Nash, "Laughing at the Almighty: Freethinking Lampoon, Satire, and Parody in Victorian England," in Jennifer A. Wagner Lawlor, ed., *The Victorian Comic Spirit: New Perspectives* (Aldershot: Ashgate, 2000), 43–66. The Hogarth comparison, of course, made evident the much-longer history of religious caricatures, including a full repertoire of anti-Catholic, anti-enthusiast, anticlerical, and anti-Jewish satires. See, for example, John Miller, *Religion in the Popular Prints, 1600–1832* (Cambridge: Chadwyck-Healey, 1986).

11. For folks who made scrapbooks out of Heston's cartoons, see *Truth Seeker*, 8 Jan. 1887, 20; 19 March 1887, 187; 11 Feb. 1888, 91; 16 March 1889, 170; 1 Feb. 1890, 74; 15 March 1890, 170; and 23 Aug. 1890, 538. One of these late nineteenth-century scrapbooks survives in the comic art collection at Michigan State University. See "Cartoons by Watson Heston: A Scrapbook of Clippings from *Truth Seeker*," Special Collections, Michigan State University Library, East Lansing, MI. For the use of Heston's cartoons as eye-catching pin-ups at a California newsstand and in a book store in Manchester, England, see, respectively, *Truth Seeker*, 13 Feb. 1892, 106 and 9 July 1892, 438. For a gallery of his cartoons in a bar, see *Truth Seeker*, 18 Sept. 1886, 602; for a doctor's office, see *Truth Seeker*, 4 Jan. 1890, 10; for a barber shop, *Truth Seeker*, 27 April 1889, 266. For use of his artwork in a lecture hall in Silverton, Oregon, and at a secularist convention in Seattle, see *Freethought*, 9 June 1888, 278–79 and 22 Feb. 1890, 120–21. For use in pamphleteering, see Charles B. Reynolds, *Blasphemy and the Bible* (New York: Truth Seeker Co., 1886); *Freethought*, 11 Jan. 1890, 23, 26; and *Truth Seeker*, 15 Oct. 1892, 660; 5 Nov. 1892, 708; and 1 April 1893, 200. Macdonald reprinted more than half of Heston's front-page cartoons in book form with commentary. See Watson Heston, *The Freethinkers' Pictorial Text-Book* (New York: Truth Seeker Co., 1890); Watson Heston, *Part II of The Freethinkers' Pictorial Text-Book* (New York: Truth Seeker Co., 1898). The back-page Bible cartoons were collected into *Old Testament Stories Comically Illustrated* (1892) and *New Testament Stories Comically Illustrated* (1903). For Gott's postcards, see the advertisements for them in his own *Truth Seeker* 10 (March 1904): 12 and 10 (May 1904): 12. Gott borrowed Heston's cartoons shamelessly from 1900 to 1915. Though in 1900 and 1901 Gott usually noted that the cartoons came from the New York *Truth Seeker*, he soon dropped even that identifier. The cartoons have, in turn, been discussed as if they were Gott's imaginings without any mention of Heston; see David Nash, *Blasphemy*

in Modern Britain: 1789 to the Present (London: Ashgate, 1999), 168–94. Gott was charged with blasphemy numerous times; his last jail term for that offense came in 1922.

12. Robert G. Ingersoll, *The Gods and Other Lectures* (Peoria: n.p., 1874), 157; Sarah A. Cope to Editor, *Truth Seeker*, 9 April 1887, 234. On the emergence of the Paine observances, see Albert Post, *Popular Freethought in America, 1825–1850* (New York: Columbia University Press, 1943), 155–59; Eric R. Schlereth, *An Age of Infidels: The Politics of Religious Controversy in the Early United States* (Philadelphia: University of Pennsylvania Press, 2013), 190–200.

13. "To Pray for Ingersoll Thursday," *Chicago Daily Tribune*, 27 Nov. 1895, 1; "Prayers for Col. R. G. Ingersoll," *New York Times*, 29 Nov. 1895, 1; "Pray for 'Pagan Bob,'" *Chicago Daily Tribune,* 29 Nov. 1895, 1; "Ingersoll Won't Weaken," *Atlanta Constitution*, 2 Dec. 1895, 3; "Prayers Are Lost on Ingersoll," *Chicago Daily Tribune*, 8 April 1896, 7.

14. Heston played reflexively with the priority of printed books versus the visual medium of his cartoons in another Santa Claus image a few years later. See "Some Christmas Suggestions, Etc.," *Truth Seeker*, 19 Dec. 1896, 801. Amid a mountain of books presented as potential holiday gifts, Heston used one of his own cartoons as a focal point for garnering *Truth Seeker* subscriptions and placed two of his picture books prominently next to Samuel Putnam's *400 Years of Freethought*.

15. H. Patrick to Editor, *Truth Seeker*, 13 March 1886, 170; unnamed subscriber to Editor, *Truth Seeker*, 19 June 1886, 395; George M. Hare to Editor, *Truth Seeker*, 11 Dec. 1886, 795; D. S. Aungst to Editor, *Truth Seeker*, 1 March 1890, 138; E. G. Abbott to Editor, *Truth Seeker*, 1 March 1890, 138; Gustav H. Scheel to Editor, *Truth Seeker*, 25 April 1891, 266.

16. F. E. Sturgis to Editor, *Truth Seeker*, 8 March 1890, 155; "New Pictorial Work for Liberals," *Truth Seeker*, 4 Feb. 1899, 66; Elmina Drake Slenker to Editor, *Truth Seeker*, 12 Feb. 1887, 106; Robert Fleming to Editor, *Truth Seeker*, 12 Nov. 1887, 730. Slenker continued to remark on how ineffaceable the cartoons were. See Elmina D. Slenker, "Our Picture Book," *Truth Seeker*, 20 Sept. 1890, 600; Elmina D. Slenker, "Thinks the Pictures Deserve Gratitude," *Truth Seeker*, 22 July 1893, 458.

17. Simeon Nixon to Editor, *Truth Seeker*, 7 Aug. 1886, 507. On the teeming devotional imagery of nineteenth-century Protestantism, see especially David Morgan, *Protestants and Pictures: Religion, Visual Culture, and the Age of American Mass Production* (New York: Oxford University Press, 1999).

18. Isaac Ivins to Editor, *Truth Seeker*, 23 April 1887, 267; J. Ildstad to Editor, *Truth Seeker*, 18 March 1893, 170; D. S. Weaver to Editor, *Truth Seeker*, 12 Feb. 1887, 106.

19. That motto was emblazoned on a statue of the pope that Heston depicted as a dark inversion of the Statue of Liberty. See "Now and Then," *Truth Seeker*, 24 July 1886, 465. For another Heston knock-off of Nast, which he acknowledged in the cartoon itself with the byline "Watson Heston with apologies to Nast," see "Trying to Keep the Sectarian Wolf out of Our Schools," *Truth Seeker*, 31 Jan. 1891, 65. For discerning a "Protestant-secular continuum" in the nineteenth century, anti-Catholicism is a very robust example. See Tracy Fessenden, *Culture and Redemption: Religion, the Secular, and American Literature* (Princeton: Princeton University Press, 2007), esp. pp. 3–5, 9, 120, 140.

20. See "A Wave from the West," *Truth Seeker*, 13 March 1886, 161, in which Heston names six Protestant preachers and evangelists, while having one unnamed Catholic cleric in the mix.

21. Henry Bisson to Editor, *Truth Seeker*, 9 Dec. 1893, 779.

22. Ess. E. Tee to Editor, *Truth Seeker*, 31 July 1886, 490. For a similarly positive assessment of another of Heston's anti-Calvinist cartoons, "The Glory of Predestination," see John McClemont to Editor, *Truth Seeker*, 4 Jan. 1890, 11.

23. For another cartoon of the sectarian cacophony that Heston aimed to quiet, see "Those Sabbath Bells," *Truth Seeker*, 23 March 1889, 177.

24. For Heston's wall, shield, and platform images of a materialized secularism, see "As the Political Smoke Rolls Away, We Find the Same Old Enemy," *Truth Seeker*, 5 Dec. 1896, 769; "The Only Safe Place for Our Public Schools," *Truth Seeker*, 4 May 1895, 273; and "Too Soon for the Resurrection of Puritanism," *Truth Seeker*, 4 Aug. 1894, 481.

25. The call for secularist chaplains also came up in World War I, though it was again "quite overlooked." See George E. Macdonald, *Fifty Years of Freethought*, 2 vols. (New York: Truth Seeker Co., 1929), 2: 470.

26. For an early indication of Heston's populist economic views, including outright endorsement of working-class revolt, see Heston, "Our Artist Uses His Pen," 566. See also Watson Heston to Editor, *Truth Seeker*, 1 Jan. 1887, 10. Heston's activism on behalf of the Populist Party was particularly pronounced in the movement's heyday in the early-to-mid 1890s; his cartoons appeared in several Populist papers, most prominently in the *American Nonconformist* (Winfield, KS) and *Sound Money* (Massillon, OH). See Worth Robert Miller, *Populist Cartoons: An Illustrated History of the Third-Party Movement in the 1890s* (Kirksville, MO: Truman State University Press, 2011), 8–9, 27–28, 35, 50–57, 66, 75, 87, 91, 96, 98, 101, 108, 122, 126, 130–32, 137, 160. Heston's Populist Party cartoons caught the eye of the national reform periodical *Arena*. See B. O. Flower, "The General Discontent of America's Wealth Creators as Illustrated in Current Cartoons," *Arena* 80 (1896): 298–304. *Sound Money* ran an account of the artist at work; it accented his political cartoons while acknowledging that the "greater part" of his work had been devoted to freethought. It was reprinted as "Heston in His Lair," *Truth Seeker*, 2 May 1896, 277. Heston brought little to none of his freethinking secularism to bear on his Populist Party cartoons; that irreligious content would have been needlessly divisive in a movement urgently trying to maintain disparate alliances. His antiplutocratic, prolabor commitments were, however, clearly part of his freethinking activism. The religious element that did shift from one venue to the next was Heston's treatment of Jews. In Populist imagery they were Shylocks, part of the financial class that was exploiting farmers, laborers, and the dispossessed. In freethought imagery, as will be seen below, Jews were more ambivalently portrayed: they were a minority, like freethinkers and infidels, who were endangered by a Christian majority, but they were also the fountainhead of much superstition, epitomized in the Hebrew Bible.

27. Watson Heston, "Thanksgiving and Giving Thanks," *Truth Seeker*, 23 Nov. 1889, 737.

28. E. C. Walker, *The Future of Secularism: When Will the Cause of Justice Triumph?* (New York: Truth Seeker Co., 1899), 1, 7, 10.

29. For the death of the gods—from Jupiter to Jehovah—see Watson Heston, "The Graveyard of the Gods—Preparing for the Next Funeral," *Truth Seeker*, 29 Dec. 1894, 817. For two scientists preparing to dynamite the Rock of Ages, see Watson Heston, "A Poor Place to Hide," *Truth Seeker*, 16 Sept. 1899, 577. The secularist train of progress was a commonplace image in Heston's work. For one example, see his "Comparativ[e] Progress," *Truth Seeker*, 15 July 1893, 433.

30. A. W. Williams, *Life and Work of Dwight L. Moody: The Great Evangelist of the XIXth Century* (Philadelphia: n.p., 1900), 149.

31. Watson Heston, "An Old Grudge—The Specter That Still Curses Woman," *Truth Seeker*, 17 Oct. 1891, 657.

32. For Heston's Slenker cartoon, see "A New Coat of Arms Suggested for Virginia," *Truth Seeker*, 25 June 1887, 401, which is reprinted in chapter 4; for his Reynolds cartoon, see "Casting Pearls before Swine—C. B. Reynolds in New Jersey," *Truth Seeker*, 4 Sept. 1886, 561, which is reprinted in chapter 3.

33. For an excellent study of these tensions over gender among freethinkers, see Evelyn A. Kirkley, *Rational Mothers and Infidel Gentlemen: Gender and American Atheism, 1865–1915* (Syracuse: Syracuse University Press, 2000), esp. pp. 118–33. As Kirkley's study makes plain, Heston's ambivalences about women's rights (including suffrage) were common among liberal secularists. For a larger critique of the widespread presumption of secularism's emancipatory force in matters of gender and sexuality (routinely juxtaposed to religion's oppressive sway), see Linell E. Cady and Tracy Fessenden, eds., *Religion, the Secular, and the Politics of Sexual Difference* (New York: Columbia University Press, 2013), esp. pp. 3–24. For an indication of the ways in which a masculinist bias continues to shape the secularist movement, at least among much of its New Atheist leadership, see Stephen LeDrew, *The Evolution of Atheism: The Politics of a Modern Movement* (New York: Oxford University Press, 2016), 197–211.

34. On racial politics—from voting rights to public accommodations—American secularists and freethinkers were divided, just as they were on other major issues of the day such as women's suffrage and the Mormon question. For an indication of this, see "Sectional Liberalism," *Truth Seeker*, 25 April 1885, 265. They could produce highly progressive voices as in Hugh O. Pentecost, "How We Treat the Negroes," *Truth Seeker*, 6 June 1903, 354–55 or harshly racist ones as in the editorial on "The Negro Problem," *Truth Seeker*, 7 March 1903, 148. On occasion at least, white secularists were able to engage black intellectuals directly and participate in lively interracial debate on these questions, as was the case when the African-American attorney James D. Carr spoke at the Manhattan Liberal Club in May 1903. See James D. Carr, "The Negro's Viewpoint of the Negro Question," *Truth Seeker*, 23 May 1903, 326–28. Interracial collaboration was also evident at the Ingersoll Memorial Meeting in Washington, DC, in 1901, in which a number of African-American leaders, including lawyer W. C. Martin, played pivotal roles. For a detailed account of the meeting, see "Negroes Praised Him," *Truth Seeker*, 20 April 1901, 246–48. Many freethinkers were eager to present Frederick Douglass as an unambiguous member of their movement (just as they were with Abraham Lincoln). Though Douglass had political and reform alliances with a number of freethinkers, including Ingersoll and Colman, and was a fierce critic of Christian hypocrisy, he was not formally affiliated with the chief organizations of the liberal secularist cause. See, for example, the debate between John S. Maiben and John Remsburg on whether Douglass was a freethinker or a Christian in "False Claims," *Truth Seeker*, 17 May 1884, 310–11. See also J. J. Shirley, "Two Important Questions," *Truth Seeker*, 6 April 1895, 219. For many years, beginning in 1888, the Truth Seeker Company offered among its "very cheap pamphlets" for broad circulation a pair of civil-rights addresses by Douglass and Ingersoll. The advertisements were frequent and ongoing; for one, see *Truth Seeker*, 11 Aug. 1888, 510. Douglass noted the humane solidarity he felt with Ingersoll in *Life and Times of Frederick Douglass* (Hartford: Park, 1882), 561–62. For critical theoretical engagement with secularism's racialized limitations, see Jonathon S.

Kahn and Vincent W. Lloyd, eds., *Race and Secularism in America* (New York: Columbia University Press, 2016).

35. "Editorial Notes," *Truth Seeker*, 29 Aug. 1885, 553; "The Freethinkers' International Congress," *Truth Seeker*, 14 Oct. 1893, 646, 648; "International Congress of Free-thinkers," *Freethinkers' Magazine* 11 (1893): 781; *Christian Recorder*, 25 Dec. 1890, n.p.; Putnam, *400 Years*, 661; "Cincore as Othello," *State* (Columbia, SC), 3 Dec. 1907, 11; "Rev. David Cincore's Missionary Tour," *Philadelphia Inquirer*, 11 Dec. 1915, 1. The spelling of Cincore's name was inconsistent: Sincare, Cincose, Cincoze, and Sincore. For an antebellum predecessor to Cincore, see the short-lived efforts of William Dunkins to promote an organization of freethinkers among the black citizens of Boston in 1844, "Union Hall Meetings for Free Enquiry," *Boston Investigator*, 2 Oct. 1844, n.p.

36. "A Colored Brother's Enthusiasm," *Freethought*, 24 March 1888, 150; R. S. King to Editor, "'Is There a God?' Asks a Colored Brother," *Truth Seeker*, 17 Dec. 1904, 809; *Truth Seeker*, 2 July 1904, 424. This last untitled note on R. S. King points to a pamphlet entitled *The Devil Vanquished* that King had published with the Truth Seeker Company. It does not appear to be extant. On Harrison's freethought connections, see Jeffrey B. Perry, ed., *A Hubert Harrison Reader* (Middletown, CT: Wesleyan University Press, 2001), 35–46; Macdonald, *Fifty Years*, 2: 421, 453. Turn-of-the-century freethinkers often saw the African-American writer Paul Laurence Dunbar as an ally, being particularly fond of his poem "Religion," in which the "lugubrious saint" is urged to "let Heaven alone" and concentrate strictly on the immediate needs of humanity. See, for example, "Gems of Thought," *Truth Seeker*, 8 June 1901, 367; Paul Laurence Dunbar, "Religion," *Humanitarian Review* 2 (1904): 745.

37. Queen Silver, "The Godliness of Ignorance," *Queen Silver's Magazine* 3 (Jan. 1927): 4. These pervasive conjunctions of primitivism and emotionalism in views of black religiosity are explored with particular acuity in Curtis J. Evans, *The Burden of Black Religion* (New York: Oxford University Press, 2008), esp. pp. 108–109, 121–35. For Heston's use of an African-American figure to show the persistence of superstition and religious ignorance, see "A Queer Trio—John Wesley, Dr. Buckley, and Witchcraft," *Truth Seeker*, 9 April 1892, 225; "Superstition the Same in All Places and Ages," *Truth Seeker*, 12 Jan. 1889, 17; and "A Hint to Beecher," *Truth Seeker*, 25 Dec. 1886, 817.

38. See Watson Heston, "An Inhuman Travesty—French Justice," *Truth Seeker*, 30 Sept. 1899, 609.

39. On the responses of the *Hebrew Standard*, see "Opinions of the Press," *Truth Seeker*, 30 Jan. 1886, 71; "The Truth Seeker Hits Hard," *Truth Seeker*, 24 April 1886, 261. Also see "A Russo-Jewish Controversy," *Truth Seeker*, 23 April 1892, 266, in which Heston's cartoons are praised for their attack on Christianity (rather than Judaism) and seen as in harmony with those Jews who have been "drifting very fast from belief to Freethought." Heston's use of anti-Jewish imagery, including the Shylock figure, is discussed in Miller, *Populist Cartoons*, 15–17, 27–28, 37, 51, 54, 66, 96–97, 122, 126, 130–31, 160. The Jewish caricatures in the leading British secularist journal, George W. Foote's *Freethinker*, exhibited the same hackneyed types. See Nash, "Laughing at the Almighty," 61–64. That was also true of other American humor magazines of the period, including Joseph Keppler's *Puck*, which displayed a tension between solidarity and demeaning ridicule similar to that in Heston's work. See John J. Appel, "Jews in American Caricature: 1820–1914," *American Jewish*

History 71 (1981): esp. pp. 110–13. Over the much longer haul, the *Truth Seeker*'s blanket contempt for the "superstitions" of Judaism and the Hebrew Bible came under strenuous attack as distinctly anti-Semitic. These debates swirled for years in the wake of Hitler's Nazi regime, being fought out between rival wings of American freethought with publisher Emanuel Haldeman-Julius and his allies at the *American Freeman* attacking the *Truth Seeker*'s leadership (especially Marshall J. Gauvin and Charles Lee Smith) as bigots. The anti-Semitic charges were collected in Mordecai T. Heller, E. Haldeman-Julius, and John D. McInerney, *The Shameful Decline of the 'Truth Seeker': How a Once Fine-Organ of Freethought Fell into the Clutches of Ignoble Bigots and Became a Sewer for Anti-Semitism* (Girard, KS: Haldeman-Julius, 1949). The defense was equally pointed, including charges that Haldeman-Julius based his initial attack on an obvious forgery. See "Forged Anti-Semitism," *Truth Seeker* 73 (Aug. 1946): 118–19; "More Forged Anti-Semitism," *Truth Seeker* 73 (Oct. 1946): 156–57; Marshall J. Gauvin, "Haldeman-Julius Raves," *Truth Seeker* 76 (May 1949): 74; Marshall J. Gauvin, "Haldeman-Julius's Hypocrisy," *Truth Seeker* 76 (July 1949): 105–106; [Charles Lee Smith], "Semitic Freethought," *Truth Seeker* 76 (Aug. 1949): 116; Marshall J. Gauvin, "The Raver Still Raves," *Truth Seeker* 76 (Sept. 1949): 139. The race theories of the *Truth Seeker* circle after World War II became increasingly reactionary and lost all connection to earlier strands of progressivism within parts of the secularist movement. This was particularly apparent in the work of associate editor Woolsey Teller, but by the late 1950s that racist rightward tilt had taken over the journal almost entirely and had largely cut this group off from broader humanist organizations. For an early indication of this turn, see Woolsey Teller, *Essays of an Atheist* (New York: Truth Seeker Co., 1945).

40. For the untitled report on persecution of Mormons in Carter County and also Bell County, see *Truth Seeker*, 19 Aug. 1899, 516. For the Mormon use of Heston's cartoon, see Patrick Q. Mason, *The Mormon Menace: Violence and Anti-Mormonism in the Postbellum South* (New York: Oxford University Press, 2011), 165–66. Seventh-day Adventists were also known to have embraced Heston's work for their own purposes. See C. L. Jacobs to Editor, *Truth Seeker*, 31 May 1890, 346. These solidarities between freethinkers and religious minorities stretched back into the antebellum political landscape, evident in recurrent battles over majoritarian Protestant efforts to enact and enforce Sabbatarian and antiliquor legislation. See Kyle G. Volk, *Moral Minorities and the Making of American Democracy* (New York: Oxford University Press, 2014), 38–39, 44–45, 53, 66, 191.

41. "In the Case of Brigham H. Roberts," *Lucifer the Light Bearer*, 23 Dec. 1899, 394. For another account of "Mr. Walker's wrath" over Heston's cartoons, see "At the Manhattan Liberal Club," *Truth Seeker*, 23 Dec. 1899, 808. Walker had been previously a big fan of Heston's work. See the enthusiastic endorsement in "Notes," *Lucifer the Light Bearer*, 7 May 1886, 2, which was reprinted in "Heaven for Murderers," *Truth Seeker*, 5 June 1886, 359. For the "Auto-da-Fe of the Picture Book" in Los Angeles, see C. H. Lawrence to Editor, *Truth Seeker*, 16 July 1892, 458. The book-burning episode was said to have increased sales of Heston's books for the store's proprietor, Max Roth. On the Canadian ban, see "Why This Paper Is Contraband in Canada," *Truth Seeker*, 19 Oct. 1895, 665; "A Scurrilous Transaction," *Truth Seeker*, 26 Oct. 1895, 684; "The Canadian Censorship," *Truth Seeker*, 2 Nov. 1895, 700. The last also has the episode from the National Reform Association convention in which a minister held up Heston's cartoons. That group was in an out-and-out war with Heston for more

than a year. See "About Present-Day Infamies," *Truth Seeker*, 12 May 1894, 293; "Is This Stupidity or Cunning?" *Truth Seeker*, 9 Nov. 1895, 708; "Still Evading the Issue of Religious Liberty," *Truth Seeker*, 14 Dec. 1895, 787–88. On the seizures at Canadian customs, see "Freethought in the United States," in *Truth Seeker Annual and Freethinkers' Almanac for 1895* (New York: Truth Seeker Co., 1895), 18, 23, 36; "The Picture Book in Canada," *Truth Seeker*, 29 Nov. 1890, 761.

42. "In the Case of Brigham H. Roberts," 393–94.

43. "Plural Marriage," *Truth Seeker*, 30 Dec. 1899, 826. Heston misread (or was at odds with) the preponderant liberal mood in the debate over Roberts. See, for example, the untitled report on Thomas Wentworth Higginson's opposition to the anti-Roberts crusade in *Truth Seeker*, 4 Feb. 1899, 68; Moncure D. Conway's letter defending Roberts in Macdonald, *Fifty Years*, 2: 189–90; and the postmortem of James F. Morton, Jr., a rising leader in free-speech circles, "The Real Issue in the Roberts Case," *Truth Seeker*, 17 March 1900, 169. Heston defended himself from his critics, including Shepherd, in "A Few Remarks on the Cartoons Concerning Polygamy, Etc.," *Truth Seeker*, 27 Jan. 1900, 58, but the tide was against him. See George B. Wheeler, "The Roberts Cartoons a Mistake," *Truth Seeker*, 3 Feb. 1900, 74.

44. Macdonald estimated that 80 to 90 percent of his readers were fans of the cartoons with Heston's detractors occupying the remainder. The hundreds of letters to the editor about the cartoons confirm those numbers; they ran decisively in Heston's favor. See "Editorial Notes," *Truth Seeker*, 17 Nov. 1888, 729; "Our Pictures," *Truth Seeker*, 14 Dec. 1889, 793.

45. Charles Remhard to Editor, *Truth Seeker*, 3 April 1886, 218; "What Other Papers Say," *Truth Seeker*, 20 Feb. 1886, 126; Paul Carus, "Notes," *Open Court* 6 (1892): 3190; "Don't Quite Suit Mr. Carus," *Truth Seeker*, 30 April 1892, 275.

46. John Steves to Editor, *Truth Seeker*, 3 April 1886, 218; E. Fowle to Editor, *Truth Seeker*, 8 Feb. 1890, 90; John Peck, "The Reason Why," *Truth Seeker*, 11 Jan. 1890, 20; John Peck, "My Say about the Pictures," *Truth Seeker*, 15 Feb. 1890, 102 103; W. F. Jamieson, "'Oh, Them Picters!'" *Truth Seeker*, 13 Nov. 1886, 734; H. B. Milks to Editor, *Truth Seeker*, 22 May 1886, 330; Albert B. Paine, ed., *Mark Twain's Notebook* (New York: Harper and Row, 1935), 198. On Twain's subscription to the *Truth Seeker* as well as his equivocal relationship to organized freethought, see Macdonald, *Fifty Years*, 2: 361–63.

47. "What Other Papers Say," 126; Mrs. F. I. Bird to Editor, *Truth Seeker*, 1 Feb. 1890, 75; Mrs. Lettie Foster to Editor, *Truth Seeker*, 28 Dec. 1889, 826; Frederick W. Peabody to Editor, *Truth Seeker*, 28 Dec. 1889, 826; "Watson Heston to His Friends and Critics," *Truth Seeker*, 15 May 1897, 309; "Death of Watson Heston," 132. When Macdonald pushed Heston aside in 1900 and began looking for new artistic talent, he deliberately sought out a cartoonist, Ryan Walker, with more polish and refinement. Lasting only a few months in 1902, Walker's stint with the *Truth Seeker* proved short-lived and unproductive.

48. Peck, "My Say about the Pictures," 103.

49. H. H. Gilman to Editor, *Truth Seeker*, 3 July 1886, 426; J.K.P. Baker to Editor, 442.

50. W. E. Walton to Editor, *Truth Seeker*, 21 April 1888, 251; Charles Bursee to Editor, *Truth Seeker*, 23 Oct. 1886, 683; J. Tompkins to Editor, *Truth Seeker*, 3 April 1886, 218. See also S. F. Woodward to Editor, *Truth Seeker*, 5 Feb. 1887, 90.

51. "The Blood of the Lamb," *Truth Seeker*, 12 June 1886, 376; "Peace with Honor," *Truth Seeker*, 3 July 1886, 424–25; schoolmaster to Editor, *Truth Seeker*, 11 Dec. 1886,

795. The offending cartoon that had compelled Gill to unsubscribe was "Jesus Paid It All" from the May 15, 1886 cover, which satirized the doctrine of the atonement—that "2½ gallons" of Christ's blood had canceled humanity's considerable debts to Jehovah.

52. "Peace with Honor," 424; William E. Renwick to Editor, *Truth Seeker*, 22 Feb. 1896, 122; F. H. Heald to Editor, *Truth Seeker*, 18 Feb. 1893, 106.

53. D. McMillan to Editor, *Truth Seeker*, 9 Aug. 1884, 507; W. W. Baker to Editor, *Truth Seeker*, 5 Jan. 1889, 10; E. N. Fairchild to Editor, *Truth Seeker*, 12 Nov. 1887, 730.

54. J.A.R. to Editor, *Truth Seeker*, 3 Sept. 1892, 571; W. D. Wiseman to Editor, *Truth Seeker*, 4 Jan. 1890, 10; W.J.N. Welborn to Editor, *Truth Seeker*, 30 Oct. 1897, 698; "Children's Corner," Eustace Eugene Bradley to Susan H. Wixon, *Truth Seeker*, 7 July 1894, 428. For other instances of Heston's name being used for christening little freethinkers, see Allen Johnson to Editor, *Truth Seeker*, 3 Nov. 1894, 698; A. D. Strickland to Editor, *Truth Seeker*, 10 Dec. 1892, 794. Allen Johnson later recalled the secular funeral for "our little son, Watson Heston Johnson," in a letter to the *Blue Grass Blade*, 8 March 1908, 15.

55. "The Freethought Congress," *Truth Seeker*, 27 Nov. 1897, 760; "A Card from Watson Heston," *Freethought Ideal*, 15 March 1901, 7; "A Card from Watson Heston," *Blue Grass Blade*, 5 May 1901, 2. On how Macdonald and another colleague had defrauded Heston, see "Mack Is Camping on My Trail," *Blue Grass Blade*, 29 Dec. 1901, 3; Homer A. Billings to Editor, *Blue Grass Blade*, 26 Jan. 1902, 4. On Heston's peripatetic ways and unending search for a more reliable income, see Watson Heston to Editor, *Truth Seeker*, 3 March 1894, 138. On Heston's recurrent financial and physical woes, see "Death of Watson Heston," 132; "W. S. Bell in Texas," *Truth Seeker*, 1 Jan. 1887, 4; "Editorial Notes," *Truth Seeker*, 2 Aug. 1890, 488 and 23 Aug. 1890, 538; Samuel D. Moore to Editor, *Truth Seeker*, 17 May 1890, 315; "Watson Heston Asks for a Loan," *Truth Seeker*, 24 June 1893, 393; "Our Duty toward Watson Heston," *Truth Seeker*, 16 Sept. 1893, 583; "Watson Heston and Wife Suffering from Poverty," *Blue Grass Blade*, 13 Nov. 1904, 2. Sales figures for the first part of his *Freethinkers' Pictorial Text-Book* were set at six thousand as of 1896—about a thousand copies a year. See "Another Great New Book," *Truth Seeker,* 28 March 1896, 195. As of 1900, his *Old Testament Stories Comically Illustrated* had sold eight thousand copies—again about a thousand copies a year. See "Some Handsome Premiums," *Truth Seeker*, 7 July 1900, 427. Sales figures for his other two volumes, both of which were follow-ups to these two, were not reported. Even with modest sales of the companion volumes, Heston's numbers almost surely topped twenty thousand by the time of his death in 1905. His books were very good sellers for the Truth Seeker Company for over a decade. The financial pressures on Macdonald were quite real. He was forced to discontinue the cartoons from February 1897 to July 1898 as a cost-saving measure—a move that caused Heston immediate financial hardship and forced him to scramble to get the job back. See "The Cartoons," *Truth Seeker*, 13 March 1897, 164; "Freethought Congress," 760.

56. "A Plea for Watson Heston," *Blue Grass Blade*, 25 Dec. 1904, 4; "Literary Siftings," *Public Press* (New Albany, IN), 18 April 1905, 1; "Watson Heston: The Infidel Cartoonist Died Peacefully," *Blue Grass Blade*, 12 Feb. 1905, 2; "Death of Watson Heston," *Humanitarian Review* 3 (1905): 111. The narrative conventions surrounding infidel deathbeds were a matter of frequent comment and dispute. See especially George W. Foote, *Infidel Death-Beds: "Idle Tales of Dying Horrors"* (New York: Truth Seeker Co., [1892]).

57. On Queen Silver, see Wendy McElroy, *Queen Silver: The Godless Girl* (Amherst, NY:

Prometheus, 2000). For the Heston cover, see *Queen Silver's Magazine* 4 (Sept.–Oct. 1929). One of Heston's cartoon books came to the Center for Inquiry Libraries in Amherst, New York, as part of the Queen Silver Collection. On the Heston cartoon in the research files for *The Godless Girl*, see P-146, Box 31, f. 7; for the mouth-stuffing cartoon idea in the "Shooting Script," see Box 1234, f. 1: 48–49, both in the Cecil B. DeMille Archives, L. Tom Perry Special Collections, Harold B. Lee Library, Brigham Young University, Provo, UT. The American Association for the Advancement of Atheism had picked up Heston's cartoon "A Few of the 'Good Old Patriarchs'" for circulation in their leaflets in the mid-to-late 1920s; that group was one of the main sources for DeMille's researchers. For more on the group's activities, see the epilogue. Also of note is the work of cartoonist Harry Fowler, who developed a rich iconography of irreligion, reminiscent of Heston's in its roughhewn style and symbolism, for Emanuel Haldeman-Julius's *American Freeman* in the late 1940s. If Heston had a visible heir after the 1920s, it was Fowler. Fondness for Heston's cartoons continued in later American freethought publications. See, for example, the reprints in *American Atheist* 31 (Feb. 1989): 37; *American Atheist* 34 (June 1992): 35.

58. "Verbatim Transcript of Expository and Descriptive 'Reading' by Cecil B. DeMille of *The Godless Girl*," DeMille Archives, Box 293, f. 8: 8, 80, 90, 96. See also the way the studio brought cartoons ("pictorial blasphemies") into play in a press release about the movie, "Devil's Angels," Box 293, f. 4. On the global controversy following the publication of the Danish cartoons of the Prophet Muhammad in 2005, see Jytte Klausen, *The Cartoons That Shook the World* (New Haven: Yale University Press, 2009). Defending the right to blaspheme has long remained central to the American secularist program, but it has taken on renewed prominence in the wake of these recent cartoon controversies. See, for example, the essays collected for the "special blasphemy issue" of *Free Inquiry* 35 (Oct.–Nov. 2015).

59. "The Mask Dropped," *Truth Seeker*, 21 Sept. 1895, 599; George Penman to Editor, *Truth Seeker*, 22 Feb. 1890, 123.

CHAPTER 3. THE BLASPHEMER; OR, THE RIDDLE OF IRRELIGIOUS FREEDOM

1. "Got Off Cheap: Col. Bob Ingersoll Fails to Clear Blasphemer Reynolds," *St. Louis Post-Dispatch*, 21 May 1887, 5; "Remarks at the Reunion of New York People," *New York Indicator*, 15 May 1901, n.p.; untitled news item, *Truth Seeker*, 31 July 1886, 489; "The Blasphemer's Program," *Truth Seeker*, 9 Oct. 1886, 645; "Reynolds Arrested for Blasphemy," *Truth Seeker*, 7 Aug. 1886, 504; "A Right Not Worth Insisting On," *Brooklyn Daily Eagle*, 20 May 1887, 4. For the photograph of Reynolds at a camp meeting, see W. L. Sutton, *Ellen Gould Harmon White Attending the Hornellsville, New York Campmeeting in 1880*, Center for Adventist Research Image Database, (accessed June 22, 2015), http://centerforadventistresearch.org/photos.

2. "Jersey's Heresy Case," *Chicago Daily Tribune*, 22 May 1887, 17. For the Protestant authoritarian lesson, see David Sehat, *The Myth of American Religious Freedom* (New York: Oxford University Press, 2011), 1–2; for its secularist inversion, see Susan Jacoby, *The Great Agnostic: Robert Ingersoll and American Freethought* (New Haven: Yale University Press, 2013), 131–36. Steven K. Green offers a more nuanced version of the secular narrative, viewing the case as a reactionary hitch in "the law's secularizing trend." See Green, *The Second Disestablishment: Church and*

State in Nineteenth-Century America (New York: Oxford University Press, 2010), 352–53. The trial's contribution to American secularism is also the implicit angle pursued in a recent examination of the case: Craig A. Leisy, *The Blasphemy Trial of Charles B. Reynolds, Morristown, New Jersey, May 19–20, 1887* (Manchester Center, VT: Shires, 2011), vii, 102. Leonard W. Levy set the scholarly tone for incorporating the case into a larger secular liberal storyline about the attenuation and eventual undoing of blasphemy jurisprudence in the United States. See Levy, *Blasphemy: Verbal Offense Against the Sacred, from Moses to Salman Rushdie* (Chapel Hill: University of North Carolina Press, 1995), 508–11. Liberal secular optimism about the case's import was evident from the earliest renderings of this "famous trial" among freethinkers; Ingersoll was seen as having dealt a "death wound" to blasphemy laws through his eloquence. See Samuel P. Putnam, *400 Years of Freethought* (New York: Truth Seeker Co., 1894), 792–94. That Reynolds's career has not been closely examined is evident in the way scholars have often casually misidentified his religious background, claiming him to be an ex-Methodist rather than an ex-Adventist. That mistake was made early on by the *New York Times,* 20 May 1887, 8, and it has lingered. The Seventh-day Adventists, with their own record of minority activism on behalf of religious liberty, lent a distinct timbre to Reynolds's transit into secularist agitation.

3. "The Conviction of Reynolds," *New York Times*, 21 May 1887, 4.

4. J. H. Burnham, "Religious Toleration," *Truth Seeker*, 30 Jan. 1886, 66–67; *Truth Seeker Annual and Freethinkers' Almanac for 1884* (New York: Truth Seeker Co., 1884), 30–31. See also "Religious Freedom," *Boston Investigator*, 1 Aug. 1883, 5. Burnham's essay lost its way in its own brand of liberal intolerance, which the paper's editor then tried to refine into greater consistency. See [E. M. Macdonald], "Religious Toleration," *Truth Seeker*, 30 Jan. 1886, 72.

5. Modest details about Reynolds's life, including his being orphaned, appeared in his obituary in the *Truth Seeker*, 22 Aug. 1896, 541. The basis for most of that account was Putnam's portrait in *400 Years of Freethought,* 792–94. The story about the acting troupe is a bit of family lore that still circulates among his descendants. See Leisy, *Blasphemy Trial*, 2. Reynolds's skill as a dramatist on the lecture circuit was widely noticed, and those well-honed talents lend some added credence to the family story.

6. "News from the Field," *Signs of the Times*, 29 April 1875, 197; "Progress of the Cause," *Adventist Review and Sabbath Herald*, 5 July 1877, 14. See also C. B. Reynolds, "Frank Admissions," *Adventist Review and Sabbath Herald*, 4 May 1869, 150.

7. J. M. Gallemore, "To the Lonely Ones," *Adventist Review and Sabbath Herald*, 27 April 1876, 135; C. B. Reynolds, "The Sabbath," *Truth Seeker*, 5 May 1883, 274–75 and 12 May 1883, 290–91 (quotations on p. 274).

8. C. B. Reynolds, "Gross Misrepresentation of Our Most Efficient and Zealous Co-Worker," *Boston Investigator*, 30 Dec. 1891, 3; "Abstract Principle Not Personal Interest," *American Sentinel*, 21 Jan. 1892, 19–20. The *Truth Seeker* monitored Adventist persecution alongside Reynolds's travails, sometimes in the same article. See "Religious Persecution in Arkansas," *Truth Seeker*, 12 March 1887, 168.

9. "Progress of the Cause," *Adventist Review and Sabbath Herald*, 10 July 1879, 22; C. B. Reynolds, "The Tent," *Truth Seeker*, 4 July 1885, 421; "Mr. Reynolds," *Truth Seeker*, 21 Feb. 1885, 116. See also C. B. Reynolds, "The Tent—Answers to Questions," *Truth Seeker*, 25 April 1885, 260. In 1884 and 1885, members of the National Liberal League were in the process of renaming themselves the American Secular Union.

Reynolds rose in the organization when it was known by the former name and was equally active in the renamed body. See "The National Liberal League: The Eighth Annual Congress," *Truth Seeker*, 20 Sept. 1884, 596.

10. C. B. Reynolds, "Continuing in Well Doing," *Signs of the Times*, 17 Oct. 1878, 307; "All Sorts," *Freethinkers' Magazine* 5 (1886): 44; C. B. Reynolds, "Salvation," *Truth Seeker*, 4 Oct. 1884, 626.

11. C. B. Reynolds, "Tobacco," *Truth Seeker*, 16 June 1883, 375; "From Mr. Reynolds," *Truth Seeker*, 18 April 1885, 245.

12. C. B. Reynolds, "Repentance and Faith in Jesus," *Truth Seeker*, 30 June 1883, 411; C. B. Reynolds, "Christian Lamentations," *Truth Seeker*, 18 Aug. 1883, 516–17.

13. C. B. Reynolds, "Drifting Away," *Adventist Review and Sabbath Herald*, 23 Oct. 1879, 138.

14. [Jay Chaapel], "Memorial Meeting in Rochester, N.Y.," *Truth Seeker*, 6 Jan. 1883, 2–3. The article identified Reynolds as a Baptist preacher, perhaps confusing his affiliation as being with the Seventh-day Baptists rather than the Seventh-day Adventists, groups that mirrored one another on the Sabbath question. Reynolds credited "Mr. and Mrs. Elias H. Gault" as decisive influences in bringing him to freethinking rationalism, though the Gaults were among those freethinkers, like Bennett himself, who also harbored spiritualist sympathies. See C. B. Reynolds, "The Tent," *Truth Seeker*, 13 June 1885, 372.

15. C. B. Reynolds, "Scandal," *Truth Seeker*, 3 Feb. 1883, 68–69. The "Scandal" essay is dated January 18, 1883, less than two weeks after the article about his speech at the Rochester memorial meeting. Reynolds's turn from the ministry to infidelity would necessarily have created suspicions about his character and moral failings, but I have found no evidence that he left the ministry under any cloud besides his loss of faith.

16. "The Rochester Convention," *Truth Seeker*, 8 Sept. 1883, 564–65, 572–73. Reynolds announced his entry into the lecture field that November and was on the road the following winter and spring and much of the time thereafter. See "Lectures and Meetings," *Truth Seeker*, 24 Nov. 1883, 741; "Lectures and Meetings," *Truth Seeker*, 19 Jan. 1884, 41; "Lectures and Meetings," *Truth Seeker*, 10 May 1884, 297.

17. "The Meeting at Salamanca," *Truth Seeker*, 20 Dec. 1884, 806; "The Effects of Reynolds on Frackville, Pa.," *Truth Seeker*, 28 Feb. 1885, 135; "Hamburg, Erie County, N.Y.," *Truth Seeker*, 23 Feb. 1884, 116; C. B. Reynolds, "The Tent," *Truth Seeker*, 4 July 1885, 421; C. B. Reynolds, "The Tent," *Truth Seeker*, 1 Aug. 1885, 485; "Liberal Entertainments," *Truth Seeker*, 7 Nov. 1885, 713; C. B. Reynolds, "Mr. Reynolds in Ohio," *Truth Seeker*, 19 March 1887, 183.

18. "Excitement at Montezuma, N.Y.," *Truth Seeker*, 17 Jan. 1885, 36–37; C. B. Reynolds, "Montezuma, New York," *Truth Seeker*, 24 Jan. 1885, 55.

19. C. B. Reynolds, "Death and Funeral of the Child of Mr. and Mrs. Ross," *Truth Seeker*, 31 Jan. 1885, 67. For the changed atmosphere the next year, see C. B. Reynolds, "The Tent in Wayne Co., New York," *Truth Seeker*, 17 July 1886, 452. For a repeat of this type of Baptist-infidel rapprochement, see "Lewis Knapp," *Truth Seeker*, 26 Feb. 1898, 139. Knapp was a village atheist in Kenosha, Wisconsin, who had made himself notorious by erecting various infidel monuments and tombstones in town; yet, upon his death, the local Baptist preacher conducted a respectful funeral service for him, praising the freethinker's good and generous heart: "Knapp was a Christian, but didn't know it."

20. Reynolds, "The Tent—Answers to Questions," 260; C. B. Reynolds, "The Tent," *Truth Seeker*, 22 Aug. 1885, 532.

21. "Lectures and Meetings," *Truth Seeker*, 27 Feb. 1886, 133. Frances Reynolds was brand new to the lecture field; she had lectured only twice before the Boonton appearance, once in Philadelphia and once in Jobstown, New Jersey, both in the previous week. At Boonton she attracted a crowd as a woman "who dared speak in public against religion."

22. "Lectures and Meetings," *Truth Seeker*, 27 Feb. 1886, 133; C. B. Reynolds, "Boonton Secular Union," *Truth Seeker*, 6 March 1886, 148; C. B. Reynolds, "The Tent in Wayne Co., New York," *Truth Seeker*, 3 July 1886, 420; Florence Hennion to Editor, *Truth Seeker*, 24 April 1886, 266. The club kept inviting infidel lecturers after the Reynolds debacle. See Florence Hennion to Editor, *Truth Seeker*, 16 Oct. 1886, 666.

23. "Reynolds Arrested for Blasphemy," *Truth Seeker*, 7 Aug. 1886, 504–505.

24. "Reynolds Arrested for Blasphemy," 504–505; "Boonton," *Iron Era* (Dover, NJ), 7 Aug. 1886, clipping in the C. B. Reynolds Vertical File, New Jersey History and Genealogy Center, Morristown and Morris Township Library, Morristown, NJ. The *Truth Seeker* carried the fullest report on the initial incidents in Boonton. The paper's editor, E. M. Macdonald, was on hand for the hearing and reprinted a transcript of the proceedings. Though Macdonald was clearly a Reynolds partisan, his account of the violent threats comport with local newspaper reports, which were partisans in the other direction.

25. "Reynolds Arrested for Blasphemy," 504.

26. "Reynolds Arrested for Blasphemy," 504–505. The sign in the prosecutor's law office is from "Boonton," *Iron Era* (Dover, NJ), 16 Oct. 1886, clipping in the Reynolds Vertical File.

27. "Reynolds Arrested for Blasphemy," 505; "New Jersey and Her Laws," *Truth Seeker*, 14 Aug. 1886, 520–21. The oath and affirmation requirements for witnesses varied from state to state, but the majority allowed "non-religious affirmations," though, as Reynolds discovered in New Jersey, those allowances did not always work for infidels. Minnesota and Michigan were especially accommodating for infidel witnesses, while Maryland, North Carolina, Tennessee, Pennsylvania, and Massachusetts were famously unaccommodating. See "Affirming," *Truth Seeker*, 8 Dec. 1888, 777; "Sunday, Oath, and Blasphemy Laws," in *Truth Seeker Annual and Freethinkers' Almanac for 1887* (New York: Truth Seeker Co., 1887), 37–91. The fight in Massachusetts, thanks in large part to the editorial leadership of the *Boston Investigator*, had been particularly sustained, if mostly fruitless. For samples of that long-running struggle, see "Competency of Witnesses," *Boston Investigator*, 6 Sept. 1833, n.p.; "Rights and Competency of Witnesses," *Boston Investigator*, 12 June 1835, n.p.; "Rejection of Atheists," *Boston Investigator*, 17 April 1844, n.p.; "Witnesses—Oaths," *Boston Investigator*, 13 July 1853, n.p.; "Atheist Witnesses," *Boston Investigator*, 9 Nov. 1853, n.p.; "Atheists, as Witnesses," *Boston Investigator*, 4 March 1857, n.p.; "Debate on the Witness Bill," *Boston Investigator*, 2 Feb. 1859, n.p.; "Atheists as Witnesses," *Boston Investigator*, 16 Nov. 1870, 228; "Credibility of Witnesses," *Boston Investigator*, 16 March 1881, 4; "Credibility of Witnesses," *Boston Investigator*, 23 April 1884, 3; "The Atheist Bill Defeated," *Boston Investigator*, 26 May 1886, 5. For a particularly substantial articulation of the case for atheist competency, see F. M. Holland, *Atheists and Agnostics: A Protest against Their Disabilities before the Law: A Lecture Delivered in Investigator Hall, Boston, to the Ingersoll Secular Society, on Sunday, March 1, 1885* (Boston: Mendum, 1885). Witness competency remained a live issue for freethinking activists through the mid-twentieth century, until *Torcaso v. Watkins*

settled the religious test question on liberal secularist terms in 1961. On that case, see the epilogue.

28. "Reynolds Arrested for Blasphemy," 505; "A Blasphemer in Court," *Milwaukee Sentinel*, 2 Aug. 1886, 2; "Boonton," *Iron Era* (Dover, NJ), 7 Aug. 1886, clipping in Reynolds Vertical File; George E. Macdonald, *Fifty Years of Freethought*, 2 vols. (New York: Truth Seeker Co., 1931), 2: 131; Robert G. Ingersoll, *The Works of Robert G. Ingersoll*, 12 vols. (New York: Ingersoll League, 1933), 11: 87. Most nineteenth-century American freethinkers knew the scriptures well and took critical exegesis of the Bible as their starting point. On the same competence among their British counterparts, see Timothy Larsen, *A People of One Book: The Bible and the Victorians* (Oxford: Oxford University Press, 2011), 67–88.

29. "Boonton Again Awakened," *Truth Seeker*, 21 Aug. 1886, 536; "Mr. Ingersoll to Defend Mr. Reynolds," *Truth Seeker*, 21 Aug. 1886, 537. The pamphlet was based on the *Truth Seeker* report, "New Jersey and Her Laws," cited above. No independent copy of it appears to be extant.

30. C. B. Reynolds, "The Blasphemer's Program," *Truth Seeker*, 9 Oct. 1886, 644; "Blasphemy: Reynolds Indicted for the Crime of Libeling a Ghost," *Truth Seeker*, 30 Oct. 1886, 696–97; "Editorial Notes," *Truth Seeker*, 21 Aug. 1886, 537; C. B. Reynolds, *Blasphemy and the Bible* (New York: Truth Seeker Co., [1886]), 2, 7. The formal indictment did not mention Heston's caricature, but it was widely seen as the most incriminating aspect of the pamphlet. See, for example, "Charged with Blasphemy," *New York Sun*, 20 May 1887, 1; "On Trial for Blasphemy," *New York Times*, 20 May 1887, 8; "Trial for Blasphemy," *Atlanta Constitution*, 23 May 1887, 1; C. P. Farrell, "Publisher's Preface," *Trial of C. B. Reynolds for Blasphemy, at Morristown, N. J., May 19th and 20th, 1887* (New York: Farrell, 1888), iv. As Farrell concluded, "This cartoon was the gravamen of his offence."

31. "Then and Now," *Truth Seeker*, 6 Nov. 1886, 712; C. B. Reynolds, "Mr. Reynolds's Program," *Truth Seeker*, 18 Dec. 1886, 804.

32. "Mr. Reynolds's Case," *Truth Seeker*, 5 Feb. 1887, 89; *Jerseyman* (Morristown, NJ), 4 Feb. 1887, 2, Reynolds Vertical File. This report cited a similar appraisal from the Boonton *Bulletin*. The *Jerseyman* suspected from the outset that the town of Boonton had made a mistake in arresting Reynolds on blasphemy charges; the paper only became more convinced of that as the case developed. See the untitled clippings from the newspaper for 30 July 1886, 2, and 6 Aug. 1886, 3, Reynolds Vertical File. In the end, the paper thought Reynolds's conviction was just, but still tactically miscalculated. See "Morris County Courts," *Jerseyman* (Morristown, NJ), 27 May 1887, 3, Reynolds Vertical File.

33. "Convicted and Fined," *Truth Seeker*, 28 May 1887, 344–45; "Trial and Conviction of C. B. Reynolds for Blasphemy," *Boston Investigator*, 25 May 1887, 3; "On Trial for Blasphemy," *New York Times*, 20 May 1887, 8. The *Times* counted sixteen prosecution witnesses; the *Truth Seeker* listed ten by name; the New York *Sun* had the number at a dozen; the *Chicago Tribune* listed eleven.

34. Ingersoll, *Works*, 11: 56, 63, 102, 115; "Charged with Blasphemy," 1. An example of just how well the speech played was the thrilled response of George Jacob Holyoake, the dean of British secularists, to news accounts he had read of Ingersoll's "eloquent and imperishable defence of Free Speech." See Holyoake to Robert Ingersoll, 21 June 1887, Robert Ingersoll Papers, reel 18, Manuscript Division, Library of Congress, Washington, DC. Ingersoll also kept a scrapbook containing some of

the favorable newspaper reports. See scrapbook #21, pp. 34–43, on reel 28 of the Ingersoll Papers. Still, as one vinegary critic remarked of Ingersoll's oratorical style in general, the Great Agnostic seemed like "a music-box" in which "ideas are subordinated to euphony." "I would as soon think of having a controversy with an æolian harp as with Col. Ingersoll." See W. C. Brann, *The Complete Works of Brann the Iconoclast*, 12 vols. (New York: Brann Publishers, 1919), 4: 276.

35. "Convicted and Fined," 344–45; Ingersoll, *Works*, 11: 92; *The People v. Ruggles*, 8 Johns, 290, Supreme Court of Judicature of New York (1811). For the tenacity of blasphemy jurisprudence in the early republic, particularly the legal weight of the *Ruggles* opinion, see Sarah Barringer Gordon, "Blasphemy and the Law of Religious Liberty in Nineteenth-Century America," *American Quarterly* 52 (2000): 682–719; Green, *Second Disestablishment*, 162–69, 174–78; and Phillip I. Blumberg, *Repressive Jurisprudence in the Early American Republic: The First Amendment and the Legacy of English Law* (Cambridge: Cambridge University, 2010), 318–35. Others have suggested the focus should instead be on the rare application and weak enforcement of blasphemy laws in the nineteenth century; blasphemy trials were aberrations that proved the rule of American toleration and religious liberty. See Levy, *Blasphemy*, 400–23, 505–12; Chris Beneke, "The Myth of American Religious Coercion; or, Failures of the Unofficial Religious Establishment, Briefly Told," *Common-Place* 15 (Spring 2015), (accessed Aug. 25, 2015), http://www.common-place.org/vol-15/no-03/beneke/#.VfMXZ32CiSo. Beneke is especially critiquing David Sehat's reliance on blasphemy jurisprudence as central to his depiction of the hegemonic force of the Protestant moral establishment. See Sehat, *Myth of American Religious Freedom*, 1–2, 5, 49–56, 164. Reynolds's story is positioned here in the ductile space between these opposing interpretations.

36. "Convicted and Fined," 344–45; Ingersoll, *Works*, 11: 108; *Abstract of Returns Concerning Jails, and of the Accounts of the County Treasurers, for the Year Ending November 30, 1877* (Hartford: Wiley, Waterman, and Eaton, 1878), 23; *Abstract of Returns Concerning Jails, and of the Accounts of the County Treasurers, for the Year Ending November 30, 1878* (Hartford: Wiley, Waterman, and Eaton, 1879), n.p.; "County Finances—Jail Statistics," *New Haven Register*, 11 Dec. 1879, 4; "Blasphemy," *Boston Investigator*, 22 March 1882, 4; "Is Knowledge Dangerous?" *Lucifer the Light Bearer*, 15 Feb. 1889, 2. The Kneeland episode is much studied: for a classic compendium, see Leonard W. Levy, ed., *Blasphemy in Massachusetts: Freedom of Conscience and the Abner Kneeland Case* (New York: Da Capo, 1973); for a recent examination, see Paul Finkelman, "Blasphemy and Free Thought in Jacksonian America: The Case of Abner Kneeland," in Christopher S. Grenda, Chris Beneke, and David Nash, eds., *Profane: Sacrilegious Expression in a Multicultural Age* (Berkeley: University of California Press, 2014), 119–40. On the Mockus case, see Levy, *Blasphemy*, 512–15; William Wolkovich-Valkavicius, "Two Lithuanian Immigrants' Blasphemy Trials during the Red Scare," *Historical Journal of Massachusetts* 26 (1998): 145–57; *State v. Michael X. Mockus*, 120 Me. 84, Supreme Judicial Court of Maine (1921). Also, see how the "blasphemy" of a street-preaching freethinker in Atlanta was suppressed through a public disturbance charge in 1897: "Denial of Free Speech in Atlanta," *Truth Seeker*, 12 June 1897, 372; "Silencing the Freethinker," *Truth Seeker*, 12 June 1897, 377. The disorderly conduct charge was still routinely used against freethinking street orators in New York City in the 1910s and 1920s. See Macdonald, *Fifty Years*, 2: 452–53, 466–67, 580, 598; "Bigotry Wins a Point," *Truth*

Seeker, 1 Sept. 1923, 549; "Catholic Manifestations," *Truth Seeker*, 1 Sept. 1923, 567. For obscenity's inheritance of blasphemy's mantle in the prosecution of freethinkers and atheists, see chapter 4.

37. "Convicted and Fined," 344–45. See also "Jersey Law Triumphant," *New York Times*, 21 May 1887, 8; "The Blasphemy Trial," *Chicago Daily Tribune*, 23 May 1887, 3.

38. J. W. Leighton to the Editor, *Truth Seeker*, 28 Aug. 1886, 554; C. B. Reynolds, "C. B. Reynolds on His Western Tour," *Truth Seeker*, 17 Sept. 1887, 597; C. B. Reynolds, "C. B. Reynolds on His Western Tour," *Truth Seeker*, 3 Dec. 1887, 772. The *Truth Seeker* and *Boston Investigator* tracked his westward itinerary in detail, and so did the journal *Freethought*, a new publishing venture in San Francisco. Reynolds estimated that during this eighteen-month tour he had lectured on all but about twenty-five nights (in other words, over five hundred times). See C. B. Reynolds, "C. B. Reynolds on His Western Tour," *Boston Investigator*, 6 March 1889, 3.

39. C. B. Reynolds, "Victory of the Washington Secular Union," *Truth Seeker*, 13 Dec. 1890, 788; C. B. Reynolds, "The Cause in Washington," *Boston Investigator*, 30 March 1892, 3; "God in the Public Schools," *Boston Investigator*, 19 Oct. 1892, 6; "Charles B. Reynolds," *Truth Seeker*, 22 Aug. 1896, 541.

40. "Ingersoll's Brief Visit," *Chicago Daily Tribune*, 11 June 1887, 1; "The Conviction of Reynolds," 4; "A Right Not Worth Insisting On," 4; "A Blasphemer Punished," *Atlanta Constitution*, 24 May 1887, 4; *Western Rural* article reprinted in "Another Curiosity for Mr. Lamar of Chicago," *Truth Seeker*, 2 July 1887, 424; "An Indecent Blasphemer Brought to Book," *Christian Advocate*, 26 May 1887, 1.

41. Ingersoll, *Works*, 11: 56; Macdonald, *Fifty Years*, 1: 423. The minister who wrote to the *World* (cited in Macdonald) was Hugh Pentecost; he became a fellow traveler among free-speech activists. Religious liberals like Pentecost often joined the cause of equal rights for atheists. A cadre of Harvard Divinity School graduates led the campaign for the equal rights of atheists in Massachusetts in the 1880s: Thomas Wentworth Higginson, Cyrus Bartol, and F. M. Holland. They were joined by Minot Savage, a Congregationalist-turned-Unitarian pastor and a graduate of Bangor Theological Seminary.

42. Samuel P. Putnam, "News and Notes," *Truth Seeker*, 14 Aug. 1886, 517; Samuel P. Putnam, "News and Notes," *Truth Seeker*, 15 May 1886, 309; Ingersoll, *Works*, 11: 114.

43. "C. B. Reynolds on His Western Tour," 723; "The Tent in Wayne Co.," 420. Toleration as a "nitty-gritty practice" (p. 11) is especially well developed in Benjamin J. Kaplan, *Divided by Faith: Religious Conflict and the Practice of Toleration in Early Modern Europe* (Cambridge, MA: Harvard University Press, 2007). Kaplan distinguishes between *tolerance* as a principle of embracing religious diversity and *toleration* as a social practice in which religious differences are grudgingly accepted as a means of peaceful coexistence. In the post-Revolution American setting, the principles of religious freedom and the rights of individual conscience had become common (if highly negotiable) coinage, but Kaplan's larger point on the local, practical, quotidian qualities of toleration remains quite relevant, even in that transformed religious and political environment; religious variety, after all, was still regularly perceived as threatening and objectionable rather than desirable, and that remained especially the case when it came to unbelievers and infidels. A similar concern with "*everyday practices* of peaceful coexistence" in war-torn early modern Europe is at the heart of Jesse Spohnholz, *The Tactics of Toleration: A Refugee Community in the Age of Religious Wars* (Newark: University of Delaware Press, 2011), 16. For the

extension of this line of inquiry to North America, see Chris Beneke and Christopher S. Grenda, eds., *The First Prejudice: Religious Tolerance and Intolerance in Early America* (Philadelphia: University of Pennsylvania Press, 2011).

44. *Jerseyman* (Morristown, NJ), 27 May 1887, 2, Reynolds Vertical File; Mount Holly *Mirror* quoted in *Jerseyman* (Morristown, NJ), 6 Aug. 1886, 3, Reynolds Vertical File; Ingersoll, *Works*, 11: 64–65.

45. "Prosecuted for Blasphemy," *Boston Investigator*, 11 Aug. 1886, 6; Samuel P. Putnam, "News and Notes," *Truth Seeker*, 28 May 1887, 340–41; "Reminiscences of Ukiah," *Freethought*, 21 July 1888, 354.

46. B. F. Underwood, "The Bigotry of Odd Fellows," *Boston Investigator*, 20 June 1877, 5; Andrew Goan, "Persecution of Odd Fellows," *Boston Investigator*, 18 July 1877, 2; B. F. Underwood, "A Note from B. F. Underwood," *Truth Seeker*, 1 March 1879, 136; B. F. Underwood, "A Letter from B. F. Underwood," *Boston Investigator*, 19 Feb. 1879, 3; B. F. Underwood, "The Arrest and Trial of B. F. Underwood," *Boston Investigator*, 30 June 1880, 1; B. F. Underwood, "Science versus Theology," *Boston Investigator,* 14 July 1880, 3. The prosecution of Underwood occasioned second-guessing, much as the attempted suppression of Reynolds did. The Christians of Irwin Station should not try to stifle discussion but seek "open and equal discussion with unbelievers," so one Pittsburg paper advised; otherwise, they were just embarrassing their religious cause. See "The Irwin Error," *Boston Investigator*, 5 March 1879, 5.

47. S. H. Preston, "No Atheist Need Apply," *Freethinkers' Magazine* 5 (1886): 368–73; S. H. Preston, "Questions for Infidels," *Truth Seeker*, 15 Sept. 1875, 7. On the Thorne case, see "God in Politics: The Case of the Quaker Mr. Thorne," *Boston Investigator*, 17 March 1875, 3; "A Case of Proscription," *Boston Investigator*, 17 March 1875, 4. On the Robitscheck case, see also "Atheism and Citizenship," *Truth Seeker*, 14 Aug. 1886, 516; "Atheists as Citizens," *Freethought*, 3 Nov. 1888, 532–33. Robitscheck pressed his case with the help of a lawyer and was then allowed to substitute an affirmation for an oath. Preston wrote his article before the denial was reversed. See "Notes and Clippings," *Truth Seeker*, 21 Aug. 1886, 529. The other naturalization case Preston cited involved Julius Nieland. His initial denial of citizenship—his appeal was successful four months later—also attracted considerable notice among civil-liberties activists. See "Appeal to the American People," *Truth Seeker*, 15 May 1875, 9; "Citizenship Refused on Account of Unbelief," *Boston Investigator*, 24 March 1875, 6; "A Meeting of the Liberal League," *Boston Investigator*, 12 May 1875, 6. Even the most zealous evangelical reformers acknowledged that "our laws make no provision for excluding Atheists from citizenship." See the admission of the *Christian Statesman*, which cited this weakness in the law as another reason to amend the Constitution on Christian terms, in "Atheism and Citizenship," *Boston Investigator*, 15 Dec. 1886, 3. On the witness competency cases Preston adduced, see also G. L. Henderson, "A Witness and His God," *Truth Seeker*, 1 April 1875, 9. The infidel editor whom Preston cited was John A. Lant, one of Anthony Comstock's targets, whose case is discussed in the next chapter.

48. On Ingersoll's political quagmire, see "A Test Case of Equal Rights," *Index*, 13 Dec. 1877, 594; "Politics and Religion," *Boston Investigator*, 6 Sept. 1876, 4; "Shall Ingersoll Go to Berlin?" *Milwaukee Daily Sentinel*, 16 Nov. 1877, 7; "Religion in Politics," *Boston Investigator*, 19 Dec. 1877, 4. For an example of how the "avowed Atheist" charge was used in one state contest in New York, see "Christian Men! Can You Vote for an Atheist?" *Index*, 19 Nov. 1874, 556. Religious efforts to remove a public official on the grounds of infidelity could backfire. See the case of a Connecticut postmaster

and judge recounted in J. P. Fenton, "Experience of an Infidel," *Boston Investigator*, 20 June 1877, 2. Among the political cases American freethinkers were watching most closely was one abroad: namely, that of British secularist Charles Bradlaugh who was elected to Parliament in 1880 but denied his seat because of his objections to the religious oath. His case dragged on for several years until he was finally acknowledged as an MP in 1886 and ultimately won a change in the oath requirement for atheists in 1888. See Timothy Larsen, "Charles Bradlaugh, Militant Unbelief, and the Civil Rights of Atheists," in Caroline Litzenberger and Eileen Groth Lyon, eds., *The Human Tradition in Modern Britain* (Lanham, MD: Rowman and Littlefield, 2006), 127–38. A still more hopeful sign abroad was the electoral success of New Zealand's infidels in 1884. Robert Stout, President of the New Zealand Freethought Association, was elected the colony's premier. See P. J. Lineham, "Freethinkers in Nineteenth-Century New Zealand," *New Zealand Journal of History* 19 (1985): 62–63. For American satisfaction with Stout's success, seen as a "first" for freethinkers across the British Empire, see "Editorial Notes," *Truth Seeker*, 25 Oct. 1884, 681.

49. On the Russell case, see "The Texas Infamy," *Index*, 22 Nov. 1877, 558–59; L. J. Russell, "A Card from Dr. L. J. Russell," *Boston Investigator*, 21 Nov. 1877, 2; "Freethought in the United States," *Truth Seeker Annual and Freethinkers' Almanac for 1895* (New York: Truth Seeker Co., 1895), 26.

50. Ingersoll, *Works*, 11: 82; T. G. Springer to Editor, *Truth Seeker*, 12 April 1890, 234; H. P. Marsh to Editor, *Truth Seeker*, 22 March 1890, 186.

51. Ingersoll, *Works*, 12: 219, 226. Ingersoll's line-in-the-sand opposition to fellow secularist efforts at wholesale repeal of the Comstock laws is documented at length in Eugene Macdonald, *Col. Robert G. Ingersoll as He Is: A Complete Refutation of His Clerical Enemies' Malicious Slanders* (New York: Truth Seeker Co., 1896), 111–34.

CHAPTER 4: THE OBSCENE ATHEIST; OR, THE SEXUAL POLITICS OF INFIDELITY

1. "Violating Postal Laws," *New York Times*, 20 April 1887, 5. Biographical attention to Slenker has been both thin and scarce, but see Hal D. Sears, *The Sex Radicals: Free Love in High Victorian America* (Lawrence: Regents Press of Kansas, 1977), 204–28; Edward D. Jervey, "Elmina Slenker: Freethinker and Sex Radical," *Virginia Social Science Journal* 16 (April 1981): 1–12; and Jervey, "Elmina Slenker: Infidel and Atheist," *Free Inquiry* 5 (Winter 1984–1985): 41–43. Jervey had access to a scrapbook of Slenker's writings, found in an attic in Snowville. He donated it to the Radford University archives, but it has since been misplaced and is at present missing. Most of the pieces he cites from the scrapbook are clippings from the *Boston Investigator*. Two helpful archival files on Slenker, again mostly newspaper clippings, can be found in the Ralph Ginzburg Papers, Boxes 5 and 22, Wisconsin Historical Society, Madison, WI. Even without manuscript materials, Slenker's career can be reconstructed through her voluminous published writings in a range of journals.

2. "Defiant Mrs. Slenker," *New York Times*, 30 April 1887, 5; "The Slenker Scandal," *St. Louis Post-Dispatch*, 30 April 1887, 12; Elmina Drake Slenker, "Mrs. Slenker in Her Own Defense," *Truth Seeker*, 14 May 1887, 311; Elmina D. Slenker, "Jail Life, or Life in Jail," *Boston Investigator*, 18 May 1887, 2.

3. "A Letter from Mrs. Slenker," *Boston Investigator*, 20 July 1887, 6; "A Letter from Mrs. Slenker," *Boston Investigator*, 3 Aug. 1887, 3; "Elmina at Abingdon," *Boston*

Investigator, 9 Nov. 1887, 3; "Mrs. Slenker's Attorneys," *Truth Seeker*, 30 July 1887, 485; "A Woman Victim," *Worthington Advance: Free Thought, Free Speech, and a Free Press*, 19 May 1887, 1.

4. "Defence of Natural Rights," *Boston Investigator*, 29 June 1887, 4; "The Obscenity Spook," *Liberty*, 30 July 1887, 8; "Mrs. Slenker's Case," *Boston Investigator*, 18 May 1887, 4.

5. Elmina Drake Slenker, "Mrs. Slenker in Her Own Defense," *Truth Seeker*, 14 May 1887, 311; Elmina Drake Slenker, "Sexual Intemperance.—No. 6," *Truth Seeker*, 7 Aug. 1880, 503; E. D. Slenker, "Queries and Replies," *Alpha* 9 (Oct. 1883): 14; "The Celebrated Slenker Case," *Boston Investigator,* 31 Aug. 1887, 3. Slenker sometimes used her full name, sometimes initials, in her bylines; I have followed her case-by-case usage except where she signed a piece only *Elmina* or *Aunt Elmina*; in those instances, I have supplied the last name and dropped the "aunt."

6. E. D. Slenker to Ezra Heywood, *Word* 12 (Feb. 1884): n.p.; Slenker, "Mrs. Slenker in Her Own Defense," 311; Elmina Slenker, "Some Good Words for the Heywoods," *Truth Seeker*, 29 Dec. 1883, 821; "Mrs. Slenker's Arrest," *Truth Seeker*, 14 May 1887, 313.

7. Elmina Slenker to Ezra Heywood, *Word* 15 (Sept. 1886): n.p.; E. D. Slenker to Ezra Heywood, *Word* 16 (Sept. 1887): n.p.; E. D. Slenker to Ezra Heywood, *Word* 17 (Feb. 1889): n.p.; Slenker, "Mrs. Slenker in Her Own Defense," 311; "Mrs. Slenker's Arrest," 312-13; Elmina Drake Slenker, "An Open Letter to Friends," *Truth Seeker*, 16 July 1887, 453; "Mrs. Slenker's Offense," *Truth Seeker*, 30 July 1887, 487; "The New Aspect of Mrs. Slenker's Case," *Truth Seeker,* 13 Aug. 1887, 520-21. The *Truth Seeker* remained contemptuous of the Vice Society in its prosecution of Slenker but saw her as having gone to "intolerable lengths" to obtain "data" on sexual relations ("Mrs. Slenker's Arrest," 312). On Green's blast at Slenker for disgracing the cause, see "Help People before Hitting Them," *Truth Seeker*, 11 June 1887, 376. Green ultimately cut Slenker more slack than he did Putnam, even as he remained convinced that her forays into sexual physiology were a clear error in judgment. See "Elmina Drake Slenker," *Free Thought Magazine* 15 (1897): 722. That partial rapprochement seems to have stemmed from his son's teaming up with Slenker on her small magazine for children called the *Little Freethinker*. Her most consistent backers were those freethinkers who shared her strong interest in sex reform. See J. H. Cook, "Elmina Slenker's Friends Tested," *Lucifer the Light Bearer*, 1 July 1887, 4.

8. "The Defense Association's Appeal for Mrs. Slenker," *Truth Seeker*, 4 June 1887, 357. See also C. L. James to Editor, *Truth Seeker*, 4 June 1887, 363, for a spirited critique of the journal's equivocation in Slenker's case.

9. "Details of the Trial," *Truth Seeker*, 12 Nov. 1887, 724-25; "The Trial of Mrs. Slenker: Examination of Barclay Concluded," *Truth Seeker*, 19 Nov. 1887, 738-41; Edward W. Chamberlain, "The Trial of Mrs. Slenker," *Truth Seeker*, 12 Nov. 1887, 724. Parkhurst briefly took the stand before being disallowed; the other sex reformer, Albert Chavannes, did not make it to the stand at all. Parkhurst wrote in defense of Slenker by way of explaining his own investigations of sexuality. See Henry M. Parkhurst, *Why I Wrote 'Diana'* (New York: n.p., [1887]). Parkhurst called his teaching Dianism, which encouraged slightly more physical affection than Alphaism, but not by a lot, at least as Slenker applied it. Sex was still only for propagation. See Elmina D. Slenker, "Dianism," *Lucifer the Light Bearer*, 14 April 1897, 117; 2 June 1897, 174.

10. "Trial of Mrs. Slenker: Examination of Barclay Concluded," 738-41; "Mrs. Slenker Free," *Truth Seeker*, 12 Nov. 1887, 728; *United States v. Slenker*, in Peyton Boyle, ed.,

The Federal Reporter: Cases Argued and Determined in the Circuit and District Courts of the United States, October, 1887–January, 1888 (St. Paul, MN: West, 1888), 691–95.

11. *New York Society for the Suppression of Vice: Fourth Annual Report* (New York: n.p., 1878), 7; J. N. Mason to Editor, *Truth Seeker*, 3 Dec. 1887, 779; "Mrs. Slenker in Her Own Defense," 311; Lucy N. Colman, "Mrs. Slenker's Arrest," *Boston Investigator*, 25 May 1887, 6; Elmina D. Slenker, "Pioneering," *Truth Seeker*, 9 July 1887, 435.

12. D. M. Bennett, *The World's Sages, Thinkers, and Reformers* (New York: Bennett, 1885), 952; Oswego Monthly Meeting Men's Minutes, 14 May 1847, 16 June 1847, 14 July 1847, 18 Aug. 1847, 19 Jan. 1848, 16 Feb. 1848, New York film box 108; Oswego Monthly Meeting Women's Minutes, 19 April 1848; New York film box 109, Friends Historical Library, Swarthmore College, Swarthmore, PA. Also see the Drake and Pinkham clans indexed in James E. Hazard, ed., *Quaker Records: Bulls Head-Oswego, Poughkeepsie, and Oakwood Monthly Meetings* (Swarthmore, PA: Friends Historical Library, 2005), 53–54, 111. Biographical accounts of Slenker, from Bennett's to Jervey's, describe her father as "a Quaker preacher," but that is not evident in the records of the monthly meeting. Slenker did describe her father that way at her trial in 1887. See "Trial of Mrs. Slenker," 740.

13. Bennett, *World's Sages*, 953; "Matrimony," *Water-Cure Journal* 19 (Dec. 1855): 139; "Married," *Boston Investigator*, 18 June 1856, n.p.; "Pioneering," *Truth Seeker*, 9 July 1887, 435; "Trial of Mrs. Slenker," 740. For a rare indication of Isaac Slenker's irreligion from his own pen, see Isaac Slenker, "A Word to Liberals," *Boston Investigator*, 19 Dec. 1855, n.p. For a sense that he shared his wife's enthusiasm for D. M. Bennett and freethought, see Elmina Slenker to Editor, *Truth Seeker*, 2 Sept. 1882, 555.

14. "Mrs. Rose—Atheism," *Boston Investigator*, 21 May 1856, n.p.; Elmina Drake Slenker, "Eminent Women: Ernestine L. Rose," *Truth Seeker*, 31 Aug. 1889, 550; "Elmina Abroad and Yet at Home," *Truth Seeker*, 17 June 1882, 382; Elmina Drake Slenker to Editor, *Boston Investigator*, 17 Nov. 1894, 6; Bennett, *World's Sages*, 952; E.P.D. Slenker, "Infidelity Is Progressing," *Boston Investigator*, 23 July 1856, n.p. That her religious misgivings began with her mother's prompt to "read the Bible through" is a point she further elaborated in her first published book, *Studying the Bible; or, Brief Criticisms on Some of the Principal Scripture Texts* (Boston: Mendum, 1870), 1–3. This was a compilation of brief and derisive scriptural commentaries that Slenker had serialized over several years in the *Boston Investigator*.

15. "A Specimen of Christian Courtesy," *Boston Investigator*, 7 May 1856, n.p. On the Bangor affair, see the introduction.

16. "Specimen of Christian Courtesy," n.p.; "Mrs. Rose—Atheism," n.p.

17. Slenker, "Infidelity Is Progressing," n.p.; "Continuation of the Letters of Bonnell Thornton, Esq., on a Female Atheist," *Boston Mirror*, 4 March 1809, 3; "Fanny Wright," *Times-Picayune* (New Orleans), 16 March 1839, 2; Ella Wheeler Wilcox, "Infidel Women," *Lucifer the Light Bearer*, 16 March 1901, 67.

18. E. P. Drake Slenker, "A Voice from Pennsylvania," *Boston Investigator*, 12 Aug. 1857, n.p.; Slenker, "Pioneering," 435.

19. Elmina Drake Slenker, "Going, Going, Gone!" *Boston Investigator*, 30 July 1890, 2; Elmina D. Slenker, "Atheist Women," *Boston Investigator*, 13 Jan. 1892, 6; Elmina Drake Slenker, "Many Atheist Mothers," *Truth Seeker*, 29 Aug. 1891, 554; Elmina Slenker, "Where Shall We Find Liberal Wives?" *Truth Seeker*, 25 Nov. 1882, 746; M.C.G. Reed to Editor, *Truth Seeker*, 2 Nov. 1878, 700.

20. Elmina Drake Slenker, *Little Lessons for Little Folks* (New York: Truth Seeker Co.,

1887), 28, 71–72; "Trial of Mrs. Slenker," 740; J. D. Kruschke, "The Children's Department," *Boston Investigator*, 15 Oct. 1884, 3. Slenker had been publishing her
lessons in the *Boston Investigator* and also through a publishing concern in the
freethought community of Liberal, Missouri; the earlier, somewhat longer collection
of her *Little Lessons* had appeared in Liberal under G. H. Walser's imprint in 1884,
but the New York edition was more widely circulated, reviewed, and discussed. On
the first version, see Susan H. Wixon, "Aunt Elmina's Book," *Truth Seeker*, 27 Sept.
1884, 611. For a very helpful investigation of freethought literature for children in
this period, particularly Susan Wixon's "Children's Corner" in the *Truth Seeker*, see
Joanne E. Passet, "Freethought Children's Literature and the Construction of Religious Identity in Late-Nineteenth-Century America," *Book History* 8 (2005): 107–29.
Passet misidentifies Slenker as "a freethinking Spiritualist" (p. 110) here and in *Sex
Radicals and the Quest for Women's Equality* (Urbana: University of Illinois Press,
2003), 159. The confusion stems from a surviving spirit photograph of Slenker with
ghostly faces in the background. A staunch anti-spiritualist, Slenker often tested
spirit phenomena, including spirit photography, only to report on it skeptically. On
her sundry trips to spirit photographers and her disgust at their frauds, see Elmina
Slenker, "A Few More Boston Notes," *Boston Investigator*, 22 Oct. 1884, 3; Elmina
Slenker to Editor, *Truth Seeker*, 30 May 1885, 346.

21. E. D. Slenker, "Children's Department," *Boston Investigator*, 12 Aug. 1885, 8; Elmina
P. D. Slenker, "A Proposition," *Boston Investigator*, 4 July 1866, 1; Elmina D. Slenker,
"The Infidel and the Christian; or, The Two Friends," *Boston Investigator*, 31 May
1871, 3; 21 June 1871, 3; 19 July 1871, 3; 16 Aug. 1871, 3; 6 Sept. 1871, 3. For more of her
early stories, see Elmina Drake Slenker, "Advertising for a Husband; or, Living Out
One's Principles," *Boston Investigator*, 23 Nov. 1870, 235; "Martha J—; or, The Victim
of Circumstance," *Boston Investigator*, 21 Dec. 1870, 267; and "Lellia's Three Lovers;
or, The Woman Who Believed in Equal Rights," *Boston Investigator*, 4 Sept. 1872, 3;
11 Sept. 1872, 3; 18 Sept. 1872, 3; 25 Sept. 1872, 3. In biographical sketches of Slenker
another piece of domestic fiction, *The Clergyman's Victims: A Radical Romance*
(1881), has often been attributed to her. While Slenker advertised that novel for sale
along with her own romances, she was not its author.

22. Elmina D. Slenker, *John's Way: A Domestic Radical Story* (New York: Liberal and
Scientific Publishing House, [1877]), 25; Elmina D. Slenker, "The 'Experience' of
Mrs. Holmes; or, Religion and Infidelity," *Boston Investigator*, 8 Nov. 1871, 3; 15 Nov.
1871, 3. "I *am* what you dread, fear, and abhor—an Infidel! an Atheist!" school-
teacher Mary Jones admits to a suitor in another of Slenker's romances, only to
win the admirer over to irreligion and marriage through her combination of keen
intelligence and spotless virtue. That story ends too in the familial contentment of
a happy home. See Elmina D. Slenker, "Mary Jones; or, The Infidel School-Teacher,"
Boston Investigator, 29 Sept. 1875, 3. *Mary Jones* was eventually published as a nov-
elette in 1883.

23. Elmina Drake Slenker, *The Darwins: A Domestic Radical Romance* (New York:
Bennett, [1879]), 5, 25, 44, 117.

24. Slenker, *Darwins*, 147–48, 183, 191, 254–55.

25. Elmina D. Slenker, "The Most Needful Education," *Lucifer the Light Bearer*, 8 Nov.
1889, 1; Henrietta L. Buckner, "How I Became Acquainted with Elmina Drake Slenker: My Visit to Her Mountain Home," *Truth Seeker*, 24 Aug. 1878, 530; Elmina Drake
Slenker, "Beautify Your Homes," *Truth Seeker*, 22 Jan. 1881, 55.

26. New York Society for the Suppression of Vice Records, 7 vols., 1: 3–4, 9–10, 19–20,

25–26, 35–36, 63–64; 2: 92–93, Manuscript Division, Library of Congress, Washington, DC.

27. Vice Records, 1: 13–14, 63–64, 179–80, 231–32, 235–36, 245–46; 2: 248–49; 3: 20–21, 126–29.

28. Vice Records, 1: 13–14; "Train off the Track," *Cincinnati Commercial Tribune*, 26 Dec. 1872, 7; "George Francis Train," *Commercial Advertiser* (New York, NY), 21 Dec. 1872, 3; "The Arrest of George Francis Train," *Boston Investigator*, 15 Jan. 1873, 6; "George F. Train," *Boston Investigator*, 4 June 1873, 6; "A Large Elephant!" *Boston Investigator*, 23 April 1873, 5. The Train-Comstock showdown is neatly limned in Heywood Broun and Margaret Leech, *Anthony Comstock: Roundsman of the Lord* (New York: Literary Guild of America, 1927), 108–14. The legal scheming, especially over Train's sanity, was elaborate. See Clark Bell, *Speech of Clark Bell, Esq., to the Jury in the Proceedings before Chief Justice Charles P. Daly and a Jury, upon the Inquiry as to the Sanity or Insanity of George Francis Train* (New York: Russell Brothers, 1873). It did not help Train's sanity plea that he had also announced his candidacy for President of the United States and then proclaimed that he would rather be the dictator of the country.

29. Vice Records, 1: 55–56; "Obscene Literature Arrest," *New York Herald*, 27 July 1875, 13; D. M. Bennett, *The Champions of the Church: Their Crimes and Persecutions* (New York: Bennett, 1878), 1023–24; Lewis Masquerier, "The Persecution of John A. Lant," *Boston Investigator*, 9 Feb. 1876, 5; "Judicial Intolerance and Cruelty," *Truth Seeker*, 8 Jan. 1876, 12; A. S. Davis, "John A. Lant and Family," *Truth Seeker*, 3 June 1876, 181; "Grant's Last Pardons," *New York Herald*, 21 March 1877, 5; "A Martyr Out of Prison," *Truth Seeker*, 17 March 1877, 86. After his release from prison, Lant tried to start a new journal called *Labor*; it was short-lived. Later he edited a local paper in Tarrytown, New York, called *Record of the Times* and had one more run-in with Comstock there in 1892. See Vice Records, 2: 222–23. Eventually, in the mid-1890s, he became publisher of the *American Moslem* and a convert to Islam. See George E. Macdonald, "Inquirer," *Truth Seeker*, 10 Feb. 1894, 89; Umar F. Abd-Allah, *A Muslim in America: The Life of Alexander Russell Webb* (New York: Oxford University Press, 2006), 250, 255. As another disconcerting instance of the instability of infidel identities, Samuel Putnam would render Lant, former martyr for liberal secularism, invisible in his *400 Years of Freethought* (see chapter 1). Lant's offending medical terms in the Toledo *Sun* were specified as "p-n-s" and "s-m-n" in "American Liberty: Is It a Sham?" *Truth Seeker*, 24 Nov. 1877, 378.

30. "Judicial Intolerance," 12–13; "What about the Constitution?" *Truth Seeker*, 5 Oct. 1878, 632; Vice Records, 1: 55–56; "Suppressed in New York," *Sun*, 25 June 1875, 1. Surviving copies of the Toledo *Sun* are scarce. This one is in the John A. Lant file, Box 21, f. 18, Ralph Ginzburg Papers, Wisconsin Historical Society, Madison, WI. Lant's report on his half-hour confrontation with Comstock emphasizes that the vice reformer repeatedly recurred to "blasphemy" as his problem with the Toledo *Sun*. On Lant being arraigned for blasphemy under the guise of obscenity, see also Lewis Masquerier, *Sociology; or, The Reconstruction of Society, Government, and Property* (New York: n.p., 1877), 137; "Christian Superstition," *Truth Seeker*, 15 July 1875, 8.

31. Vice Records, 1: 63–64, 75–76; "Are We Really Progressing?" *Truth Seeker*, 15 Jan. 1875, 4; Joseph Treat, *God, Religion, and Immortality: An Oration Delivered at the Paine Celebration in Cincinnati, Sunday, January 29, 1860* (Cincinnati: n.p., 1860), 3. For Treat's close association with Slenker, see E. P. Drake Slenker, "Making a Beginning," *Boston Investigator*, 4 Dec. 1867, 245; E. P. Drake Slenker, "Free

Meetings—No. 3," *Boston Investigator*, 26 Feb. 1868, 341. On Treat's early free-love connections, see Joanne E. Passet, "Beyond Berlin Heights: The Free Lovers in History and Memory," *Communal Societies* 25 (2005): 95, 97, 103.

32. Vice Records, 1: 105–106, 127–28.

33. Bennett, *Champions of the Church*, 1062–66; Slenker, "Some Good Words," 821; D. M. Bennett, *An Open Letter to Jesus Christ* (New York: Truth Seeker Co., n.d.), 5–6, 8, 22.

34. Vice Records, 1: 165–66, 193–94, 199–200; "Truth's Sunday Sermons," *Truth Seeker*, 19 Feb. 1881, 117; "What 'The Truth' Thinks about It," *Dr. Foote's Health Monthly* 6 (June 1881): 14; "Lectures and Meetings," *Truth Seeker*, 10 Nov. 1883, 709; "Books," *Truth Seeker*, 2 April 1887, 222; Louis F. Post, "Postal Censorship in the United States," *Truth Seeker*, 26 Aug. 1905, 535. On Post's changing religious views, see Louis F. Post, *A Non-Ecclesiastical Confession of Religious Faith* (Chicago: Public, 1905), 7–8.

35. Vice Records, 2: 106–107; T. R. Kinget, "A Proposition to Liberals," *Boston Investigator*, 26 Oct. 1859, 213; "A New Liberal Lecturer," *Boston Investigator*, 1 Feb. 1860, 326; "Commission to Lecture," *Boston Investigator*, 22 Feb. 1860, 351; "Minutes of the Proceedings of the Infidel Convention," *Boston Investigator*, 14 Nov. 1860, 235; T. R. Kinget, "Independent Order of Liberals," *Boston Investigator*, 31 Jan. 1866, 306; T. R. Kinget, "The Independent Order of Secularists," *Boston Investigator*, 28 March 1866, 374; George Mortensen, "Secularism in Minnesota," *Boston Investigator*, 6 March 1867, 349; "I. O. S.," *Boston Investigator*, 18 Nov. 1868, 321; "Dr. Kinget's New Book," *Truth Seeker*, 3 July 1880, 430. Kinget also had his own upstart periodical, the *Health Journal*, derailed through postal regulations in 1881. See "America or Russia?" *Truth Seeker*, 30 April 1881, 276.

36. Anthony Comstock, *Frauds Exposed: How the People Are Deceived and Robbed, and Youth Corrupted* (New York: Brown, 1880), 426, 443, 453, 486; Flora W. Fox, "Moses Harman in the Penitentiary," *Freethinkers' Magazine* 11 (1893): 108–10; "Shall Such Things Continue?" *Truth Seeker*, 11 Feb. 1893, 87; R. Frankenstein, ed., *A Victim of Comstockism: Being the History of the Persecution of George E. Wilson, by the Agent of the Western Society for the Suppression of Vice* (Chicago: Wilson Publishing, [1894]); Vice Records, 2: 222–23, 240–41; 3: 42–43, 184–85, 212–13. Two other cases—those of editor Charles Chilton Moore and sex reformer Ida C. Craddock—are relevant as well, for the way they intermingled freethought, blasphemy, and obscenity. See John Sparks, *Kentucky's Most Hated Man: Charles Chilton Moore and the Bluegrass Blade* (Nicholasville, KY: Wind, 2009), esp. pp. 251-74, and Leigh Eric Schmidt, *Heaven's Bride: The Unprintable Life of Ida C. Craddock, American Mystic, Scholar, Sexologist, Martyr, and Madwoman* (New York: Basic, 2010), esp. pp. 181-85, 205–206.

37. J. B. Wise to Editor, *Truth Seeker*, 17 Oct. 1891, 666; John R. Charlesworth, "My Lecture Trip," *Truth Seeker*, 5 Dec. 1891, 775; J. B. Wise to Editor, *Truth Seeker*, 10 Sept. 1892, 586; J. B. Wise to Editor, *Truth Seeker*, 15 Oct. 1892, 666; J. B. Wise to Editor, *Truth Seeker*, 5 Nov. 1892, 714; J. B. Wise to Editor, *Truth Seeker*, 24 June 1893, 394; J. B. Wise to Editor, *Truth Seeker*, 14 Oct. 1893, 650; J. B. Wise to Editor, *Truth Seeker*, 2 Dec. 1893, 762; "Christians Attack Their Own Fetich," *Truth Seeker*, 7 July 1894, 421; "Is the Bible Obscene?" *Truth Seeker*, 14 July 1894, 436–37; J. B. Wise, "Wise vs. Vennum," *Truth Seeker*, 18 Aug. 1894, 517.

38. "The Prosecution of J. B. Wise," *Truth Seeker*, 28 July 1894, 469; E. B. Foote, Jr., "Time to Be Moving," 4 Aug. 1894, 489; "The Case of J. B. Wise—Its History," *Truth Seeker*, 11 Aug. 1894, 500-501; "A Strange Case," *Atlanta Constitution*, 16 Aug. 1894,

4. For a direct reply to the *Atlanta Constitution*, see "A Prophet Come to Judgment," *Truth Seeker*, 8 Sept. 1894, 565. Freethinker H. L. Green stayed true to form, denounced Wise, and followed Vennum's Comstockian logic. See H. L. Green, "Freethought and Liberalism—J. B. Wise and Obscene Literature," *Truth Seeker*, 6 Oct. 1894, 631.

39. "Mr. Wise, His Trial, and the Preachers," *Truth Seeker*, 20 Oct. 1894, 660; "The Approaching Trial of Mr. Wise," *Truth Seeker*, 23 March 1895, 179; "The J. B. Wise Case," *Truth Seeker*, 20 April 1895, 245; "Is the 'Holy Bible' Unmailable?" *Truth Seeker*, 27 April 1895, 264; "The Wise Case," *Truth Seeker*, 25 April 1896, 261; "Note and Comment," *Truth Seeker*, 10 Oct. 1903, 641.

40. Vice Records, 1: 117–18; 2: 236–37; "More Comstockism," *Truth Seeker*, 18 May 1878, 313; "The Career of Dr. Sara B. Chase," *New York Tribune*, 13 May 1878, 2; "Dr. Sara B. Chase's Case," *Physiologist and Family Physician* 1 (June/July 1878): 42–43; "Dr. Sara B. Chase Placed on Trial," *New York Herald*, 25 May 1893, 13; "Dr. Sara B. Chase Tells Her Story," *New York Herald*, 30 May 1893, 16; "Dr. Sara B. Chase Sentenced," *New York Tribune*, 15 June 1893, 11. On Comstock's harassment of Chase for publishing the *Physiologist*, see S. H. Preston, "Another Comstock Outrage!" *Boston Investigator*, 22 May 1878, 2; S. H. Preston, "Mr. Preston to the People," *Truth Seeker*, 30 April 1881, 277; E. D. Slenker, "Our 'Physiologist,'" *Truth Seeker*, 23 July 1881, 473; "America or Russia?" 276; S. H. Preston, "The Inquirer," *Physiologist and Family Physician* 3 (March 1881): 109–10. The whole June 1881 issue of the *Physiologist* was also devoted to Comstock's campaign against the paper.

41. Anthony Comstock, *Traps for the Young*, ed. Robert Bremner (Cambridge, MA: Belknap, 1967), 158–60, 184–85, 205; Comstock, *Frauds Exposed*, 443–44.

42. Elmina D. Slenker, "Woman," *Physiologist and Family Physician* 3 (March 1881): 101; Elmina Drake Slenker, "The Prevention of Conception," *Physiologist and Family Physician* 3 (Jan. 1881): 54–55; E. D. Slenker, "Woman," *Physiologist and Family Physician* 4 (Oct. 1881): 85; Elmina Drake Slenker, "Woman and Her Mission," *Physiologist and Family Physician* 4 (Dec. 1881): 103; Elmina Slenker to Sara B. Chase, *Physiologist and Family Physician* 1 (May 1878): 30.

43. Slenker, "Woman and Her Mission," 103; Elmina D. Slenker, "Womanhood," *Truth Seeker*, 5 May 1888, 279; Elmina Drake Slenker, "Scholars of Infidel Color," *Truth Seeker*, 30 June 1888, 405; Elmina Slenker to Editor, *Truth Seeker*, 29 Aug. 1885, 555; Elmina Slenker, "Leaves of Grass," *Truth Seeker*, 2 Dec. 1882, 765. Her "Eminent Women" series appeared regularly in the *Truth Seeker* in 1889 and 1890.

44. Slenker, "Many Atheist Mothers," 554; J. Francis Ruggles, "To the Benevolent," *Truth Seeker*, 8 June 1907, 362; "'Aunt Elmina' Dead," *Truth Seeker*, 22 Feb. 1908, 117; E. B. Foote, Jr., "A Free Speech Trio Drop Out Almost Hand in Hand," *Truth Seeker*, 22 Feb. 1908, 120.

45. Mary Antin, *The Promised Land*, ed. Werner Sollors (1912; New York: Penguin, 1997), 190–91. Antin's memoir remains complexly religious even as it stands out as a secularist manifesto; in time she became more of a freethinking seeker than a diehard atheist.

EPILOGUE: THE NONBELIEVER IS ENTITLED
TO GO HIS OWN WAY

1. Will Herberg, *Protestant-Catholic-Jew: An Essay in American Religious Sociology* (1955; New York: Anchor, 1960), 46–47, 52–53, 60–61, 259–60. The 1950s imperative

for religiosity that Herberg documented has now become the object of growing historical attention. See Jonathan P. Herzog, *The Spiritual-Industrial Complex: America's Religious Battle against Communism in the Early Cold War* (New York: Oxford University Press, 2011); T. Jeremy Gunn, *Spiritual Weapons: The Cold War and the Forging of an American National Religion* (Westport, CT: Praeger, 2009); Jason W. Stevens, *God-Fearing and Free: A Spiritual History of America's Cold War* (Cambridge, MA: Harvard University Press, 2010); and Kevin M. Kruse, *One Nation under God: How Corporate America Invented Christian America* (New York: Basic Books, 2015).

2. "A Word from Dr. York," *Humanitarian Review* 1 (1903): 292-94; [Singleton Waters Davis], "Death of H. L. Green and Wife," *Humanitarian Review* 1 (1903): 295-97. "I shall not have so many deaths of the Freethought captains to report in 1907. There are not so many left," editor George Macdonald remarked after his dispiriting necrology for 1906. See George E. Macdonald, *Fifty Years of Freethought*, 2 vols. (New York: Truth Seeker Co., 1929), 2: 286.

3. Stephen D. Parrish, "The Village Infidel," *Humanitarian Review* 4 (1906): 53-57; Charles Smith, "An Unhonored Hero," American Association for the Advancement of Atheism, *Fifth Annual Report 1930* (New York: n.p., 1931), 7; Van Wyck Brooks, *The Ordeal of Mark Twain* (New York: Dutton, 1920), 89. See also Robert F. Hester, "The Village Atheist," *Fifth Annual Report*, 14—a poem in which the eponymous figure is hailed as "the most scorned" as well as "the queerest, strangest, and most odd" man in town.

4. Clarence Darrow and Wallace Rice, eds., *Infidels and Heretics: An Agnostic's Anthology* (Boston: Stratford, 1929), vi-vii; "Lewis Dares Deity to Strike Him Dead," *New York Times*, 20 April 1926, 2; Sinclair Lewis, *Elmer Gantry,* ed. Jason Stevens (1927; New York: Signet, 2007), 14, 26, 36-37, 64, 256-57. Darrow presented his own irreligion as an inheritance from his father, "the village Infidel" in "a small country town." See the reminiscence in Macdonald, *Fifty Years*, 1: 288-89. The dramatic episodes of unbelief in the mid-to-late 1920s could be multiplied at some length beyond Darrow and Lewis. A fine example is the role that botanist Luther Burbank played among secularists of the period as a self-proclaimed infidel. See Frederick W. Clampett, *Luther Burbank, "Our Beloved Infidel"* (New York: Macmillan, 1926). Another in the same vein is journalist Herbert Asbury, a descendant of the revered Methodist bishop Francis Asbury, whose memoir *Up from Methodism* (1926) celebrated his scoffing triumph over the grim sanctimony of his boyhood faith. See Charles Willis Thompson, "Methodism in American Life: The History of a Sect and the Story of a Personal Revolt against Its Authority," *New York Times*, 7 Nov. 1926, BR4. For two more assertions of unbelief that captured considerable attention at the time, see Rupert Hughes, *Why I Quit Going to Church* (New York: Freethought Press Association, 1925), and Carl Van Doren, "Why I Am an Unbeliever," *Forum* 76 (Dec. 1926): 864-69.

5. "Methods," American Association for the Advancement of Atheism, *Second Annual Report 1927* (New York: n.p., 1928), 20. For the survey of the 4A membership, see George Vetter and Martin Green, "Personality and Group Factors in the Making of Atheists," *Journal of Abnormal and Social Psychology* 27 (1932): 179-94. The researchers had the cooperation of the 4A in conducting the survey; they received 350 completed questionnaires out of the 600 distributed. Of religious backgrounds they found Methodists and Jews making "the largest proportional contribution to the ranks of the Atheists" (185). They found the Northeast and Far West to be the

regional bases of the 4A, with the South "far behind" (184). The whiteness of the 4A was a result of its own racial myopia; it was not for lack of engagement with atheism and agnosticism among African-American intellectuals and artists of the period—among them, Nella Larsen, James Weldon Johnson, Langston Hughes, and George S. Schuyler. See, for example, Anthony B. Pinn, ed., *By These Hands: A Documentary History of African-American Humanism* (New York: New York University Press, 2001), esp. pp. 137–45.

6. "In Darkest Arkansas," American Association for the Advancement of Atheism, *Third Annual Report 1928* (New York: n.p., 1929), 7–8; Charles Smith, "Report on Arkansas Campaign," 17 Dec. 1928, Widener Library, Harvard University, Cambridge, MA. Marcet Haldeman-Julius, wife of publisher Emanuel Haldeman-Julius and niece of Jane Addams, also showed up in Little Rock to picket the jailing of Smith, adding to the media attention. See "Woman Picket Baits Arkansas in Atheist Row," *Chicago Tribune*, 27 Oct. 1928, 9.

7. Chapter 24 of Arthur May's "History of the University of Rochester, 1850–1962" tells the story of the Society of Damned Souls in more detail than any other source. It is available from River Campus Libraries, University of Rochester, Rochester, NY, at http://www.lib.rochester.edu/index.cfm?PAGE=2330&TheClass=0&Subject=&O MID=0&StartLtr (accessed April 29, 2015). See also Homer Croy, "Atheism Rampant in Our Schools: How Propaganda Works on the Youthful Mind," *World's Work* 54 (June 1927): 142–44, and the clippings on the group in the Department of Rare Books and Special Collections, Rush Rhees Library, University of Rochester, including "Damned Souls Rightly Named, Minister Says" and "Irrepressible Youth." For alumni reaction, see "Those Damned Souls," *Rochester Alumni Review*, Feb.–March 1926, 83, in the same collection.

8. Homer Croy, "Atheism Beckons to Our Youth: How Unbelief Is Being Spread in Schools and Colleges," *World's Work* 54 (May 1927): 19; "Freethinkers' Club Is Formed at Yale," *New York Times*, 28 April 1926, 3.

9. "School and College Branches," American Association for the Advancement of Atheism, *Second Annual Report 1927* (New York: n.p., 1928), 6; Croy, "Atheism Rampant," 140–41. The archive for *The Godless Girl* is extensive, part of the massive Cecil B. DeMille Archives, L. Tom Perry Special Collections, Harold B. Lee Library, Brigham Young University, Provo, UT. DeMille's researchers had done extensive background work on the 4A, including a local young operative, Queen Silver. On Silver and the 4A clubs, see DeMille Archives, Box 292, f. 1–3; Box 293, f. 1. On DeMille's faith, see the *Guideposts* pamphlet from 1957, *Religion Guided My Career*, Box 912, f. 22.

10. "Shooting Script," DeMille Archives, Box 1234, f. 1: 17, 44–49, 54, 61, 263. DeMille wanted to have it both ways—a sensationalized critique of the imminent threat of atheist clubs in the nation's schools with a caution against Bible-thumping over-reactions to that peril—but he was clearly more concerned to see religion vindicated than to have the rights of an atheist minority protected. See "Verbatim Transcript of Expository and Descriptive 'Reading' by Cecil B. DeMille of *The Godless Girl*," DeMille Archives, Box 293, f. 8: 3–4, 80, 90, 96; Harry Carr to Bill Sistrom, 29 Dec. 1927, Box 293, f. 5. When Governor Henry S. Johnston of Oklahoma wrote DeMille in support of *The Godless Girl*'s mission to protect American youth from the "evil" of atheism and to note that his state had refused to allow the 4A to incorporate a chapter there, DeMille wrote a heartened letter commending the state's refusal to condone the 4A's organizing. See Henry S. Johnston to Cecil B. DeMille, 22 Nov.

1927, and Cecil B. DeMille to Henry S. Johnston, 9 Dec. 1927, DeMille Archives, Box 293, f. 5. DeMille repeatedly encouraged ministers and community leaders to help stop the "unlawful" distribution of atheist propaganda, so poisonous to "tender minds." See, for example, Cecil B. DeMille to David R. Wylie, 24 Feb. 1928, DeMille Archives, Box 293, f. 2. One minister, Julia N. Budlong, wrote the director to express her worries that his depiction of a riotous gang breaking up an atheist meeting had the potential of inciting "mob violence" and "religious intolerance" against perfectly "quiet and orderly gatherings" of questioning youth, atheist and otherwise. Her worry left DeMille unconvinced. See Julia N. Budlong to Cecil B. DeMille, 5 Feb. 1928, and Cecil B. DeMille to Julia N. Budlong, 10 March 1928, DeMille Archives, Box 293, f. 2.

11. "Notes," DeMille Archives, Box 292, f. 3; "Script and Re-Writes for *The Godless Girl*," DeMille Archives, Box 1253, f. 5; "Announcing the Junior Atheist League," DeMille Archives, P-146, Box 31, f. 7; Croy, "Atheism Rampant," 142–46; Croy, "Atheism Beckons," 19; Charles Lee Smith to Cecil B. DeMille, 28 Oct. 1927, DeMille Archives, Box 293, f. 1.

12. American Association for the Advancement of Atheism, *First Annual Report 1926* (New York: n.p., 1927), 5–6; "The American Anti-Bible Society," *Second Annual Report*, 6; "Journals," *Second Annual Report*, 12.

13. *First Annual Report*, 2; "Other Lectures and Debates," *Second Annual Report*, 2.

14. "The Martin-Smith Debates," *Second Annual Report*, 1–2; *There Is a God! Debate between Aimee Semple McPherson Fundamentalist and Charles Lee Smith Atheist* (Los Angeles: Foursquare Publications, n.d.), 46. These Fundamentalist-atheist debates of the 1920s and 1930s had a rich history behind them in the American religious marketplace, especially in intra-Protestant doctrinal showdowns. See E. Brooks Holifield, "Theology as Entertainment: Oral Debate in American Religion," *Church History* 67 (1998): 499–520.

15. Charles Smith, "Godless Evolution," 4A leaflet, New York, n.d., Widener Library, Harvard University; Smith, "Report on Arkansas Campaign."

16. Charles Smith, "The Bible in the Balance," 4A leaflet, n.d., Widener Library, Harvard University; "The Revolt against Sex Taboos," *Third Annual Report*, 12; "In Sexual Matters," *Second Annual Report*, 15–16.

17. *First Annual Report*, 3; "Law Suits," *Second Annual Report*, 9–11; "Law Suits," *Third Annual Report*, 9; New York Society for the Suppression of Vice Records, 7 vols., 4: 62–63, Manuscript Division, Library of Congress, Washington, DC; John Roach Straton, *Fighting the Devil in Modern Babylon* (Boston: Stratford, 1929), 259, 260, 266. The legal maneuvering in the Smith-Straton case was prolonged, which helped keep the tandem's back-and-forth jabs in the news for over a year. See, for example, "Straton to Fight Atheist in Court," *New York Times*, 2 April 1927, 10; "Atheist Hits Back in Straton Row," *New York Times*, 3 Jan. 1928, 13; "Atheist Convicted on Straton Charge," *New York Times*, 15 May 1928, 1, 10.

18. "Law Suits," *Third Annual Report*, 9.

19. "Blamegiving Day," American Association for the Advancement of Atheism, *Fifth Annual Report 1930* (New York: n.p., 1931), 3. For the liturgy of a "Blamegiving Service" the group held on Thanksgiving 1931, see "The First Annual Trial of God," American Association for the Advancement of Atheism, *Sixth Annual Report 1931* (New York: n.p., 1932), 3–9.

20. Smith, "Report on Arkansas Campaign"; "Law Suits," *Second Annual Report*, 9–11; "Law Suits," *Third Annual Report*, 9–10.

21. See "Mr. Smith's Federal Question" in Frank Swancara, *Obstruction of Justice by Religion* (Denver: Courtright, 1936), 117–23; Frank Swancara, "A Legal Leper," *Dicta* 17 (1940): 81–85; Frank Swancara, "Charles Smith Was Rationalism's Dred Scott," *Truth Seeker* 76 (Oct. 1949): 156. Swancara's Dred Scott analogy ended up being densely ironic as Smith spent the last several years of his career in the late 1950s and early 1960s spouting a right-wing, eugenicist, and racist message against the equality of African Americans and other minorities. He pushed the slogan: "Liberty—Quality—Fraternity." See, for example, Charles Smith, "An Atheistic Rightist," *Truth Seeker* 84 (March 1957): 39; Charles Smith, "Contra Equalists," *Truth Seeker* 84 (June 1957): 89–90. Along with his colleagues Woolsey Teller and James Hervey Johnson, Smith wound up effectively destroying the credibility of the *Truth Seeker* in wider humanist circles. D. M. Bennett's nearly century-old journal never recovered. Swancara, for his part, dwelled tirelessly on the civil liberties of atheists and nonbelievers. An amateur scholar, without an academic affiliation and working out of a law office in Denver, he is now little recognized. But, from the 1930s through the 1960s, Swancara poured forth dozens of books, pamphlets, and law review articles in his chosen field of study. See, for example, Frank Swancara, *The Separation of Religion and Government: The First Amendment, Madison's Intent, and the McCollum Decision* (New York: Truth Seeker Co., 1950); Frank Swancara, *Thomas Jefferson versus Religious Oppression* (New York: University Books, 1969).

22. *First Annual Report*, 1–2; "Law Suits," *Second Annual Report*, 9–11; "Opposition," *Second Annual Report*, 12; "Repeal Campaigns," *Second Annual Report*, 19; "Law Suits," *Third Annual Report*, 10; "The New Jersey Oath Case," *Sixth Annual Report*, 10.

23. "Spread of Atheism," *Second Annual Report*, 13; Rev. Fred W. Hagan quoted in Macdonald, *Fifty Years*, 2: 563; Van Doren, "Why I Am an Unbeliever," 867.

24. "Joseph Lewis, Champion of Atheism, Dies," *Boston Globe*, 5 Nov. 1968, 37; "The Enemy of God," *Time*, 11 Nov. 1935, 28. For Heywood Broun's editorializing in support of Lewis's case, see Arthur H. Howland, *Joseph Lewis—Enemy of God* (Boston: Stratford, 1932), 74–76. Howland offers a biographical portrait of the first half of Lewis's life; his sixth chapter details the church-state battles. For a broad sampling of court challenges, see "Darrow Offers Aid to Freethinkers," *New York Times*, 11 June 1925, 2; "Freethinkers Open Attack on McKee," *New York Times*, 8 Feb. 1926, 21; "Freethinker Sees Hot Religious War," *New York Times*, 22 Feb. 1926, 7; "School Dismissal for Children Legal; Freethinkers Lose," *New York Times*, 25 April 1926, 1; "Seeks Writ against Religious Teaching," *New York Times*, 27 April 1926, 14; "Files Suit to Force Tax on K. of C. Hotel," *New York Times*, 28 March 1931, 11; "Suit to Bar the Bible Pressed," *New York Times*, 6 May 1931, 2; "Sues Over School Buses," *New York Times*, 11 Dec. 1936, 7; "Freethinker's Suit Dismissed by Court," *New York Times*, 20 Oct. 1951, 14; "Pledge's 'Under God' Is Opposed in Court," *New York Times*, 10 Nov. 1956, 40; "'Under God' Phrase in Pledge Is Upheld," *New York Times*, 3 Dec. 1960, 20; "No Legal Bar Found to Airport Chapels," *New York Times*, 6 Dec. 1961, 37.

25. "The McCollum School Suit in Illinois," *Truth Seeker* 72 (Oct. 1945): 148–49. I have relied especially on the collection of Arthur G. Cromwell's papers in the hands of his grandson Dannel McCollum, which include a substantial number of Cromwell's published and unpublished letters. I have drawn as well on the Dannel Angus McCollum Papers, Illinois History and Lincoln Collections, University of Illinois Library, Urbana, IL. The first two boxes in the latter collection focus on *McCollum v. Board of Education*, particularly newspaper clippings about the case. Arthur Cromwell offered a sketch of his life in *Memoirs of a Freethinker*, which the American Rationalist

Federation published as a pamphlet in 1964. Two other short autobiographical sketches survive in typescript in Dannel McCollum's private collection, one from 1956 and one from 1977. Cromwell gives the date for the founding of the Rochester Society of Freethinkers as 1938 in the *Memoirs*, but, in the 1977 sketch, he gives the date as 1929; certainly, he was involved in freethinking activities before 1938. In his *Memoirs* he also dates his *Rationalism vs. Religious Instruction* pamphlet to 1938, but the copyright date is 1940. For a careful examination of the case, written from the family's papers, see Dannel McCollum, *The Lord Was Not on Trial: The Inside Story of the Supreme Court's Precedent-Setting McCollum Ruling* (Silver Spring, MD: Americans for Religious Liberty, 2008).

26. "Anti-Bible Mother on Stand Today," "Woman Atheist Opens Battle against Religion in Schools," "Boy, 10, Says Being Atheist Makes Him Feel Different," "Storm-centers in Bible-Teaching Trial," newspaper clippings, Box 1, McCollum Papers; "McCollum School Suit," 149.

27. *Everson v. Board of Education of the Township of Ewing*, 330 U.S. 1 (1947).

28. McCollum, *Lord Was Not on Trial*, 29, 49–50, 70, 101, 105, 155–56; Vashti Cromwell McCollum, *One Woman's Fight* (New York: Doubleday, 1951), 72, 82–83, 97–102, 155–59, 185–87. For the defaced pictures of her, see scrapbooked newspaper clippings, Box 1, McCollum Papers.

29. *Illinois ex rel. McCollum v. Board of Ed. of School Dist. No. 71*, 333 US 203 (1948).

30. *Zorach v. Clauson*, 343 US 306 (1952); Herberg, *Protestant-Catholic-Jew*, 257.

31. *Zorach v. Clauson*, 343 US 306.

32. "Compulsory godliness" is a phrase from Jackson's dissent in *Zorach*.

33. *In the Matter of Joseph Burstyn, Inc., Appellant v. Lewis A. Wilson, as Commissioner of Education of the State of New York*, 303 NY 242 (1951); *Joseph Burstyn, Inc. v. Wilson, Commissioner of Education of New York*, 343 US 495 (1952). *Burstyn* was settled on free-speech grounds rather than on an explicit basis of religious neutrality, but the latter principle remained critical to this larger reorientation. In a last-ditch blasphemy case in Maryland, for example, the Court of Special Appeals took the neutrality principle—that the government is not to favor believers over nonbelievers—as decisive (rather than the Free Speech Clause) in deeming the state's blasphemy statute unconstitutional. See *State of Maryland v. Irving K. West*, 9 Md. App. 270 (1970).

34. *Torcaso v. Watkins, Clerk*, 162 A. 2d 438, Maryland Court of Appeals (1960).

35. *Torcaso v. Watkins*, 367 US 488 (1961). A small file of newspaper clippings and another file of legal correspondence on the case are included in the Leo Pfeffer Papers, Box 13, "Job Oath of an Atheist—Torcaso 1959–1961," and Box 18, "Job Oath of Atheist—Torcaso Case 1961," Special Collections Research Center, Syracuse University Libraries, Syracuse, NY.

36. Robert Bendiner, "Our Right Not to Believe," *Saturday Evening Post*, 10 Feb. 1962, 10, 12; Billy Graham, "Our Right to Require Belief," *Saturday Evening Post*, 17 Feb. 1962, 8, 10.

37. *Engel v. Vitale*, 370 U.S. 421 (1962). For the hate and harassment directed at the Engel plaintiffs, including the cross-burning episode, as well as at the Schempps, see Bruce J. Dierenfield, *The Battle over School Prayer: How Engel v. Vitale Changed America* (Lawrence: University Press of Kansas, 2007), 138–43, 163, 167–68. The Murrays experienced similar forms of harassment (Dierenfield, pp. 173–75), but Madalyn Murray, at least, relished the notoriety and ceaselessly exploited it. See Bryan F. Le

Beau, *The Atheist: Madalyn Murray O'Hair* (New York: New York University Press, 2003), 47–50, 98–103.

38. Mark Twain, *Pudd'nhead Wilson*, ed. Malcolm Bradbury (1894; New York: Penguin, 2004), 52; Paul Blanshard, "The State and the Rights of Religious Conscience," (Sept. 1961), clipping from publication of Protestants and Other Americans United for the Separation of Church and State, in American Civil Liberties Union, Washington, DC, Office Records, 1948–1970, *Torcaso v. Watkins*, Box 16, f. 2, Seeley G. Mudd Manuscript Library, Princeton University, Princeton, NJ; *School District of Abington Township, Pennsylvania v. Schempp*, 374 U.S. 203 (1963). A notorious critic of Catholic teachings on sexuality and papal authority, Blanshard was also a vaunted civil-liberties watchdog and humanistic freethinker: "When I am called by conscience to vote on the categories of unbelief, I will vote atheist because I think it is the most honest vote," he commented late in life. "I do not relish the awful associations of that word in an allegedly pious society, since I am not yet a murderer, a Communist, or an all-around blackguard. In fact I still believe enough in ethical associations to be a creedless Unitarian, Ethical Culture, and Humanist atheist because men who defy the dragons of orthodoxy need mutual support." See Paul Blanshard, *Personal and Controversial: An Autobiography* (Boston: Beacon Press, 1973), 290.

39. "Is God Dead?" *Time*, 8 April 1966, cover. On postman Bill Moore, see Mary Stanton, *Freedom Walk: Mississippi or Bust* (Jackson: University Press of Mississippi, 2003), esp. pp. 41, 80–81, 83, 86. Though the news media downplayed it in covering his death, Moore's atheism was well known, and his religious views, along with his integrationist commitments, loomed large in the mind of his presumed killer. See also Madalyn Murray's aggrieved, self-serving tribute to him in "Malice in Maryland," *Realist* no. 59 (May 1965): 18, 32, and in Madalyn Murray O'Hair, *An Atheist Epic: Bill Murray, the Bible, and the Baltimore Board of Education* (Austin, TX: American Atheist Press, 1970), 256–68. For Daniel Seeger's case, see *United States v. Seeger*, 380 US 163 (1965). The "Death of God" movement in liberal Protestant theology was often conflated with outright atheism, though it owed more to a kind of Christian existentialism. The distinction was lost in the hubbub over the cover story in *Time*. One of the chief theologians *Time* highlighted, William Hamilton, found his life turned upside down. He received death threats and was ostracized at church and seminary. See Paul Vitello, "William Hamilton Dies at 87; Known for 'Death of God,'" *New York Times*, 11 March 2012, A20. Likewise, his principal collaborator, Thomas J. J. Altizer, also received ample hate mail and faced widespread calls for his firing from the faculty of church-related Emory University. See Thomas J. J. Altizer, *Living the Death of God: A Theological Memoir* (Albany: State University of New York Press, 2006), 12, 16–17; Walter Bugaber, "'God Is Dead' View Arouses College," *New York Times*, 5 Nov. 1965, 34; Christopher Demuth Rodkey, "Methodist Heretic: Thomas Altizer and the Death of God at Emory University," *Methodist History* 49 (2010): 37–50. Altizer's correspondence files on the controversy are filled with outraged, prayerful letters over his public espousal of what he termed Christian atheism. See Thomas J. [J.] Altizer Papers, Boxes 1 and 2, Special Collections Research Center, Syracuse University Libraries, Syracuse, NY.

40. "Toward a Hidden God," *Time*, 8 April 1966, 60; Laurie Goodstein, "In 7 States, Atheists Fight for Removal of Belief Rule," *New York Times*, 7 Dec. 2014, 21, 29; Herb Silverman, *Candidate without a Prayer: An Autobiography of a Jewish Atheist in the Bible Belt* (Charlottesville, VA: Pitchstone, 2012), 98–103; Richard John

Neuhaus, "Can Atheists Be Good Citizens?" *First Things* 15 (Aug.–Sept. 1991): 21; Natalie Angier, "Confessions of a Lonely Atheist," *New York Times*, 14 Jan. 2001, SM 34. For various cases of harassment and intolerance aimed at atheists, see Margaret Downey, "Discrimination against Atheists: The Facts," *Free Inquiry* 24 (June/July 2004): 41–43. Downey, a Philadelphia-based activist, continues to document such cases through her Anti-Discrimination Support Network. For further indicators of ongoing discrimination and distrust, see Caroline Mala Corbin, "Nonbelievers and Government Speech," *Iowa Law Review* 97 (2011–2012): 347–415. Corbin uses the evidence of stigmatization and intimidation to make the case for a strong rendering of the constitutional protections afforded nonbelievers.

41. *McCreary County v. American Civil Liberties Union of Ky.*, 545 US 844 (2005); *Town of Greece, NY v. Galloway*, 134 S. Ct. 1811 (2014). The cavalier exclusion of atheists was especially noticeable in the oral arguments in the *Town of Greece* case, though Justice Elena Kagan pressed against this point in her dissent as well as in the oral arguments. Andrew Koppelman characterizes Scalia's approach as an "atavistic synthesis" in *Defending American Religious Neutrality* (Cambridge, MA: Harvard University Press, 2013), 39–42. For overviews of the recent legal terrain facing secularists and atheists, see Nelson Tebbe, "Nonbelievers," *Virginia Law Review* 97 (2011): 1112–80; Alan Payne, "Redefining 'Atheism' in America: What the United States Could Learn from Europe's Protection of Atheists," *Emory International Law Review* 27 (2013): 661–703. For a broad-ranging critique of the conservative judicial tilt toward the Religious Right by a leading lawyer with the American Humanist Association, see David Niose, *Nonbeliever Nation: The Rise of Secular Americans* (New York: Palgrave Macmillan, 2012), esp. pp. 191–202. For growing efforts to forge atheistic networks and communities out of the media success of the New Atheists and the growth of the Nones, see Richard Cimino and Christopher Smith, *Atheist Awakening: Secular Activism and Community in America* (New York: Oxford University Press, 2014).

42. Abby Goodnough, "Student Faces Town's Wrath in Protest against a Prayer," *New York Times*, 27 Jan. 2012, A11–12; Hemant Mehta, "Even Today, Jessica Ahlquist Is Facing Condemnation for Her Successful Lawsuit," (accessed Sept. 22, 2015), http://www.patheos.com/blogs/friendlyatheist/2013/09/24/even-today-jessica-ahlquist-is-facing-condemnation-for-her-successful-lawsuit/. For a collection of first-person narratives of contemporary American atheists navigating their minority status outside the kind of media spotlight Ahlquist gained, see Melanie E. Brewster, ed., *Atheists in America* (New York: Columbia University Press, 2014).

INDEX

Note: Page numbers in *italics* indicate figures.

Abbot, Francis Ellingwood, 38–40, 201, 206; on free-love movement, 45–46, 64; Heston and, 106; Kinget and, 240; "Nine Demands of Liberalism" by, 39, 53, 59, 106, 135, 263; on obscenity laws, 213

Abington v. Schempp (1963), 278, 279

abortion, 243–44

Adams, Robert C., 58–59, 67

Adler, Felix, 47, 144

Adventists. See Seventh-day Adventists

African Americans, 20, 127, 135–42, 138, 139, 302n34, 304n39, 323n5

agnostics, 19–21, 189–90, 277–82; bookshop for, 240–41; Boy Scouts and, xiii; Chainey on, 57; as freethinker label, 12, 13, 17, 253, 291n32; Heston's cartoon of, 106, 108; Reynolds on, 180; Swancara on, 24

Ahlquist, Jessica, 283

Aikenhead, Thomas, 3

American Association for the Advancement of Atheism (4A), 250, 253–54, 263–65, 322n5; Fundamentalist debates of, 258–60; Heston's cartoons used by, 169; Ingersoll Forum of, 261; legacy of, 265–66; theodicy debates of, 262–63; youth groups of, 254–55, 257–58

American Bible Society, 258

American Civil Liberties Union (ACLU), 254–55, 259; on church-state separation, 276, 283, 290n31; on right to testify, 265

American Secular Union, 28, 51, 263; African American members of, 140; Putnam and, 52; Reynolds and, 202

Andrews, Stephen Pearl, 47

Anthony, Susan B., 10

anti-Catholicism, 98–101, 99, 100, 106, 108

Anti-Evolution League of America, 259

Antin, Mary, 248, 321n45

anti-Semitism, 142–44, 143, 145, 301n26, 303n39

Asad, Talal, 290n28

Baird, Robert, 9–10, 287n16

Baker, R. L., 55

Bakunin, Mikhail, 77–78

Barkley brothers, 232

Bartlett, Samuel Colcord, 34

Bartol, Cyrus, 313n41

Beecher, Henry Ward, 36, 160, 234, 235, 289n38

Beers, Henry A., 14

Bell, W. S., 16, 59

Bellows, Henry Whitney, 38, 293n20

Bendiner, Robert, 276–77

Beneke, Chris, 312n35

Bennett, D. M., 16, 41, 47, 52, 67; Comstock and, 232, 237–39, 245; death of, 75; Lant and, 235–36; *Open Letter to Jesus Christ* by, 238; Reynolds on, 182, 183; spiritualism and, 295n41, 309n14

Berlinerblau, Jacques, 288n21

bestiality, 217

Bierck, Adolph, 243

Bigelow, Herbert S., 15

Bird, Henry, 59

birth control, 217, 231, 232, 244, 248, 261–62

Black, Hugo, 269–73, 276, 278, 282

Blanshard, Paul, 279, 327n38

blasphemy, 274; heresy and, 173, 196, 274; legal definition of, 196–97; obscenity and, 198, 220, 232, 236–37, 244–45; Reynolds's trial for, 132, 170–74, 188–98, 200–203, 207, 308n2

blue laws. See Sunday blue laws

Boonton (N.J.) Secular Union, 186–87

Boy Scouts of America, xiii, xvi

Braden, Clark, 78, 89, 101

Bradlaugh, Charles, 52, 315n48

329